"*Many Paths* is the astonishing re
it mildly — rare for a successfu.
his muses and spiritual guides as well as to the intricacies of banking, mergers and acquisitions, Bruce McEver has written sheaves of well-observed poetry and taken a master's in theology to go with his master's in business administration. Along the paths he has suffered grievous hurts and betrayals yet has been able to surpass these to take joy in life and love, and to express it all in this inspiring autobiography."

--Tom Shachtman, author of *The Founding Fortunes: how the wealthy paid for and profited from America's revolution*; and *Skyscraper Dreams: the great real estate dynasties of New York*; and *The Day America Crashed*.

"In *Many Paths* Bruce McEver candidly traces the warp and weft of his life's journey, from his boyhood in Georgia to the boardroom in Manhattan, around the world many times and back again. His is a remarkable life, sustained by knowledge, art, literature, poetry, nature, music, faith, and love. You won't forget this testament to finding the ties that bind."

--Lisa Bayer, Director, University of Georgia Press

"Bruce's gifts for telling vivid stories and writing evocative poems coalesce in this delightful memoir about a fascinating life and the adventures that made it such. Like the carvings on the totem pole that signify the paths of his life, Bruce's poems, peppered throughout the book, stand as colorful markers of the events and people that collectively give life meaning and purpose."

--Bob Chapman, Chairman & CEO of Barry-Wehmiller, co-author of *Everybody Matters: The Extraordinary Power of Caring for Your People Like Family*.

"It's said that it takes a rich and varied life to produce a robust soul, and that few meet the challenge. Bruce McEver has, and with wings on. As detailed in his gripping autobiography *Many Paths*, in one lifetime he has not only successfully explored the world of finance as a pioneer of investment banking but has also ventured deep into the world of the spirit. He has known triumph and personal tragedy, war and peace, and makes what he has seen and the lessons he has learned vividly available in a book that, once read, won't be forgotten."

--Jeff Zaleski, Editor and Publisher, Parabola

"*Many Paths* begins with a wrenching account of loss, then becomes something somehow even more affecting and profound: a search for truth and meaning in every facet of a life fully lived. Measured in the full conscience and grace of a gifted writer, thinker, and business visionary, McEver succeeds, at every stage of his life, as his own idiosyncratic and true self. Yes, as *Many Paths* attests, McEver was "in the room when it happened." But what will surprise, and always reward, readers who have not yet discovered his writing and work is the power of his insights and lyricism. McEver's voice is bright, curious, charming, authentic, funny, and humble. *Many Paths* is a book to be savored for all that it can teach us."

--John W. Evans, The Phyllis Draper Lecturer in Non-Fiction, Stanford University

"From Eagle Scout to philanthropist, from naval officer to entrepreneur, from Wall Street dealmaker to poet and spiritualist, my friend Bruce McEver has lived a rich, colorful and fascinating life. In these pages he tells his own story, with feeling, fidelity and, yes, poetry."

--James Grant, Editor, Grant's Interest Rate Observer

"Bruce McEver's story is proof that focus and discipline can accomplish anything. He has built a global and well-respected financial firm, become a published poet and established an unmatched legacy with his work to create better understanding among religions. McEver evokes in his writing, a tangible sense of life's journeys. His travels have taken him around the globe and back again. Yes, he has had his fair share of heartbreak and disappointment. But he has stayed the course and is finishing well. *Many Paths*, Bruce's entertaining recounting of his life, is a must read for anyone who has high hopes and big dreams. I highly recommend it! "

-- Chip Mason, Founder and Former CEO, Legg Mason

MANY PATHS

A Poet's Journey
Through Love, Death,
And Wall Street

BRUCE McEVER

C&R Press
Conscious & Responsible
Winston-Salem, NC

MANY PATHS

A Poet's Journey
Through Love, Death,
And Wall Street

To Bertis —

Keep up your life long learning
and good works. Best wishes.

Athens, Ga

May 5, 2022

"Yet isn't it a miracle, the oddity of consciousness being placed in one body rather than another, in one place and not somewhere else, in one handful of decades rather than in ancient Egypt...or the Ob River Valley in the days of woolly mammoths? Billions of consciousnesses silt history full, and every one of them the center of the universe. What can we do in the face of this unthinkable truth but scream or take refuge in God?"

Self-Consciousness, Memoirs
John Updike

Georgia Nunnally Johnson McEver 1990s

Chapter I
Augury

Some days are steeled in memory. On a cold, clear morning in November 2000, I was at the top of my game. I'd grown up in red-dirt Georgia and was now running in Central Park under the spires of Manhattan, confident I knew how to get to the top of some of them. Like Rocky Balboa, I bounded up the stairs of the Natural History Museum in sweats toward the rear-end of the statue of Teddy Roosevelt seated on his horse. There, I found a pigeon who seemed to be mourning over another bundle of grey-blue feathers lying in an empty corner. It was flapping its wings and cooing, trying to gather up its partner, bring it back to consciousness. Finally, it was shaken from its task by my presence and flew off, leaving the sad bundle of a former mate with what looked like a broken neck. I mused on this scene for weeks, not knowing what spirit or randomness put it in my path. Ancient Romans who interpreted omens from the flight of birds were called augurs, but this signal was beyond me that morning.

A few weeks later, at year-end on Wall Street, it was time for bonuses, when the all-important pie is cut up among the partners. The scramble for funds was sometimes nasty, proceeded by a certain amount of puffery for deal credits usually adding to over 100%. Running a firm, a financial gauntlet thrown down by my wife's stepfather when courting her, stuck in my mind: "Have you ever met a payroll?" he asked, as a test of real economic arrival. This year I was not only going to meet the payroll for about forty people but raise salaries and pay bonuses!

We were an investment banker's investment banker and in the middle of the action at the core of the economy. The numbers were in, showing we had a record year, and I had bonuses of over several million to hand out. However, what was always remarkable to me about this process was the hubris of those who received such sums—the expressions of resentment and dissatisfaction with whatever was rewarded. We had assembled a great team, but it was only my original partner Bruce Cameron who ever thanked me or expressed any gratitude for what he received. Looking beyond the satisfaction of building a business and the bounty we'd reaped, my attitude toward work and what I was building, soured around these issues of compensation and greed.

This year proved no different, and after a less-than-inspiring morning handing out more than we'd ever made, I called my wife Georgia to say I was coming home that Thursday evening—a day early, the day before Christmas Eve. I asked her to please make a dinner reservation and to order a bottle of champagne.

She reported there was snow in Salisbury, Connecticut, the little town we lived in on weekends. That meant a white Christmas. We'd gotten lucky this year, choosing to spend the holiday there rather than with our parents in the South. Retiring from her full-time opera singing career, Georgia made this town her home and the home of a new opera company she was starting.

We had dinner at the Holly House, the finest restaurant in Salisbury, and sat at a table by the fireplace in the old, converted pocketknife factory. Georgia met me, and we opened a bottle of champagne. I caught up on her news for the week, the health of the horses and goats on our farm and the organization and progress of the Light Opera Company of Salisbury (LOCOS), her new non-profit phenomenon. I expressed my dismay with the bonus granting. She was used to this gripe and assured me I was still on the right course.

"They'll get over it and move on. It's just natural from all those high-spirited prima donnas you manage so well, like me," she said.

She was the woman behind the big moves in our lives. She'd pushed me into the entrepreneurial world where I flourished and wondered why I hadn't done it sooner. I so admired this woman's common sense but was still struck by her statuesque silhouette and long blonde hair against the backdrop of the roaring fire. She was like some goddess I'd been blessed to have dinner with after a distinctly disappointing day. We finished the bottle and, a bit giddy, went home to our little cabin at Utopia Ltd. Farm (named for her favorite Gilbert & Sullivan light opera) and lit another fire in the Franklin stove that heated the house. Putting on some light classical music, we kissed and snuggled on the couch in front of it, and soon were in bed passionately entwined until, exhausted, we both slept.

I was up early the next morning to fix coffee. We lived in an Acorn Deck House constructed by a boat builder who said he'd never located a home so perfectly. It overlooked the river—a dark line beyond the trees at the edge of the snow-white harvested cornfield below. The Housatonic runs into the meandering Blackberry River just south of this view. And beyond, across the river, looming ominously like a priest taking confessions was Canaan Mountain rising over the blue-collar town it's named for, and yes, someone had started the Land-of-Nod Winery on it slopes across the river. It was looking out at this view—the day after we bought this house—that changed our lives. That view, in fact, had inspired me to start writing poetry. In 2000, I was commuting every weekend to Salisbury. Georgia sang as a soloist at the Congregational Church and would that night to celebrate Christmas Eve. The church's music director Aly Sly—living up to his name—recruited Georgia as soon as he heard she'd arrived in town. Salisbury had become our home, our community, and Georgia had decided to live there most of the time, out of the opera rat-race of continual auditions. She still answered calls from regional companies around the country that were mostly run by friends who'd become impresarios and wanted her to sing. She'd been a child prodigy in grammar school with a voice that sounded like an adult's. At only sixteen, she'd been a soloist for the famous Robert Shaw Chorale in Atlanta. She was a natural on stage and made singing or comedy seem effortless.

I had no inkling this little cabin would re-center our world, becoming our home for seventeen years, nor what would happen that day. Georgia awoke with a slight headache and a chill and was still not feeling 100% after our celebratory evening. After a light breakfast, she said she wanted to go down to the barn and see the horses. When we got there, I decided to take my horse Cinnamon out for a bareback ride across our snow-covered pastures. She wasn't up for riding her horse Windsor and followed on her cross-country skis.

Georgia lagged behind. I thought she was saving herself for the Christmas Eve church service. With her behind me, I trotted out across the pasture, opening the gate to cross into the larger field formerly owned by the nature writer Hal Borland when Georgia signaled me, and I trotted back to her.

"I'm too cold. Let me take Cinnamon back to the barn," she said. I hefted her up to the horse and walked her skis back to the barn.

When I reached the barn, Cinnamon was loose, standing outside the barn with his reins dragging, and Georgia nowhere to be seen. Something was wrong. This was not the way an experienced horsewoman left her mount. I put Cinnamon in his stall. Curious and worried, I ran to our caretaker Eli's restored barn where Georgia laid on his couch. She held her hand to her head, moaning. Eli had prepared a bag of ice, and some friends, Darry and Zenith Arreglado, who were there checking out the guest cabin for their visiting relatives, suggested other remedies. We all hovered around Georgia. I thought to make tea in Eli's cat-shaped teapot with a paw up for a spout. My wife was dying. The aneurism in the back of her neck that killed her was filling her brain cavity with blood, which, even for a few minutes, is deadly for brain cells. To me, in that moment, she seemed to be fading fast with no explanation.

I called the hospital and asked for an ambulance, but I couldn't get the emergency room to send anyone since it was Christmas Eve. The dispatcher said I could bring her to the emergency room, so I ran to get the car. I called Dr. Bruce Janelli, our regular doctor, who said to get her to the hospital, and he'd meet us there. Eli and Darry helped an almost unconscious Georgia into the car, and I sped away with her to Sharon Hospital. She had ceased speaking and only moaned as we drove at breakneck speed on that surreal morning. The roadsides were piled up into snowbanks. I didn't know what was happening but gave up on trying to talk to her. Georgia wasn't responding. I grasped her hand and squeezed it, she squeezed mine in response—our last communication.

When we got to the emergency room, I tried to help her stand, but she collapsed. I carried her in. The admitting nurse wanted paperwork and ID.

"My wife's unconscious. Please help," I pleaded.

My distress energized the doctors on duty and the crew rushed Georgia into the emergency room where they began to try to resuscitate her. All I remember is the doctor screaming, "I'm getting no response here…" and then starting to cut off her sweater. Nurses scurried to assist and shut off my view as confusion ensued.

Dr. Janelli arrived and went straight into where the ER team worked furiously on Georgia. I tried to use my cellphone to call her mother and sisters, but there was no coverage in Sharon, CT. I was livid and was forced to go to the cafeteria to get quarters to use the only payphone. Finally, a sympathetic nurse let me use her phone to call Georgia's close relatives. My mind was split, half in panic and half in denial, hoping someone could revive my wife, and the other half picking up on the word "aneurism" my thoughts turning to the bleak embankments of snow on either side of the car when she last squeezed my hand, and then to Georgia's odd chill she'd shrugged off that morning.

Dr. Janelli emerged from the ER looking stoic, and quietly took me to an office where rather than explain hope was fading, empathetically showed me a CT scan of Georgia's brain. I immediately fixated on the image of her totally white skull filled from blood loss. It was the head of a ghost. I'd never seen anything like it but couldn't process the conclusions. He told me she was still alive, but they'd transfer her to the neurological ward of Hartford Hospital—the only facility in the state that could deal with this. She'd suffered a major stroke, was probably brain dead and mostly likely would never recover. Neurologists had to confirm this. I was to contact whoever needed to be there and pack to spend the night at Hartford. I was in denial and couldn't process the gravity of our situation.

Stunned and shaking, I called Georgia's mother, Alma, and explained Georgia's severe stroke-like event and told her that she might not recover, while not believing the words myself. I told her to get on the next plane. I also called Georgia's sister Holly who was ready to board a vacation jet to Jamaica with her family; she took the next plane from Baltimore. Georgia's oldest sister Suzy was initially hesitant about finding a flight at this late hour considering the last-minute cost. Almost losing it, I don't remember exactly what I said, but all three of them would arrive at the hospital in Hartford the following morning. This was a hell of a Christmas present for us all.

When I began writing this narrative, I knew there was no other way to begin other than to describe the great chasm that opened before me that day. Looking back, it was the time of turning, a change of seasons— the winter solstice when the days shorten to depressing, and cold wrings out all hope. In BCE times, pagan rituals were enacted to return the light, to hasten spring. In our time, we celebrate the birth of Christ, the birth of the Good News and the Word incarnate. But there was no hope before me that afternoon, only the deepening and widening darkness of a vast valley that I couldn't see across. This was also the turn of a century, the end of the year 2000, when the greatest tragedy of my life unfolded before my eyes.

Chapter 2
Purgatory

When I got to the Hartford hospital, I found my way to Georgia's room where she was wrapped in a white sheet and breathing on a ventilator, or, as I learned later, a life support system, destined to become infamous during our later pandemic. My split brain was hardly functioning, and my heart leapt at seeing her. I hoped that in one of the most sophisticated neurological facilities on the East Coast a miraculous procedure could somehow revive her. No—this was her playing a bizarre role in some strange theater of the absurd, and she'd snap out of it. On the other hand, my practical side was skeptical, telling me to brace myself. I soon learned the full extent of the damage and would share it with her mother and sisters. Jointly, we'd decide her fate.

To my surprise, my business partner Bruce was sitting in the ward. I'd alerted him something was terribly wrong. He drove up from his home in Katonah, finding the emergency room where Georgia had been admitted. Tall, mustached, and always savvy, Bruce had gone to college at Trinity College in Hartford and knew his way around. He'd been with me since the founding of our firm. Ironically, he was the person I needed right then, the person I could turn the running of the firm over to. My anguish was paralyzing, preventing rational decision-making. After a brief conversation, we agreed he should become interim CEO and raise enough cash to withstand any emergencies for the next six months. I knew and told him that wasn't why he'd come, but I thanked him for being there. I turned my attention to Georgia, who quietly wrestled with the angel of death, while I could do nothing but watch.

As the evening wore on, I began talking to Georgia, believing she could understand me on some level. I asked her forgiveness for all the selfish things I'd done and our silly arguments. Even lying down with the ventilator over her nose and mouth, she was stately—a blonde goddess resting at peace somewhere in a purgatory, but also listening to her sniveling husband's confessions. I'd been angry (and jealous) of her being a real artist and not bringing in any money (but that was my job). I'd never cheated on her but had taken time away from our relationship to build my business. I was a workaholic, and she called me on it by having an affair to get my attention. Having remarkable common sense, she took us to therapy where we worked it through. If there was a problem, it was both of us being so busy. We never got around to having children. There seemed to be plenty in the world already—something I regret now.

A nurse checked in on me periodically. Otherwise, I was alone with her breathing. When my remorse and confessions were complete, I began to pray to God to somehow restore her to me. Then exhausted from prayer and supplication, I read aloud Corinthians 13:1 slowly and with great feeling. I believe this is one of the greatest love poems ever written, though it's not a love poem, but Paul's treatise on love, included in his instructions to one of his churches:

> If I speak in tongues of mortals and of angels, but do not have love, I am a noisy gong or a clanging cymbal.... And now faith, hope and love abide, these three; and the greatest of these is love.

Georgia had been God's gift to me, and I felt like I hadn't loved her enough or spent enough time with her. Was this the reason she was being taken from me? I felt most clearly that the love of my life was there before me, breathing and conscious on some level. Hopefully, she understood the message of devotion I'd read and knew I'd loved her as best I could. My guilt spoke, chastising me for selfishly building my company and taking time away from us. All she'd wanted was my love and attention. She was a stunningly beautiful, witty and talented person. What more could I want? She'd given me most of her life, helped me build my business, followed me wherever I wanted to go. She had an uncanny ability to see inside me, see the shy poet and pull him out to play and rejoice in our world together. Her life and our love were fading. I was losing my lover, best friend and playmate. The world as I knew it was coming to an end. The one person I wanted to spend my life with was a breathing corpse.

Chapter 3
Gotterdammerung

Exhausted from my almost all-night vigil, the following morning I returned from a nameless nearby hotel to find they'd moved Georgia into a brighter room with a panoramic view of Hartford. Her mother and Holly were at her bedside—I no longer had to go through this alone. Our caretaker Eli, who'd driven me to Hartford, was there as well. We were all visibly changed by the shock of our once-vivacious Georgia wrapped in a white sheet and breathing through a ventilator. She breathed peacefully as if she were asleep. She was always the star of the show. This was the death scene from one of her operas, and she was playing it to perfection, but would get up soon. Nothing bad could happen on Christmas, I repeated to myself.

A nurse informed us that a neurosurgeon had been summoned to assess the situation but wouldn't be there until later that afternoon. Suzy would finally arrive from Fort Worth that afternoon, and the preacher from our church where Georgia had been scheduled to sing that Christmas Eve would arrive after the morning service. All we could do was sit around her bed, each in a state of disbelief, trying to comfort one another through small talk, and by recalling happier holidays together.

Most visibly affected was Alma Black, Georgia's mother, who was also a vivacious lady and who'd lost her second husband not two years earlier. The potential loss of her youngest child was more than she could bear, though she kept a brave exterior. Alma was a musician—a pianist who'd forfeited her promising career for a family. She'd also won the audition for Scarlett O'Hara's part in *Gone with the Wind* among the debutants who tried out for it before the studio ultimately chose Vivien Leigh. This lady gave Georgia her spunk, musicality, and beauty.

A dark-haired beauty like Alma, Holly was Georgia's middle sister and the tomboy of the family. A great golfer, tennis player and raconteur on her own, she'd married into one of the old monied families of Baltimore—the Lanahans. Like the scion of that family, she loved horses, rode well, and they shared investments in Maryland Hunt Cup champions. After she'd injured her shoulder riding, she'd sent me her horse, Cinnamon. She was a type-A personality, and I learned to agree with her. She always had something witty to say, but not that day. That day she was shaken. The sibling rivalry between competitive sisters was suspended. Tough Holly was tearing up.

Eli was 6'3" tall, angular, and well-muscled. He was a horse whisperer who became the caretaker of our farm. Georgia had met him at a farm down the road from ours. He kept three racehorses there, Manny a mare, and her offspring—Perfect Timing and Elijah's Profit, who had been sired by the famous racehorse, Mr. Prospector. But Perfect Timing was paranoid and came in last in every race he ran, while Profit showed real promise until he was injured at racehorse training. Georgia realized Eli's potential. He raised horses as a hobby while working full-time in a paper factory. Eli was of mixed parentage, had ten siblings, and was raised near the coal mines of West Virginia where his father died of lung disease. Though always cheerful, that day the sun didn't shine for him either.

Preacher Dick Taber arrived, and was initially upbeat, but became increasingly sad, telling us of the congregation's shock at hearing the news. He assured us of the congregation's and community's support and prayers. He led us in prayer, as we joined hands around the bed. I wish I could better remember what he said, but at that point I was looking for any help we could find, particularly divine intervention. His presence was a comfort. He wanted to stay until the doctor arrived, though he had another service that evening. Dick had gone to Yale Divinity School and was, at core, a biblical scholar. He and Georgia had become particularly close, and her singing had become part of his ministry. It was a Congregational Church—the original pilgrims' church—established before the town of Salisbury began. In 1744, as was the evangelic order of the day, the church had been built and then the town around it. Liking the preacher and community, it was only after we joined the church that I researched and discovered that these were the Puritans.

Suzy finally arrived, and the two sisters and their mother hugged and were deeply grieved by Georgia's state. That we were all there—appalled and anxious—on Christmas Day in a sunny room overlooking the city of Hartford with the grim reaper hovering was surreal. I couldn't believe this was happening and that everyone got there as quickly as they had. I remembered much happier family Christmases at Alma's farm drinking the syllabub that their grandmother traditionally concocted for the holiday. I could have used some right then.

A hell of a day it turned out to be. Midafternoon, the doctor, whose name I have since forgotten, arrived. He seemed polite, but serious and got right to work. He was very business-like in examining Georgia and her records. Then he turned and faced us all sympathetically, yet firmly delivered his verdict. It was then I understood why Georgia had been sent to this hospital, and it wasn't because there was any hope of her survival or return to semi-normal living. He stated that Georgia was brain dead, and he was one of only three people in the state who could make that determination. She'd had an aneurysm, probably caused by the drug Tamoxifen she'd taken after her breast cancer surgery three years before.

For a woman like Georgia to have breast cancer had been a physical and mental trauma. We were thus very conservative in its treatment, maybe too much so. But she'd been cancer free for three years, and we thought we were out of those woods. The doctor explained that she currently wasn't in pain or discomfort and could continue to live on a ventilator indefinitely because she was otherwise healthy. She'd suffered a massive stroke and would never recover consciousness. But we could decide to shut the machine off, and she would pass away. He stepped out to let us decide. We all looked at one another in shock.

"Bruce, let her pass. It's her time," Eli said and stepped outside with the doctor.

I asked Dick if he'd pray with us. "Dear God, help us in our time of trial," he began, a truly centering prayer, and I was in a trance thereafter, in disbelief that I was asking the good Lord for His wisdom and under-standing for this ending that was to be done by our hands. It seemed hours passed in that profound facing of reality and of God. I turned to Georgia's mother who tearfully nodded, and through tears, each of her sisters agreed. I stepped outside to get the doctor. He came back in, and we asked him to shut off the machine.

Georgia's beauty was as radiant and statuesque as ever when they removed the mask. She continued to breathe, and then, just as peacefully, stopped. There was no struggle or difficulty; she just stopped the rhythmic inhaling and exhaling, the metronome that measured out our last hours, then minutes together. We were all around the bed touching her, like a laying on of hands. I touched her warm arm and then held her hand—the one that squeezed mine the day before—as it became ice cold and then stiff.

I could almost feel her spirit leaving the room. In fact, it seemed as if she left as soon as we decided she should seek her heavenly path. It was the end of love and life as I knew it. We all hugged and sobbed uncontrollably.

Half of my split brain, the hopeful part, ceased to function, taken over by this awesome reality. It wanted to follow Georgia's spirit. The practical side was congratulating itself for getting everyone there and was now trying to figure out what to do next. Dick Taber pulled me aside and began to feed me important information, principally the name of the local funeral director. He said he could call him, or I could. I asked him to do so, and to request to have her cremated, as was her wish. I couldn't believe I was still able to make another decision. I thanked Dick for coming over to be with us. He expressed his profound sympathy and said I should call him about any problems and certainly when we were ready to have a memorial service.

The doctor and the hospital staff assured us Georgia's body would be taken care of. The undertaker had already been in touch with them and the arrangements made. I wanted to be with her a little longer, as did her mother and sisters. We sat in an unmeasured silence. Eli went down to get the car, and Alma, Holly, Suzy, and I gathered our things and went out into a cold, waning Christmas day to drive west on Route 44 from Hartford to Salisbury.

I was numb. None of us said much on the way back home, though we eventually realized we hadn't eaten all day. We asked Eli to stop at the first place he saw, which was a Kentucky Fried Chicken outside of Winsted, CT. We pulled up in front of a white square building, as welcoming as an ice cube. We bundled inside to be greeted by a picture of the goateed founder who was probably neither Southern nor military. In the linoleum-floored lobby, we picked a screwed down table with hard benches and ordered a tub of chicken. We all recognized the greasy waft of deep-fried chicken, certainly not cooked as well as it had been by all our mothers. With the chicken came sides of mashed potatoes and slaw. We just grabbed for whatever was there—something to fill the hunger, but which left and even magnified the unfathomable emotional void we all tried to deny. After this tasteless meal, all I remember was that I wanted to go outside and see the last light.

The sun was setting, and there was a pink, shading-to-amber glow on the horizon. Here we were at this fast-food franchise, all equally guilty of having pulled life support from Georgia. The woman whose life I'd just taken was my wife, lover, confidant, playmate and soulmate. I thought it was the end of my life, then I strangely began to feel brave. Something inside wanted out. It was a good thing I wasn't driving because I was emboldened like never before. The hopeful side of my brain was now angry at God. I wanted to die—death didn't disturb me anymore because if I passed, I'd be with her. It had turned to Gotterdammerung, the twilight of that fatal day, the pink glow of the world's end radiated all around me. Nothing could hurt me because my heart had been taken out before my very eyes in that hospital room, and I was astonishingly still standing. I knew what those Germanic gods felt before going into that final battle. I was transformed into one of them at sunset at a Kentucky Fried Chicken, living, and facing squarely their dark ominous hell, about to fall into despair with no way out or back.

Georgia and Windsor at Utopia Farm, 1990s

Chapter 4
Hierophany

The next morning the numbness of Georgia's dying was wearing off, like waking up in real pain after your wisdom teeth are extracted. A piece of my heart had been torn out. My whole being ached. I needed to get out of the house. The morning was bright, cold, and I was in a house with some highly organized women, who were all in different degrees of shock, but, as was their nature, there to help me and each other through it. I was up before anyone and made coffee, feeling the full impact of my wife's absence in our bed the night before, and wondered how I could cope. I tried not to notice Georgia's notes, knick-knacks—all the reminders around the house. My mother had arrived the evening before and was already talking of getting me away, of me coming with her to Hawaii.

I can't remember who made breakfast, but I ate heartily, then put long johns on under my clothes, and announced I was going for a walk. I loved these people so but couldn't wait to get out of our small cabin and down to our barn where Georgia and I had spent many joyful hours, thinking that remembering or reenacting our happy rituals might help numb the pain.

I left in snow boots and backpack and took the trail by the swimming-hole pond. The pond was frozen, and I walked across it with a death-defying confidence that nothing could hurt me that morning. The most someone could inflict had already happened. I was an open wound. Like a pilgrimage to a holy shrine where I was once happy, I trekked the long route to the barn, unphased by six inches of snow. It was where she gamboled with and groomed the animals and where I'd last seen her alive. Uncharacteristically, Eli had let all the horses out loose that morning and was nowhere around.

It was a stunning sunny day, but bitter cold. I put on sunglasses. I opened the slightly sagging, handmade cedar gates, and they closed behind me with a slam that startled the horses. They all eyed me strangely, and Cinnamon moved first, loping over to me from many yards away. He came up and nuzzled me, something he never did unless I had an apple or carrot. I didn't have either. He was enthusiastic in his nuzzling, then was joined by Windsor and then Eli's horses. Our two goats Bongo and Ditto, and the neighbor's dog Zinger followed the four horses, and all surrounded me in a sympathy circle. I couldn't believe it—it was as if they knew of Georgia's passing and were expressing their sympathy—they did and were grieving with me! They had never behaved like this before, nor did they ever after.

Our animals loved Georgia. They were openly displaying sympathy beyond my human understanding. I was moved. I could do nothing but open my arms and look up at the blinding sun. An energy and understanding of something beyond me raced through me like an electric current. I think I heard something said aloud, or perhaps I only understood a realization repeating itself like a well-known tune: "Many paths. Many paths." I still puzzle over the phrase's meaning. I think that in my emotional condition I experienced what is termed a hierophany—an encounter with the sacred. I have no idea how long it lasted, and many months later, I wrote about the experience:

Many Paths
"...that very Spirit intercedes with sighs too deep for words."
Romans 8:26

After Christmas morning, below zero,
the day after she died,
my breath freezing, I am dazed
as I walk into the barnyard,
to recall our happiness with the animals there.
Sagging cedar gates close behind me.

My quarter horse Cinnamon
spots me over a hundred yards distant
and begins his long lope. Soon,
his soft nuzzle is rubbing my face, warm,
then her horse and soon, the whole herd,
joined by the goats, and the dog.
They ring me in a circle of compassion.

Touched, yet unbelieving, I look up
into a blinding, cold sun and feel a release—
an energy courses

the length of my body,
and something unnamable
says again, then again:
There are many paths.

Nothing has ever been so clear.

    I didn't know what I experienced, but walking stunned from the barn after petting and hugging each of the animals, I pondered its implication. I sat on the event, afraid to tell anyone what I'd just experienced the day after my wife died. Maybe I'd hallucinated, but it felt real and left me speechless. Was this how life would be? I walked down our road by the frozen river, watching the sheets of ice slide together and crash over one another. I was overcome by sadness and a dull ache. I tried to capture some of that feeling though writing poems that came out slowly afterwards.

Dark River
In memory of Georgia Nunnally Johnson McEver
January 20, 1947 – December 24, 2000

It was winter, like now.
We searched long for a place by water.
The first night in our unfurnished house
we lay in a sleeping bag
joyful on plain pine boards.
Through sunrise's haze,
we overlooked the river
defining the valley.
It wound south
between bare tree-lined banks
fresh with snow.

You said the river had moods,
would change color with each season
and it did: olive springs,
summer's green, and amber falls.
It took all the sorrow
from highland people to the sea.

Four days past
the solstice the river flows
dark south
to where the sun sinks
red on the horizon.

I don't feel it can rise again.
Ice floes scrape and spin—
blown by raw wind,
pieces of a cold puzzle
freezing this river over.

Out of clear dusk,
Venus rises, so bright
I could climb
that gloam-etched tree,
and pluck her from the sky.

I cannot fathom
this early darkness, my love…
I want to go away,
anywhere, till the river changes
colors. But I stay
here, where we were going
to grow old
together.

The grief seemed like it could and would pull me down. I cried a lot
and uncontrollably, and I drank more than I should have to numb the
pain, which didn't help. My doctor wanted me to take antidepressants,
but I didn't want drugs. I found that the most helpful balm was my
meetings with many others who'd experienced the death of a close loved
one. More than anything, their sharing helped me start to come to terms
with it—that and writing about it. So many came forward to share their
experiences of loss. Death is all around us, but we seem to cover it over.

I heard a classic story of the Buddha, who encountered a grieving
woman so distraught that she carried her dead child around with her

and could not be consoled, nor would she let go of the child who had, by this time, putrefied. The loving Buddha calmed her and took her dead child away. He then instructed her to go around the town and countryside and collect from any family who had not experienced death a mustard seed. When she had a handful, she should return to him. In a week, she returned empty handed. "You mean you found no family that had not experienced death?" he inquired. "No," she mused. The Buddha had made his point. It is said this was the Buddha's first female devotee. Death is all around us, a part of life just like a birth, but hard to look in the face, as I was finding out.

Georgia & Bruce McEver with PK Johnson and T.O. & Susie Allen, NYC, Spring 1978

Chapter 5
What Train Sets Out for Yesterday?

After my river walk, I clomped back to our cabin home where my mother and Alma were in high gear, taking care of organizing things for a memorial service and informing friends and relatives of the tragedy. We met later that morning with the preacher to plan the memorial service, and I was impressed with how the older women and preacher knew the proper rites and songs. My sisters-in-law were busy, dutifully cleaning out Georgia's closets and drawers. They cooked and cared for me, and I appreciated them because we were all zomboid from our loss. For Alma, it was losing her beautiful baby, and for her sisters, with one of the three muses gone, they couldn't complete their dance of life liked they used to. When I could sleep, I kept waking and searched for her when I did, just wanting to touch her once more.

The service was on a Saturday. It was snowing, promising a white-out day. Despite the snow, the church in the center of the town was surrounded by cars—strange for a Saturday. New England towns were founded around their Pilgrim (now Congregational) churches, and this seemed like a re-founding. We went into the back of the church as a family and were ushered into a waiting room, staying there until we were led single file into an overflowing meeting house with people standing in the back, both downstairs and in the balcony. I saw familiar faces, some I hadn't seen in years—employees from my company, friends from Atlanta and elsewhere—all to honor Georgia. The news had spread further than I ever imagined. Georgia's mother designed the music program, and the songs were Georgia's favorites. The preacher Dick Taber choked up initially. Despite his emotion, he presided masterfully. Particularly haunting was his reading of a poem by Robert Hillyer, a poetry professor at Harvard, who'd also lost his wife. I had found it by chance earlier that week:

Nocturne

If the deep wood is haunted, it is I
Who am the ghost; not the tall trees
Nor the white moonlight slanting down like rain,

Filling the hollows with bright pools of silver.

A long train whistle serpentines around the hill
Now shrill, now far away.
Tell me, from what dark smoky terminal
What train sets out for yesterday?

Or, since our spirits take off and resume
Their flesh as travelers their cloaks, O tell me where,
In what age and what country you will come,
That I may meet you there.

Having traveled Europe on trains and through many dark, smoky stations, the poem spoke to me. I was in a cave from which I thought I'd never emerge, but everyone being at the service helped pull me out when I truly realized their presence and the subtle power of the ritual being performed. I found the power of communal rites with friends and family strange in how it girded the grieving. I was in a dark hole, but in the receiving line shaking everyone's hand, I was lifted from a yawning chasm—one friend at a time—all there to honor Georgia. I was a different person when I walked out of that meeting house, somewhere uphill from the bottom of the pit I was free-falling into when I'd first walked in. The sun even broke through the thick cloud cover as we walked to our cars.

More extraordinary, and unbeknownst to me, there were two other simultaneous services for Georgia in Fort Collins, Colorado and Chapel Hill, North Carolina where that summer she'd sung the leading role in *Suzanna* with their regional opera company. In a few weeks, we were also to have a service in Atlanta at my mother's church that would be another full sanctuary of people. This outpouring, along with the letters and the condolences was all a bit overwhelming. I started to assemble all of it into a scrapbook.

The paralysis wouldn't go away, however, and I was learning this was a long-term affliction. Having too much wine to make me sleep at night didn't help. I tried to go back to work the week after my mom and Georgia's family left. I had lunch with Bruce and my assistant Marilee, both who'd been with Berkshire since the beginning. The business was thriving. Though I tried to work as much as I could to keep my mind off things, I concluded after a day that I was impaired and couldn't concentrate enough to work full-time. It was good I had Bruce, and he could assume leadership until I climbed out of this funk. The rest of my partners took up the slack. That was also a good thing because my mom wanted to take me to Hawaii where she and Dad had spent so many happy winters after he retired. My mother was sage enough to see what I needed most was to take my mind off the reality of Georgia's death and away from our regular haunts.

The weekend before Mom and I left for Hawaii, I went back to the country. It was cold, empty, and full of memories of the Saturday service. I was called and visited by friends, but most memorably by Georgia's friend Isabel who sang in her opera choir. Isabel was an artist and someone who'd had an out-of-body experience when she almost died in a car crash. Isabel had missed the memorial service and wanted to express her sympathies, so reluctantly told me about her experience of seeing a vision of Georgia, that she was even starting to paint on account of the profound effect of it. Art was in her veins as a member of the Livingston family of New York, who'd signed the Declaration of Independence and had married into Fredrick Church's family and even lived beneath his famous home, Olanna on the Hudson. I was skeptical at first but listened patiently and saw too many dots connect. It prompted me to go and see the place where her unusual vision occurred.

The Vision

i
High cirrus dimmed Christmas Eve's sky.
Isabel went to pray for an ailing friend
at the old quay, out on the Hudson
and was surprised to find her sitting
on a bench in a white fur coat,
facing the half-iced river and the mist-
draped mountains beyond...

iv
Isabel's story was curious
because the white mink coat,
bought on a birthday whimsy,

was my wife's favorite.
One night, she enticed me in it
to skate with her on a black-iced lake.
She pirouetted like a polar bear,
her icecapades spotlighted by passing cars.
She was wrapped in this coat, chilled and sick
after chemo in our window seat,
smelling of the treatments,
I pretended not to notice.

v
It's here, Isabel said as I turned
the car onto the snow powdered path.
Her dog, following fresh deer tracks,
led us down to the river beneath
her great-grandfather's home, Olanna.

vi
*It was a day like today, about the same
time in the afternoon,* she remarked, not knowing
it was the same time my wife died
or that we came to Olana to toast
sunsets on special occasions.
I chilled recalling the oil of its grand view
hanging above my wife's piano.

vii
We pilgrimaged, silent, afraid our footsteps
crunching snow would frighten the spirit
waiting at the end of the dock.
The wrecked iceflows
piled up around the quay,
a hard-edged tribute to the simple bench,
of cinder block and bleached board
sided by cedar and thorns—
heaven's gate.

viii

So, what did you say? I asked.
There were no words spoken,
but a complete understanding
something horrible happened;
then, the deep peace shared between us
assured me she was all right.
There was an emerald glow
around her head,
and when she turned toward me,
there was no face.

Initially I discounted this incident, but Olanna was our favorite place, a place where Georgia and I went for sunsets with champagne on the hill beneath the Moorish mansion Church created. Its picture windows and manicured lawns were like his great painted landscapes. Isabel encountered Georgia's spirit there at the same time she passed. It seemed a natural place for her spirit to have fled to from that grim hospital room in Hartford, and I, strangely enough, began to or, more likely, wanted to believe it. I went there before I left for Hawaii on the chance, I'd reconnect with her spirit. If nothing else, I became more open to such reverberations in the future. I stood on the end of that ice-bound quay watching the magnificent sunset I'd follow west.

Chapter 6
Hawaii and the Absolution Lick

Mom arranged it all. I left from New York, and she flew from Atlanta. We met up in LA, took a flight to Honolulu together staying at the US military resort hotels that Mom and Dad had visited every year in Dad's retirement. The Hale Koa on Waikiki beach on Oahu was one of these resorts and was where we started our trip. We ate at the officers' club there and at other bases around the island, sometimes accompanied by Mom and Dad's friends who were on vacation. Dad had stayed in the Navy Reserves to get his retirement benefits, one being the ability to use the officers' clubs and PXs on military bases worldwide. It was not without its price, however, as he'd been recalled to active duty during the Korean War. We drove around to see the sights. It's a magical island if you overlook some touristy aspects. I was there to tune out and be with Mom, and while I found myself diverted, I couldn't shake my grief. Instead, I found I'd developed a new attraction for graveyards and rituals honoring the dead.

Fallen Flowers

I
At 4:00 AM, under Diamondhead's
worn molar, my light is an orphan
on this high-rise reef
ringing Waikiki.
I tend a little memorial
on my dresser. Next to a candle: your toy
lamb and yellow beach bonnet,
the hotel's welcome lei, a heart-shaped
box of candy, and a photo
of us with friends in the country
and our pet goat.

All's quiet now at Hale Koa,
the house of warriors,
as far away as I could go to heal.

The large orange and yellow koi
feather in the lobby pond beneath lotus pads.
The soft breeze motions
the air-borne roots of the central banyan
like pendulums recounting time
and rustles palms like dancers' hips
weary of the hula...

II
I climb to the Punchbowl,
a necropolis of our fallen
in an extinct volcano crater
overlooking Honolulu.
On its north rim, the first were laid here
with columns of oily smoke rising
from the battleships still burning in Pearl Harbor...

Over a hundred manicured acres—
smooth-bark banyans shade
the remains from each avenging step
across the Pacific islands to a setting sun:
Midway, Guadalcanal,
Rabaul, Coral Sea,
Bougainville, Leyte Gulf,
Surigao Straight, Saipan,
and Mt. Suribachi.

Reviewing the long march of crosses,
the multitude of markers decorated
with Valentine flowers strikes me.
My father's fallen comrades initiate
me into that left-behind legion
who are to ration out petals
with our sorrow for the rest of our lives.

III
The Jains believe only fallen flowers
are suitable for worship.

At first light, I walk the hotel gardens
gathering wind-trimmed flowers
for your memorial. I take back fresh
tropical fragrances and bright colors:
purple, azure, and saffron.

Not bad for my second day on the job.
I have some coffee and wonder
what the maid thinks?

I began to understand the power and importance of ritual in dealing with death and seeing its enormity across our culture, even though we don't want to deal with it directly. We traveled around the island, visiting some of the historical sites, the most memorable being the Pearl Harbor Memorial. At the visitor's center, the film of the Japanese attack and the black smoke column rising like a dark angel from the Arizona that we'd just boated and walked over in the pale blue waters of the harbor was unforgettable. Particularly poignant is the journey over the old sunken battlewagon still oozing oil, leaving a rainbowesque scum on the water around it. The plume in the film was ominous and etched in my memory, as I vividly recalled it the following year watching the World Trade Towers fall from my office window in Manhattan.

Afterwards I walked up into the cemetery for those sailors killed at Pearl Harbor and noted the flowers on the graves. Cemeteries were becoming friendly places. I found now that I could relate to the departed, had no fear of the dead, but wanted to strangely be and commune with them. I looked over the hills of Hawaii and could imagine the Japanese planes droning over them like swarms of bees. It was around Valentine's Day and reminiscing angels had scattered roses on many of the tombstones of their loved ones.

One evening at the hotel, Mom and I happened upon a dance for widows and widowers, giving me a preview of social life awaiting me. I knew I'd never be the same. I couldn't shake her absence but saw how others coped with that reality as well. I'd joined a club I never wanted to join, "the widowers," and found myself to be a card-carrying member of it.

Line Dance Heaven—

a bright blue banner
in a Honolulu shopping mall proclaims.
A western fling where
Asian ladies in cowboy boots
and hats step, clap, turn, and sway.

Center stage, their leader croons
to the twangy tunes
in turquoise tassels.
Held Wednesdays at seven
this is a widow's stomp:

the single male is a Hawaiian
under a Stetson who attends
his lover drooling
in a wheelchair near the DJ.
Rejoining the ladies' lines,
he causes a twitter,
a bodhisattva
with a blue bandana...

Nice postcard cowgirls!
I can join your club.
Get in line and face
the music.

After a week in Oahu, we decided to hop to the big island, Hawaii, to see Mauna Kea and other sites. There we splurged, staying at a luxurious hotel. It was a distinctly different island from more tropical Oahu, with a dry, almost desert-like climate. During the day, I explored the island while Mom sat at the pool reading, content in the sun that was good for her arthritis. The evenings became a time for us to catch up with each other and for mom to regale me with our family history, I here-to-fore hadn't paid that much attention to. The hotel dining room was a gourmet delight—a fusion of native Polynesian, Japanese, and American. I'd lost weight from my emotional ordeal and didn't feel guilty at the luaus, testing the poi from taro root and suckling Kalua pork. These were long fascinating discussions with my mom.

The next day I went out to size up the big island, and learned something of the remarkable history and culture of the Polynesians at a national park. I also had a moving experience at the little, but famous Painted Church not far from there.

Refuge

I
The ancient Hawaiians revered
places of refuge like this black lava flat
by an old royal compound at Honaunau Bay.
It's staked with some straggly palms and crossed
by a pumice block wall divvying
the refuge, or pu'uhonua,
from the thatched-roofed royal
reservation and temples
by the king's landing lagoon,
now occasioned by sea turtles.

A park ranger in breechcloth
coolly weaves a mat of palm leaves
telling the story of his ancestors—
Polynesian Vikings,
who followed a great shark
and the luminous constellations
of these latitudes. They crossed
hundreds of ocean miles in hand-hewn canoes
full of breadfruit, pigs, and dogs,
searching for new islands,
a place of refuge.

Here, the defeated or those who
had stepped on the king's shadow,
(believed his essence, or kapu)
were saved and granted absolution.
If they could make it to this home.

II
On the road back to Kona,
I visit the Old Painted Church
guarded by a friendly dog.
The white wooden-latticed chapel
and its necropolis—dug
from rust-red volcanic slope
overlook the azure bay.

The interior is a shoebox Sistine
giving the illusion of St. Peters
with columns of palm trees.
Through this sacred space
whispering tourists wander
snapping cameras.

I pick a pew next to a mural
of St. Francis' epiphany.
After a day of dragging grief
around, I prostrate myself.
Sobbing overtakes me.
It happened so suddenly,

had I stepped on God's shadow?
I imagine Jesus comes
down from his cross
and offers a fresh flower lei.
There's breathing next to me,

a cold nose on my thigh,
then a paw on my knee
and mutt gives me
the absolution lick.

While there, I took an expedition, a pilgrimage really, to the obser-
vatories at the top of Mauna Kea. I went up the mountain in a tour van
and was supplied a fur-hooded heavy coat because it's so cold up there

at 13,000 feet. From the floor of the ocean, this is the tallest mountain in the world. What was remarkable was the first view of the naked night sky because it demonstrated the reality that the sky is really nothing but billions of stars. I'd never seen a naked sky like that—it was solid stars—the appeal of astronomy was never stronger. I couldn't help but think of Shiller's poem, "Ode to Joy" (Beethoven uses it to close his 9th symphony), asking, *Is there a heavenly father beyond the stars?* I was looking up in awe, saying: *Yes, dear Lord, Yes!*

It was during this time in Hawaii that I bonded with my mother in a way I never had before, understanding we shared the same pain over the loss of our spouses. Knowing this hurt lasted a lifetime, she took me away to her paradise to ease its onset. In her case, she'd been married to my father for over fifty-two years when he passed. Georgia and I gave them a surprise fiftieth birthday party where Georgia—wearing Dad's leather flying jacket and captain's hat—played a musical version of Harold singing of his life with Lucille, while Lucille was played by Georgia's best friend Paula. My parents were delighted at the performance. I'd only been married thirty-one years when Georgia passed. Mom told me she still envisioned him and regularly talked to him when she was in the kitchen fixing dinner. I remembered the Iroquois saying about the departed being as close as the other side of a leaf. Given the number of experiences I had after Georgia's passing that seemed more than synchronicity, I came to believe that as well.

That evening, Mom talked about her and Dad's early life together. She recounted her life and my early childhood. I didn't know much of their courtship until this trip. Mom had been a farm girl whose ancestors left Germany to avoid the Kaiser's draft and came to the rich rolling hills of Nebraska where they got a section (360 acres) of land. This was pioneer stuff. My grandfather had a sister who was the sole survivor of her family after a Sioux massacre. Aunt Anna, whom I met, had been hidden under a large cooking pot and was a community icon. So was the legend.

My grandfather raised prized Poland-China pigs, and my mother and her sisters had been important to running the farm. It was constant work with no vacations, feeding crews of hired men and managing the farm chores, along with her schoolwork. Winters had been long, cold and snow-buried, while summers were hot, much too brief and carried threats of twisters. When it was time for my mother to go to school, her father bought her an Indian pony at a Sioux City fair for her commute. They had a house in the town of Carroll, Nebraska with a barn where my mother stabled her horse during the day, complete with a pulley to raise and lower her saddle onto the horse's back!

The stories continued. I remembered that house and barn fondly from our summer visits when I was a child. Mom was one of three sisters, the middle child. Eva, the oldest, had a dark cloud about her, and probably suffering from depression, eventually took her own life. The youngest, Margaret Anne, or Peddy, was a fireball. As young women, all of the girls moved to California where their cousins had preceded them, escaping the Midwest winters. They were part of the exodus from the Midwest that largely populated California prior to the war.

My mother graduated from a small local college, Wayne State University, and was teaching high school English in Wayne, Nebraska, before she migrated with her sisters to Long Beach, rich in oil around Signal Hill and teeming with military personnel. The Douglas aircraft factory was there, so Long Beach centered as a jumping-off port to all points west before the Pacific War.

There was such a rush of folks to California from the Midwest, my mother couldn't get a job as a teacher right away, so she worked as a bank teller. Then one morning a group of Navy flyboys came into the branch, and one of them struck up a conversation with her. He came back the next day to ask her out to dinner. It turned out he was a flying instructor, temporarily stationed at a nearby naval air station. He was from Georgia. My mother recounted how polite he was and his drawl. He talked slowly, and she could barely understand him. The other girls giggled, but she thought he was damn handsome.

She was smitten and so was he. I have my father's letter to his twin brother saying he was head-over-heels about this woman from Nebraska he'd met in Long Beach, though she was "a little plain." Whatever his hesitation, war time and his impending deployment overseas soon swept it away. With the Pacific War raging, romance was compressed, and after less than a year, they were married in April 1943. Luckily, my father's younger brother Charlie was on leave from the Army and served as his best man. All Dad's wedding party were in uniform. Mom was in a tailored suit, and her sisters were in attendance, as well as Muriel, her best friend who I would get to know. More than the marriage was hastened because my mother disclosed to me after a couple of drinks that I was a "diaphragm baby." She got pregnant during their brief honeymoon in the fancy hotel on Long Beach Boulevard. I have since surmised that my father resented my unplanned arrival in the world, maybe accounting for our long-strained relationship.

Since my father was a flying instructor and was needed to train a continuous stream of pilots vital for air combat, he didn't go off to the war right away. My parents were soon sent to the Navy Training Airfield at Olathe, Kansas, where those mass-produced freshmen flyboys had nothing but flat cornfields to destroy while earning their wings.

I was born at three in the morning on February 8, 1944. My mother's suitcase was already packed, and my father drove her to the municipal hospital in Kansas City, Missouri. Mom told me that he was so nervous they wouldn't let him in the delivery room. I was a healthy eight-plus-pounds, delivered without any real problems.

Around the time my father was called to go into the Pacific theater to fly transports, we had an old Ford with a rumble seat in the back where I traveled as my parents drove cross-country over the Rockies to the naval base at Alameda. (During Vietnam, my ship was stationed at that same base.) I've always liked the San Francisco Bay Area, possibly from this early introduction.

In 1944, Dad was flying transports, the ubiquitous C-47, in the action around the Philippines. He landed the first US plane on those islands after we retook them. He was so exhausted from his mission, he went right to bed, unaware a Japanese attack came in overnight behind him. The next morning, he discovered they'd shot off the top of his tent. He didn't make it home until over a year after I'd been born. He'd survived being shot at by the Japanese, but I threw a tantrum upon first meeting the "new" man in our house, and that tension remained between us throughout most of our lives.

After four days on the big island, we hopped to Maui, where we stayed in a beautiful hotel. It was on the beach, and we were entranced by the surf and surfers there. There's nothing like watching the unfurling curl of those blue-green waves and the surfers who harness their power and ride them, go with the flow, so to speak. We found a beach front café there for breakfast, and I asked Mom to return to her history, but first she insisted that I should explore a particularly old volcano crater this morning, then we'd continue to talk.

She was right. I had another remarkable experience walking across the crater of Mauna Loa. Late morning, I left Mom by the pool, where she was content to sit in the sun and read. I took the car up to the National Park on the edge of the long dead volcano. It was a moonscape that could have been where the Apollo astronauts conducted their pre-lunar landing training (or a fake one was staged?). I hiked across the most barren landscape I've ever walked in. The multi-colored dust, ash and stone made it desolation exemplified. It was the shape of my soul at that point—desolate and burned out. As I walked, I wondered how I'd ever reinvigorate it. I realized my mother was the key. The history of her life and my early life that she relayed while we were together was beginning to put things back into place for me—to examine my past life, help me relive it, and possibly suggested a future. I'd have to find my way through it without Georgia now, but hadn't fully appreciated the extent of my mother's strength and her perspective as a guide on my paths.

She continued her history saying after the war was winding down, my father's next duty station was in Coral Gables, Florida where he flew transports down to South America. We lived near the beach and with my father's twin brother Bill, who was a Navy pilot as well, who flew PBY's or the "flying boats" out of Miami. In Florida I took to the water like a pro, but also ended up in the ER having swallowed our neighbor's rat poison, an incident recorded in the Miami papers.

After my father was discharged from the Naval Air Corps in Miami, we soon went back to Georgia and stayed for a while in Gainesville with my grandmother and my father's two sisters, Lucy and Mary Lou, who adored and took care of me before my father went to Atlanta and interviewed with the then-fledgling Delta Airlines. My grandmother was a pianist and painter. She was a graduate of Brenau College there in Gainesville, an artist who had to give it up to take a bus to Atlanta daily to support her family after my grandfather died suddenly. She was a devout Baptist who played for her church on Sundays. She was also a rabid member of the Women's Christian Temperance Union (WTCU) and pledged me on as a baby. I still have the certificate but became a backsliding disappointment.

There was a glut of pilots after the war, but with his war record and instruction skills, dad got the job and went "on the line," flying the milk runs to Baton Rouge, Jacksonville, and Brunswick. Mom related those days he confessed navigating with roadmaps, following the major highways to those towns. Pilots' salaries were not what they are today, but my father was happy to have a job. My parents rented a basement apartment near the airport in College Park on Rugby Avenue. It was all they could afford at the time. The landlady was nice and allowed them to have me—not all places took young children.

This turned out to be a lovely community, too. Its streets were named for colleges, a planned community—the first of its type. There was a private boy's school, Georgia Military Academy—across the railway tracks at the end of Rugby Avenue. The streets were oak-lined, and on spring Sundays, my mother walked me up the shaded lane to watch the parades there. I remember the cadets dressed in grey with white trousers and spiffy starched white "X's" across chest and backs. They marched company by company, like human blocks, across the grounds there. Little did I know I'd be attending that school and marching in those parades not fifteen years later.

My father's dream job with Delta was not secure. There was a terrible recession during Eisenhower's presidency that forced the fledgling airline to lay off junior pilots, my father among them. It was a struggle; he found a job as a bill collector for the Commercial Credit Corporation as delinquencies rose. My mother had almost needed to return to teaching, a social no-no for married women at the time. It was a tough time for us. Mom reminded me of my little wheeled black-and-white pinto toy horse named Queenie. I recalled my knees were skinned from careening down the driveway to our apartment. I also nearly died from a bout of bronchial pneumonia, coughing in this damp, little basement apartment. My parents tried everything to heal me and eventually had to move.

When my father got rehired as a pilot, I went with him to the airport and rode in the jump-seat behind him. You could never do that now. Off to those little Southern cities, I'd go, getting used to flying and feeling really proud of my dad. He did it with such quiet confidence. I loved it, but I was resentful of his not paying more attention to me. I don't think he ever understood what I wanted to do. He did his best. He was a man who loved his work and his family. He wanted me to be a pilot as well. It was only natural, but we never seemed to be able to see eye to eye.

Flying

The first star burns
in the western sky,
bright over the fading aurora
that was today:

A navigation beacon
emitting in the shadowy zone
of ultraviolet space
that is tonight.

Above the weather's patch quilt
and the just-bejeweling sporelike cities
we fly, safe,
up here
in my father's place—

where he worked and watched
this continental cyclorama
of earth, cloud, and sky
for all those years,
but never told me.

Tonight, I, too, see
the same silent spectacle,
spread a full horizon,
up here
in my father's place.

My father died of kidney failure in November 1996 after decades of taking aspirin for the chronic back pain he experienced from overexerting himself as a stock boy when he was a teenager. Because he was a pilot, he avoided opioids, but the aspirin he took in its place, gradually destroyed his kidneys. When discovered, it was too late for a transplant, so he radically changed his diet and became a vegetarian, that extended his life seven years. He was seventy-six when he died peacefully in St. Joseph's in Atlanta. We were all with him. His last words to me were to take care of Mom and to reconcile with and look out for my sister Sharon.

Sadly, Dad never seemed to understand my ambition or encourage it. Maybe he was jealous. I later learned that after his own father tragically lost his business, he died suddenly of a heart attack overstressed from that loss at the family dinner table when my father was only fourteen. Dad never had his blessing, nor did he ever fully give me his. After my father's funeral in Atlanta—a sunny winter afternoon—several of his pilot friends told me what a great man and pilot he was and the inspiration they'd taken from him. Mom reminded me of the Summer Olympics of 1996 in Atlanta some of which we attended before dad passed away. Through the lottery, I had gotten tickets for all the track and field events, so we went every day or traded for other venues around the city. That was a grand time for all of us and a great memory of dad still vital before he was unable to get out of his bed.

Captain Harold B. McEver, 1970s

Chapter 7
Georgia's Youngest Eagle Scout

Our verbal journey back into my childhood continued the next evenings at dinner, Mom and I recalled our move to an ordinary red brick apartment complex in East Point from our more airport convenient, basement apartment in College Park because of my illness. At the time, she was pregnant and big as a barn with my sister, Sharon. I remembered her waking me up late one night on her way to the hospital, suitcase in hand with Finley Smith, our neighbor who was standing by as my father was, of course, off flying. She recalled clearly: "Those apartments were temporary, one step up from public housing, you know, clotheslines full of laundry, kids screaming…something inexpensive, but clean while your Dad was completing building our first house, on Pollard Drive, in Cascade Heights." This was a subdivision in Atlanta where many pilots were building. The builder, Ed McGriff, lived across the street and would build yet another house for us, as was my fathers' way with contractors.

She continued: "As I said there were other pilots in the same neighborhood, whose children became your best friends – "Zeke" Fanning and his son Steve and Doug Volk and little Dougie. Charlie Dolson, the president of Delta, lived in a little bigger house and not very pretentious, either, at the end of the street." This company grew from its origin as fraternity of military pilots, but amazingly maintained many of their related values.

"That was your first year in school. Because you were born in February, you had to wait a year before you were six and could enter first grade, but that didn't hold back your schooling. I was a teacher and all your doting grandmothers, uncles and aunts made sure you could read. We had an early TV set; you never watched much, but your favorite programs were "The Lone Ranger" and "Hop-Along Cassidy.""

I discovered I even had the black cowboy suit with accompanying twin pearl handled pistols like Hoppy, and speculated maybe I was attracted to their honor code or their common sense solving the outlaw problems.

"I think you just liked shoot-em-up westerns," she concluded, always practical and realistic.

She described me riding my bike to school through Adams Park where there was a neat little library I would stop at regularly to check out and read books. She observed I was an avid scholar and consistently exceeded their 10-book summer reading goals, speculating this is where I got my 'curiosity gene'. I recalled an illustrated volume of Nordic mythology and poring over this colorful text, imagining the cosmic origins and struggles of those ancient gods that fascinated me.

Mom said it was then I became a member of the Cub Scouts and I remembered one meeting after school when struck by an awful pain in my side. Our "den mother" Mrs. Volk tried to give me a laxative, but luckily it was so bad I refused to swallow it. When we finally got to the emergency room, I was found to be having appendicitis. Mom commented that taking the laxative could have killed me, rupturing the appendix, spreading infection. I only succinctly remembered the crude screen mask of that day and horrible smell of ether.

It wasn't soon after my recovery from surgery that we heard shocking news that Doug Volk's Sr.'s plane went down in a tornado. He and all his passengers were killed. Mom said this was her greatest fear. It was one of Delta's first tragedies. The outpouring and memorial were unforgettable. We felt so bad for Helen and her family, who had to move out of our pilots' neighborhood, sell their house and go back to live with her parents. I lost a good friend, Doug, Jr. and our den mother. I had not encountered death up close until this and didn't fully understand sadness, particularly Mrs. Volk's grieving. Mom said again we never truly understand this until we experience it, first- hand. Our eyes caught each other's in acknowledgement.

Mom said I really enjoyed my school, Cascade Heights Elementary. She rated it "a good public school with teachers, who in those days were very competent." She always honored the profession, being one. She added: "You were largely unchallenged academically, maybe got a little lazy, but I remember you always reading a lot on your own. You sang in the boys' chorus where you were a soprano soloist, until your voice changed, then you took up the clarinet, of all things; maybe because I had told you I played the clarinet in my high school band. That was your last musical challenge… well until you met Georgia."

At the time of the Korean War, Dad being in the Navy Reserve and a needed pilot, was recalled. We were to report to the Naval Air Test Station at Patuxent River, Maryland, not far from Washington D.C. I did not want to leave my comfortable home and bike ride to school, nor the cub scouts after school. Mom said this transition was a huge trauma for me, but a good one for me after I adapted. It was winter after selling our house when we moved and experienced our first snowfall. Initially we couldn't get base housing, so we lived in a town called "Tall Timbers" Maryland, in a modest wooden two-story frame apartment near a remote cove of the Chesapeake Bay. I had to take a bus before first light to ride for an hour to the Navy base elementary school and came home with lots of homework.

I remembered my new 'Yankee' classmates were also much sharper than my laid-back Southern pals. The smartest person in the class was a woman who was ahead of me to begin with that I caught up with by the year end. These "Navy brats," used to the vagabond military life, were more worldly wise than sheltered me.

Mom said Dad did some exciting flying to Europe via Newfoundland and the UK in a domed (to navigate by the stars) DC-6, bringing back great photos and presents from Pompeii, Naples, Capri and stories of trans- Atlantic flying to our naval bases over there. I still have on my library shelf, a hand carved destroyer Dad brought from Naples, Italy.

The principal hidden benefit of our move, hands down, were my trips to Washington D.C. to visit my cousin, Phil Landrum, a long time Dixiecrat Congressman whose sister, Sarah Landrum ran his office. Sarah could open any door in Washington and relished taking me around with her to show me the wonders of our Capitol. Mom agreed: "She was a go-getter and loved you. Also, when you would later go up to D.C. with your aunt, Mary Lou or me, and Sarah would guide us, but soon you knew your way around the Mall and had visited every museum.

It was an early education, just touring these places and I used every minute I could there. Mom added: "Sarah took you over to meet Richard Nixon, who was the Vice President then under Eisenhower. He was always the politician and gave you a pen with his name on it. You did not wash your hands for a week after you shook his. Mom added. "Little did you know you would later serve in his administration at the end of his last unfortunate presidential term."

Despite the rough start at Tall Timbers, I began to flourish on the Navy base when we got officers housing. I remember dad and I going out fishing a spring evening before we left that cove on the Chesapeake Bay with one of dad's friends who rowed us mid-channel in his boat. "We must have had the word straight from Jesus to fish on the right side of our boat, because I've never caught so many fish."

I also remembered singing in the boys' choir at the base chapel and being soloist until my voice began to change. I bonded my new companions – we were a sort of a bicycle gang like those kids on bicycles in the ET movie and went all over that base on our wheels. These Navy brats taught me much about the world. The Blue Angels were stationed there, so we had our heroes close at hand. By the time the war wound down and Dad went back to Delta in Atlanta, I was sort of sad. I liked our time in the Navy, especially being close to DC and those museums.

Mom continued: "Before we moved to Maryland, you became seriously engaged in scouting first through your cub scout connection in Helen Volk's pack in Adams Park. You progressed directly through the Cub Scout ranks to Webelos, its highest rank, and were extremely fortunate on our return to join Harry Price's Troop 110. That's where you made you first real mark on the world."

I remembered, our lodge was rather humble and inauspicious, a brown-woodened-shingled hut, behind the Gordon Street Presbyterian Church in Southwest Atlanta. We met on Friday nights sitting on a wooden bench around the inner circumference of our hut with one of four patrols stationed in each corner. Summers were spent at Camp Bert Adams near Kennesaw Mountain on the outskirts of the ever-burgeoning central civilization of Atlanta. Our scoutmaster who was known as Harry Price. Mr. Price was a clerk at the Southern Railroad with an ordinary desk job that he translated into meaning beyond his office time, producing in his lifetime an astounding 72 Eagle Scouts.

As a scout I would visit Mr. Price at Southern Railroad headquarters in the middle of its vast freight yard in downtown Atlanta. I would find Harry Price at his desk lined up with other clerks in a large open-space office in an upper floor of the Southern Railroad building. Before computers, he was one of many schedulers for the railroad who kept the freight moving from the North through Atlanta to points South into and from Florida and to and from the ports east, Savannah and Charleston taking it to Birmingham and points West. His was an important job, but you could tell his life was all about his scouts.

In my mind, in that open-air office was a man as great as Lincoln, my scout master Mr. Price, a humble, a similarly unassuming person that produced so many Eagle scouts and who got me so fired up for all things scouting that I eventually produced more merit badges than I needed by the time I was 12 years old. Old enough to get my Eagle and becoming the youngest in the state at that time. I don't remember him being demanding or a disciplinarian, rather a rock-solid quiet example who showed us how scouting could open your eyes to new worlds and challenges.

There were several exceptional guys in that troop, some I went both through elementary school and scouting with such as my good friend Sam Lyons, now a renowned aviation artist. His father, Sam, Sr., who'd graduated and played football at Georgia Tech, was one of the more active parents in our program. He got our troop involved in selling cokes Saturdays at Ga. Tech football games. Watching Bobby Dodd's championship teams at that time fostered a future alumnus. Also, a fellow eagle scout, and a true Vietnam war hero, my friend, Steve Fanning, who recently passed away, was in this troop. His dad, Zeke and my father were pilots and participated when possible. Likewise, my neighbor Don Arnold whose parents were separated. A traveling salesman, Don's dad had been banished to a small frame house behind the Baptist Church in Cascade Heights where he had an incredible collection of books stacked in orange crates about Native Americans and Mesoamerica which he would let me borrow; I credit him for my archaeological interest, particularly all things native American.

My mom really encouraged me and took me religiously to our scout meetings. I loved it because it involved outdoor activities I lacked with dad gone flying so much. Most boys were into little league, hunting and fishing, or other sports, but I was involved with getting as many merit badges as I could accumulate. I worked my little tail off, interested in the education it provided out of doors and outside of school, that I had begun to tire of. Working on a merit badge was an ideal introduction and instruction to a diverse range of skills such as: marksmanship, drama, the arts, and the natural sciences, particularly geology (I had a big rock collection), also they taught crafts, such as wood carving and painting, each course opening a new world. Every badge was a mini course in a skill. Many just needed individual skills, but there were group activities such as conservation projects requiring leadership to organize folks to get these projects done. I was a whirlwind of activity and seemed to thrive better at this level of activity. I needed 21 merit badges, but by the time I finished and was old enough to get my Eagle, I had 32 merit badges. Still, I had to wait until my 12th birthday, February 8, 1956, to be declared an Eagle

Scout. I had enough momentum to eventually accumulate 45 merit badges, today preserved on a sash in my home office.

Reflecting on my dedication to scouts and later building my investment banking business, I think this early training was great for helping me to multitask, undertake running several deals simultaneously, and seeing them to completion without stressing out over running several jobs at one time.

Though I had the required number of badges and was approaching my twelfth birthday, to be declared an Eagle Scout was not without its own trials. Sort of like defending a dissertation, I went before an august board of fellow scouts and scoutmasters who drilled me about my woodland skills and subject knowledge. Because I was so young—and would become the youngest Eagle Scout in Georgia—the examination went on for a couple of hours, longer than what was standard practice; the qualification board wanted to be sure I was worthy. I must have handled it okay, and remember the last question: If I were in a rain-soaked forest with only flint and steel to light a fire, how would I start one? Luckily, I remembered the ubiquitous plant in Georgia called wild mullein that's sort of like a lamb's ear with a soft hairy underside, usually dry in a downpour and luckily plentiful in Georgia's countryside. I passed! And remember today my Mother and Father beaming at me from the audience of the ceremony held at the courthouse in downtown Atlanta.

One of my grandest adventures in Scouts happened the summer after I turned fourteen. I went back to Bert Adams Boy Scout Camp—a preserve on the edges of Atlanta that was a whole mountain—where I was to be the "nature counselor" and where I learned every tree, plant, rock, snake and animal I still reference in natural environments worldwide. It was a staff of great guys. I was one of the ranking scouts and enjoyed the other counselors, many of whom had been there several years. Before camp started, I led teams up all the creeks on the property to catch as many snakes as we could in order to save them from the campers and to populate the nature hut that had a pet raccoon, skunk and a python—feeding time for the python was an event of high interest for the camp and campers. I think this experience has helped me even today in becoming acutely aware of the natural environment around me, what is growing and living in it, and to appreciate its increasing scarcity and its transformation due to our warming weather patterns. I clearly see this in my current conservation efforts in Connecticut with the explosion in invasive species and an impulse for overdevelopment at the cost of perservation.

We counselors also divided ourselves into two parties: the Conservatives and our rival Communist party, headed by "Moose" Davis, the head cook. Early on, we decided to one up his group by stealing their "manifesto" they foolishly painted in red with yellow lettering and hung on the wall of Moose's hut. We took it and nailed it to the floor of the nature hut under the python's case where it stayed all summer despite reprisals. One night, our camp was ambushed and hosed down after one of our meetings, but no one snitched where the manifesto was hidden. My late wife used to sing a Gilbert and Sullivan opera—*Yeoman of the Guard*—whose central aria summing up the state of the world laments every boy and girl as being either "a little liberal or conservative." Nothing much has changed.

The highlight of our summer as camp counselors came when we closed camp. I let out all the snakes I'd captured, and those the campers had caught as well, returned the python and raccoon, as well as a de-skunked skunk, "Petunia." We were given the use of all the canoes and taken to the Chattahoochee River for a three-day-long trip. To sweeten the excursion, we were given all the leftover steaks and full rations we would cook for ourselves. Set for a great adventure and party differences aside, we'd completed a successful season—no camper had gotten lost or sustained any major injury.

Off we went down the slow, muddy green stream flowing around Atlanta and south to the Gulf Coast. It was a beautiful day, a good one for a canoe trip. We were all pretty proficient canoers, even shot some rapids. Bone tired from a day of paddling, we found a large island with a beautiful beach and pulled our canoes up on shore. Moose and his boys began to unpack the steaks (we were too young for wine in Georgia) and were almost hungry enough to eat the steaks raw. The counselors who were to keep the matches dry had, of course, gotten them wet, but one of the fathers along with us was a smoker and had a lighter. We pigged out and went to bed early after some campfire singing. Great trip, or so we thought.

What we hadn't anticipated was the new dam at Lake Lanier releasing water that was in overabundance from summer rains at midnight. We were sound asleep and didn't discover that our canoes—all of them—had been taken downstream by the rising tide. We calmly fixed breakfast and set out in shorts and tennis shoes, walking the edges of the river. Our reward for service was not the outdoor vacation we'd anticipated, and we recovered all the canoes, though it took most of the day. These senior Boy Scouts weren't as prepared as they thought, and luckily the campers didn't find out.

Mom told me that upon returning from Maryland, our new house was in southwest Atlanta on the edge of city development where dad liked to build before land values went up. He had pioneered our first house this way and it was shortly surrounded by suburbs of rapidly growing Atlanta. This house was a ranch built out of 'old brick' The contractor was again Mr. McGriff. It was set back with a sweeping lawn, aesthetically set off by tall pines dad left in the front yard despite the hazard of wind and ice. One of my jobs was continually pick up their branches the weather trimmed every storm from these trees. She recalled: "You also had a lawn service summers, a neighborhood monopoly that paid your bills."

Here I got my first dog, a male collie, a beautiful animal named King. I was impressed by the TV show 'Lassie' who we actually traveled with in the first- class section on a Delta flight on our way to Chicago. I loved that dog. King became my constant companion as he and I 'explored' the new wilderness of largely pine and mixed hardwood forest in South Atlanta – nearby and the now developed extensive Confederate trench works built to defended the South of the city. We used to stage our own battles there and camp between the embankments in our winter boy scout overnights. Mom observed: "You generally stayed out much too long but were always back for dinner; that I could count on. King being a very smart dog, brought you back for his dinner. He would wait for you at the end of the road where the bus would let you off after school and walk proudly back with you.

King was my guardian and constant companion. I really bonded with that animal that seemed like another human with different sensitivities to me. He was tragically killed by wild dogs roaming the outskirts of Atlanta at the time. My father broke that news to my horror on the way back from my summer's counseling at Bert Adams Boy Scout Camp. I was distraught for days thereafter. For many, the loss of a pet is our first encounter with that knot in the stomach we'd like to forget, never really leaves, but girds us larger challenges later in our lives.

Chapter 8
High School & Westward Ho!

Those dinner conversations with my mother and the beauty of Hawaii's landscape helped to loosen my straitjacket of grief. We talked at length about our family history and mine, examining through the process my early proclivities and development, as well as people that influenced me. This walk through my family's and my history, reliving my earlier adventures was helping restore my soul's currently burnt-out landscape.

Mom then brought up our first and subsequent trips to California when I was a young teenager, with my grandparents moving to Long Beach, California, across the street from my Aunt Peddy and Uncle Dwight, who I adored and bonded with as second parents. The feeling was mutual. They had no children, and so let me stay up late, eat as I pleased, and drive their souped-up cars. Dwight ran an auto parts company and had the hottest Chevys. This, of course, was a delight. What I didn't realize was that Dwight was a drunk.

On weekends, he took his boat out to fish around Catalina Island. We'd leave before the sun was up and drive across the channel to the island where the US Navy had formerly tested its ordinance. The fishing was great, but so was the thirst of my uncle and his buddies who drank most of the way and were snockered by the afternoon. When our boat was filled with bonito—a small yellow tail tuna—we headed home with me driving the boat. Dwight and typically a couple of his buddies slept under the front deck. Being unacquainted with people drinking that much and starting at breakfast, I used to dismiss this as them being "tired" from a hard work week. Luckily, they were sober enough to help me get the boat safely home, though I relished driving it anyway.

At thirteen, it was in California that I learned to drive. My aunt and uncle took me to flat streets, back of Signal Hill and let me drive their Chevy with close instruction. Soon they were letting me drive to the supermarket and around the neighborhood, though I hadn't gotten a learner's permit. They were pleased to be teaching, and I was delighted, learning ahead of my class. When I got back home, my parents were not so liberal, though I had my eyes on my father's forest green '54 Chevy coupe that he'd sell me (not give me) for $400 as soon as I could legally drive at sixteen.

After the summer I learned to drive, I came back to Atlanta to start my first year at Southwest High School and found my locker was the center of the universe—where I stored books and clothing. I was a good student, challenged with the greater competition, and by the end of the year was at the top of my class. I did have to study but also read a lot on my own. I continued to be involved with Boy Scouts, graduating to the Explorer Scouts that came with a cool green uniform, but school events and social life would become more prominent in my life. That year I also joined the chess club, beating our faculty advisor in a game—he was our math teacher and a nice fellow. However, wizening to female sensibilities, chess did not seem to engender the same attention as football and track, or so I thought.

My first real serious sport was track and, the first chance I had in the spring, I went out for the team. We all tried out in PE, taking the field in grey shirts and red shorts. There I learned I could run and was soon at the head of the pack in the middle distances—the 220- and 440-yard races. I continued to run throughout high school and into adulthood until my knee joints started to ache running up and down those stairs in Central Park.

My PE teacher, Bob Greer, who also taught woodshop, was the line coach for football, and he encouraged me to be a guard on his squad and a linebacker on his B redshirt team. I began to lift weights and drink protein in my milkshakes to bulk up since I was six feet tall and lanky. I gave up chess and sat on the bench but played some in practice and scrimmages. I was much more popular with the ladies and enjoyed several invitations to the spring prom. My social life was looking up, though I had no steady girl. There was one girl, Diane Long, who was quite intelligent and whose parents brought her over to talk while our parents socialized. That was a purely platonic intellectual relationship. I also dated Katherine, whose last name is lost, but who was much more sporting. We took a lifesaving course together and became more intimate in our wet bathing suits than was probably prudent at that stage of our lives.

The summer before I was to start tenth grade, Mom and I visited her parents in the little house that backed up to a park in Long Beach and was across from Aunt Peddy and Uncle Dwight's. The last time out there I'd learned to drive, but this summer was to be even more special since Dwight had purchased a portable camper that slid right into the back of his truck. We were going to tour the Western National Parks!

Mom and I had a real surprise and send off when we reached Chicago. TWA had just inaugurated jet service on its new Boeing 707s, and Mom and I were able to get two seats in first class. It was an incredible flight, and I could tell, even then, that this would revolutionize air travel. The previous trip we'd flown on the old Constellation. The flight had taken over six hours and was noisy and prone to much turbulence from summer thunderstorms. In contrast, this flight took half as long, was smoother, quieter, and of course faster. The service was superior, as was the food, and the cabin attendants took real pride in their new aircraft. We weren't as tired after the trip either. It was the dawning of the Jet Age.

We spent a couple of weeks in Long Beach, going one day to visit the new phenomenon Disneyland and its Magic Kingdom. I thought it wouldn't be cool for a mature teenager like me, but soon reentered childhood, plunging into the pond in an automated pirate ship, hanging on to the rails with my aunt screaming beside me. We also visited Knotts Berry Farm. One Sunday, we went out to visit the remarkable Crystal Cathedral to hear Dr. Schuller preach. That was awe-inspiring: a cathedral of glass risen out of nowhere. A refugee from the Midwest, Schuller had begun by preaching to congregations in California he'd gather in drive-in theaters. He was a great preacher and developed quite a following, starting one of the country's early mega-churches. My aunt was a member of this congregation and was an occasional attendee. When she passed away many years later, the Crystal Cathedral sent a mourner, a deacon, to be at her funeral, a lonely affair. After Dwight died, Peddy seldom socialized, and the friends she did have had passed away.

Before we left for our National Park tour, we spent a couple of weeks visiting Dwight and Peddy's friends and our cousins from Nebraska who had migrated when Mom and Peddy had moved to California prior to the WWII. Many were employed in the aerospace industry, principally at the big Douglas aircraft factory in Long Beach. Some nights we went to the top of Signal Hill that at the time was still an active oil field, but Dwight knew the workers since he supplied equipment to the companies, and we'd park, have a picnic, and watch until the lights outlined the vast harbor and refineries beneath. It was quite magical, above the edge of the LA's then nascent smog that captured the city's shimmering lights like watching a distant galaxy.

We spent many days preparing for our trip and at the end of two weeks were driving northeast out of LA. I said goodbye to Mom, my grandparents and their aging, but still remarkable, dog Jimmy. I was going to bond with my aunt and uncle, and we were going to explore the West. It was to be a great adventure; in retrospect, I was anticipating something like Steinbeck's adventures he describes in his book *Travels with Charlie*, a book I'd read years later.

Our first stop was King's Canyon—quite remarkable because of the geological formations. I was an amateur geologist and began to collect all sorts of specimens, particularly a kind of crystalline layered rock that looked like a sandwich, as well as some excellent geodes from rock shops along the way. The next stop was Sequoia National Park to see the magnificent trees there. It was a religious experience going through those woods. The trees were pillars of a great natural cathedral, as splendid and taller and more spectacular than the largest and most ornate found in Europe (though at that point I had no basis for comparison). The grandeur and majesty of those living monuments, over two- or three-thousand years old, was moving.

We were three Musketeers, continually kidding one another. They got me for speaking with a Southern drawl and being a rebel, and I got them for living in a desert with so many cars and traffic-bound commuters. It was one joke after another. Dwight was a skilled fisherman who'd taught me. He'd spot a likely stream and pull the truck over, cast out, and soon we had dinner. Peddy fried up what was usually a beautiful trout, and we feasted before finding a camping ground, or staying along the road if we were in a safe place. Every fourth or fifth day we treated ourselves to a motel and a shower.

Yosemite was the highlight. Though summer, the snowmelt still spilled into the incredible glacier-sculpted valley, and it was awe-inspiring to drive into the valley. We found a campsite near the famous Ahwahnee Lodge and that first night indulged in a big dinner in the log-beamed dining room. The next day Dwight, Peddy, and I climbed the trail to the top of Bridal Veil Falls. Both Dwight and Peddy were smokers and soon turned back, but I kept going because I had to get to the crest.

What I found when I got there were the rangers building a massive bonfire that they'd light at sunset then push over the falls for the evening's spectacular show. I had to run back down valley to tell Dwight and Peddy. Luckily, I didn't sprain an ankle in my enthusiasm, though I knotted my thighs and calves so badly that I could hardly walk the next day. Excited and breathless, I didn't notice my legs were sore. In honor of the event Peddy went to the commissary for steaks and potatoes. We feasted, watched the festivities, and weren't disappointed. It was all very romantic—Peddy and Dwight snuggled up, and I took a long walk around the camp to let them go to bed early.

When I returned and climbed into my bed by the camper's upper window, I heard a noise and looked out to see a huge bear looking for the remains of our dinner in the garbage can. They didn't have animal-proof trashcans like they do now, and he scavenged all the cans, inspecting each in turn. He trashed the whole camp, and, memorably, we had to police the mess the next morning—Oh! My legs were beyond sore.

From there we were off to Lake Tahoe, Nevada and the Hoover Dam. These sights were impressive, but the desert and countryside between there and Yellowstone were less appealing. Dwight never ceased to fish along the way. It was getting to be a long trip until we pulled into Yellowstone and witnessed Old Faithful and ate a big meal in the lodge. It was the end of the trip and time to head back to Long Beach. What an introduction to the West. More important was that over the course of the summer, I felt I'd acquired another set of parents that I needed at this stage of life, particularly since I felt misunderstood. I could tell Dwight and Peddy things I'd never tell my parents, and they, in turn, shared things about their lives and interactions, specifically my aunt's sibling rivalry with my mother.

Peddy was the youngest of three sisters and the beauty. She was spunky, cursed, and sometimes went around in her bra or more revealing tops, which she was chastised about by Dwight. She and Dwight adopted me as their surrogate son—Peddy couldn't have children because she'd been kicked by a horse as a young girl. She was also a worker—kept everything very neat—and had an incredible sense of humor. She loved animals.

Dwight was talented, a real talker-salesman. He'd been in a band in high school and turned entrepreneur with his own auto parts business that also serviced oil field suppliers and international construction companies, which meant he frequently traveled to Central America. He taught me about automobile repair, having the right tools for the job, honesty in business, and how to fish. How he liked good fish stories. He was also an alcoholic, but that summer, under the watchful eye of my aunt and inspired by nature, controlled himself well. I wish I'd known then what I know now about alcoholism. My family had no idea it was a disease and treatable or that it was so difficult for him. He was also a high-degreed Mason and most loyal to them—that was his church and it sometimes kept him sober. Later, they buried him. I loved Dwight and Peddy very much and was sorry when they delivered me back to the LA airport to take a TWA jet back home to Atlanta via Chicago.

Georgia's Youngest Eagle Scout, Bruce McEver & Parents, February, 1956

Chapter 9
Master Cadet

Our last night on Maui, mom wanted to talk about my high school experiences, saying she and dad were concerned with me going through desegregation in an Atlanta public school and at the quality of those schools. From my vantage point, things had been pretty good for me at Southwest High School. I was becoming worldly from my air travel, and Scouting was being replaced by athletics and a social life. I was sixteen, feeling it, and sporting a red-and-gold football and track letterman's jacket. Academically, Southwest had been relatively easy, and I could walk or bike to school, with its typical red brick and sandstone facade, a long city block from our home. I'd gotten two invitations from young ladies to the prom my sophomore year and drove the '54 Chevy, now with spinner hubcaps that I'd bought from my father. I was mobile, and gas was a quarter a gallon. Life was good. I saw no need to change things, but mom said otherwise.

The events in the South, particularly in Atlanta, were about to change the complacent lives of the white middle class. We thought we had no issues but were quite frankly blind to what was happening around us. It was the cusp of the sixties and a time of racial unrest in Atlanta. It was a stage set for a larger racial opera. A restauranteur in Atlanta named Lester Maddox was running for mayor and handing out axe handles to prevent his establishment from being desegregated. Meanwhile, brave African Americans were trying to non-violently integrate lunch counters and were being hauled away to jail for it. It was time for change and my life along with it.

When the courts ordered the public schools in Atlanta desegregated, our local politicians played brinksmanship, threatening to close schools rather than integrate them. With the real prospect of public schools closing, all the private schools were full because white parents scrambled to enroll their children for the upcoming academic year. Since my dad was a former Navy pilot, he knew Captain Brewster, the President and son of the founder of Georgia Military Academy (GMA) from their days together in the Navy Reserves. I wrongly thought they conspired to change my life, thinking the discipline and academic rigor of GMA would be good for me. In fact, I was lucky to even get into the school.

Ironically, I'd been given a preview of the school when I was about five or six—those spring Sundays when my mother walked me up Rugby Avenue to see the GMA parades. When Dad came home to tell me the "good news," all I could picture was me—a drudge in grey regiment marching to the boom-boom parade band. I'd been impressed but never dreamed I'd be one of those grey-uniformed cadets with red sash and sword. I was less than excited about the prospects of giving up my budding social life at Southwest High School, commuting to school, and wearing a uniform for daily inspection. I realized I had no choice and set about getting a uniform to become a member of the Corps of Cadets.

Over sixty years ago when I arrived on GMA's campus, I felt awkward in my used uniform (bought from a former cadet) and crewcut. I plunged into classes and went out for the football team. My fall from grace was swift. This school was hard academically, and for the first time, I had to study. Because of the fear of integration, they could take their pick, and the school had nearly doubled its class size, taking in a full class of academic and athletic talent from all around Atlanta. We outsiders presumed that military schools were full of problem students whose wealthy parents couldn't control their kids. What I believed to be rich delinquents were actually smart, tough guys, thoroughly versed in social graces. They knew good alcohol and cigars; whereas, we strait-laced fellows from the Atlanta middle class were uninitiated and naïve. This was a new class of student-athletes who took the school a gigantic step forward and up, both athletically and academically. Today Woodward Academy is one of Atlanta's most prominent schools because of this cathartic time they wisely took advantage of.

Cadet officers worked us new plebes over. Their passion for shined shoes and belt buckles wasn't mine. I tried so hard on the athletic field that I sprained both ankles in preseason football practice and was immediately demoted to the B team, coached by a totally unsympathetic Major Garland Watkins, known as "the Wedge," because he looked like one. The futility of my new life climaxed early on with me sobbing, sitting helplessly on the bench outside the old gym watching Westminster (the wealthy northside private school I couldn't get into) demolish us 74-0 with my swollen ankles taped and throbbing.

GMA would gradually administer its balm for my mind, body, and spirit. This institution treated the whole person. It did have a soul. That soul was its faculty and coaches, who made you work and think, and cared when you made the effort; the classes were small, and the teachers really paid attention to students. There was no place to hide or skate. There were some unforgettable characters like the Wedge who tried to make us into scholars (he taught history) and athletes. This was a military school, so the teachers were known by their rank, that was hierarchical and organized according to their tenure.

One of the most senior faculty members and an actual Air Force Colonel was Col. Russell, known as "the Moon," for his bald head. He taught geometry with a long pointer, used both for blackboard illustration and on unwary cadets not paying attention. Under him, I began to see Euclid and the beautiful truth of his mathematics. Lively ballroom dancers, Russell and his wonderful wife Lottie performed ballroom exhibitions at our formal dances.

Our English teacher was Capt. Jackson Farabee, who loved the romantic poets. He passionately recited long passages from memory with his eyelids fluttering. He showed us the wonder of a Shakespeare sonnet and persuaded me into being a member of his debate team. I was not a good public speaker at the time, but he was patient and helped me get over that crippling shyness.

My favorite teacher was Capt. Stephen Hatfield, who taught Chemistry wearing his white lab coat. For many an hour after class, he painstakingly coached me to excel in the subject, that, from a sterile world of beakers and test tubes, was no easy task. Yet he transmitted his enthusiasm and tutored me to love this science the way he did. For a while, I seriously entertained the idea of becoming a scientist instead of an engineer. In reviewing my old yearbook, I found that in my last will and testament I'd left him my slide rule, a precious object I learned to use skillfully and still have it today—a real relic. Stephen inspired me to win the Bausch & Lomb Chemistry Award for the school in my junior year.

Then there was Major A. T. Ferguson, who taught us Latin and Classics. He looked like Ichabod Crane. On Fridays he sat with his long, thin legs crossed, reading us Caesar's conquest of Gaul in Latin. The wars were exciting enough, but even more exciting was the part where a nude Cleopatra is unrolled from a rug before Antony. He got every cadet's attention! Suffice it to say we learned Latin. I'm not sure what good three years of it did for me, but Major Ferguson's performances were unforgettable.

Some teachers excelled in both the classroom and athletics. Col. Paget, who taught American History, was a stimulating teacher, and a favorite of mine. He was also our track coach. The 440—one complete loop around the track—was my race. I had to run it and a leg of the mile-relay; I was thoroughly exhausted at the end of every meet, sometimes crawling on the turf to catch my breath, sometimes throwing up. During my senior year, we had a state championship mile-relay team with every member running under a fifty-second leg.

When I arrived at GMA, the institution excelled in track, swimming, and gymnastics— traditional prep school favorites. It was not long after we'd been defeated by Westminster that the administration hired William "Bill" Lundy from Marietta High School (the Georgia state champion) to build a football team and athletic program that could compete beyond the traditional Mid-South prep school league. I understand from West-minster friends and alumni our dominance continues today. We are still getting our revenge! Captain Lundy had two great assistants, Capt. Frank Giles and Capt. Franklin Brooks. Capt. Brooks was an all-American, 165-pound guard from the famous Georgia Tech team that was national champion in the fifties. I would have gone through a wall for that man and often did. Tragically, he passed away from cancer young, but he, Giles, and Lundy taught us teamwork, and how important that is to winning anything in life.

These guys took us down to pre-season football camp in Palmetto, Georgia. There was a big lake that we never got to swim in but had to run around first thing every morning after beating ourselves up the previous day. Our big event was one night off to go to the movies in town. I retell this story in a poem written for our 50th reunion that gives some color to that time and names for my teammates.

Reunion
for the Georgia Military Academy Class of 1962

I.
Our class bugler Jimmy Sims,
blows *Taps* and breaks down.
One hundred graying men, some saluting
and others with hand over heart
have come to attention around

their former bull ring, bounded
by knee-high pyramids of cannon balls.

Like a graduation procession
through heaven's gate, our chaplain
John Brinsfield reads the names
of departed classmates—each underscored
with a prayer-gong, struck
thirty-three times and left
to resonate into silence.

Each name surprises,
like an "incoming" round—
a memory of a camaraderie
when time didn't seem to count—
in class, on the sport or drill field,
or screwing off in refuge
from the discipline meant
to make us men.

The Commandant meted out punishment
in wasted time and shoe leather
for the pranks, we played.
Before we went off to war,
we practiced here.

Unrecognizable, except by our tags,
fifty years has etched our faces.
But I can't recall the story
I saved to tell after all these years,
when it's my turn at the cocktail party.

II.
The faces of my departed mates and the story
come back with the reading of the names:
football camp in South Georgia,
steamy August, up at dawn to run
a mile and a half around a tempting lake

we couldn't plunge in.
John Reeves, our skinny half-back,
ran in combat boots and always won;
Big Don Kirkpatrick, who caught
many a crucial pass, and our tight end,
also, up front. Duncan Dunn
star fullback, we always counted on
for yardage, coolly lagged behind.
We were state champs until Dunn
went down ramming in for the score.

With whistle in square jaw,
Franklin Brooks, our line coach,
an All-American from Georgia Tech urged us on.
For him, we would go through walls;
he made us forget the heat
and hunger for combat.

Bruised and exhausted
from two weeks of internecine combat,
pushing sleds and hitting dummies,
we were allowed one night
out to the movies. We dreamed
of something with lots of Hollywood cleavage.

We drove into Palmetto, searching
for the marquis at the Dixie Theater.
Damn!
We rubbed our eyes—
there in black and white:
Snow White and the Seven Dwarfs.

   The training and sweat paid off. We had a Cinderella team in our
senior year. We'd come back. Our first three games we held the other
teams scoreless, and we knew we were headed toward regional cham-
pionship. The Atlanta high schools were tough teams. At a game with
our neighboring Russell High School, I tackled their star halfback for a
loss, and he angrily swore he'd "pay me back." After the game, he took

me aside in what I thought was a friendly gesture and pulled a knife. I was rescued by my teammates and police. Our ranks had thinned as the season wore on, and we didn't have the student body depth or bench of the larger rival schools. At the end of the season, there were some unfortunate late season injuries that put us in second place in our division.

During summers between my junior and senior years, I worked in the construction gangs that were renovating GMA. The football coaches recommended this labor to keep us in shape and earn some extra dollars. Sam Lyons—the now-famous aviation artist (whose brother was Tommy Lyons, the UGA All-American football star)—and I, as well as some others took up the challenge and reported for this sweaty, dusty duty. Our bosses and the other laborers were all African American. We'd never worked harder, and we got to know a group of guys who we wouldn't have normally met in our segregated Atlanta lives. Because I was entrusted with the keys to the dump truck, I was particularly popular, since I took these guys around to see their girlfriends at lunchbreaks.

Eddie, our mason foreman, was built like a fullback. He had a mild disposition and a natural leader who was in love with a local beauty, who rather coyly kept playing him. Jerome was his number two bricklayer, rather lanky and played the field, occasionally being caught. This made for joking and horseplay during afternoon breaks. By the end of the summer, we were all friends sharing emotional experiences. It was also face-to-face encounters in a segregated culture that stuck with me. At that point I saw the festering prejudice and the tragedy of the separated South that I'd blithely participated in.

I don't recall at what point in high school I first became interested in the stock market, but I'm certain it was because of my father's and his twin brother Bill's interest in it. Both savers, they'd invested their money, and by the time they'd died, had acquired surprisingly large sums for an airline pilot and traveling salesmen. They hadn't been doing this unadvisedly but had a savvy broker in New York City named Allen Wood. Allen had been with Atlanta's Courts & Co. but had moved to New York with Hayden Stone. Beyond being a competent broker, Allen had been a diplomatic courier in WWII and could speak fifteen languages. That's why he went to NYC—to practice those skills live.

Allen and my father convinced me to begin to follow good companies, those that would benefit from economic trends. One of my early stocks was the defense contractor, General Dynamics, whose electric boat division was building our nuclear submarine fleet. I invested in its growth and followed its development. I also became enamored with the technical aspects of the market and began to read up on it. One of my early gurus was Joseph Granville whose price and volume theory I subscribed to even carefully charting my stocks. A devotee, I was interested because I could follow national economic trends and profit from them. Little did I suspect the games Wall Street played on "the public," but I had Allen looking out for me. He turned out to be a major influence on my life.

After the last season parade of my junior year, we came home to celebrate in our backyard on our cement turnaround crowned by a basketball hoop. It was a beautiful spring day in Atlanta, abundant in dogwoods. Dad grilled steaks on his bar-b-que—a silver-painted 55-gallon drum sawed in half with hinges welded on so the top lifted to reveal a generous bed of coals. Dad had his traditional scotch and was attending the steaks.

"I was really proud of you today, son. You've done a great job in school, but you know the cost of GMA was more than I'd been expecting to pay for your education. You'll need to figure out how to finance college. I can help some, but you need to seriously consider the service academies or an NROTC scholarship," he said.

"Yes, sir," I said and walked away, knowing it was useless to argue. I was dumbfounded. I was neither a good enough athlete nor genius enough to get a scholarship, and because Dad wasn't poor, I couldn't get financial aid. Mom was more sympathetic and helped with my applications. Military service solved the dilemma, but as all things, it had its price. Vietnam was raging. Since I was healthy, I'd either go into service or be drafted. My father advised me to join the Navy, not to see the world, but because "I would always have a dry bed," as he counseled.

It was this and the military experience at GMA that led me get to appointments to both the Naval and Air Force academies. I applied at Harvard, MIT and Rice, but was rejected. I got into Vanderbilt, but I took a Navy ROTC scholarship at Georgia Tech, my default standby because I'd had my eyes on the stars at the time. I'd abandoned ideas of being a scientist. After much back and forth, I thought I wanted to be an engineer since I might have a chance at being an astronaut in the developing space program.

The Russians had launched Sputnik. I'd become enamored with all things astronomical after my father took me to hear Dr. Werner von

Braun from Huntsville's rocket program speak. I was a good all-around student athlete and would somehow get into the developing space program. All I needed was an aerospace degree from Georgia Tech. I was on my way and most immediately needed to get a summer job to help me pay for it.

It was early during my junior year at GMA at one of our formal dances that I first beheld Tina McGaughey. These dances were a part of our education at a private prep school, but also a bit stiff. Imagine a room full of cadets in full dress uniform and red sashes, and the ladies in long formal gowns. Or was it hoop skirts at the time? From across the room, I saw a lovely creature with a French twist standing with one of the upperclassmen, an officer and one of my then-superiors. He didn't deter me. I found out she was the daughter of a respected local entrepreneur who owned a well-known sporting goods store in Atlanta—Reeder & McGaughey—and her brother Cliff had attended and graduated from GMA. They lived in Rugby Lane, but in a much nicer and larger house than I grew up in. She was the belle of the ball, and I had to be her beau.

I forget how I broke the ice, but I think we were introduced through one of her girlfriends. I got up the courage to ask her out on a date, and by the following year we were dating steadily. Tina was interested in literature, so I immediately stepped up my extracurricular reading to stimulate our conversations, and we even began reading novels together. Delighting in each other's company, our romance evolved, and we encouraged and were proud of one another's achievements. Being in the same neighborhood, we walked around College Park a lot and met after school to study and hang out. We invented picnics in romantic places, since neither of our parents had places we could be alone. It was the time of the drive-in, and unromantically, romance was practiced on wheels. By my senior year, I'd upgraded to a '57 Chevy with a floor shift and truck mufflers. I thought I was so cool. We parked in her driveway after dates and moving to the backseat, made out passionately, observing unspoken limits. This woman and our relationship became special. It seemed we were destined for one another, but it was too soon to do anything about it at this age; it was time to take a break.

It was our senior year, and tired of the South, Tina decided to study journalism at Stephens College, a private girls' school in Columbia, Missouri. Turning down my service academy appointments, I'd determined I was going to go to Georgia Tech but would live at home my first year. It was going to separate us, but we pledged ourselves to "staying in touch."

By the time I graduated, I was in much better spirits than that early awful night on the bench at the Westminster game. Though a pain to dress for, those Sunday parades were stirring on a fine spring afternoon. Yes, I was proud of the fact that I was graduating from GMA, and more confident of my future because of the training I received. At graduation, I was named the Master Cadet, the best all-around student and also salutatorian of my class. Totally surprised, it was Zeke Fanning, one of Dad's pilot buddies and my classmate's father, who was the first to leap up on the stage to shake my hand and congratulate me heartily.

Georgia Military Academy's Master Cadet,
Bruce McEver, May, 1962

Chapter 10
Back from Where I Came

High school memories and our Hawaii trip came to an end. Mom and I flew back to the San Francisco airport together where we also flew from on my father's last flight as a Delta Captain. We recalled that event saying our farewells. I went nostalgically into the city and checked into my favorite hotel—the Huntington on Nob Hill. I always stayed there when in town and knew all the staff, who made me feel like I was coming home. I also had my running and walking path out to Poet's Corner, atop Russian Hill. Sometimes when I had time, I walked down to Ghirardelli Square to the Fontana where Georgia and I first lived after we were married. My memories of us there were still so strong.

While Hawaii had been incredibly therapeutic, and my mother gotten me away from what turned out to be a catastrophic snowstorm that would have made being in Connecticut, or even New York, a devastating landscape to grieve in, I was not near to being healed. Some comfort had come from memorial services in Salisbury, and after our return from Hawaii, Mom held a service at her church in Atlanta. Before Easter we finally scattered Georgia's ashes along the river in front of our house in Salisbury during the day. Alma attended, and the service was presided over by Reverend Taber. Despite the respite, I was still gripped by grief. My journals from this period are pages of sorrow, candle lightings, and always watching for signs of her presence. I oscillated between disbelief and denial—each day, a religious trial. I felt as though I had a millstone hanging from my neck. I cried at the slightest provocation or remembrance. This grief was lingering.

I had some remarkable dreams where Georgia would return. In one she came down the road from our hilltop in a Russian princess outfit, complete with high boots and fur hat. She looked radiant and was accompanied by two guardian bears costumed to show they meant business. She approached me smiling, but I was leery of the bears. She informed me she had a mission now and had gone away to protect the animals. What was my mission now? I should move on without her and find my calling. She loved me, she explained, but I should not wallow in my grief.

Dreams like this and good friends woke me up, as did my writing. I was trying anything for relief. I had composed a series of poems about her death and my feelings thereafter. The writing was cathartic. I took those sad poems over to my poet friend Kevin Pilkington, and he went through them, making minor corrections, but mainly encouraging me to pull them together into a chapbook and publish them. I found another friend from the writing group at Sarah Lawrence, Ron Egatz, who was starting Camber Press there. He said he was willing to help me edit and publish these poems as the press's first publication. Other friends helped and piled on encouragement as well; Tom Lux, also a poet friend, wrote the introduction. My neighbor, a famous photographer of the Berkshires, Bill Binzen contributed the cover photo. It took me about a year to write the poems and another year to edit and have the book published, but it was a therapeutic process and helped pull me out of my slump. It also pushed me into really delving into writing poetry and showed me its power to re-order the chaos. One of those early poems from my first chapbook describes a presence I experienced not long after Georgia died:

Snow Geese

Sometimes there were signs.
After the March maelstrom,
I snow-shoed up
our mountain in morning sun
and tracked into another storm.

At first, I thought the yappings
were coyotes chasing me.
But vee-ing overhead—
all white with black-tipped wings,
calling me,
then disappearing
into the oncoming blow—
was a flight of snow geese.

By the time I got down,
the cottoned forest was prismed
in the thawing light. Drops glistened
and draped every tree
like the diamond necklace

adorning my wife
singing *The Merry Widow.*

For a moment, Vilia
was in the mist between tall pines.
The wood nymph's presence,
was fresh and chilly,
a rush of rivulets.

Winter loosened its grip—
like the last squeeze
of her hand
as she slipped
into unconsciousness.

Later, this poem was set to music by a local composer to be performed at a Berkshire Choral Festival. it was gratifying to hear my work shared and played publicly to honor Georgia.

During this time, I tried to go back to work and soon learned I was still seriously grief-stricken. Like the Fisher King in the Grail legend, I had a festering wound that wouldn't heal. I talked at length with my former psychologist Tom Waller who assured me it was a process that only time healed and encouraged me to watch my healing progress in those dreams about Georgia. I also talked to Bev Jones, the Methodist bishop, then at the Candler School of Theology. He told me to tell God I was mad at him for taking Georgia from me. I had many starry nights of confrontation. So many tried to counsel me. The best by far was a clairvoyant named Gail Kontz (Angel Gail), an ordinary-looking Detroit housewife who had some shamanic experiences as a young woman and who, within a few minutes of meeting me, could tell me my life history and Georgia's. She helped me interpret dreams and gave me hope for a future without Georgia. Gail told me to call Georgia with a candle. This is the end of a poem I wrote about it:

Think about it.
Meditate on the flame.
Feel its heat,
the energy.

It takes you back
to the light
from where you came.

The outpouring in letters and goodwill visits were overwhelming. One of the most memorable was my classmate and shareholder, Tom Barry, who, not three years earlier, had lost two children in a tragic fire in his new Manhattan townhouse. Once a month, he took me to the Links Club for lunch where we talked the grief out between us. Also, my partner Steve Sheppard, who had lost his first wife to a rare disease that struck her when they were on a trip together in London, came forth to share his experience. Many others came forward to share their stories, slowly teaching me death is part of life that we so often deny, not wanting to face its stern reality.

I was seriously considering reordering my life about this time and began working with Ken Knoespel to design a course in Religion and Literature at Ga. Tech we would jointly teach. Ken had been trying to persuade me to do this for a number of years and with my no longer being CEO of Berkshire I could consider it seriously. While in Atlanta working with Ken, I also spent time with Tom Lux who wanted me to take the next summer course available at the Warren Wilson School, where he taught. He thought I should get an MFA and begin writing more poetry, but also start my life story he thought worthwhile putting down on paper.

This all took me back to my time as an undergraduate student at the North Avenue Trade School as it was affectionately called by Georgia Tech's rivals.

Chapter 11
The Rat

The summer before I went to Georgia Tech, I worked construction again, this time building bridges in Atlanta for Eisenhower's interstate project. Construction pay was the best a teenager could make at the time, and I needed the money. I had received a full NROTC scholarship that paid for books and tuition, but no spending allowance. The company hired both white and black laborers, so the crews were integrated. These were tough, experienced guys, and it was an education—understanding how working men made ends meet and coming to appreciate their joys and concerns was an invaluable lesson for me in later life.

Up early and dressed in heavy boots, jeans and a tee-shirt that I'd take off and stick in my back pocket by the end of the day, that Atlanta summer I was tanned and in excellent physical condition. The construction routine became a ritual. We built the forms for the bridge's concrete backbone during the week. Then, on Friday, the cement arrived. We'd push incredibly heavy wheelbarrows of concrete to fill wire mesh sculptures, sort of like filling your coffin. No one had invented hydraulic lines that deliver concrete the way it's poured now. Fridays were back-breaking and ruined me for any kind of Friday night fling.

Then it happened. I was stuck on a cement pier after a pouring one Friday. In a hurry to get home, tired, and with no one in sight or earshot to help me down, I stupidly decided to jump off, thinking the pile of dirt below would cushion the fall. After I landed, I looked at the bottom of my foot for a brief second then felt incredible pain. Remarkably, I hadn't broken anything, but I'd pulled my Achilles, perhaps a more painful and enduring wound. In a cast, I hobbled around for the rest of summer. My mom and Tina were sympathetic, keeping me down and fed, and I got more reading done than I ever planned.

I was reading voraciously at night and had a list that included much of Faulkner mixed with Ian Fleming's James Bond series for excitement. Tina was in town and through her father's contacts had a job as a guide at the state capital. We'd meet up with friends who were staying in Atlanta until they left for university. Ironically, Tina had relatives in Good Hope, where Georgia's parents had their farm, but I had no inkling of that future then. We liked going off to see our country relatives. I had some in Gainesville we visited as well. It was wonderful having her around for my convalescence, and our relationship deepened, but she soon left for her freshman orientation in Missouri.

Even though I'd live at home and commute my freshman year, I was looking forward to getting to Georgia Tech. Was I in for a big shock. First, I was a freshman, and at Georgia Tech that meant you were a "rat," obliged to wear a little gold cap with your name and the word RAT inked on the bill, designating your status. A freshman found without his cap was subject to harassment and further hazing by the upperclassmen.

Also, the math and science courses were without quarter, and, as the Dean pointed out, with Vietnam escalating, we all knew we needed to stay in school with a draft deferment or we'd be sent to the jungles. The Dean of Students used to take pride in saying at orientation, "Look to your left and your right because one of you won't be here at the end of the year." There was much incentive to running the gauntlet since in 1962-63 if you didn't, that usually meant a pass to Vietnam. There was a famous Calculus professor, "Bootcamp" Bailey who was notorious for flunking unsuspecting freshmen. I was in his class and somehow got by, but it wasn't easy. I learned if I was going to get through Tech, I had to study like I never had before. Aerospace Engineering required Calculus and Physics as prerequisites, as well as Mechanical Drawing, Chemistry and Thermodynamics. Computers and calculators were not yet miniaturized, so we all carried slide rules.

There were few women and fewer black students, but that would change in the not-so-distant future since Atlanta was a center for the Civil Rights movement. We had NROTC on Thursdays and had to dress in our uniforms for drill and inspection. During our freshman year, our Navy class navigated across the Pacific Ocean and around the world, and it was damn interesting. The scholarship obligated my summers for training, midshipman cruises and four years of active duty after graduation. It didn't seem that onerous at the time.

Commuting made school seem routine, but there were a few memorable experiences. One of the most physical classes was Drown-Proofing, a holdover from WWII when we lost far too many men because they couldn't take advantage of their natural buoyancy.

Freddy Lanoue—a fish in the water but who'd had polio as a child and walked with a limp—taught the class. He wore a bathing suit, but no one else did—a hundred naked men learned buoyancy with their arms tied behind them. You had to stay up for the hour-long class and then swim the length of the pool underwater with your hands tied behind you. Many didn't make it. It proved quite a screen, as was Mechanical Drawing, which had room for half as many students at their drawing tables the following year.

Though I was going to live at home, I rushed a fraternity, as at that time at Tech, there was no social life without joining one. Rush was quite an experience for me. I didn't drink then, so partying wasn't my aim, but comradeship and a nice house to hang out in was. I eventually pledged ATO, an outstanding group and well-represented on campus. They seemed to have the combination of student, athletics and campus involvement I was seeking. It was my first club experience since Boy Scouts.

The ominous Hell Week lived up to its name. We had to wear burlap bags as a tee-shirts all week, were forced to drink cod liver oil, recite ridiculous statistics about our fellow brothers, and if we got their hometown or girlfriend's name wrong, dropped for pushups. Luckily, we didn't do anything truly destructive. When the week was over, we pledgers were bonded. We were allowed to clean up, burn our burlap tee-shirts, and given the fraternity grip and secret words to the lodge. Going through that together did strangely make brothers out of us!

My freshman year ended with me very concerned about my future as an aerospace engineer. It wasn't that interesting, and it was damn hard. I didn't appreciate, much less comprehend the Bernoulli Principal. I had to swallow my ambition and get very practical, realizing I wasn't cut out to design aircraft, much less spacecraft but could possibly still be an astronaut as an engineer. I was interested in being a leader and by the end of that first year, I thought it more likely I would run a business or be an investor with my stock market interest. Industrial Engineering (IE) seemed much more practically suited for that. Tech was one of the top engineering schools and had the number one IE course in the country, but not in business, the school all the football players graduated from. I don't remember if it was then or at the beginning of my sophomore year that I switched majors to Industrial Engineering, allowing me to take more electives and was less rigorous than AE. I was wrestling some tough angels of pride—ambition and talent—but unable to see at that age I wasn't cut out to be a real engineer. Though many of my classmates relished machine building and savored this work, I didn't. Importantly, I hadn't yet realized, I could or wanted to write. Half-aware, I made a life-changing decision and switched majors.

Ensign Bruce McEver USN at Georgia Tech, May, 1967

Chapter 12
Midshipman Cruise: Earning My Sea Legs

Since the US Navy paid for my college education, my college summers were also theirs for much-needed basic training. I had never been to sea, and the Navy's institutional wisdom starts candidates on the bottom rung and works them up through experience. This was my third-class midshipman cruise, and I was to be a swabbie—an ordinary seaman in a sailor's suit on a combat ship for the summer. The plan was I rotated over the cruise with my fellow midshipmen through all the ship's divisions: engineering, deck, gunnery, ASW (Antisubmarine Warfare) and operations. I got orders to the USS Ingraham (DD694), a destroyer that saw distinguished service in WWII and was currently stationed at the huge Navy base in Norfolk, VA. After the end of my freshman year at Tech, I flew up from Atlanta and reported for duty in my dress whites, ready for a sea adventure, toting a duffel bag full of bell-bottoms. I'd never ventured further on water than across the Catalina Channel off California, but not out of sight of the land.

I was assigned a hammock and was initially put in the engineering division working in the engine room. This was to be a *real* basic training from the bowels of the ship up. The next morning we put out to sea into a storm and got orders to return to port. It was my first night at sea in my hammock, and surprisingly, I liked it as my body embraced the swells, adapting to the ups and downs of the wavy road—the vast fact of ocean's endless life. My brain was incorporating those gentle rolls. It must have been ingrained into my body's coping mechanism, but I never got sick at sea.

The following day, we set out with the full fleet—an anti-submarine carrier task force. The Ingraham was part of the eight-odd destroyer screen and rotated being plane guard behind the carrier; we also had some auxiliaries, principally a couple of tankers for endurance. We were to practice anti-submarine maneuvers and cruise up the coast to a Royal Canadian Navy base in Nova Scotia, then out to a former British base in Bermuda and back to New York for Fleet Week exercises. The Atlantic complied, and we had a pleasant initial voyage while I got used to the watch routine in the engine room. Generally, I rotated eight hours on and eight hours off. I became familiar with the ship's propulsion system

and its operations. The ship was powered by two steam turbines fired
by two huge boilers to produce the steam, heat and everything else. We
were to clean out one of the boilers on the voyage to the delight of
the engineering department, who, with the arrival of new swabbie crew,
would be spared the dirty work. Wearing asbestos suits like firefighters,
we blasted down the steam pipes inside of the boiler with hot steam
hoses, though I can't say I relished being like Jonah swabbing down the
ribs of this whale.

Beforehand, we pulled up to the Royal Canadian Navy (RCN,
once known as Her Majesty's Canadian Service) base in Sydney, Nova
Scotia where famously, during WWII, supply convoys were staged for
the torturous Atlantic crossing through vicious German U-Boat wolf
packs. It was ironic we were there, the too-late protectors of these ghost
convoys. These flocks of ships even had the prefix "SC" for "Slow
Convoy." The infamous Convoy SC7 typified the dangers inherent with
Nazi U-boats stationed off the coast of Cape Breton and Newfoundland
during the Battle of the Atlantic when twenty of the thirty-five merchant
cargo vessels were sunk on their trip to England. I hoped arrival was not
going to be that fateful, and eventually the town's people turned out to
watch the fleet come into port. We put on our dress whites and marched
with the performing local RCN band from the Navy base to the end the
town surrounded by a cheering crowd of curious onlookers.

It seemed a long way to march on a hot summer afternoon, and
afterwards the sailors and midshipmen headed to a local pub. I remember
it well because I was nineteen and had never had a drink, but it was a
bright summer day and we'd marched there after I'd spent the past week
in the boiler room, and what the hell, I was going to try one of the local
beers on tap. It was Schooner, I believe—a Canadian lager. It was a little
bitter at first, but delicious and certainly more refreshing than water.
I enjoyed my first draught and tried another, maybe another with my
shipmates' urging. We were soon singing and playing darts and had to
return boisterously to the ship after dinner, me newly initiated into the
drinking fraternity by my shipmates.

We spent the weekend in Sydney, a pleasant, sunny town that seemed a
throwback to a time right after WWII when those slow convoys gathered.
It had one of the largest steel factories in the world, the Dominion Steel
& Coal Works that was to close before the decade was out, throwing
the town into a depression. It was a factory town, but as I remember

it—filled with quaint picturesque houses, some surrounded with picket fences and flower beds abloom that time of year. It sprawled up from the harbor, like a vast amphitheater of neat middle-class Canada. I imagined stories about the lives of the hardy folk that populated them, maybe my ancestors from Scotland, and conjured up times and stories when those pubs were lively and full of local ladies and sailors about to make the dangerous passage—those passionate nights before their departure. If only those quaint dwellings could tell their tales, of the comings and goings from those neat picket fence gates.

Monday morning we headed out to the open Atlantic, and the destroyer twisted down to meet the swells that greeted it head on, then torqued gracefully to the other side. We were on our way to Bermuda with some major anti-submarine exercises ahead of us. The commodore—a thin serious man—came aboard our ship to observe operations from one of his escorts rather than the carrier, so we proudly carried his flag. However, the officers and crew were a bit tense with his spit-and-polish presence, and were more used to our captain, himself an experienced salt, but a little more laid-back. The commodore was out to get good marks on this exercise, and our ship was to be an example for the rest of the fleet—the bar was raised.

These maneuvers took a week at sea. I was in the engineer room answering the bridge's continual calls for more or less speed as we maneuvered. This was automatic, but we kept vigilant. It was hot down there. I imagined being in hell but was to rotate to the deck crews soon and was getting a new experience when the word came we were to literally "batten down the hatches." There was a storm, an early season hurricane, coming between us and Bermuda.

What's remarkable is just how moody vast water is and how quickly it can change. The sky darkened; the swells grew, and the ship twisted sometimes up over the waves then crashed down, creating a huge white "V" of water, dipping into the next mountain of water, and struggled to rise up and throw that off, over the top of the next even larger mountain of water. It seemed endless. Soon from the continual motion, the crew sickened while nothing stayed on a table and we had to secure everything. By the end of the second day, I was one of the few crew members still standing, so I was called to the bridge and given instructions for steering the ship. I just followed the deck officers' or the captain's orders: "Right ten degrees rudder," "Steady," "Hold your course." It became pretty exciting, especially when we were plane guard behind the carrier in a ripping hurricane.

Dramatically, the huge flat top would dive into a mountain of water, and the back of the carrier would come out of the water with six screws rotating uselessly and then the monstrous craft would breast another wave, and the screws would take it up and over a watery alp again. Our officers kept us safely back, but it was skillfully choreographed to maintain course and proper distance in formation like a close drilled unit. The radio traffic from the bridge with the commodore watching his brood around the carrier was dramatic and had distinct language: "This is COMDESRON 6, come left to zero-nine-zero, stand-by, execute," and a flotilla of a dozen ships turned into the face of the storm—a well-rehearsed chorus. We rode this storm out for the rest of the week. I was energized being up on the bridge—actually driving the ship—and returned to my hammock exhausted. I ate, but the ship smelled of vomit. Men were strapped in their bunks and hammocks like zombies. We'd survived a real storm at sea.

We pulled into Hamilton Harbor, and I don't think I've seen a more picturesque and welcoming site—white beaches, a lighthouse, and a town of red-tiled roofs facing the water. Still a British colony at that time, it was an exotic port of call for me. I couldn't wait to explore as the ships lined up, our signal flags flying, and the band playing as we pulled in. We anchored in the bay around the carrier, and soon a flotilla of launches took us to our storm-earned liberty.

We midshipmen had bonded, and six strong, we rented bikes in our dress whites to ride over to the Elbow Beach and Surf Club. Word soon got around; this was the place to be. What a sight: Six strapping midshipmen in dress whites biking on Bermuda with the friendly local dogs sometimes chasing after. This club was to be our headquarters. The social director sought us out and declared he had over a hundred secretaries from New York City there that weekend. He was happy for us to entertain his guests and passed out meal and drink coupons with a schedule of club entertainment. I thought I'd died and gone to heaven. Biking back to make curfew in the evenings was like Ichabod being chased by the headless horseman or by those damn dogs.

When we got back to the harbor, we lined up for a launch, and the commodore arrived in his car. He'd had a few too many with the British at the officers' club, lessening the tension of getting his fleet through a hurricane. We dutifully helped him aboard the launch. The bay was still choppy, and to the embarrassment of the other officers in his party, he was singing. We sat quietly in the back of the launch while he commanded the coxswain onward and urged us to join his chorus.

When we got to the ship, there was a most proper bosun's mate (the chief enlisted deckhand) on duty. The commodore had dressed him down during the cruise for some minor infraction, but this was the bosun's moment. The commodore, who could barely stand on his own, started up the ladder that was swaying with the left-over storm waves in the bay. As he almost got to the top of the bucking ladder, he slipped and grabbed the side of the ship—the gunnels to be accurate—and hung on for dear life, screaming for help.

The bosun saluted snappily and before rescuing the floundering commodore—who, by that time, hung over the side of the ship in full dress whites and medals—went to the ship's PA system, piped the commodore aboard and slowly and properly announced him, as he was formally to do for a dignitary boarding: "COMDESRON 6, arriving." He let the commodore struggle for a few seconds more before reaching down and pulling him up. The commodore blustered, reluctantly returned the salute and went below. The bosun winked at us as we saluted and requested permission to come on board.

Our next port before returning to Norfolk was New York City. It was "Fleet Week," and we were the entertainment. What a sight to pull up to Manhattan Harbor lined in formation—passing by the Statue of Liberty and parading up the West Side of the great city with fireboats arching a spray. The "Weekend Warriors" (local reserve units) were out flying as well, buzzing the fleet with their squadrons that included helicopters. I had been to the city with my parents, but we flew in, so nothing as dramatic as this with the bunching of Wall Street towers and then the midtown skyscraper cluster seeming to salute our entrance. I was inspired and awed by the size and the grandeur of the city from my harbor view.

My companions all knew places to go, so we split up upon docking. I went to see my and my father's broker, Allen Wood. He was a bachelor and frequented the part of New York where he was learning yet another language—I think he had a girlfriend in each section of NYC. I'd been trading stock throughout high school and had a nice nest egg. Allen supervised and advised. He thought it would be interesting for us to visit

Yorkville, near where he lived and have some German food and beer. As a new beer drinker, I thought that a capital idea, and we went to Lorelei where Allen engaged the bartender and half the patrons in conversations. I had taken freshman German and tried to follow their discussion.

Allen looked out for my family and an Atlanta contingent. He was their northern intelligence point and market advisor. He was bullish on America and told me to relax about changing majors. He confirmed IE (Industrial Engineering) was much more practical for business than AE (Aerospace Engineering) and wouldn't be subject to layoffs due to government spending cycles. He advised: Meet a lot of people and keep a circle of connected friends and contacts—that was important. Business loved Georgia Tech graduates and Naval Officers, be sure to become both and keep up my grades, but most importantly, when I got out of Tech and the Navy, I should come to NYC first to get my experience in the financial world before going back to Atlanta as I'd naively been planning to do up to that point. I did like researching companies and investing in the market. Allen was planting seeds that would later sprout—a great mentor for me at that time.

Soon, the rest of my fellow midshipmen caught up with us, and we had another round with Allen before going back to the ship. The summer had been much more interesting than I'd anticipated, and I entered my sophomore year at Georgia Tech with my sea legs under me.

Chapter 13
Coming into My Own

When I returned from my Atlantic adventure for my sophomore year, it was promising to be lively as space opened in the fraternity house. I would finally leave my parents' nest and live on campus for my sophomore year. My roommate was to be Ben Jordan, a handsome football player from Murfreesboro, TN. Ben had come to Tech on a football scholarship but had suffered a knee injury that ended his collegiate athletic career. Determined to stay in the action, he tried to pay his way through Tech playing cards. Though without the funds for it, Ben was incredibly creative and the consummate playboy. The "shades of the prison" house—as coined by Wordsworth—were closing in on him, and if I wasn't careful, me too. After Ben predictably flamed out, luckily by the end of the year, I had a more suitable roommate, John Robertson, who was a Chemical Engineering major from New Orleans. John became a lifelong friend and was the best man in my wedding to Georgia.

Besides moving into a new environment, my first order of business was to get acquainted with my new major—Industrial Engineering. At the time, this meant factory design, efficient distribution systems, and linear programming. It was systems design—observations of how things worked, interacted, then making common sense out of them and improving the hell out of the way they functioned was its objective. I'm still impatient at inefficient operations whether in a restaurant or in city traffic. The world can always be better organized and that became my mindset.

My challenge was getting through basic science and math classes that were incredibly hard in my sophomore year at Tech. I could do the math but was in denial about engineering overall. It wasn't that interesting for me, nor could I peruse any latent literary interests because there weren't any liberal arts classes at Tech at that time. Physics was particularly opaque to me, and instead of studying a little every day, I let it slide under Ben's and the frat's influence. Really, it was my fault, but midterms were suddenly upon me. I tried to cram for the exam. About that time a wonder drug called Dexedrine (aka Speed) appeared. With one of these marvelous pills, I could stay up all night and study right through until the exam. I decided that's how I would conquer physics. A couple of my similarly struggling brothers and I went to my parents' house and stayed up, (against my mother's protest) working in the dining room. Up all night, I was still wired for the test the next morning.

When I got to the exam, I knew the answers to the questions but forgot the acceleration of gravity was thirty-two feet per second per second and halved it—a blurry mental slip, and used it throughout the exam, thus failing completely. My instructor caught the error and pointed out the outrageous mistake but failed me anyway. I had one more chance on the final where I pulled it out but got a C in an important course. My grades began to average down. I was hoping I could keep a "gentleman's B" and get through the year.

In the spring semester I moved in with John, who was a true fraternity man plus a rare human being who put others first. His father had been an infantry officer in WWII. John was also a contract NROTC student, applying for a regular scholarship like mine that would pay his way, as his family didn't have the funds for all their children to go to school. John and I moved into a room together on the second floor of ATO, overlooking a huge oak tree in the front yard. We kept a neat room. I was a book-a-holic, while we both liked classical music, and the more engaging John sang in our fraternity's country and western group. Being from New Orleans, he also liked good food (and could cook), and soon we were into wines. We went to our local liquor store and were advised we should buy a case of Monopole—white wine that we sipped for cocktails after class in the evenings. Knowing nothing, we came to find out that Monopole was really crap wine that the French threw together out of the grapes they didn't squeeze for the good vintages—we were drinking a blend of "vin ordinaire" that we thought was fine wine. So much for our pretentions.

John and I were both busting our chops to maintain and even improve our grade point average, trying to keep above 3.0. Mine was down to 2.7, and John's was sagging further, but his courses were much harder. We worked hard during the week, took advantage of the extras the fraternity "file" of previous quizzes provided, but weekends would party hard, beginning Friday night. The idea was to drink Friday nights at the house and go easy at parties off campus on Saturdays at Snapfinger Farm or other such haunts. The fraternity would have lively bands, like The Hot Nuts—real jivers. We held a hell of a party to impress the ladies, locals from Emory or Agnes Scott, sometimes imports from UGA or other colleges. I missed Tina though and after one of these bashes, in late spring 1967, I wrote what was probably my first poem bemoaning her absence, touching on that mystic longing for the other while the party roars around you.

In the meantime, Tina excelled at the Missouri School of Journalism at Stephens College. It had been her plan to escape Atlanta, and our occasional rendezvous in Missouri were heartfelt. I soon discovered staying at the University of Missouri's ATO house next door to Stephens was most convenient. Those were special weekends, but we were dating other people, and the distance strained the limits of our friendship during our freshman and sophomore years. A more serious relationship developed in my junior year when she transferred to Emory in Atlanta.

John got involved with the Tech YMCA that sponsored a unique exchange program—the World Student Fund—between Georgia Tech and six German universities. It started after WWII when returning Tech students brought promising German students to Tech for a year, housing them at a fraternity house, and supporting them with funds taken up at a football game. A German exchange student from Stuttgart, Frank Rusch was currently resident at the ATO house and got me fascinated with this program and all things German.

The World Student Fund committee that chose the Georgia Tech students for the exchange program had taken John in. It was comprised of a group of campus intellectuals and some remarkable personalities: Tom Hall who ran alumni affairs, Dr. James Young, an English Professor from Stanford who first taught at MIT, then Rice where he met and became a friend and a collaborator of James Dickey's, who also taught briefly with Jim at Tech. Dr. Sandra Thornton was also a member of this cadre. Thornton taught German and ran the Modern Languages Department. With his outgoing and candid personality, John was a favorite.

I was wrestling with what to do about my flagging engineering interest and met with Tom Hall, a member of the WSF committee, who John Robertson thought could help me. To get to know Tom and Jim Young were life-changing events for me. I was struggling with getting away from my parents and finding my way in the world. I found it wasn't only the subject matter, but the personalities of those around me—my friends and fraternity brothers—who shaped my future. I groped for what that might be and hadn't found it yet. I was trying to find myself believing I was a mystical seeker at heart, and thinking existential philosophy was a key to the meaning of life at that time. In reality I had many interests, including spiritual, philosophical and literary that would take me years to discover and confused the finding of myself in the meantime.

I again spent that summer in the service of the US Navy, but on shore, first at Little Creek, Virginia for Marine Corps training and then in Brownsville, Texas for preliminary flight training. The range of our training was broadening; though I lacked the motivation for Marine training, I came out in better shape than I'd ever been. At Little Creek we were greeted by a gunnery sergeant who chewed on us both individually and as a group. He had us "drop for ten" at the most minor infraction. Somehow his shirts and fatigues stayed starched and dry in the summer heat and humidity, while we all looked like we'd come through the Bataan march.

We formed up with fifty-pound backpacks and M-1s for a little "walk" to a swamp where we were to surround some "insurgents," who were suspected of being up to no good. Our mission was to bring them back for "interrogation." This was a five-mile hike at double speed with full gear, including combat boots. By the time we got to a clearing in the swamp, we were exhausted—a full company of second-class midshipmen in thirty-odd-man platoons, three or four squads were promptly disbursed through the backwoods with guns that fired blanks. Our instructors were cool, running right along, but carrying no equipment, only a holstered pistol and swagger stick. We divided up and went down the many trails with maps and compasses to find the insurgents.

Somehow, we all got back—mainly because it was lunchtime. We never found the insurgents. One platoon went slightly off-reservation and captured a local farmer and his son who protested vigorously but were brought back hands-up by a proud platoon that was summarily dressed down for their stupidity. The colonel, no less, went out in his command jeep when the faux pas was reported to headquarters to apologize to the farmer.

The next day we watched another class perform a dramatic amphibious landing with full bombardment using blanks. We were really playing war. We were briefed on their mission that soon would be ours and marched bleachers onto the beach where we could view the full operation. The amount of planning was impressive. There were obstacle courses we had to run in order to ready for our assault. Every morning and afternoon we were climbing ropes and walls, or rappelling down them. We were ready!

Finally, our time arrived. We were loaded onto the landing ship at pre-dawn and readied our gear, cleaned our weapons and waited for the bombardment to begin. Then it started: first the destroyers opened with their five-inch guns, then the aircraft strafed and bombed the beach just like the real thing. It was dramatic, and we got the word, "Away all boats," and over the side and into the landing craft we went. It was exciting, and the water was choppy that morning. Then the steel gate went down with a splash and out we ran. I ran up a sand dune and jumped into what I thought was beach grass but turned out to be a poison ivy thicket and had to violate my orders, stand up, and relocate. My company commander was in a tizzy when I stood up, even though we were firing blanks. I got a dressing down and a bad case of poison ivy.

Our next base was Brownsville, TX—I don't know why the Navy has an airbase there, but it must be for the same reason it has one in Olathe, Kansas where I was born. It's flat and desolate, so student pilots have nothing to run into if they crash. There were squadrons of squat T-38 trainers along the runways, and we were to get our fill of flying them.

I must give the military credit for its training because the time we spent in the classroom was invaluable. We learned everything a basic pilot needs to know about aircraft flying and flight safety—how the engines and the craft works and how to take the plane up and, most importantly, how to control the crash that's called a landing. These little aircraft were ideal for clumsy trainees. It was hot in Brownsville and that beer at the officers' club was welcome at the end of the day. We got a couple of nights to cross the border into Mexico, but that was less appealing and tragically impoverished. Some of the guys visited prostitutes who were readily available, but disease seemed too big a risk. After two weeks in the little T-38s, we were to graduate and begin two weeks training in jet aircraft. We were instructed carefully for this moment. We put on the blue flight suits, our helmets with oxygen masks and went up with our instructors for the big one.

Some of our class were really counting on jet training since they were looking forward to going into Navy aviation after graduation, that was to be an additional two years of training, starting with flight training in Pensacola. I got my assignment and went up with an experienced pilot, who took the plane right off the deck and straight up, then we dove, spun, barrel rolled, tried a mock dogfight. An exciting flight, but the instructors were trying to find out who had it for jet training, who could survive the g's and twists and turns required for "jet aptitude." I passed and was encouraged to take further training. Though my father wished nothing finer for me, it would have cost another two years of my life.

Home from the desert waste of rural Texas and the shores of Virginia, my junior year at Tech arrived. I thought myself much cooler and was more experienced in many ways. I got to spend some time with Tina, who'd spent the summer in Atlanta working at her father's downtown sporting goods store. It was good to be home and discover Tina was transferring to the English Department at Emory, just a short drive from Georgia Tech.

At Tech, the ATOs saw hundreds of freshmen in their little rat hats and quickly separated the wheat from the chaff, selecting a class of about thirty more pledges who were an astounding crop of promising students, engineers, and athletes. As rush chairman, I was proud of the class I recruited with my brothers and was told it was our best class ever. Afterwards, I ran for student government and was selected as class representative then assigned to the committee to look into building a student union. There wasn't one at Tech at the time, and it was needed, particularly for the majority of the student body who didn't belong to one of the fraternities or, rarer, the sororities on campus. I was to work with Dean of Students James Dull.

Dull and I worked together as a team and traveled to other universities around the Southeast, reporting on student centers and the kinds of issues they ran into. We got the grand tour of universities. Jim was a man with a dull exterior like his name. He looked like a sad sack but was passionate about students and their activities. He supported student theater, particularly Drama Tech, that continues today with excellent student drama.

One of my junior-year guiding principles was improving my grades. Maintaining my grades above the gentleman's B of 3.0 was imperative, yet I had some ball-busters like Thermodynamics, Linear Programming, and Computer Science that required taking boxes of punch-cards to the Computer Center and waiting almost a week for the results, something unimaginable today.

My favorite class was James Dean Young's class on William Butler Yeats and Wallace Stevens. I'd never read poetry, and the classic forms of Yeats and his mythical, beautiful Ireland romanced me, yet it was the poetry of businessman Wallace Stevens that intrigued me. I wrote a paper on "Cuchulainn's Fight with the Sea" that I would love to find today. I was still writing the paper at the three-o'clock Friday deadline when Jim took it from me. I got an A. I loved everything about that class, including Jim who was one of the wisest, most intelligent men and teachers I've ever encountered. Jim's class was one of the few electives outside the Engineering School. Georgia Tech now has Ivan Allen College, the School of Liberal Arts realizing, as many other major research universities, that real creativity comes from interdisciplinary collaborations.

I was also introduced to Dr. Peter Sherry, a professor of Chemistry who'd been on sabbatical in Sweden and at Oxford my sophomore year. Peter was an erudite, bow-tied intellectual with a great sense of humor, and a prince of a man. With his nudging, I decided to put my hat in the ring that year for a WSF exchange scholarship.

My grades were looking up. I was active in student government, my fraternity and intramural athletics and was being talked about as one of the rising leaders in my class. I thought of running for senior class president but first wanted to see if I could get the exchange scholarship to Germany. It was a longshot, forcing me to think deeply about my future and how to explain those thoughts to some highly intelligent people. I was closely interviewed by the committee and chosen as first alternate.

Disappointed, I decided to run for student government as Senior Class President. I really got to know students in my class through campaigning and visiting the dorms and other fraternities. An eye-opening experience, I saw and heard issues I'd never noticed before as well as a genuine desire on the part of Tech students to quietly and effectively integrate and diversify the campus. There was a strong concern for a kinder, gentler administration and for a new school with curriculum that allowed more electives outside the vigorous technology regime. I was helped by my fraternity brothers and friends. "McEver for President" posters went up all over campus. I spent a lot of time campaigning, talking to each student, face-to-face as much as time would allow, and it paid off. I was elected President of the Class of 1966.

I was feeling confident. It was a beautiful spring in Atlanta. It began with early harbingers—daffodils that come out of nowhere from the cold rain and then the yellow forsythia and then the red buds that are wild in the forest surrounding the city. This is a prelude to the magnificent symphony of white and pink dogwoods populating lawns and the woodlands—followed by the finishing chorus of azaleas.

School was going fine when I received a strange formal invitation under my door in elegant calligraphed letters with my name on it. I was to come dressed in black tie to an address in Ansley Park in order to be inducted into something called the Jabberwocky Society. This was mysterious. My roommate John was also invited, so we sprung for a black-tie rental and went to the appointed address. It turned out this was the home apartment of Dr. Peter Sherry. He and Dr. Young and Tom Hall were all there, as were a notable group of students: John Cowan, Guinn Leverett, Jim Simpson and our German exchange student Frank Rusch, Drew Blanchard, who was going to be the World Student Fund exchange student in Hanover, and some others. They were all enjoying martinis to a backdrop of Mozart. After a lively cocktail discussion, we were invited into a sumptuous French dinner with excellent wine and were told the reason of our being there was to be inducted into this secret society whose purpose was the heightened awareness of the culture on an otherwise bland technological campus. That was badly needed at the time!

Lewis Carroll's poem "Jabberwocky" was read, and we all signed our names around the non-sensical poem in the membership book, a worn copy of *Through the Looking Glass*. We were told never to reveal our membership except at our deaths. This was a gathering of the like-minded. John Robertson still has the book, and there are over 100 names inscribed in it.

At the end of the semester, I received an urgent message from Tom Hall and found my way to his office on the hill. He asked me to sit down and came right to the point. Drew Blanchard had contracted hepatitis and wouldn't be able to travel to Hanover. I was the first alternate and had to decide within a week if I was able to go. I seriously needed to talk to my parents, Tina, and the US Navy. Suddenly I had a true dilemma on my hands.

Chapter 14
Ausländer

I knew I'd take the exchange scholarship to the Technische Hochschule Hannover. Having grown up in the inward-looking culture of the South, at this time of my life, I felt I needed and wanted another, more classical world view. It would be my second departure from home, but this time feeling guilty having just been elected class president, and also having to leave my girlfriend, family and fraternity brothers. I finally reasoned, however, all of this was worth risking for an inside view of a European culture as an exchange student. Especially since, with my navy obligation, I would not have another shot again soon to get to Europe.

I had no idea what I was getting into or how hard that would be in a new language. I'd only taken German my freshman year at Tech. I also needed to get the permission of the US Navy to put off my pending first-class summer midshipman cruise. Vietnam was raging, and men flunking or dropping out of college were being sent to the front, while I was asking for a cultural reprieve to go to school at a German university. The Navy commandant Captain Woodfin was so proud I'd gotten this scholarship that he personally saw to it I got the deferment. It came through, and I was set. Though not easy to walk away, the student council had a strong bench and the plans for a student center were already underway; also, I was to be Tech's exchange student representative to Hannover. Tina was more difficult as our senior year would have been spent together in Atlanta and she was to be my fraternity's sweetheart. We talked it out as best we could. She'd taken her sabbatical from Georgia and encouraged my European opportunity. We reluctantly decided it was my turn for a break from the South.

What I needed was a cram course in German, and there was an advanced basic course, Grundstuffe II, starting in Passau in July, that would give me three months training through September when university began. I spent the month of June packing and saying goodbye to family and friends. Frank Rusch, still at Tech from Stuttgart, was helpful in advising me and packing my trunk, including a 35mm camera and a few books. Then, late one June afternoon, I boarded a Lufthansa jet in Atlanta and was in Munich early the next morning.

After arriving, I spent the week in Munich getting a cultural lay-of-the-land, visiting the art galleries and then taking a train out to see the concentration camp at Dachau—I had to see it for background before moving into this new culture where I could barely speak the language but was to go to one of their leading universities. I was like a duck in that my feet were paddling furiously under the surface to learn every scrap of German and the country's history I could so that I would be able to stay afloat. I was going to immerse myself and conquer it in the middle of my college life.

An hour south of Munich by train, Passau is known as the Three Rivers City, a city at the confluence of three rivers—the Danube, the Inn and the Ilz—that come together at the Austrian border. It's an ancient city—mostly baroque with a huge cathedral topped by onion-shaped spires typical of Bavarian churches. St. Stephen's Cathedral has the largest cathedral organ in the world—its 17,974 pipes came alive for services and concerts. The twisting stone streets were ideal for wandering and poking into quaint stores and shops. This charming city was to be my first real taste of European culture. The people were welcoming—characteristic of Bavarians and southern Germans—unlike the more reserved Prussians in the north, as I was to find out. At the time I was there, the population was about 15,000, but there were three breweries that kept the population happy, slightly soused and supplied taverns competing for customers throughout the town and the surrounding countryside.

I lived over a bridge and up a hill outside the city, renting a room over a small grocery store owned by a large, friendly widow, Frau Knopf. My roommate was Daniel LeClair, a sincere Frenchman with a desire to speak German and a pale and jowled Norman face. This was the first time he'd been out of his home country, so we were novices exploring Deutschland together. The bohemian countryside was delightful, quaint, and hospitable. Like me, he was a biker, and had even brought his own.

Our class was mostly made up of Fulbright scholars, who, also like me, hadn't studied much German, but were about to be thrown headlong into German university and its social life. These were bright, diverse, and serious students. Our instructor was a jovial German who had a bit of a beer belly and ate pretzels for lunch. He was polite and funny. When he spoke to us, it was a bit theatrical because he always pronounced everything precisely, the way he wanted us to speak back to him. He was a living Rosetta Stone who spoke English, French, some Norwegian, and even Italian.

The class rapidly bonded into cliques and friendships. My circle contained Owen Davis, a philosophy student from Oklahoma, who was going to Marburg; Elsa Rossbach, from Radcliffe, who was going to Berlin; Vinca Nagelgaard, a charming Norwegian redhead who was going into the hotel business in Frankfurt, and my roommate Daniel. We lunched together at a little tavern down by the river that had a slogan painted on its walls: "Im Bier lieght Kraft; Im Wein lieght Warheit; und Im Wasser leight Bacillian," which translates: "In beer there's strength; in wine, there's truth; and in water there are germs!"

We became good friends struggling with the language and practicing it on each other constantly. We also took some trips, one most memorably to Munich for October Fest and another to Vienna for a wine tour. Living in the language and constantly speaking it with everyone we met was amazing for improving our language skills. We went to German Westerns at night and listened to soap operas on TV, testing our comprehension constantly with the most basic of conversations. It was amazing how even children talked circles around us! Soon the idyllic summer in Bohemia was over. We were given our Grundstuffe certificates and were about to go out into the real world where the people we were talking to weren't patient. They cut us no slack—a rude awakening.

Hanover was a northern German city in the center of Prussia where they spoke Hoch Deutsch or High German. I was spoken to formally, not in the familiar as I was addressed in Bavaria. Because of its proximity to the channel, during the war the English and then Allied bombers had pounded it mercilessly and left it in rubble. When I saw the city, it had been rebuilt; streetcars were running (on time!), and it looked like a modern city, but scars remained, and ruins scattered in vacant lots were occasionally visible. It was the home of the Continental Tire company and some insurance companies that I understood were the first towers to rise from the rubble.

The university was in the former castle of the Guelf family of Saxony. What was left of the restored castle, also leveled by the bombing, was fronted by an erect and well-known statue of the Saxon Horse, the state's symbol. In front of the castle was the famous formal baroque Herrenhausen Garten where the court musician Handel wrote Music for the Royal Fireworks—a royal barge carried the family between downtown and their home in the castle on the canal to great fanfare. The small studentenheim where I would eventually live was in this garden on the canal.

I wanted to live with the students in the dorms. My wish was accommodated, but because I was the only American, I was considered "Auslander," a foreigner, and assigned to live with the other Auslanders—Turks, Norwegians, and other non-Prussian Germans who were at the university. The administration would not mix us, though I protested. The other foreign students were now my friends and fellows; the German students wouldn't speak to us informally, as I found out my first day at lunch when I tried to speak with my tablemate, who set me straight about being friendly or informal with anyone at the university. I soon got to know what being an Auslander was all about. It was another perspective and education I needed to receive and understand quickly. In fact, as a white male Southerner, it was healthy psychology for me to have to walk in these shoes on the other side of prejudice's street.

My first roommate was an East German who just laughed and shrugged off this incident. He confirmed what it was like on the other side of the wall as well. He'd courageously escaped during a soccer game through barbed wire with the border guards shooting at him. He'd left his family and girlfriend behind, possibly never to see them again for the "freedom" and education of the West. The West German government paid for his education, but his classmates still treated him like an Auslander. His freedom mattered most to him, not his social life.

We soon had another roommate who was Norwegian and a member of their Olympic cross-country ski team. He was friendly and had come to Hanover to learn shipbuilding because Norway had only one technical university then, and its capacity was limited. Hanover was known for its shipbuilding engineering and was where the Germans developed their submarines and torpedo prowess. The Norwegian ambassador to Germany owned the local brewery in Hanover, so our student parties were well supplied, and our Christmas party was over the top. The Norwegians didn't let being ausländers get in their way either. After that party, we went downtown to see the just-released film *The Vikings*, starring Kirk Douglas. We almost took over the local movie theater, and we all cheered as Kirk climbed the shut portcullis of the besieged Norman castle on axes thrown like steps into the great closed gate.

Classes were large and formal. They were in huge halls with the professor lecturing formally while students dutifully took notes. There was little give-and-take or questioning like I was used to in the much smaller classes at Tech. In fact, I found out the students worked in informal circles with one student going to class and taking very precise notes that the others would copy. Then they would go away and study together before the exam or paper was due. Many of the students drove taxis to supplement their income or worked other jobs. Going to the university was not a four-year affair but went on for many years, almost a profession. The Germans, however, only educated a small fraction of their intellectual elite. Many students were weeded out early and sent to technical or trade schools.

This was an austere and seemingly unfriendly place. I was used to many friends and having a brotherhood. There, I had few friends outside of my roommate and the Norwegians. Then I went to a student council meeting out of curiosity and met some of the student leaders, telling them about Tech's student government. While I was there, a heated debate about the pricing of beer sold on campus ensued. At the end of the discussion, one huge German stood up and declared what the price would be. He did it so forcefully that no one argued. It turned out, he was the student body president, Ingolf Meyer-Plate. Afterwards, I introduced myself, and we became friends at that moment and remain so today. I told Ingolf about my background on the student council at Tech and confided my isolation. He was sympathetic and said I should move into his smaller studentenheim called the Lodiheim. There was a vacancy since one of the students had to leave school suddenly mid-term. Ingolf saw to my moving in because he was interested in working in the States after he graduated and possibly being an exchange student at Georgia Tech. I was in luck that I spoke up, made a friend of Ingolf, and that his new group of roommates took me in.

About that time this group alerted the basketball coach there was an American on campus, and the coach recruited me for the team. This sent me around Germany with *zug und bier geld*—train and beer money. The camaraderie of an athletic team was welcoming. Life had changed, and I was on the other side of the social wall at the German university. Things felt and looked much more normal.

It was still unusual being away from home, family and being unable to express myself thoroughly. Early on, I'd bought a TV that I watched during the day to get the hang of ordinary language. My whole raison d'être was to improve my language skills. I couldn't go to language school now and had to learn on the job. There was no one in Hanover to speak English with, so I was forced to speak German. It worked.

After a while I strangely began to dream in German. After my first German dream, I thought I'd arrived.

Not only was communication difficult there, but I hadn't anticipated how difficult communications with home would be as well. We didn't have a telephone. To call my parents, girlfriend, or friends at home, I had to go to the post office on Saturdays and make an appointment for a phone booth. I was writing mournfully long letters to Tina. Not much was coming back. We'd agreed on my leaving we'd see others, but we had a close relationship and seemed made for each other. I should've gotten the hint because soon only my mother's letters arrived; she wrote faithfully, a good mother, with Mid-West training. Today it's hard to understand the enormity of the communications gap that previously existed in the world without computers and cell phones, bridged then only by pen and paper.

Sometime after a lonely Christmas, I decided to go see my friend Elsa Rossbach. She'd written that I should come over and see the "glories of East Berlin." By then I'd acquired a used 1962 blue Porsche (a fine machine) for only $1000. My father sent me $100 per month that translated into 400 DM and made me a pretty rich student. I had some savings, so I sprang for the Porsche. This was much discussed by my fellow classmates.

I drove the car proudly to Berlin but was detained for hours by the East German border guards who were curious that a student would be driving it. Elsa found the Humboldt University in East Berlin with its free arts programs attractive. She took me over at our first opportunity and preached to me the "glorious revolution of socialism," emphasizing the communist support for the arts in a country that was obviously falling down economically. The contrast between East and West Germany was like night and day, yet Elsa sang the East's praises. At first, I thought she was putting me on, then I realized she was indeed serious and was a true socialist. Thoughts of me losing my NROTC scholarship flashed before my mind, but this was going to be a different experience whatever happened, so I sat back and enjoyed it. I spent one of the most interesting weekends of my life seeing East Berlin from the inside and its "glories," mainly the university and the arts and cultural events—the ballet and concerts where Elsa knew some of the producers and performers.

We went to brunch with some journalists on Sunday and talked up the progress of the Eastern regime and its support for the arts and people's revolution. I was speaking pretty good German by then and was able to mimic an accent but was spotted as an American not long into the conversation. I got up to go to the bathroom and was followed by the most alert and talkative of the journalists. He sidled up beside me at the urinal.

"Do you have any dollars? I notice you are an American, and surely you have some dollars? That socialist bullshit is just that—those people are crazy. How did you get involved with them?" he asked.

"Well, Elsa and I went to the language school together—"

He cut me off. "Look, I'm trying to leave this place and am planning to escape through Yugoslavia in a few weeks. Could you please change some East German marks for some of your dollars? As an American they make you change at the border before you leave. I'll give you the black-market rate, so you don't lose anything. Can you help me out? I can get in real trouble, so please don't say anything to Elsa or anyone. You seem to be someone I can trust."

I changed a couple of hundred for him and went back to our brunch and wondered how my friend had been so altered. I left after we ate for the ride back on the Autobahn to Hanover, having seen the inside of the other side. I was detained an hour at the border while my gas tank was checked for contraband, and I was questioned about my bundle of East German marks. I was glad to be out of East Berlin, a culture that had to wall its people in.

School was easier now that I could speak the language. I was asked to give a presentation to a Mechanical Engineering class on industrial and systems engineering as we practiced it at Georgia Tech. My fellow students seemed rather interested, and I made some new friends.

Spring break was approaching, and I'd been corresponding with another of my classmates from Passau, Oren Davis, who was studying philosophy at Marburg with Rudolf Bultmann, Martin Heidegger's famous student. We both agreed to go to Greece for the break, where many German students flee. I drove to Marburg, an ancient college town, to pick up Oren who brimmed with his academic experience and meetings with Bultmann. Existentialism was our topic, and Oren was a knowledgeable guide, pulling together all I'd been reading the past lonely winter from Hesse, Kafka, Dostoevsky, Kierkegaard, Sartre, and Nietzsche.

Chapter 15
Retsina, Tina, and The Kerry

Oren and I drove to Munich where we had the Porsche thoroughly overhauled for the long trip and experienced the *gemultichkeit* of the bier halls there. We would go to the center of town where the great halls are, find a table, and strike up a conversation in German. There were no class distinctions in these places where the "brown shirts" had congregated. All tables are mingled; you could be sitting next to a doctor, lawyer, or company chief and his family. The city remains unique in this social institution of communal dining.

We set off for Athens via Trieste where we went inside a communal cafeteria the city had and tasted yogurt among other unfamiliar foods for the first time. It was a dark trip through the frontier on sometimes unpaved roads, navigating our way to Thessaloniki across the Greek frontier. We drove through one guard post after another, crossing into Yugoslavia. We stopped for fuel at an armed camp, where the gas station attendant came out in the middle of the night, tired and malcontent with an automatic weapon on a strap across his back. We had driven all night across the country and came to the Greek frontier and into the city of Thessalonica. We were glad to finally be in Alexander's capital, in fact stopped to honor the statue of him and his great horse, Bucephalus on the city's quay.

There was an upside—at that time, Greece was dirt cheap. We'd stop at a taverna, and the host would let us inspect rooms and pick the one we liked, then when we came down to dinner since we didn't speak the language, and thus couldn't read the menu, we were escorted to the kitchen and introduced to what was for dinner through a ritual of lid raisings where we responded with a nod, and the food would be served in generous portions on our plates. We were given half a large basketed bottle of local wine, Retsina, tasting slightly of turpentine from the pine kegs that age Greek wine. These were happy places and below $5 a day!

Athens was a jumble of traffic and slightly polluted but overarching all, is the ruin of the Parthenon, dramatically illuminated on its stone mesa overlooking the city and can be seen from all approaches. What a reminder of the civilization that came before with its appreciation for beauty, grandeur and grace. I had to stop the car when we got our first good view, coming into the city at dusk. Despite its age and wear and tear, it stood a noble old lady: its gravitas and spirit undiminished. It's the symbol and expression of a Greek democracy at its pinnacle of power, when all of a society's forms of creative expression flowered simultaneously, reaching a climax that subsequently remained unsurpassed for some time.

We spent the next few days in Athens walking up to and around the Parthenon and its ruins and museums. We went to other monuments and museums like the impressive temple of Poseidon at Sounion, that I'd view later that summer from the bridge of the *Kerry*. We cast about for where in the Greek islands we could take our car and came up with Crete. We booked passage on a large, Minoan Line car ferry, and we were there within one pleasant afternoon's cruise and off on another adventure.

We landed in Heraklion, the capital city of the Minoan's. We had to visit the Palace of Knossos and the Heraklion Archaeological Museum; Oren was particularly keen since he'd studied quite a bit about this ancient civilization. Oren led me through the museum and was so intent that he backed into one of the Minoan rhytons in the form of a bull and knocked off one of its horns. We were aghast, and I backed him up as he went to the museum director's office, broken horn in hand. The museum director was a large man with a huge black moustache. He looked at Oren who was turning red holding the prehistoric horn in his hand and let out a surprising laugh, then motioned to show us something downstairs—dozens of bulls' heads dug up from around the prehistoric site. (Oren said he went back thirty years later to find they'd just glued the broken horn back on.)

Once we finished our scholarly duties, it was time to party, and we took off in the Porsche for a little coastal town with a beautiful beach and a taverna on it that took on tourists. We spent four or five of the most idyllic days there joining forces with a group of California co-eds on spring break as well. We ate in the kitchen picking our meals from the various pots, brought ample supplies of Retsina, and had a hell of a time. The highlight of the stay was a pig roast out on the beach our last night there. We'd had a grand time exploring the nearby towns, beaches, and—up into the hills—some of the archeological remains from the Mycenaeans, Greeks, Roman, Byzantine and Turkish civilizations that at one point occupied the island.

Oren and I went on to rendezvous with my parents in Rome on Easter. The plan was to hook up with them in Naples first and visit Capri together. We drove northeast from Athens across Greece, stopping in mystical Delphi, and spent a half-day exploring the ruins—the stony valley had real presence that I certainly felt. We had lunch and walked around the ruins, trying to take it all in and imagine what had gone on there.

Driving on to Corfu, we spent the night before taking the early ferry to Brindisi. There we ran into another most memorable surprise—the Maundy

Thursday services in Corfu. The town comes out dressed in white sheets with pointed white hats and face coverings with holes for the eyes, nose, and mouth. It was surreally like an island of Ku Klux Clansmen. They gather to take the saints and relics out of the churches in torchlight and march them in procession about the town, to mournful chanting accompanied by a band playing the most sorrowful music ever heard. This was an amazing demonstration of piety on a full-city scale.

The next morning we drove from our landing in Brindisi across the peninsula to Naples where we met up with Mom and Dad. Dad had flown from a near-by base during the Korean War, and he'd take the ferry out to Capri, he was eager to show us, as well as impress my mother. Oren and I'd been ferrying quite a bit, but this trip was spectacular with the Aegean incredibly blue on the way out. We also visited Pompeii when we returned, viewing a slice of civilization frozen in time where the museum and the mosaics were the most memorable, particularly the victims' forms molded as they burned to death in the lava.

Moving on to Rome, I forget where we stayed, but my parents had taken care of the arrangements. We went to St. Peter's for the Sunday Mass, even though my parents were Protestant. It was a most impressive site, particularly the Pope's address and blessing. It was also great to see my folks, who were thrilled to see me after such a long absence, and they took Oren in as another son. Dad and he compared political notes, and Mom asked all about my life in Germany. My mother broke it to me that she'd heard through the grapevine that Tina was dating someone else. That's why I hadn't received any mail or gotten any calls. This was the woman I'd planned to ask me to marry me when I returned. Her long silence was strange. Oren and I said goodbye to my parents and began the long drive back to Germany. After Germany, I lost track of Oren until he contacted me about ten years ago via the internet. He'd been a philosophy professor and recently retired nearby; we united at a Tanglewood Beethoven performance and remain close friends today.

I enjoyed finishing my year at the university and became more proficient in German, reading more of Gunter Grass, Kafka, and Hesse. I enjoyed the baroque spring concerts in the Herrenhausen Garten and the late nights of almost dusk as we went into summer. One most memorable trip was to Stuttgart to visit my friend Frank Rusch from Georgia Tech, and together we went to Heidelberg to the famous Feurball—the student graduation ball. Frank and I stayed out almost all night at this festivity held with rock bands in the illuminated castle at Heidelberg. This was a graduation party extraordinaire, and I was graduating from Germany!

Returning to Hannover, I got a letter from Tina saying she was coming to Europe on a tour as a graduation present and would be stopping in the Neckar Valley on her trip. Could we get together? With much anticipation, I found us a hotel and met up with Tina for a few of days she was in Germany. It was a heavenly time in the spring in the Rhineland and wonderful to reconnect. I drove my little blue Porsche all around and showed off my new German prowess. Strange, it seemed as if we had never been apart—it was as if we were old friends and lovers, but this time together turned out to be a just a dream. The sand was running out of our hourglass as we said goodbye. She was going to Paris the following week, and I couldn't join her because I had to go to Rota, Spain to catch my ship. After that magical few days, I never heard from her again. Fate overcame our intentions. I found out when I returned to Atlanta, she had married someone from Emory and was living in Athens, Georgia at the UGA's Law School. Our paths never crossed again until over fifty years later in Washington, DC where she had raised her son and worked on Capitol Hill and later, the Kennedy Center.

Back in Hanover, I received a duffel bag of midshipman uniforms in the post. I tried them on, and my mother had them sized correctly. My newly made friends and I had a final party. I'd spent a year in another culture and came out able to speak the language and maybe better understand a rich, complex and formidable culture.

The next morning from the Hanover airport, took a flight to Madrid, and spent the next day touring that city, mainly visiting the Prado. I remember El Greco's works, in particular. I took an overnight train to Barcelona where I was to join my ship. I missed a connection because the announcements were in Spanish and finally took the correct train with the help of a friendly English-speaking conductor. Luckily, I had my duffel bag and all my clothes with me and arrived in the city in the middle of the night. I took a cab to the Navy base, but we were stopped by a crowd of sailors and gendarmes. I got out of the car. A sailor had been shot at one of the local bars outside the base, and his body was out on the street where he'd been killed. The police and sailors were faced off against each other. I got back in and directed my cab around the gruesome sight. At the gate, I found my orders and was escorted to a beautiful frigate, the *Kerry* at the quay. Its superstructure rode high and bristled with armament and electronics. I was bone tired, and the bosun showed me to the junior officer quarters where I undressed and passed out.

The next morning was Sunday, and I slept in. My fellow midshipman clued me in—this was the spit and polish Navy, and this boat was the flagship of the blue Navy. The Mediterranean fleet was to divide in two parts—the other half of our fleet was already underway and somewhere out there on the other side of the Med. We were in a war game for the summer, and our goal was to find the other half and engage in maneuvers to destroy that part of the fleet. A junior admiral was on board and led a flotilla of ships, including a carrier and ten other vessels. Through the Gates of Gibraltar, we went into the mouth of the Mediterranean to find our prey.

War Games

When our fleet divided for nuclear exercises,
I was focsle watch aboard the missile frigate *Kerry*.
We sailed for the opposite ends of the Med to search out
and annihilate one another.

We spearheaded the Blue Navy, sailing near Point Sunion,
beneath its Poseidon temple ruins,
where for millennia, Greeks, then Romans
incensed and petitioned victory prayers.
I feel the sea-weed festooned god,
astride the prow of our sleek warship, steaming
full ahead to battle alongside ancient brothers
I imagine I'm a citizen oarsman on an Athenian trireme
staying the Persian onslaught; I'm with Ptolemy
in the mayhem at Action;
or I'm on forecastle with Nelson,
about to cross the "T" at Trafalgar.

But then, a dot on the horizon.
In my binoculars, an F-4 screams into focus,
supersonic, straight at us, topping the swells,
rendering our radar impotent.

Before I can shout: *Bogie at 12 o'clock*!
he nails us, kicks in his after-burners,
goes vertical in a roar.
Less than an hour after the war began,
the game was over.
We were nuked,

our pretension vaporized
to a soft sea breeze.

I imagined myself an ancient sailor. On this cruise we dropped anchor at some classy ports, such as Monaco and Cannes, full flags flying. We had two Italian exchange midshipmen with us who were only animated when we were about to pull into port and would fight on the bridge for binoculars to spot potential dates in the crowds that lined the docks when the fleet pulled into port. They were auditioning for Don Giovani's role; we American midshipmen had something to learn from this pair.

I felt proud being part of the Navy both as a foreign policy embassy and as a working and fighting unit. I was also sobered with the speed of modern warfare. I left the ship in August after sailing back to Barcelona and flew out of the base in Rota, Spain, on a Navy transport plane, back to Norfolk, then on to Atlanta to begin my senior year.

Ingolf and Marie Ange Meyer-Plate, front
of Cologne Cathedral, 1980s

Chapter 16
A Beatitudes Vision

It was good to get home. My father came to pick me up at the airport and asked me what I'd like to do after being out of the country for a year. I craved barbecue. He took me to the Old Hickory House—a chain no longer in existence in Atlanta, and I ordered a plate of pulled pork and ribs. I don't believe I've ever tasted such a delight—it recalibrated my Southern taste buds instantly. My father had missed me, I was surprised.

As it turned out, John Robertson hadn't graduated on time and had another quarter in school, but the fraternity house was full, so we rented an apartment—actually half a home—near Piedmont Park on Carl Allen Drive, not far from Georgia Tech. It was furnished and modest but soon streamed with fraternity brothers and friends in and out since John was a real socialite.

I tried to get credit for the courses I took in Germany, but many didn't translate into the Georgia Tech system, so the bad news was having to have to take another full year of classes but was bonused with an abundance of electives. One of the courses I took was Dr. James Young's on James Joyce that included a close reading of *Ulysses*. We met weekly at Manuel's, a local pub, enjoying a beer with books, as was a senior's prerogative. Jim was a man with an encyclopedic mind, a great sense of humor, a big laugh and bowtie. Some years later when Jim passed away, we set up a memorial for him that his good friend James Dickey spearheaded after I tracked him down.

I got back into playing intermural football and looked forward to our Saturday afternoon games. One weekend it rained, so John and I accepted a cocktail party invitation from Bruce Fitzgerald and Walter James. Bruce was the editor of the school newspaper, and Walter was one of the smartest guys on campus with a 4.0 in Math. I was disappointed not playing football but decided to suck it up and enjoy the party. I walked into the kitchen—there before me was a blonde vision, simply the most beautiful woman I'd ever seen, like a Beatitudes vision—truly an angel. I asked her name? Georgia! She was Walter's date and was back from South Carolina University visiting her family in Atlanta. I was very shy but had to know more and began to tell her about myself. I'd just returned from Germany. I was beginning to get comfortable talking to this vision of a woman. She had the most remarkably soft but precise voice. She looked right through me. Letting down my guard, I sat down on the glass table in front of her, and it broke.

I was horrified and embarrassed. Shamed, I headed to tell Walter of my faux pas, but first I asked—like a drunken man for one last favor—her phone number. She gave it to me! I went off to apologize to Walter for breaking his table. Georgia was talking to the rest of the guests when I got back. I think I waved at her and went home to dream. When I got home, I discovered I'd lost her number. How could I have been so stupid? I also owed Walter for the table.

I could think of nothing else but Georgia. Two weeks later I was at a Tech football game, and at the stadium, there was another of Walter's fraternity brothers with Georgia. I went up to her, and she snubbed me, saying, "Thought I would hear from you." I apologized, and the next day in class grilled the poor guy she'd been with about her. He unwisely told me where she lived, and using directory assistance, I breathlessly called her home. Her mother answered, and after I asked for her, Georgia came on and said something like, "The exchange student?" but agreed to go out with me.

She was home from South Carolina University where she was a voice major and in Atlanta was a debutant that year at the Piedmont Dining Club, something she did for her mother she later explained. She had a remarkable voice and had been one of Robert Shaw's soloists when she'd been just sixteen. Because of college, she wasn't in Atlanta much. The next time she had available was a family gathering, a Christmas Eve service at their church. She'd been struck by our conversation and wanted to introduce me to her two sisters who'd just returned from traveling in Europe. Could I come to their apartment on Peachtree Road at five on Christmas Eve? This was more of an introduction than I'd anticipated.

This was also a great social leap for me. I'd grown up on the south side of Atlanta, going to GMA (the rival of Westminster where she and her stepbrother had gone to school), so I was basically from the other side of the tracks. As I would soon learn, this distinction meant nothing to Georgia but was a distinction for me and another social hurdle to get over.

I showed up in coat and tie at the appointed hour, and her mother opened the door. Alma was the most gracious of Southern ladies and hostesses. She immediately made me feel right at home. What would I like a drink, or better yet, would I like some of their homemade syllabub?

In came her husband David Black—a tall gentleman most gracious with great stories who also made me feel at ease, then there were two dark-haired beauties—her sisters, Suzy and Holly, who immediately began to ask me about my European experiences, and I was ringed by them when Georgia walked in looking radiant.

"I see you know everyone," she said and came over, pecked me on the cheek and winked. "Hope you like Episcopal services, a bit stiff and formal, but I love the carols. Oh, this is Fred." Being cool, a skinny kid slouched in and didn't shake my hand. Fred was her stepbrother and sized me up immediately as a kid from the other side of town he'd be protecting his stepsister from and began to ask some penetrating and embarrassing questions. I was saved by her sisters who'd spent the last two years traveling Europe, skiing in Switzerland and vacationing down on the Riviera, not studying away at a cold German university.

The family shared a tragic loss, however. David's wife and Fred's mother had died when an Air France jet crashed on take-off from Paris, taking a planeload of Atlanta's social elite with it. Alma's husband and the girls' father had suddenly passed away in the prime of his life, and they moved to Atlanta as a result. David had been Alma's high school boyfriend, and got lucky, sort of like me with this lovely creature who'd invited me this evening into her world. I hoped I wouldn't spill anything or say anything untoward while Fred was hovering, looking for any opening to expose this boy from the wrong side of the tracks. Life deals strange cards indeed; that night I was concerned for my social status and about impressing this woman when I had stepped into this new family only gathered together because of the tragedy they both had experienced. The hurtful reality ironically would not wrench my gut until I lost this woman who invited me into her family's tragedy and then became the center of my life.

After a beautiful and moving service, I said goodnight to Georgia at her door, and she asked me to call her again! I was smitten. I went to my parents' for Christmas and explained about this beautiful girl I'd just met and been to Christmas Eve service with. They nodded and smiled, probably feeling sorry for me because I'd lost Tina.

When I got back to school after the break, concentration was hard. I wanted to go out with Georgia but had few opportunities since she was only in Atlanta some weekends and had dates on the debutante circle that lasted until spring. I got invited to a party at a wealthy Atlantan's home one Saturday afternoon and asked Georgia to join me. Dillard Munford was an Atlanta scion, and his son was a friend. I picked her up in my little blue Porsche coupe that I was sure would impress her, but she seemed unfazed. She knew most of the people at the party since she was from the north side. There was a pool table in the games room, so we drifted in, and I asked her to play.

"Sure. You break," she said. I did, nothing dropped and when it was her shot, she cleared the table and smiled. There were things this woman did to perfection: sing, ride horses, waterski, and shoot pool. She'd had a pool table at her house as a little girl. I was not going to impress this woman; it would be on her terms. Then one evening when I walked her to the door of her parents' apartment, she let me kiss her. I had been anticipating this moment in our relationship, but don't think I've ever kissed anyone who had softer lips. I walked away stunned—that simple kiss conveyed passion and a beckoning beyond youthful intrigue; we had bonded and the kiss portended a promising future. After this, it was hard to get my feet back on the ground and my mind around school.

However, to graduate I had to get through my Industrial Engineering classes, whether I liked them or not, and signed up for Plant Design—this was a practical, hands-on project for a carpet cleaning company in northwest Atlanta. The owner was a Turkish immigrant with a good business, but woeful plant engineering. I was part of a team that was to significantly redesign his plant, make the flow much more efficient, and balance his production as well as also look at his business. I was interested, but my heart wasn't in it or the details.

I could see his errors and knew I could run his business, better. I wanted to run things myself, also invest in new ideas. To do this right…I knew I needed to go to business school. Like a sunrise, I realized my next step was to get an MBA. I had premonitions of this in Germany but being hands on in a real business confirmed it. I went to see my Navy advisor Captain Woodfin, who was thankfully still there after I returned from Germany. He reluctantly said he'd do what he could to get yet another deferment and came back to report that the Navy wanted me to have blue-water training as soon as I could, meaning go to sea or Vietnam on a river boat. The only way they'd give an exception was if I could get into either the business school at Harvard or Stanford—the two most difficult to get into in the country.

I had to try and had a shot. My grades had improved. I had above a 3.2 average, and I'd been in student government, showing leadership on campus and at my fraternity. Moreover, and importantly, I had gotten an exchange scholarship. Also, Harvard seemed to like Georgia Tech graduates—indeed, Tech was becoming a primary feeder school. They liked entrepreneurial engineers, so I had a chance and took great pains filling out my application but also sent one to Stanford.

John Robertson was graduating at the end of the winter quarter, so I needed a new roommate. Walter James was available as was Ingolf Meyer-Plate, who'd come to Georgia Tech at my urging. On scholarship, he was teaching math with Walter. He was so tall he'd been approached by the Georgia Tech basketball coach "Wack" Hyder but had never played. So, Walter, Ingolf, and I decided to room together and found an apartment on the Prado in Ansley Park—the same place where Margaret Mitchell had written *Gone with the Wind*. We moved in one weekend, when I discovered Georgia was at the Driving Club right across the street on a debutante date. We'd had a few beers and decided that stormy night to go across the street in our raincoats and crash the party.

Georgia spotted us across the dance floor and was perturbed. She came over in a beautiful white gown, chastised us, and showed us out but agreed to come over later after dumping her date. Ingolf was dating Marie Ange, a French girl (later his wife) working at the French embassy in Atlanta. Walter, with no love interest, had his guitar at the time. We all stayed up late that night and became a trio. Later Georgia came over and partied with us; she drank scotch and could hold her liquor. We were less adept but managed to get her home late. This was our gang for the rest of the year—Georgia was becoming my girlfriend. Soon, in Atlanta, we went everywhere together. My friends were delighted— she seemed to fit right in. She got along with the Jabberwocky crowd because she knew classical music and opera inside out, could match their knowledge and beat them on most musical topics. James Young was the head usher when the Met came to Atlanta at the Fox Theater and had us all ushering performances.

One Friday I was playing tennis with Walter on the courts at the Driving Club across from our apartment. I went back to get a lob, and with a desperate shot, I hit my front tooth with the racket, knocking it out. It was replaced with a temporary to hold off the pain. Saturday came, and Ingolf took my car to pick up Georgia, who was to be a bridesmaid at a friend's wedding we were all attending. Suddenly a car stopped in front of them, and he ran into the back of it, smashing the front of my Porsche, but sadly also knocking out Georgia's front tooth! Both snaggle-toothed, we were the source of jokes for weeks.

The real trauma I faced was being waitlisted at Harvard and as far as I knew at Stanford as well. This meant Navy sea duty or Vietnam. I was really interested in the economy and the effect the war, with its horrendous expenditures, was having on it. Dr. Peter Sherry had me over for drinks one afternoon and probed me as only he could on the subject. I must have explained for an hour and concluded I was concerned about the level of debt we were getting the country into, and the reaction it caused in the capital and stock markets. I could see the big picture and was concerned for my investments. Peter was silent, then said, "You need to go to Harvard Business School next week and explain to them just what you've just explained to me. I've never had anyone explain the workings of the markets better. Just go talk to them, and they'll understand you deserve to go there and that you're ready." I picked up the telephone and called the admissions office, talking to a sympathetic secretary hearing my accent was like hers and my insistence. She said "Dr. Athos, the Dean of Admissions can give you half an hour next Thursday afternoon. Can you come up?" I called Dad and got a ticket to fly up to meet the Dean. "All you have to do is just tell them what you told me." Peter smiled as I walked out.

The next Thursday morning I was in Boston and took a cab to Harvard Square. I walked around in awe. This was the famous university I couldn't get into as an undergraduate, and now I was going to try to get into the mighty Harvard Business School. I had to be kidding myself, but I walked around and observed the students, mostly long-haired and un-conventional, it seemed. After having a turkey sandwich, I walked across the river and waited outside the Dean's office. Dr. Anthony Athos was a professor of Human Behavior (that was Psychology once) and had become Dean of Admissions. My appointment was at 2:00. It was 1:30. The secretary smiled, recognized my name and said, "Relax, you'll get in. Not many take the trouble to come see him."

Soon it was time, and I sat in Tony's office where he pulled my file from the bottom of a large stack on his desk—the on-holds—and said, "Now, Bruce, why do you want to come here?" I began to explain. Then he asked, "What do you think about this war? What do they think about it in Germany? What was that like?" I was off, and two hours later we finished. He looked at his watch. "I enjoyed our time together. You'll be hearing from us." He put my file on top of the pile on the right-hand side of his desk. That small gesture changed my life. Dr. Sherry had been right. I had to convince them I had the maturity and drive to get through Harvard Business School (HBS) and the desire to do something with the degree other than get a good job.

I got my acceptance letter in the mail the next week and felt relieved and celebratory, calling Georgia and my friends. Peter asked Georgia and me over for dinner at his apartment, and we celebrated with martinis and champagne. It was going to be a great future. I dutifully went to see Captain Woodfin who put in my two-year deferral. I went out to Stanford, who also admitted me. Stanford had such a beautiful campus, but at that time, Harvard was the number one business school in the country. Honestly, I thought I couldn't study as hard in California and needed to get through the B-school experience.

The Navy came through as they said they would, and now I needed to get a job to begin to pay for HBS. I had some investments that had gone well, and Dad even said he would chip in some for living expenses, but I was going to have to pay for tuition with student loans. I got a job for $600 a month with Oxford Industries in Atlanta, a local conglomerate and was looking forward to a hot summer in Atlanta with my new girl. Georgia was going to take summer classes at Oglethorpe University to make up for some courses she didn't do so well in at Carolina.

I got a surprise call from a guy in Houston named Harry Lucas who ran an executive recruiting business for engineers in Houston. He'd seen on my resumé that I was going to HBS and was impressed. "I see you're going to HBS. That must be expensive. How much is that job going to pay you in Atlanta? I could use you here in Houston," he drawled. I told him.

"Well, I'll pay you $800 per month and your ticket over and back from Atlanta. I need you to start next week. I'm in the oil business and recruit engineers too. Can you be here?" I told him I appreciated the offer but wanted to go to graduation. He just laughed. I missed graduation to fly to Houston. When I arrived at work in one of the older towers in downtown Houston, I found that Harry Lucas was a famous man whose family had discovered the Tea Pot Dome in Houston, making a fortune in oil. He was in London buying offshore leases in the North Sea that he'd trade out to big companies to drill on. He liked engineers, having a degree himself, and the company I was working for was a recruiting firm for engineers in the petroleum refineries and aerospace industries in Houston. It was a friendly group of recruiters I worked with. They were hail-fellows-well-met and loved to go on long lunches with a couple of martinis. I learned I couldn't do that and just worked, soon making my first recruit and going from there.

Harry was an odd duck—very conservative and security-conscious. He had all our correspondence shredded and was afraid our phones were tapped. He ordered a weekly search for bugs. The secretaries were full of Harry stories. He was a multi-millionaire who sent his underwear back for re-elasticizing rather than buying new. He thought out-of-the-box, about the big picture. All of the executives had special research projects. He wanted me to work on a fuel cell project to understand the feasibility of the automobile industry's abandoning oil and beginning to use fuel cells and battery power to propel cars. A true futurist!

I went to a Georgia Tech alumni event one evening and met Leslie McGrath, a thin, elegant redhead. She lived in River Oaks, a posh area of town she convinced me was a better area to live in for the summer than where I was living near NASA with some Tech engineers whose project for the summer was building a beer can pyramid. We became good friends, and her mom had a house in Galveston where most Houstonians escaped for the weekends, but it was unique in that her neighbors were the Bushes—George and Barbara. At the time, George ran an offshore oil drilling company called Zapata. They were the most gracious people, and George Jr. and I were about the same age and went out with Leslie and her friends. George was friendly, and we shared crab, beer, and college stories. He was going to Yale but wanted to go to HBS eventually. We were just good friends, and politics didn't enter the picture at that time, but he wasn't going to Vietnam.

At the time it was impractical and expensive to fly home, but Georgia and I managed to take a long fourth of July in New Orleans where we rendezvoused and were coached through the restaurants by John Robertson. I didn't know what to do about Georgia. It was a true dilemma as I was going to HBS and marriage was premature for us both at the time. Though Georgia wasn't 21 yet she had uncanny beauty and common sense. She seemed to understand but had no end of men attracted to her. She decided she wasn't going back to South

Carolina but would continue her education at Oglethorpe University
in Atlanta where with her natural beauty she was easily selected their
May Queen. My only consolation was she moved into an apartment
with her sister, Holly, who drove around in a silver Corvette, and they
both spent a lot of time riding horses at their mother's farm, Little
Sandy in Good Hope, Ga.

Georgia & Bruce McEver at their Engagement Party,
Atlanta, November, 1969

Chapter 17
A Well-Known Eastern Business School, 1967-1969

At the end of the summer of 1967, I returned to Atlanta with some savings and investments in the bank from my time in Houston. I visited with my family, friends, and Georgia. Her parents had moved to an ancestral farm outside the city in Good Hope—a town east of the city—where we cooled off in the shoals and rode her horses on the red dirt roads around Little Sandy Farm. I made ready to embark on my educational dream—Harvard Business School—still not believing I'd been admitted.

I was going in my blue 1962 Porsche coupe from Germany that I'd stored at my parents' for the summer and that looked something like a turned-over blue bathtub. The little car and I headed up US 95. I drove alone, listening to a classical music station on the radio when I found one and thinking hard about what I was about to undertake. Going through the Baltimore Tunnel, the gear shift broke off, but I managed to find a welder open on Friday afternoon in the city and was on my way again. Nothing was going to deter me. The next day I stopped on the top of a hill when the spires of Boston were first visible over the hazy morning horizon and thought: "Well here I am, a Georgia boy." I wondered if I could get through the Yankee school. I said a prayer to the business school angel I was about to acquaint myself with—no, more like wrestle. My self-esteem needed work too, but HBS heaped ego out in abundance to its graduates.

I found the Business School, saw the gold and weather-veined domes of Harvard University arrayed across the banks of the Charles, like they were aligned in opposition. I was to find out the difference. It was the day right before classes started. The B-School is centered around the Georgian cupola-topped and columned Baker Library, endowed by the founder of Citibank. I found my way to check-in at the well-organized central office. They'd assigned me to a ground floor room in Chase Hall with a Frenchman, Jean Francois de Chorivite. Because I'd been an exchange student, I was now his American ambassador and guide. There were six other "can-mates" because the suites—if you could call these sparse dorm rooms that—were organized around a central toilet, bath, and shower.

We began classes soon after getting to know one another. Our section advisor was Dr. John McArthur, a finance professor and former forester from Canada. He was nice, unassuming, and disarmingly smart. His specialty was pipeline financing, and he'd written his dissertation on the 1920s and '30s pyramiding of the public utilities that almost brought down the American financial system. He shepherded us through our two years, becoming a mentor and eventually dean of the school. I was so lucky to have him as an advisor.

We divided ourselves into study groups, proving important for all our cases—the raison d'être of the school. We went through nothing but cases, and through these real-world challenges, learned how businesses run, and then suggested and argued how best to solve the companies' problems. First, we had to read and discuss the cases and dissect them together with our study groups to try out these solutions before presenting and defending the solutions in class. By the time we finished, we'd gained vicarious experience; whereas before, we had little. Most of the people in the class had some business or military leadership experience under their belts. Preparation was key, and sometimes when cold-called— the bane of HBS classes—thinking on your feet proved golden. I was fresh, raw, right out of college. However, the Harvard Business School learned Georgia Tech graduates had a lot of practical problem-solving experience and weren't afraid of numbers. Probably one reason I got in were the thirty-five-plus Tech graduates who proceeded me.

My study group included Jean Francois, who was a graduate of the elite French HEC Business School. He brought along Dominique Heau, who was also a graduate of HEC and who became a Professor of Finance at Fontainebleau. I brought Butch Harris, who was, like me, a Tech grad and a real Industrial Engineer, who was just back from the Army and had practical co-op experience. Pipe-smoking Jean Francois adorned our wall with a large poster of Charles de Gaulle. His father was a doctor in Bordeaux, and Jean Francois was a scholar, good tennis player, and a snappy dresser, though he, being French, as we joked at times, wore no deodorant.

The first week or so I was so intimidated that I hardly spoke in class. The professors hinted I needed to participate. As I listened, I began to realize it was the Northern Harvard and Yale guys who spoke up, but their initial opinions were really bullshit or anecdotal. As we got to know one another, the older and wiser business-hardened folks began to voice opinions. Common sense helped too!

I also learned the real crunch were the WACs or Written Analysis of Cases due each Friday by midnight in a slot on the side of Chase Hall. In writing, we were to take apart an entire case and put it back together with real, practical solutions. This was a new exercise for me, but I found a good typist who'd been a former WAC reader, and we became good friends. Loring Lowe helped me get through this course, turning my scribbled handwriting into meaningful text.

We had one case that featured an analysis of advertising ethics for *The New Yorker* involving apartheid sanctions. Was it ethical for the magazine to accept advertising from South African Rock Lobster Co., South African Airlines, or De Beers Mines Ltd., when each had different racial policies and employee practices? I wrote the winning WAC, slated to be published. It never was, but the award was flattering. I had taken the approach of taking apart a history of the company and its experience with apartheid to their matching employee profiles to determine a policy, or a bottom up rather than a top-down approach to the problem.

We were seven sections of a hundred students each, and being a super competitive group, we worked very hard. There was little time for recreation except Friday nights after the WACs were finished, or on Saturday nights. I slowly got to know others in my class and found out what a remarkable group of people they were. In fact, they were the best part of the school. My classmates bonded through this experience, and we've remained close throughout our business and personal lives. It was hard to believe a whole year had passed. I was much more business savvy, or at least I thought so. At the end of that first year, with all my interest in the stock market (and we were in a roaring bull market) and the capital markets, coupled with my German experience and French roommate, I now wanted to study international finance.

One morning a former B-School professor from the Investors Overseas Services (IOS) empire in Geneva, run by the now-infamous Bernard Cornfeld appeared in my dorm room. They hired two B-School students each summer to apprentice at headquarters and had their eyes on me. I milked my exchange student credentials and new relationships with my French friends for all they were worth but was also sincerely interested in the international money management they practiced. I got a job offer and began to plan the summer in Switzerland. Determined to try an international business experience, my friend and section-mate Peter Huri and I were going to set up an international consulting firm, however after my offer he decided on working for his family's firm there.

Georgia didn't want to wait until after the summer to see me. She wanted to accompany me to Switzerland and match her sisters' experience in Europe. She asked her mother, who answered affirmatively and who even came to NYC to see us off. Having never lived with a woman, Georgia and I would really get to know one another in Geneva and understand our compatibility together. I didn't dare share this with my parents. We had a wonderful weekend in New York with Alma and Georgia's sister, Suzy, who was dating a spiffy guy—T. O. Allen who drove an Excalibur. I also saw my friend and broker, Allan Wood. He gave us the names of good restaurants in Geneva. Off we flew to Switzerland with well-wishers waving.

We arrived in Geneva in the middle of the night and found our way to our hotel on the lake where we were rudely initiated into European living—the couple in the next room made love noisily all night long. When we finally woke up, lines of people clutching suitcases circled in front of the banks on the streets below. The French were in crisis, and before the currency devalued, citizens fled to Switzerland with bags of cash to exchange for Swiss francs. Such was the state of the currency markets at the time. Welcome to international finance where the solution at that time was a suitcase of money.

We found a local bistro for breakfast. Later, though jet-lagged, we went to visit Peter Huri and his wife YuYu at his parents' home on the lake. Peter Huri's father, a Swiss banker, had some concerns about IOS, but couldn't put his finger on them directly, just cautioned us.

On Monday I found my way to IOS headquarters, a chalet (more like a castle) on the lake. It was fabulously appointed with oil paintings and antiques, and also oddly endowed with a bevy of beautiful secretaries. So, this was what international finance attracted?

My investment management division met first thing to discuss the markets and their current asset allocation policy. There was a currency crisis in France, but would it affect the rest of Europe or the US? Those assembled around the conference table began to argue about how we'd switch the asset allocation around between the hotshots on Wall Street who managed part of the money in NYC and London, and continental international managers who played on the various exchanges in Europe. What I learned that summer would be an invaluable lesson for the rest of my life.

At the time, it was only the Scots in Edinburgh and these guys in Switzerland who were attempting international investing. This was leading edge stuff but complicated by managers who jealously guarded the money they managed, and they were reluctant to share with their rivals, or operate on the schedule we, as central managers, dictated. Both my fellow HBS trainee Rob Drake and I could see that the managers' delays in trading and transferring money led to average profits instead of the outstanding results that were possible.

Comparing notes after work, Rob and I realized this place was a bit too contrived—the beautiful women, exquisite oil paintings and antiques. Bernard and his partners turned out to be on the edge of legitimacy. They and their formidable salesforce owned and traded their own stock with regularity and promoted it to their clients, and a year after I left, the company collapsed under the market decline. The company was then looted by a major international criminal—Robert Vesco—who absconded with the remaining funds to Latin America, eventually fleeing to Cuba where he died in 2007.

In the meantime, things were heady. Their salesmen were pulling money from under mattresses, and out of safe but stodgy Swiss bank accounts all over Europe and putting it into IOS mutual funds. Success bred success, we had to keep up our investment results. IOS had some of the best asset managers at that time working for them, but they weren't coordinated. Yes, the answer was international asset allocation. I was fascinated but couldn't solve the practical problems of moving the funds on a timely basis between our diva-like managers.

One weekend Georgia and I and my classmate Neil Keltner, also working in Geneva and a recently returned Vietnam veteran, as well as his girlfriend went to an IOS soiree out on the lake. Many of the women partygoers in their tiny French bathing suits were soon waterskiing and doing figure eights, making for a lively discussion on the lakeshore. At that time, the lake was polluted, but this didn't stop Georgia who was determined to demonstrate her skills as an excellent water-skier. She started from the dock, catching everyone's attention, and many of these boys thought shapely Georgia with her long blonde hair was certainly going to make a big American splash. She deftly jumped off the pier and took off to the amazement of the people driving the boat and the onshore spectators. She went for a spin around the lake and then let the rope go, perfectly timed to glide back into the pier without getting wet. Champagne was sent down from the castle we shared.

While Georgia was the heroine of that moment, the real hero with us that day was Neil who was the only Bronze Star winner in our class. I wrote this beginning of a reflection for him after his interment at Arlington Memorial Cemetery:

No Ordinary Hero

I got to know him in Geneva that summer
between our B school years, where we interned.
We'd meet Sundays to picnic on grassy banks
by the lake shore with our girlfriends
(mine who later became my wife).
When Neil took off his shirt to sun,
his stomach and chest looked
like tank treads were tested on him.

After cutting cheese and the uncorking wine,
the girls left to swim,
and I asked him what happened?
He had a crew-cut then and drawled
with a grin: "Viet Cong ambush."
Distant, the symbol of the city
the *Jet d'Eau*, arched
a summer spray celebrated by
a circle of half-moon sails skimming
the lake in light breeze, far
from the jungles of Viet Nam...

I walked to my car turning
the honoring over in my mind:
That there, in the chapel, you could feel the souls
of fallen heroes gather around us,
invasive, curious and like the heat
of the morning, sneaking in between
the silent intervals in the service,
listening...

As one after another, of the remaining
members of Neil's brigade came forward
to witness how, if not for Neil, Captain Keltner
they would not be there, talking on this day,

directly disobeying their commander's last order,
whose instructions for his memorial,
before he died of lung cancer,
were there be no mention of any hero,
other than Christ.

We had a great time in Geneva and touring around Europe on
weekends. We sublet an apartment for the summer that was owned by
a former furrier who also collected rare books. He'd gone into a nursing
home, assuring us he would be back at the end of the summer. There was
one closet in our apartment always locked where he kept his books. Sadly,
he died before we left at the end of our summer, and when his relatives
came to get his possessions, his daughter opened the closet and showed us
an actual Gutenberg Bible. We'd lived with it all summer.

At the end of that summer, we drove across the Alps and down to the
Italian coast where we rented a villa overlooking Porto Venere where Lord
Byron swam the bay. We shared this idyllic spot with Dominique Heau
and his artistic wife, Gisella, who was over-animated and later tragically
institutionalized for mental illness. We drove from there and across France
(I was not impressed with the French roads after that drive.) to visit with
Jean Francois at his family's place in Bordeaux where we had oysters and
the excellent local wine. His mother kidded Georgia about being squeamish
about eating the fresh oysters she served. The wine was memorable.

Our European summer was over, and we flew back to Atlanta out of
Paris and once rested, had dinner with my parents. I had no idea how to
handle explaining this experience with my parents, but Georgia and I were
a couple, and headed toward getting married. No one spoke for a while,
but I was covering our tracks nicely, talking all about traveling in Swit-
zerland and how my experience there was so brief. Inevitably Dad asked,
"Georgia, what did you do for the summer?" To which she quipped:
"Followed Bruce around Europe." There was dead silence, and then Mom
said, "Well, I hope he took good care of you," and we all laughed nervously.

My second year I lived off campus and buckled down to finish business school. I knew I was going into the military because I couldn't defer my NROTC scholarship repayment any longer, so I got to know Ron Fox who'd been Assistant Secretary of the Army for Logistics and was teaching at HBS. He was a great guy to work for, and I helped him when I could by doing logistical research. Ron told me about the Systems Analysis Group (OSA) and got me an interview in DC; they were interested in me joining them when the Navy released me from sea duty and offered me a job.

I was also fascinated by what was happening in the South with voter registration. Vernon Jordan was a guest lecturer at the Harvard Kennedy School, and I got to know him through taking his course. I was taken by the non-violent and voter registration strategies. About that time radical, Harvard students protesting the war occupied Harvard Yard, and Peter Lavery and I went over to the Yard to witness the event. Vietnam, was a morass that kept escalating, reverberating across American campuses. Maybe I could do something about it in OSA?

Toward the end of my B-School experience, each section divided into three corporations, and we played a live business computer simulation game. This was as close to a real business as we got—a scrimmage before the live game. I was elected president of my company by my teammates. We took on tasks depending on our talents and had a great team. After a month's competition, we were the leading company! We had three divisions, and each division head, the CFO, and I pledged we'd all get the same grade if we won. There was one move left, and we were miles ahead. It looked like a shoo-in, but when the teams opened the envelopes, another team had beaten us. There went our Distinction! As it turned out, the winning team had fraudulently obtained (hacked) the simulation model and manipulated the last week's move. Ultimately, we were declared the winners. The professor informed us he only had one Distinction that he offered me, but I took the High Pass along with the rest of my team as we'd pledged one another.

Now, there are annually over 11,000 applicants for the 1000 slots at HBS. I'd been just damn lucky to get in and winning this game was a nice way to finish. I didn't stay for graduation. Ordered to Athens, Georgia, I'd start the Navy Supply Corps School in early June. The whole senior year at HBS had been about getting a job for most students, but going into service for four years, I only interviewed with a few of the big investment banks and learned I'd have to start all over when I returned from the Navy; military service didn't count for seniority on Wall Street. The rest of my class were on their way to Wall Street. This was the largest class to go into the investment banking business of all time—some 40% of the class—just in time for the market's decline and a massive consolidation of the industry. Thinking I was being left behind, I was actually lucky but didn't realize it as the capital markets collapsed and with them many of the traditional investment banking firms and my classmates' early careers.

Lucille Paulsen McEver's Parents & Grandparents
(The Paulsen Family)

Chapter 18
Porkchops and Champagne

Whether I liked it or not, I was destined for sea duty, or Blue Water Experience, my detailer—the person who controlled my fate for the next four years of my life—explained before I left HBS. Even though I'd interviewed with and been accepted to work in the Systems Analysis Group for the Secretary of Defense in the Pentagon, I had to go to sea first, just in case I ever changed my mind and decided to stay in the Navy and wanted to take the admiral track. It had been the US Navy who paid for my education, and I owed them, particularly since they'd generously deferred that service for three years, even while we were at war. Sea duty became the first hurdle I had to clear in order to work in the Pentagon.

Thus, the Navy having waited long enough for my services, sent me to join the next class of the US Navy Supply Corps School in Athens, Georgia, starting June 1969. For me, however, this was like sending Brer Rabbit into the Briar Patch. What a location because about forty miles southeast was Georgia's parents' farm in Good Hope, and it was also close to Atlanta where my parents lived.

The US Navy takes training seriously and Athens is their version of business school for the active-duty Supply Officer, to teach the intricacies of their supply system so you can utilize it effectively as the on-board businessman and fixer. I would be paymaster; run the ship's storerooms, laundry, and mess; as well as arrange for any parts and supplies we needed. Also, the supply officer determines which merchants are allowed to sell their merchandise to the crew on board your ship; that's real power. As a supply officer, I always pictured Milo Minderbinder (also a supply officer) of *Catch-22* who arranged everything from scotch to sex for that storied bomber squadron.

Ours was a class of mostly undergraduate business majors, but also a few MBAs like me. First order of business was fitting into our uniforms, then we were soon organized into platoons for morning quarters and marching between classes. For us Porkchops, as we were called—a derogatory name for the golden flowered Corps emblem on our sleeves—discipline was gained by osmosis. We formed into platoons and carried only .45s that we'd someday use to protect the payroll on payday. I had to get my own housing unless I wanted to stay in the limited and stark dorms on the University of Georgia campus. Searching the local paper, I found a great place—an upstairs corner apartment in the palatial white-columned house of Mrs. Foss and her sadly overweight and sweet daughter Stephanie.

At every opportunity, I was over at Little Sandy Farm. Our experiment in living together had worked—I'd fallen in love with Georgia; we seemed destined to be together, even though I didn't know where I was about to be sent. Georgia was only twenty-one, and one of the most delightful creatures the Lord had ever placed on earth. She was beautiful, intelligent and quite a wit, and very quick on her feet, but totally unassuming, except when on stage where she transformed it, radiating energy. She had uncanny judgment, and her stepfather David always bragged about her solid common sense. She was just fun to be around, but also cared for me, was proud of what I'd done, and always encouraged me. I realized it was my good fortune to have her love. I seemed to perform at a higher level just being with her because her elevated energy level was uplifting.

In 1969, we went to Sea Island for Labor Day weekend where we stayed in the old Cloisters Hotel. It was a charming antique, though when modernized, the act broke the family who owned it. We biked around the romantic island, and after returning to our suite from a thrilling horseback gallop along that wide beach, I finally got up the courage to propose to her. We sat on our terrace overlooking the Marshes of Glynn. We didn't know where the Navy would send me, but Georgia pushed aside the uncertainty and said yes, and asked me to help her break the news to her parents.

She and I got a little nervous at this prospect. I hadn't told my parents yet, who liked Georgia, but thought her a little young and not a serious enough student. Though my mother agreed that she was certainly a remarkable personality and a most talented and attractive young lady, she wanted me to wait out the Navy experience and become settled in business before taking this leap. I didn't know what Alma or David would think. She was their baby, their youngest charge, and none of her sisters were married yet. It seemed right to both of us, but would everyone else think it was too early?

The following weekend was a beautiful specimen of a Georgia fall. I screwed up my courage and decided not to ask them directly but do it by telling a story before dinner about a young man and his girlfriend. When I came to the part about them getting married, Alma got what

I was doing right away and jumped up to get a bottle of Champagne she'd been saving for just such an occasion. Dave was also delighted, and he seemed to really like me. Soon we were into a second bottle before dinner was served. It was truly a celebratory event. I was glad that Alma and the stern but approving David had so readily accepted the idea. Mit, Georgia's 100-year-old grandmother, a life-long Baptist, was also into the Champagne with us. As it began to grow dark, Alma urged me to stay over, but I had school in Athens starting at eight the next morning. I needed to be spit-polished and in formation early the next morning. Unwisely, I said I had to go. My stubborn streak was almost tragic.

Outside Good Hope, I approached the crest of the hill that dead ends into the highway going into High Shoals with its spectacular falls on the way to Athens. I was traveling at high speed, left the road, and luckily lodged between two trees on the other side of the road. The impact was shock enough. My knee smashed into the ignition, shutting down the engine. If I hadn't had an across-shoulder seatbelt on, I would have eaten the dashboard. After the shock, I reflected I was alive, that my knee hurt, but there was no bleeding. I was stunned. The car wasn't going to restart. Luckily, I'd missed a large tree and power pole. I had to find someone who could pull the car out and repair the ignition. I should have laid down but stood on the other side of the road on the crest of the hill surveying the landscape with both waning day light and my options for getting back to the farm or fleeing to Athens fading. There wasn't much traffic on this back-road shortcut.

Soon enough a couple of good-old-boy farmers in a truck stacked with full chicken crates crested the hill. I waved them down. They grasped the situation immediately, and one of them said to the other, "Lem, where'd you put that chain last time you used it? In the tractor shed?" They knew exactly what to do and took me back to their farm to find a chain. They got a tractor, pulled me out, and hotwired the ignition. How lucky could I be? They even shared their six-pack with me to help with the shock. I wanted to buy them a case, but all the stores were closed.

I was on my way back to Athens, thank God. I couldn't stop because the ignition was rigged. What I didn't realize was that when I didn't call Georgia upon getting home and my landlord reporting my absence, set Georgia and her mom out to find me, and to their horror saw the rear of the car wedged across the road between the tree and power pole and no Bruce. They went back home and called the State Patrol. I somehow missed everyone, and when I did call, got a frightening lecture. I was appropriately shamed and felt like a fool. Where the accident had taken place was henceforth known as "Bruce's Corner" in family parlance.

The time at Athens went quickly. It was important to do well in Supply Corps School, taking endless multiple-choice tests on every aspect of naval logistics, because your duty assignment was determined by your standing. While I didn't graduate at the head of my class, it was high enough to be eligible to pick my ship and avoid the river boats in Vietnam. I chose the USS Neptune, a cable layer out of San Francisco (that seemed innocent enough), and we were both enthusiastic about that city—the center of the new age and flower children at that time.

We wanted to get married in Atlanta and before I went away, so Georgia and I agreed on December before Christmas. Georgia's mother was such a sweet and respected person in the community and an expert at organizing such affairs, so, soon, we were the subject of several luncheons and cocktail parties since Alma's friends were eager to host such events. Since Georgia was in the inner circle of Atlanta's serious music set, our wedding was to be a concert at the Ponce de Leon Presbyterian Church where Jerry Black was organist and concert impresario.

We shook up the Atlanta social circuit with our international set of wedding guests. I had HBS classmates as groomsmen, almost all from abroad or Yankees, while Georgia had her sisters and a few local friends. John Robertson was my best man. Other attendees were Dominque Heau from France and his artist wife Gisela, Ingolf Meyer-Plate from Germany, and his fiancée Marie Ange from Paris. My HBS roommates Joe Henderson arrived fresh from a round-the-world tour and brought all of us fashionable Thai silk ascots to wear. Peter Lavery, my HBS roommate, and his wife Jan came from Melbourne, Australia. It was an international crew that enchanted the Southerners, who, not to be outdone, turned on their charm and hospitality for a week of festivities.

It was a sunny, cold day—December 20, 1969. The wedding was a concert of musicians and singers orchestrated by Jerry Black, the Druid Hills Presbyterian Church's impresario Georgia often soloed for; the ceremony was almost a sideshow. Georgia looked amazing. The groomsmen and I were in morning suits. After the wedding, the reception was held at the Peachtree Golf Club, where David was a member. We drove in a limo and had a flat tire on Peachtree Road, pulling into an Arby's. The driver was Eastern European, could barely speak English, and had no experience changing a tire, so I had to do that in my tails. It was great for us to see all our family and friends at the reception. Georgia and I soon retired from there to the top of the new Regency Hyatt downtown that overlooked Atlanta sprawling and sparkling below, brightened with its Christmas lights. On our pillow was a note Holly had written from Attila, the feisty Siamese cat I had given Georgia for Christmas that year, wishing us marital bliss and safe travels. We were on top of the world.

The next day we boarded a Delta jet to the Caribbean where we met up with our schooner for Christmas. I wanted to do something different and exotic for our honeymoon, so proposed a barefoot Windjammer cruise to the Caribbean—a three-mast schooner sailing out of Martinique. Georgia never having been on ocean swells, didn't know she got seasick, moreover, the first two days we were in a gale. It was not an auspicious beginning for a honeymoon. Once the wind died down, it was beautiful sailing between the Grenadines to Grenada, the nutmeg island. Besides tropical islands and sandy beaches, I recall on one island, acting macho, I speared a bright orange fish one morning, much to Georgia's distress. I learned quickly; she was a guardian of all animal life. Living with her required respecting her love of all animals. We returned to the States rested and sunburned and ready to get on with our new life together.

We sold Georgia's blue Mustang known as "Magnolia" and courtesy of the US government, packed our wedding gifts for our new life together. We got a lot of china and silver, and for some reason, a plethora of Chinese bowls. Alma and Mom helped us sort what we'd need and what we would store with them. Driving my forest green 911 Porsche (with a white racing stripe!), we decided to take the southern route through San Antonio before heading to the Grand Canyon. We arrived at night in a lightly flaking snowstorm with our headlights eerily projecting out into the eternal darkness of the canyon's abyss as we drove the curving road to our lodge on the rim of the canyon that January of 1970. When we awoke the next morning, the sunrise pinked and reflected off the new snow that draped the mesas like freshly laundered tablecloths. After opening the curtain we just stayed in bed looking out the window in disbelief. So romantic! I hugged my new bride, and we set out for breakfast at the main lodge—a wooden-logged and stoned-hearth Western showcase itself.

We drove on to San Francisco over the next two days, crossing the desert and stopping briefly in Reno at the impressive Hoover Dam.

However, seeing the looming rusted towers of the Golden Gate was the finish flag and the start of our new life there. When I checked in with my orders at the impressive Commander of the Western Sea Frontier's offices on Treasure Island, we were assigned temporary officers' housing on Yerba Buena Island. This was a one-bedroom bungalow without a view or insulation but on the lovely neighboring island. We were eligible for permanent housing on the island, which was also a bird sanctuary and in the middle of SFO Bay, but it would be several months before we could get in. It was suggested we might want to find some other temporary housing until then.

The next day, while Georgia met with the faculty at the San Francisco Conservatory to follow up on her application, I sought out the USS Neptune. Normally tied up at the base in Alameda with the carriers and the rest of the fleet, I discovered the ship was tied up in a dry dock at the South San Francisco Navy Yards for repairs.

Not the safest part of town, but in the bustling shipyard, I saw what I thought was the beached grey steel whale, looking something like an arc tended by hovering cranes and illuminated by welders' sparks patching the hull. I climbed the steel ladders to the quarter deck and reported aboard. Lt. Casey, who I was replacing, greeted me took me to his office and hurriedly counted the cash in the safe after giving me the combination. He'd assembled the department members who were on board and introduced me, then took me up to meet the Captain and other officers. The Lieutenant was eager to get away once all the formalities were taken care of. He was leaving the Navy and couldn't wait to spring for freedom.

Capt. Miguel was eager to meet with me after Casey left. "Lt. McEver, I've been looking forward to you arriving. Casey left us with the lowest rating in the Pacific fleet. You've got nowhere else to go but up. You ever driven a ship?"

"No, sir," I said hesitantly, as supply corps officers didn't have to stand watch.

"Well, I know you don't have to, but we're headed across the Pacific when we get out of here, and at twelve knots that'll get really boring. I'll teach you some seamanship. You'll find it exciting. Welcome aboard." He saluted and dismissed me.

While Georgia had been at the San Francisco Conservatory to follow up on her application, they held an impromptu audition, and informed her she'd be one of only seven Voice majors admitted at the school for 1970.

We went down to the Buena Vista Café, famous for its Irish Coffees, to catch our breath, celebrate our arrival, and Georgia's good fortune. On the way, we walked by a new and spectacular dual apartment development—The Fontana—curved high-rises cupping around the small bay just up from Fisherman's Wharf and down from Ghirardelli Square with a front-and-center view of Alcatraz. I saw they were selling condos and boldly walked into the sales office to introduce myself. It turned out the marketing manager was an HBS grad like me. He admitted sales were slow, so we worked out a deal. Georgia and I rented one of the nicely furnished model apartments that looked right out over the bay with that spectacular view of Alcatraz. This was a honeymoon in the dreamy city while the ship stayed in port. She and I also discovered the Sea Witch Bar in the square next door, run by Joe Fix, an entrepreneur who had several bars around the city with singing waitresses. Soon Georgia and some of her other Voice major classmates were employed. Others were street musicians we saw around the city singing with the impromptu bands that sprang up weekends in good weather.

While celebration was in order, back on the ship, I was still shocked from the condition of the Supply Department I'd taken over, as well as the news that we'd soon be putting to sea on a long voyage, going God knows where, and to boot, the Captain expected me to stand watch. Welcome to the real Navy! I was blessed however, with good men who were bored. Lt. Casey had never organized them. Before we left, I went through every assignment, reviewed every man's task with each chief or first class, so they understood, and let each man run his department then report to me. These were good men, and if I paid attention to them, let them be responsible for their jobs—once those were clear—they'd excel. They were all well-trained and needed something to fill the days while they were imprisoned onboard. We began to develop pride in our department and work. I really saw the morale rise when we went to sea because shipboard life running smoothly depended on us. At sea, I tried to be fair and available. We were all in the same boat together. Boy were we.

Chapter 19
Blue Water Experience

The bow of the USS Neptune (ARC-2) headed out into the Pacific Ocean with Captain Miguel skillfully bisecting the counter-veiling tidal currents ripping in from the Bay's mouth under the bridge's orange arc. On one side were the concrete bunker ruins of the Presidio's old batteries, on the other, the green slopes of Mt. Tamalpais. A white cleansing surf beat both shores, painting an idyllic landscape. I wouldn't see this headland nor my dear wife again for at least three months, likely more as we headed out to cross the vastness on the horizon.

The USS Neptune was a cable-laying ship that carried no cable. Built in Norfolk in the fifties, the 350-foot long, drawing-twelve-feet-of-draft ship weighed over 8,000 tons. It had a nub nose for laying cable and a helicopter-landing platform. Entirely nondescript, it was perfect for espionage. The Neptune carried a crew of 250 men and thirteen scientists; the latter crew had a cesium beam clock that, at the time, (before navigation satellites) was the most accurate navigational system in the world. We were looking for submerged mountain tops in the Pacific— those that could host an array of listening devices keen to the sound of ship and submarine props. The system tracked the whereabouts of the Russian Navy. Our mission was to follow Soviet submarines carrying ballistic nuclear missiles. We knew their signatures and ours—really any ship's in the world if we wanted to. Pretty impressive for this old tub that'd be my home across a vast expanse of ocean for the next quarter. Other than visits from a mail- and movie-dropping helicopter, we operated independently. We ordered whatever we needed cryptographically, and the supplies were either delivered when we got into port or via a chopper.

The problem was that the max speed of this ship was twelve knots, and we cruised about eight comfortably. Our initial objective was Japan, but we made intermittent stops to find those mountain tops and then arced around to Adak, Alaska with a pass by the main Soviet submarine base of Vladivostok before we came home. During my duty tour, we made three such voyages, as well as a brief trip to San Diego for "nuclear refresher training" with the rest of the Pacific fleet units. There were six officers, including me—the supply officer.

Capt. Ted Miguel was by far the most interesting officer on the Neptune. He'd invited Georgia and me and the other officers and wives to his home on Yerba Buena right before we put out to sea. He was flat-topped, tanned, lean, and a man of few words, though polite. He said to Georgia, "We're going to take Bruce across the Pacific—and I want to teach him to drive a ship." Though not required to stand watch, I wanted to because of Ted and the chance to really learn how to pilot such a big vessel. I learned it was damn boring out at sea but also dangerous. Ted was a "mustang," having earned his way up from the enlisted ranks. He was also a former UDT (Underwater Demolition Team member)—one tough man.

The XO (executive officer) was a happy-go-lucky leather-jacketed lieutenant commander, whose first act was to take me out to a San Francisco bar to play darts, his favorite sport next to driving his convertible with his sheepdog as copilot. Thank goodness for Capt. Miguel. We were constantly undoing the XO's hairbrained PODs (Plans of the Day) that regulated shipboard life. The Operations Officer was Don Bisbee, from Phoenix, Arizona. Don had a reasonable intellect and was very knowledgeable about electronics. Lt. Bisbee was my roommate. My best friend on board was Rob Drake who was the Deck Officer. Lt. Drake oversaw the "swabbies"—the ordinary sailors who kept the ship clean, safe, and running. He could discuss philosophy, was a good athlete, and had good common sense. He had his men—most of the men on the ship were ordinary seamen—paint one end of the ship to the other, timed to be finished by the time we'd crossed the Pacific and back. Such was the eternal naval clock, painting the ship to pass time.

My division was forty men. I had Filipino stewards headed by a senior chief about to retire. They took care of the officers, a tradition that dates to the Spanish-American War when Filipinos became a ship's stewards. I also had all the cooks, the most capable being the first-class head cook. He checked in with me occasionally but was totally squared away, even saving the eggshells to put in the powdered eggs once fresh supplies began to run out. My men and the crew were well fed, and the cook was a crowd pleaser, sometimes cooking the sea's bounty caught off the fantail, particularly off Alaska.

I was also the paymaster and had a pay clerk, Caple, who was not that capable. When I first came on board in SFO, the following day was payday. Sailors are always paid in cash, so Caple and I went to the bank near the shipyards in South San Francisco—not the best neighborhood. He strapped on a .45 while I took the leather cash bag handcuffed to my wrist. I gave the teller the check to cash. I noticed Caple had his hand on his gun, and it was shaking. He had a palsy. After that we switched roles. He carried the money, and I carried the gun. Paydays were always interesting because I saw the whole ship and watched the loan sharks prey on the down-on-their luck guys to get their cash advances back.

The scientists were the navigators to get us to the right spots on the ocean floor, and the sonar men dropped the listening devices to see how well and how far they could hear underwater since the sound was magnified by the cold water deep. Our first goal was Japan, though it was delayed twice. We had a sailor who tested positive for tuberculosis before we left and were ordered into Pearl Harbor to let him off after we'd quarantined him. Pulling into Pearl Harbor is a memorable event. We were there long enough for me to appreciate wanting to come back. We soon had another case of TB—his friend. We discovered the second case after leaving Pearl Harbor, so we were forced to pull into Guam. That proved a more interesting stop than I'd figured. I had anticipated a few boring days at the officer's club, maybe meeting some of the pilots flying the B-52s out of there over Vietnam. Instead, I had another surprising adventure.

When we pulled into the harbor, there was a sailor on the docks waving at me. The ship's manifest was pre-posted, and a former GMA classmate of mine who happened to be stationed there saw my name. Stuck on an island in the middle of the Pacific, he also ran the dive shop. After we docked, he reintroduced himself and asked me out to his beach house. Once there, we equipped ourselves and waded out through a coral-carved path onto the reef before plunging into the azure waters of the atoll. The expanse of that reef was beautiful. He shot an octopus we tenderized in his washing machine and cooked up on the beach along with some other fish. I spent that week diving and starting to understand how our magnificent coral reefs were beginning to die and now, more environmentally sensitive, I'm sorry about the octopus.

Sailing on, we made some submerged mountain-top stops with Capt. Miguel expertly maneuvering with the advanced navigation system for precision. We had to get to the right spot in the middle of nowhere and take readings of the potential sites. I was the official tracking officer. Here's an excerpt from a letter I sent Georgia describing this region I later found:

This is indeed a strange area of the earth. We are at 11 degrees N latitude, about 600 miles north of the Philippines in what is known as the Tropical Conversion Zone. Here the sea is calm and glassy. Around are magnificent cloud formations—pink, yellow, black, and white, stretching miles into the heavens. It looks loke several atomic bombs have gone off all at once and all that is left are those beautiful mushroom clouds. Beneath, the billows are rain storms that periodically flood the ship. You can watch them coming at you over the glassy still deep azure blue sea. Occasionally a shark will swim by.

We made our way to Japan and pulled into Yokosuka Harbor. A month and a half away from home, I called Georgia who reported she'd become a singing waitress three evenings a week at the Sea Witch Bar in Ghirardelli Square. She assured me tips were good and so were the girls she sang with. She missed me a lot, as I did her. I was concerned but glad she was gainfully employed.

Next, we sailed to Nagasaki to take on cable. I took the week off and went via first-class train to Nara and Kyoto. At that time of year, there were marriages all along the route. I could tell the arranged ones—the couples who sat rigidly next to one another in their seats to Kyoto, politely chatting, versus the couples in love who were all over one another as soon as the train pulled out of the station, their parents waving in the distance.

I'd read Reischauer, Fairbank, and Craig's *A History of East Asian Civilization* on the voyage over, and the book which described the rich Kamakura period in Japan, the time of the first shogun and the samurai, came back to life for me at Nara—a step back into history. I toured the city and strolled its silent ancient temples and fortresses, loving wandering the antique stores that hadn't yet become overpriced. I bought many wood-block prints and some small porcelain vases. I fell in love with Japanese art, with its simple, elegant aesthetics. From there it was on to Kyoto and its many temples. I read Yukio Mishima's *The Temple of the Golden Pavilion* and had to visit this golden perfection reflecting on its placid pond. I stayed in a grand Victorian hotel with porch rockers, cold beer and sake served while I rocked. I was

debating a journal and almost sprung for one but wrote long letters to
Georgia instead, letters that describe these wonders and long for a day
we would be sharing them together. By then I was missing her badly.

These are excerpts from a letter on Nara Hotel stationary, dated May
25, 1970:

> This delightful old town's full of temples and shrines. It
> is unusual that in Japan, the historical places are preserved,
> [but] most of the temples are actually new—everything was
> constructed of wood and fire has taken its toll...
>
> For all its beauty, I feel that Japan would be much
> better with you. I am so lonely that much seems empty...
> My travels to date remind me of much of my latter days in
> Europe—part of me is missing...
>
> Tonight, I played elegant, put on a suit, and went to
> the hotel dining room for dinner. It was sparsely populated
> with Germans, French and English who all seemed well off.
> After a sumptuous meal and a cup of tea, I retired to watch
> a samurai series on TV.

Before leaving for Alaska, we took advantage of the Navy exchange
system and stocked up on every conceivable electronic device. I got a
miniature TV that looked like a space helmet, a tape recorder, stereo,
record player—the works, including headphones. I got all the women in
the family pearls and Georgia a particularly beautiful peacock brooch. We
loaded all our treasures into a storeroom, and Capt. Miguel put a lock on
it. This was our overseas bounty we'd have to navigate through customs.

Back at the ship in Nagasaki, I walked through the shipyard where a
group of businessmen were stationed at tables, proudly displaying their
calligraphy. Their artistry was appealing, even though I didn't understand
the words. Again, the Japanese aesthetic—businessmen on a Friday
afternoon displaying their artwork, even poetry brushed-stroked into a
piece of art. It was a good send-off.

We went into the real ocean. The Pacific had lived up to its name,
been relatively calm up to that point—a vast water with regular swells
and endless constellations whirling around the pole star at night. Except
for a few thunderstorms, nothing dramatic. There was the constant up
and down of the vessel plying its way east. But now we were headed

outside of Vladivostok, careful not to stray too close to the Russian, Chinese, or North Korea borders, but close to the submerged peaks conveniently located so as to get the far-ranging sounds of a busy harbor. The skies darkened, the temperature dropped, and the swells increased in size. We made a couple of precise stops and got the readings we were looking for, making this a successful voyage. Another ship would come to put in the instruments, but from then on, we'd be able to tell when the "boomers" were leaving their ports. We headed home!

Our return to the States was Adak, Alaska, which sat on the horizon as a green pearl half cloud-shrouded in a blue-grey sea. Adak had been a remote outpost in WWII and was not the post you wanted for your two-year assignment since it was known as being awarded to the lowest members of the Supply School Corps. As we approached, I could see the duty customs officer standing at the end of one of the long piers that jutted out into the bay. Capt. Miguel saw him as well and nodded to me, "Take care of him, Porkchop." And thus, I was assigned to get the ship with its vast hoard of loot past the only customs inspector between us and the mainland.

I saluted him and welcomed him aboard when the gangplank went down. Sure enough, he was a fellow supply corps officer. He'd been a couple of classes ahead of me in Athens.

"I need to inspect the ship, Lieutenant."

"Sure. Want to come to the officers' mess and have some coffee first? Where're you from?" It turned out he was from Ohio and was badly missing his wife who chose not to accompany him to Adak. "Like to look around?" I asked the obvious.

"Sure," he replied. I tried to divert him. "First try one of these cinnamon buns. My cook is a pro." Before we got to the storerooms, I told him I was awfully thirsty having been at sea, asked if I could buy him a drink.

"Well, the only rush on this island is getting off it. Why not?" he said.

He didn't care what was on this ship really but wanted someone to talk to. I bought him a double martini at the officers' club. We talked about his adventures with the University of Georgia girls in Athens that beat the hell out of his experiences at Ohio. We had another, and I told him about the cache of great movies I'd have brought over to the club for us to watch. They were starved for good films in Adak. He was soon joined by his fellow officers and never checked the storeroom as it became movie night. I later got him to sign the customs form—a mere formality after several doubles—and took it back to the Captain.

We set sail on a beautiful morning. We'd taken on a group of new recruits fresh out of the Great Lakes (the Navy boot camp). They were shown around by our bosun (the officer in charge of equipment and the crew). He was a cocky body builder and was giving them a shakedown tour of the boat as we headed south to home. We were now over three months out and dying to see our spouses and loved ones. The Captain gave me the deck.

"Mr. McEver you have the con. I'm going below for a nap. Wake me if there're any problems."

"Aye, aye, Sir. Have a good sleep, I have the con," I announced, as was bridge protocol.

I had binoculars around my neck and could see the eagles working over their prey and the neighboring island of Amchitka where we tested nuclear devices underground. I could see the whole ship from the bridge and watched the party of recruits wind to the fantail where the bold and boasting bosun was about to sit on the fantail chain, where he shouldn't because it was used to dump the garbage and chum for sharks. My last thought before I turned back to the vast blue sea and the magical stretch of the snow-capped Aleutian chain was that the damn bosun shouldn't do that. But what a fine day to head home, I was thinking when I heard the shouts from the fantail, "Man overboard!"

I ran to the end of the bridge and saw the bosun flailing in the wake. He had less than fifteen minutes to live in water this cold.

"Hard starboard. Get the Captain," I ordered. This was no time for a novice to be a hero.

Only Ted Miguel could turn this 300-plus-foot vessel around and put its nose next to that bosun.

Ted was there in a minute. I pointed.

"That damn fool," he growled. By then we were coming around. Ted backed the engines down and put the nose right on the bosun, who, with his last bit of strength, climbed in the life buoy thrown down to pull him out. That was enough excitement. The bosun survived. He could have been court marshalled, but the Captain figured he'd seen his maker and learned a lesson. We made it home five days later.

The Golden Gate was the sweetest sight I'd ever seen—that magical rusted orange arc framing the city by the bay, that gleaming white in the afternoon sun. The currents were strong, and we took on a pilot to take the ship directly into Alameda, all the way under the Bay Bridge and past Alcatraz, Treasure Island, and eucalyptus-crested Yerba Buena. There was the Navy base with its grey line-up of destroyers—a cruiser, two aircraft carriers, and all sorts of tenders and big container ships.

On the pier, a woman with long blonde hair in a flowered dress waved joyously with the rest of the crowd. I never had a hard time picking Georgia out of a crowd. For me, she was the most beautiful thing in it. I couldn't wait to get down the gangplank, kiss her, and take her home. I couldn't wait to hold my wife, but there was also a tractor trailer truck waiting. At first, I thought they were advance supplies that either we or our engineers had ordered. We'd put them up when we came back after a couple of days of home leave. We weren't so lucky. My chief clerk came up to the bridge and said, "Mr. McEver that truck is for us, and you need to sign for it before you leave."

The joyous family reunion for 250 men had spread like wildfire all over the ship and around me on the bridge. The men were showing their wives or girlfriends the odd hulk of grey metal a little worn after a pan-Pacific voyage. The carnival atmosphere continued. My first class had put out cookies and coffee, but we couldn't wait to get home. What the hell was in that truck? Capt. Miguel was with his wife and was leaving the ship with her. He looked back at me and said, "You're taking care of this, McEver?"

"Yes, Sir! Don't worry about it, Captain." I saluted and walked down with my chief clerk to talk to the driver who wasn't going to leave the pier until he had my signature.

"What've you got there, sailor?" I asked, walking up to the purring truck. The welcoming crowd milled around it, all unconcerned and headed home for a drink or probably something more passionate—my primary thought at the moment. A huge man stepped down from the cab with his clipboard and pen. His bicep had a rose and anchor across that glared one word: *Mother.*

"We've got your cups, Lieutenant. One-hundred cases of them. You're a priority ship, so we scoured the Pacific fleet's supply basement to put them together for you. You guys must drink a lot of Coke?" He stuck his clipboard under my nose.

"What?" I looked at the order. I realized one of my store clerks—and I thought I knew who—had ordered cases rather than boxes of cups we used for our one-of-a kind and temperamental Coke machine on the mess desk, the ship's main social meeting point. "There must be some mistake."

"That's not my problem, Lieutenant. You can take it up with the commander on Monday.

I need you to unload my truck because I can't take them back."

We'd run out of cups halfway back home. It caused a social disturbance, so the Captain had growled at me, and in turn, I growled at my clerk. What goes around comes around.

It was Friday afternoon. I turned to my clerk, "Johnsen, organize the men, and let's get those below."

I ran into the crowd, kissed my beautiful wife and said, "Hold that thought. I'll be right back." She looked at me questioningly.

There was plenty of space from the long voyage since the men had emptied the "treasury" from Japan and Hawaii and were carrying it down the pier—it looked like we'd looted an electronics store. I was on the phone to get the cases returned before the Captain discovered them, but it would take a while, so I dropped by his house on the way home.

"Captain, we have a problem." Captain Ted thought he'd never heard anything as funny and asked me to let him know when they were gone as I was leaving. I discovered that the order had been wrongly entered—even worse, the order form had been filled out correctly, and no one involved in fulfilling the order had bothered to check the absurd and obvious error. These weren't robots filling the order, but clerks up and down the West Coast and all over the US searching their warehouses for cups to fill a priority order from a priority ship. Our needs were top secret. An order was an order!

For this brilliant performance when our storerooms emptied, the Captain told me I was promoted to lieutenant from lieutenant junior grade. Ted held a brief ceremony in the wardroom and gave me new bars. We were to make two other cruises and changed skippers. On our last trip to Adak, I had some time off coming and got lucky, taking a military air transport back to San Francisco ahead of the ship. Georgia and I got a chance to explore the town and linger at our favorite restaurants, starting with the Buena Vista by Ghirardelli Square.

I was waiting in the crowd on the pier at the Alameda Navy station when the Neptune came back under the Golden Gate. We could see it come under the bridge, and I cheered along with the welcome committee of wives, friends, and family. There were two huge aircraft carriers there, as well as a cruiser and assorted destroyers, but it was Neptune's day, and the band played, and the flags flew. But the top mast was bent, and the ship looked like it had been run over. What happened? I ran up the gangplank, saluting the bosun, "Permission to come aboard?" I ran to the bridge where the captain was shaking the pilot's hand and thanking him for safe passage. "What happened, Sir?" I asked.

My fellow officers gathered around and told the story. South of the Aleutians, they were overtaken by a giant wake, possibly a tsunami. It was large enough to engulf the ship from the rear. The stern watch had just enough time to dive down the aft steering hatch, a spout of water behind him, and the officers watching the evening movie in the wardroom had witnessed a gush of water push out the air conditioner. Water engulfed the ship, but the boat righted itself, and the timing was lucky since no one was out on deck or had been washed overboard. I was indeed fortunate to have missed this event but was amazed no one was lost and by the seaworthiness of our "old tub" tested to its limits.

Georgia and I had a great life in this city. We eventually got into officers' housing on Yerba Buena. The officers' club at the top had been a sea-plane control tower, and drinks were a quarter. We'd also go to Fisherman's Wharf, pick up some crab to bring home and eat on newspaper spread in the backyard and watch the container or naval ships pull into Alameda or go south to the shipyards. This duplex with a bay view cost me my housing allowance, all of $125 per month. This poem written many years later reflects this time:

The Stress Reduction Center

I climb the creaky stairs
of a white frame walk-up on Clement.
The hostess, in a side-split gown,
oversees a desk with a plastic waterfall.
She ushers me, after cash payment,
into a room with a sheet-draped table
and face cradle and tells me to disrobe.

Jasmine enters and in halting English
introduces herself. With talented toes,
she walks down my spine,

holding onto a jungle gym
bolted to the ceiling. She tramps
out vintage sorrow, while "the words of the prophets
are written on the subway walls"
plays in the background.

Thirty years ago, that same song blared,
driving my bride across the Bay Bridge
to our first home, a Navy duplex
on Yerba Buena Island.
There, under fragrant eucalyptus,
in our backyard we ate local crab
off newspapers watching
the container ships maneuver to port.

Like the China Hauler I watched
last evening, bisect the orange spans
of the Golden Gate and fade
into the Pacific fog bank,
so, I watched my wife fade
into unconsciousness.

Before we left on our first trans- Pacific crossing, a Bschool classmate
introduced me to a broker with White Weld —Claxton Long—who knew
everyone of consequence in San Francisco and introduced me to Charlie
Crocker. A venture capitalist, Charlie invested his family's funds from an
office he maintained at the Crocker Bank, where he also worked with its
CFO John Boyle, an HBS graduate. Charlie and I seemed to hit it off, and
he introduced me to John, who let me work part-time on some venture
capital deals, doing the needed background research and birddogging.
John and I became close, and his wife Mary and Georgia became friends.

Charlie was an early-stage venture capitalist, investing in scientists
and inventors with patents. This was really rolling the dice, but the Bay
Area was full of these folks. I'd leave my ship after duty hours when
it was in port and go downtown to work on venture capital deals with
Charlie Crocker and John.

Charlie was the grandson of Charles Crocker, one of the Big Four
who founded and funded the Central Pacific Railroad: Leland Stanford,

Mark Hopkins and Collis Potter Huntington. In their lifetime, these four men were referred to as nabobs or "nobs," referring to their wealth and influence. All four built mansions in the same neighborhood on the same hill, known as Nob Hill today. Charles Crocker (1822-1888) was construction supervisor and later founder of the more extensive Southern Pacific Railroad built in 1883. After the 1906 San Francisco earthquake destroyed all their mansions on Nob Hill, Crocker donated his land to the Episcopal Church, and it is now the site of the Memorial Cathedral.

Charlie had also inherited a round house, complete with some old iron horses from one of his grandfather's railroads in the Sierra Mountains outside of San Francisco. He rented them out to movie companies and tourist groups, but he also held movable cocktail parties for his friends in train cars. Georgia and I attended one of these with John and Mary. I remember vividly, both ladies looked beautiful that afternoon in similar yellow dresses and big floppy hats they had to clamp down when the train got going. Later, having cocktails at John and Mary's, Mary came up to me and wondered why I looked so sad in the middle of all the frivolity. I had no explanation, but maybe I had foreseen our future.

Later when I began working in NYC, John and I worked together to finance a device called the Speedine Oven, which, before the invention of the microwave oven, was a similar device. It could cook a TV dinner in less than a minute and was patented by a British inventor with numerous patents to his credit and who Charlie backed from time to time. We were all sure this one would revolutionize the way America cooked. With the Speedine oven, American housewives would put their dishes into little tin trays and prepare them in less than a minute after being popped into the Speedine oven. It seemed most plausible. The big showdown was at the McGraw Edison plant somewhere in Missouri, where Speedine lost out to what now we know as the Crockpot.

In early spring 1972, my orders finally came through to report to the Systems Analysis Group in the Pentagon. I was happy to get them before another deployment but would miss my men, my fellow officers, and working with Charlie. I'd really miss the idyllic and romantic life Georgia and I had in San Francisco for the first two years of our marriage. Georgia was going to stay to finish her sophomore year at the Conservatory, but she applied to the Peabody Conservatory in Baltimore with endorsement from her teachers at SCM and was accepted. Late April, I headed back East. As it turned out, I was just in time for the Kentucky Derby, and as

I approached Louisville, I called my friend and classmate Vann Pell, who informed me he had an extra ticket and was in the process of preparing a mint julep for my arrival.

Twins Harold and William McEver with Parents and Relatives,
Family Home, Gainesville, GA

Chapter 20
The Pentagon: War from the Inside Out

After a long drive, I arrived in DC in May of 1972. I was too late for the cherry blossoms that had mostly turned green. There was already a hint of the upcoming muggy summer. I hadn't seen the capitol dome or the Washington monument since my childhood visits, but I was there to work—the serious work of war-watching and making. Daunting because of its size, a layer-cake four stories up, and who knew how many down to protect it from atomic attack, the Pentagon was to be the new center of my life. I noticed right away how the concentric five-sided rings radiated out like a pentagon-shaped pond splash that started from the central hamburger stand, affectionately called "ground zero," where I would later lunch with colleagues.

My first day was filled with basic tasks: where to park; how to get to my Navy detailer's office; find where I needed to check in and where I'd be working for the next two years. It wasn't called The Puzzle Palace for nothing. First, I found my detailer—the man who held my fate in his hands. It was good to finally meet him in person. An Academy graduate, he welcomed me aboard, but lamented that I was joining what he called "that group"—a collection of irreverent non-career MBAs and PhDs that Secretary McNamara had set aside to keep the services on their toes. I knew it only as the Office of System Analysis (OSA). My detailer preferred that I work on a Navy career path, doing such jobs as procuring ships or honing my skills for eventual command at sea. OSA reviewed the Navy's procurement programs, I was informed, so the Navy was glad I was there to take up their side. The services fought among themselves over every million-dollar budget decision, but we were specifically chosen to be non-partisan because OSA was staffed with non-career officers. When my time was up, I was getting out of the military. He encouraged me otherwise and kept doing so.

After our discussion, I was escorted to OSA's Asia Division on one of the inner rings of the Pentagon, and more importantly, as we were at war, on the same level as and close to the office of the Secretary of Defense. Deeper into the office rings, everything began to look the same: the same pea green walls and doors, only distinguished by a different number on each door, and, as I would later learn, according to their relative distance from the Sec. Def.'s office.

The head of my group was Paul Brands—a civilian, who was large, oval-faced, and smart as a whip. He was welcoming enough and introduced me to my co-workers, then to Joan, an overworked, centrally shared receptionist and my assistant as well. Paul was all business and got right down to it. My pea green, windowless office contained a grey metal desk. My three-drawer, combination-locked file cabinet was my storage safe. The first thing Paul did was throw the old Pueblo incident file on my desk. For a warm-up, he suggested I go through it to see examples of the types of memos I'd be writing to the Sec. Def. (Melvin Laird), the NSC (National Security Council), headed by Mr. Kissinger, and the White House staff. He asked I review the file and take a cut at a memo to the SECDEF on the situation. We'd go over it together at ten the next day. Joan showed me the central files and put me on the document circulation list. This was in the days before laptops, but in OSA we were starting to use a precursor to the internet called ARPANET that DARPA had developed. I learned everything in the Pentagon was in acronyms, and mostly "Top Secret."

I soon discovered to my delight that I had an HBS classmate—Dick Radez—in my division. Dick was a West Point graduate and a recent Vietnam veteran, who'd joined the Asia division a year earlier and knew the ropes. We were soon lunching, playing squash, and running through the parks together. That first day, a hospitable Navy commander in his dress whites invited me to dinner with his family. I was informed that we usually wore civilian clothes to work, but occasionally went to service functions in our uniforms. So Bob Higgin took me under his wing. Since Georgia wasn't with me yet, he invited me to dinners.

Bob explained we had all the intelligence on the war we wanted. Any military situation, system or armament, just say the word, and we got the background. Each day we compressed a ton of information into a succinct report and sent it via our official OSA editor to the Sec. Def. The war situation was more dire than I imagined. We had vast amounts of intelligence that needed to be sorted through and made sense of for whatever project the Sec. Def. was attacking or defending that day. Important articles, new intelligence, body counts, and specs on new weapons all circulated through in- and out-boxes. Most of it was dire reading, but there was occasional levity, such as the weekly piece of intelligence circulated on the meetings between the King of Cambodia and his pimps reporting on the royal concubines. We got the full report of who was in favor with the king, got pregnant, or was to be banished from court. It was a comic relief gossip column that came along with all the grim statistics, the continual casualty reports, etc. that were to be ground into neat intelligence morsels for executive consumption.

Paul Brands was deceptively polite, but brilliant. I'll never forget submitting my first memo backgrounding the Pueblo situation as Paul requested. Full of intelligence reports and cryptographic equipment, the Pueblo looked a lot like the Neptune (that made me shudder) but had wandered too close to the North Korean shore in 1968. That's what the North Koreans really wanted—not the ship or men but the crypto machinery and codebooks. Unthinkably, the captain and his crew didn't destroy the files or the equipment before they were captured. They also didn't defend themselves well. When the North Koreans got the files and the crypto machine, our entire Pacific fleet's intelligence codes were compromised and probably shared with the Russians or, more likely, the Chinese. The captain and his crew were mercilessly tortured by the North Koreans. The men were not court-marshalled because of what they'd endured. It was a grim reminder of the wrath of an absolute dictator in a totalitarian society.

I tried to describe the background and situation as briefly as I could, but it still took me two pages. I was the crypto officer on the Neptune, knew the situation and was proud to prove it; however, it was my job to include nothing personal, just the hard, cold facts. One page over the one-page limit, Paul ripped it apart. With no mercy he created the most succinct one-page memo I've ever seen. Paul's memo had all the facts, then four neat options at the bottom of the page, including a nuclear option that I later learned had been seriously debated. Ours was not to reason why. All options were on the table. This was war. Paul was a good writer, and he quickly taught me his standards and method. The goal was to compress large amounts of data into a one-page message that could go to the Sec. Def. or the President as an action memo, something they could execute. Anything else would fall well short. My decimated memo on the Pueblo was a warm-up, another chapter in the education of a poet, Pentagon-style.

A mild-mannered man with gold-rimmed glasses and a solid blue suit, Gardner Tucker succeeded Alain Enthoven to run Systems Analysis. The day I met him I'd been in OSA less than two weeks. Gardner Tucker led a study about the strategic nuclear weapon gap that our immediate boss Phil Odeen would chair. Phil was a great guy, very inspiring, down to earth, and it was Phil who gave me the background on our Systems Analysis group as we drove to a luncheon at the State Department in his Volkswagen Rabbit. This all started in 1961 when Kennedy was elected president and made a campaign promise to do something about the RAND-inspired predictions of a looming missile gap between the USA and USSR. To handle this challenge, Kennedy appointed the forty-four-year-old wunderkind, Robert McNamara as his Secretary of Defense. McNamara had begun as a professor at HBS but was soon recruited by the Statistical Control Office (SCO) at the Army Air Corps to apply Operations Research-type analysis to our bombing raids first in Germany, then Japan. He succeeded brilliantly and made a name for himself resulting in Henry Ford's hiring him to reform Ford Motor Company. (Where Georgia's father worked for him in the treasurer's office.)

As the new SECDEF, McNamara, asked RAND economist Charles Hitch to be the Pentagon's comptroller, and together they created the Office of Systems Analysis (OSA). Another RAND economist, Alain Enthoven, was selected to direct OSA. The Pentagon Systems Analysis group also became known as the "whiz kids." Phil explained our purpose was to try to rationalize DoD by forcing the services to justify their procurement requests in terms of roles and missions that is the exact strategic and tactical purpose each military element would be expected to fulfil under US foreign policy. OSA emphasized the importance of managerial techniques especially cost-benefit analysis based on "data" rather than judgments of experiences. He said McNamara only wanted facts and told a story that, once when informed that the Vietnam War was doomed to failure, McNamara reportedly shot back: "Where is your data? Give me something I can put in the computer. Don't give me your poetry.'"

I wasn't writing poetry then; I was churning out factual, concise memos that could have a tremendous impact if implemented. It gave me pause, and I became reverent of the power of the word. I also knew there was a region of heart and soul that lies beyond the numbers. Possibly that's what was beating us in the jungles of Southeast Asia and probably the reason for our massive miscalculation. The whiz kids frequently defended their attitude by characterizing quantitative assessments as merely background for value judgments. We insisted in quantifying everything that might serve as an input to the analysis. This is similar to what I learned at Georgia Tech. However, even McNamara admitted as he was leaving the Pentagon: "No significant military problem will ever be wholly susceptible to purely quantitative analysis."

We were assigned projects and one of mine became the Thai insurgency, a group of about 25,000 opium bandits in Thailand's northern highlands, near the border with Burma and Laos, that the Thai military couldn't seem to squash. I worked with Dick Radez, who'd been on the ground in Vietnam. Dick was a savvy insurgency fighter and analyst; his common-sense advice added reality to my analytics. Another of my projects was tracking and reporting on the South Koreans (ROKs) in South Vietnam. They were fierce warriors doing a magnificent job. The Vietcong (VC) steered clear of them because of a chilling reason: when the South Koreans in Vietnam captured VC soldiers, they skinned their bodies and then displayed them around their perimeter. War precipitated extreme conditions and such brutality was not unprecedented as Genghis Kahn had practiced the same horrific war psychology sweeping across China and into Europe.

Another of my major projects was developing a strategy for the ROK force after we "won" the war in Vietnam. They were much too powerful to send home, but they could go north, so we had to disarm half of them and, in return, pay off the South Korean government with a squadron of our F-5 fighters.

This was the plan and another project I was to work on during my entire career at the Pentagon. Developed by Northrup, it was a lightweight, all-purpose, relatively inexpensive and easily maintainable fighter, thus ideal for fledgling air forces. Most of our allies were buying them from us. Brazil had some, as did the Saudis, Koreans, and the Thai (for their insurgency). I became very familiar with this aircraft. Northrup invited me out to an airshow at Dulles airport one Saturday, suited me up in a flying suit and helmet, and took me for a test ride. Clearly, the pilot had been told to impress me. He took the plane vertically off the runway, cutting in his afterburner, then spinning out when he began to stall. I was impressed, and it was one exciting ride. The Koreans would get a couple of squadrons of these for disarming half their ground forces, an expensive trade off.

One of the more fascinating studies I worked on right after arriving in DC was an analysis of fighter aircraft technology and armament versus pilot aptitude and kill rates. OSA was a champ at grinding up facts and data to drive decision-making for selecting military hardware. RAND was doing a comprehensive study of fighter aircraft as part of their efforts to get a single fighter aircraft for all the services but were coming up with a sideways conclusion that the pilot and not the plane made the real difference in kill rates. In other words, a real ace shot down more planes than anyone else, regardless of the equipment. So, if you put an ace in any fighter aircraft irrespective of the armament or power, he'd succeed. The key was pilot-training and discovering the aces. The report was volumes thick, and I spent several weeks reading it and compressing it into my one-page conclusion. I'd learned my lesson. I also learned human beings in a machine and technical age still count. There are aces that shoot down more aircraft and "stock pickers" that still beat the indexes. I have my funds invested with the latter, remembering this study and what I've learned from my years "on the street."

Though there was a small group of us grinding away at processing these big projects, we also got to know our brethren in the other divisions quite well, especially consulting with them when projects overlapped. Systems Analysis was an extraordinary group of people, I became close with Garen Staglin and Larry Briscoe, both Stanford B school graduates, who remain friends today.

Some of my co-workers, lived nearby in apartments in Virginia, typically a large brick building with a swimming pool, but otherwise unappealing. I was drawn to the "new" area of DC being pioneered and redeveloped by local contractors on Capitol Hill, utilizing a stock of well-built and quaint townhomes that filled old DC and Baltimore. Townhouses had grown up along its patterned avenues and inner grid of numbered and lettered streets, especially in the center of Capitol Hill, behind the Library of Congress, Congress, the Supreme Court, and the magnificent Folger Library. There was the community's Eastern Market—an open farmer's market designed to center the neighborhood—and I discovered there was one of these in each quadrant of the district. Also, the highway system around the district was overtaxed, and traffic caused delays. Why not stay in town with good local transportation or walk or bike to work on nice days?

Paul Simoes a typical civil servant, worked his desk job by day, then afterwards and on weekends was one of these Nuevo-contractors, renovating a block of well-built townhouses on South Carolina Avenue behind a former Baptist Church. These were former Sunday School buildings, and he bought the whole block when the church went bust. This was happening all over the city but particularly on Capitol Hill where young workers, tired of commuting, were moving in. Even homes that needed much repair were quickly sold for a full price, a bargain for everyone including the original owners; the wealth was spread all the way around.

Paul had recently finished the green house in the middle of the row at 921 South Carolina Avenue needing the least work. He was promptly starting the one next door that needed gutting. I was intrigued. At 921, he'd left the red brick inside exposed and had added attractive exposed wooden beams. The houses had fourteen-foot ceilings, and each were three stories with a master bedroom and guestroom on the second floor and an office and extra guest bedroom at the top. There was an open floorplan, making the living room, dining room, and kitchen a large family area. High windows looked out on the wide street with elms and oaks and plenty of parking. I was tempted to use my GI bill mortgage. The Navy Federal Credit Union processed the mortgage promptly through its headquarters in the Pentagon. I negotiated with Paul to be sure the house was finished before he moved his attention next door. He was asking $37,500, and we shook hands at $35,000, a nice round figure for our first house. I put $1,000 down as earnest money and put in an application to borrow the rest. I'd bought us a new home. Feeling like a pioneer, I called Georgia to tell her.

"You did what?" she said, shocked. "I'm not even there yet. Shouldn't you wait to see if I like it?"

"You'll love it. And it was a deal! The contractor has a whole block he's developing and needed the money to move on. When are you coming to Washington?"

Georgia was finishing her sophomore year at the San Francisco Conservatory and then hoped to transfer to the Peabody Conservatory in Baltimore she had been accepted to, pending an interview. Serendipitously, her sister had married Wally Lanahan, who came from a prominent Baltimore family there, so Georgia could see her when commuting as well. Georgia would be visiting her family in Good Hope, Ga., before coming to join me.

I missed my wife. I couldn't wait to show her our new house. It was another week before Georgia would arrive, and having solved the housing situation, I urged Paul to clean up the yard and tidy his construction site. Capitol Hill was still up-and-coming, but not quite there with trash blowing about and an old tire on the front lawn; the sort of third-world tired look. I went to the airport excited to see Georgia. I drove her directly to our new estate.

"Is this neighborhood safe?" She noted right away the general rundown nature of the housing and the bars on most windows.

"This is the nation's capital; police are everywhere. You don't have to worry," I said.

I proudly pointed out our new house in the middle of the block. "Only $35,000!"

Georgia began to cry. "What is it?" I asked.

"I don't know if I could show Mom and Holly this." She sobbed, pointing to the unkept yard with the tire. With a hug and some cajoling, she soon got over it. Almost on cue, Paul came out to greet her and explain his plans for the block he never carried out, just as he hadn't cleaned up his damn construction site. We moved on, going by the Eastern Market, where a Saturday farmer's market was in full progress. We shopped for dinner and a good bottle of wine to get Georgia over her new home shock and celebrate our first meal in our new abode.

When Paul finished construction, an FBI agent and his wife moved in next door, and there began to be real demand for in-town housing. Soon the block was fully occupied. Across the street was an African American woman, Patricia Press, who was involved in the DC art scene. She brought a pecan pie to welcome us, and she took Georgia around the neighborhood, introducing her and us to our neighbors who were diverse and welcoming.

Still, we had to be alert. A few months later we were robbed at gunpoint on our doorstep by some local teenage residents. Not seeing the gun pointed at my stomach, Georgia hit the young man with her white knit purse, almost knocking him over, and surprised, the mugger fled with my wallet, that, along with my ID cards, was later "abandoned" in a nearby mailbox.

Georgia found a local dinner theater in Alexandria where she performed and sang weekends. It was owned by a musical entrepreneur, Lou Resigue, whose wife Barbara sang the leads. In fall of 1972, Georgia began to commute to Baltimore on the train, out of Union Station, just down Pennsylvania Ave. she could walk, bike or take the bus easily to.

Peabody was a great school, and Georgia loved her fellow students and musicians. It was quite a crowd of young artists, very different from my Pentagon set. Her fellow students loved Georgia as well and we sometimes hung out together, making for some interesting parties and conversations. Georgia and I fell into a routine of my working late and her commuting to Baltimore, but we had exciting weekends, exploring the environs of both cities to exhaustion.

Richard Nixon won the election, and the protest over the war stepped up a level. As the war went on, I became closer to my State Department counterparts—young foreign service officers who were also working on the Thai insurgency problem. Spiro Agnew had just visited Bangkok and given that government a fleet of helicopters. That wasn't in the plan, so we had to backfill and justify his expenditure with analysis, as was increasingly the systems analysis way.

One of the benefits of working in the Office of the Secretary of Defense was our periodic access to his boat, docked at the Washington Navy Yard, next to the presidential yacht. I found out we could use it on Saturdays when the Secretary and his senior staff didn't claim it. Being at the bottom of the totem pole, I didn't think I had a chance, but one beautiful Saturday we were having a bloody Mary party with our friends and had invited Lou and Barbara Resigue—the Longworth Dinner Theatre owners—along. Just in case, we took our coolers down to the dock with extra bloody Mary's, eggs, and bacon. We waited with the crew and became friendly. When no one showed up by ten, they invited us on board. We sailed down the Potomac to Mt. Vernon, turned around, getting back by mid-afternoon, a most memorable day.

Later that same afternoon I was working on a new basement apartment I was constructing for some extra income, when Georgia got a call. Barbara was sick and couldn't play the lead role of Marian, the librarian in *The Music Man* that evening. It was Georgia's big break. Lou now had an issue with his wife sharing future roles. Georgia was born for the stage and her star had risen.

I went back to getting us out of Vietnam. Watergate reared its ugly head. Rumors abounded. We re-learned the hard way the power of North Vietnam during the Easter Offensive in 1972, when they were able to send regular infantry and tank units under cloud cover against and through our South Vietnamese allies—like a hot knife through butter. For some reason, they were so surprised at their success that they stopped before reaching Saigon and rested instead at the old capital Hue. That was a big mistake; when the clouds cleared, our superior airpower rained hell on them and stopped their advance. This was a shock to everyone's system, causing a reassessment of our strategy. President Nixon was disgraced, and so was the US's reputation abroad.

The war protests stepped up. I'd seen it in Cambridge at Harvard Yard before I graduated in May 1969. I'd signed petitions with other HBS students protesting the war, but I saw the truth inside the Pentagon, where the news was grim indeed. There was a VC plan to dominate Southeast Asia, and North Vietnam was going to carry it out. They were a very effective guerrilla army fighting for their homeland who were much more disciplined than the South Vietnamese we supported. Despite our firepower and technology, we weren't going to win this conflict. All we could do was punish their population to try to get them to the bargaining table and conclude the most honorable peace we could negotiate.

Every day there was a new revelation about Watergate. We were in touch with the NSC staff, and they reported disarray at the White House. We were at an HBS alumni gathering at the Dumbarton Oaks mansion one beautiful spring afternoon in April of 1973 when the rumors ran through the crowd. We were on the back portico, smelling the fragrant boxwood that pervaded there. There were tapes! It was unbelievable. The new evidence had so much weight. Here was a man who'd been at the height of his powers. After his inauguration, our office had worked on getting some of the briefing memos together for his trip to China. What a brilliant move, and a tragedy we didn't pursue it further. Nixon had opened a country. Eventually we learned that not China, but the Russians were behind the North Vietnamese. The Chinese and the Russians were antagonists, and the Vietnamese had cleverly played them off each other. Significantly, two years after our exit, the domino theory, so derided by the US media would have been fully executed but was thwarted by China, who wasn't about to let the North Vietnamese dominate Southeast Asia. It cost China over 125,000 casualties, but they put the VC back in their boundaries the Chinese wanted and would maintain in SEA.

We saw my cousin Congressman Phil Landrum one last time before we left Capitol Hill for New York. He'd walked from his office and was having dinner alone at the Hawk and the Dove, a tavern on Pennsylvania Avenue we frequented. We asked him to join us. He lamented the tragedy, turmoil, and trouble Watergate was causing Congress in getting any legislation passed or in getting the country back on track. He asked what I'd been doing, and I told him about my education in foreign affairs and global politics, as well as the art of war—whether for good or bad—from my eagle's nest vantage point in OSA. I never again had so much intelligence cross my desk, nor had direct contact and influence over political decisionmakers at that level. In addition, I'd adjusted the military budget by billions as well. We all agreed that was pretty heady stuff for a twenty-nine-year-old Georgia boy. Phil Landrum, however, left a real legacy in his twenty-one years in Congress, being the author of the Landrum-Griffin Labor Act and the Economic Opportunity Act of 1964.

Harold & Lucille McEver, Genuine Members of the Greatest Generation

Chapter 21
The Fall from Grace: My Early Career in NYC

The heady experience of watching the end of Vietnam from inside the Pentagon and the downfall of the Nixon administration was over and so was my military obligation. I was a service veteran, and Georgia was a college graduate with a Voice degree from Peabody Conservatory. We headed to New York City with great expectations. Not wanting to part with it, we decided to rent out our townhouse on Capitol Hill. While job interviewing, I searched for apartments but found it depressing and distressing, looking at not much space for a lot more money compared to DC.

Like the good Eagle Scout I'd been, it seemed destiny drove me. I had to follow my dream that upon finishing my military service I'd go to New York to get experience in the financial big leagues—try out the bright lights and big city. Hadn't my broker and mentor Allen Wood advised me to do so? Most of my HBS classmates had come to Wall Street after graduation, but there weren't many left after the crash of 1969, and the ensuing consolidation of the securities industry. In its wake, I found there weren't a lot of jobs, despite a market recovery. Maybe this move wasn't so wise?

Still, I wanted the New York experience. I started interviewing at the Equitable Insurance Company and passed up offers as a private placement analyst with them and in the corporate finance department of Smith Barney, as well as with some other investment banks. These positions would give me experience, but I was now focused on the venture capital business where the action was. I thought I'd gotten a great job offer in with Bessemer Securities Corporation, and I was going right to the top of the world in venture capital with no experience at all. Financial success was assured—after all this was the Phipps' family business, and they had the insight to invest in all the right deals. I was greatly impressed by the background due diligence Pete Bancroft, the head of Bessemer Venture, did before hiring me, even calling Peter Sherry my former professor at Tech to check me out. I couldn't wait to get to work and start making money.

To speed along the process of apartment-hunting, I finally did it the NYC way and got a real estate broker who produced a unique property. Though rent-controlled, it had a fireplace and sunken living room and was strategically desirable, being on the upper East Side at 73rd & 3rd. Like everything in the city, to get this great property, I had to not only pay a broker's fee but enrich the seller—attorney Dan Pollack (Harvard Law School grad), who also wanted me to pay for a piano and some beautiful built-in bookcases that came with the place. I didn't quibble with the great attorney who was to help me through some tough future scrapes. We bought the apartment, when later, I negotiated as a board member on its conversion to a co-op.

Bessemer Ventures was in the middle of the venture capital business, investing in the hottest start-up technology firms. At the time, this was the semiconductor business and involved such firms as Intel and Advanced Micro Systems, as well as computer companies using these chips and microprocessors in distributed systems, such as Four-Phase Systems. There were two other Vice Presidents working for Pete—Neal Bronstein and Bill Burgin. Neal couldn't know enough and was tough, cigar-smoking, and distant. Bill was cool, knowledgeable and classy. I spent time on the West Coast looking at firms with them. I was in Palo Alto early in its history when there were still fruit orchards there and stayed at Ricky's Hyatt House where we had high-powered breakfasts with famous entrepreneurs and venture capitalists. They all seemed to know one another, and all invested together in the same deals. I wondered what the risks were, since they all seemed to dive in the same pool together after one of them did exhaustive due diligence. I loved kicking the tires of these firms since, in the beginning, I could put my Georgia Tech education into the job. However, knowing what I did, I never got comfortable with projections that always seemed inflated in order to get the financing.

Pete didn't pay me much to begin with—basically the same as my Navy salary, $16,000 annually, but it was alluring to work for this prestigious family and firm. In addition, they encouraged their employees to invest along with them, and thus have some skin in the game. Pete had me taken down to the private bank at City Corp where he introduced me, and the bank lent me $35,000 to invest in Bessemer venture deals. Soon I'd be a millionaire by investing on the ground floor of these businesses. I worked late almost every night and wasn't paying much attention to my health, my wife, and certainly not to my soul.

We all forgot how long the bull market had run and developing world events. It was 1973, and the stock market was about to crash. The middle eastern oil producers had formed a cartel (OPEC) and tripled the price of oil overnight, causing an economic shock wave felt around the world. Earlier in the year, I'd been given $1,000,000 of company money to invest in public technology companies, and by the end of the year, it was down to $300,000. I'd lost $700,000 and was one of the only bids remaining in the marketplace. I could now buy anything at any price. Brokers called and threw stock at me. The facts about these companies hadn't changed, so I kept buying, but my boss wasn't impressed.

By the new year, the market turned, and my portfolio was worth over $2 million, but I'd failed the venture capital test. I couldn't invest in some of the deals the other venture capitalists invested in—marketable securities were easier to invest in than the illiquid venture capital deals. I was hesitant about their projections in this environment and afraid of being locked into them. In short, I wasn't cut out for taking risks with other people's money. Pete Bancroft called me in one Friday afternoon and told me my services were no longer required. He was sorry, but they were cutting back their venture investing because the world looked uncertain. He wasn't sure where they were heading, but for a while, no action or further investments seemed prudent. He was sure I could find other employment and would be happy to give me a recommendation.

The only problem was that I'd borrowed $20,000 to get through HBS and hadn't paid that off yet. On top of that, I'd borrowed the $35,000 Bessemer had arranged. I'd promptly put the $35,000 into promising deals, foolishly holding back no reserves and was sitting with illiquid paper probably worth half of what I'd invested. I was broke—technically bankrupt. As I was leaving his office, shocked at this reality, I had the good sense to ask Pete if he'd call the bank and ask them to give me a year or, better, two to repay my loans. Thankfully he did.

Somehow, I'd forgotten my earlier path and was on one that wasn't the real me, but like Icarus ignoring his father's instructions not to fly too close to the sun, I went right for the big leagues, got burned, tumbled out of the sky and fall into the sea where I almost drowned. Dante's words at the start of *The Inferno*, came to mind: "Midway upon the journey of our life I found myself in a dark wilderness, for I had wandered from the straight and true."

Calling off the bank kept the wolf from our door. Georgia was becoming a brilliant star of the Light Opera Company of Manhattan

(LOOM) on 74th street, where they featured operettas, particularly those by Gilbert and Sullivan. Georgia excelled as the soprano ingénue, and she was also a natural comedian. Our woes were just beginning, however. She wasn't being paid much—her troop was constantly struggling for audiences and funds. We'd been barely able to pay our rent with my Bessemer salary. I had three months' severance pay but needed to find work immediately. We had the mortgage on the house in DC that was covered by its rent and Georgia had a modest trust fund we couldn't touch until she was 30. We decided it prudent to sell the house in Washington to cover our mortgage and put the rest in reserves. In hindsight that was a mistake, one that many others made too who'd been forced to downsize from the market crash. Finding work was almost impossible, and the market was flooded with experienced MBAs. We were a dime a dozen.

Being unemployed, I thought I'd have some downtime, but finding work was an all-consuming, tedious grind. I got to know recruiters, worked on my resumé and letters of application. I sent dozens of these out with few responses. I lived with rejection and became part of a vast army of unemployed. It was a full-time job waiting in line for the few interviews held—to get an interview was a success. Georgia tried to keep my spirits up, but I was depressed. It was a great time to reflect and write, but I despaired and drank. I'd come to New York to get experience and then go back to Atlanta and maybe start my own business because independence meant more to me than money, but I had neither and couldn't even get a job interview. Increasingly, I felt I'd blown a real chance to get in on the ground floor of the developing technology business and kept kicking myself for it. In retrospect, I can see from the time I've recently spent in Palo Alto, I did blow it, but what a different life it would have been for me. The Good Lord and the Fates had other plans for me.

The only solace we found was going home back to Little Sandy, where we were welcomed by her parents and at cocktail hour regaled our woes with Alma and David on the back porch. I loved wandering those fields, and out in that nature I found God and sanity again. My parents were overly anxious for me, while my in-laws were much more relaxed and laidback. These are excerpts from a poem about our time at Little Sandy Farm, I would later own:

On May afternoons like this
we'd coax the horses out of their shade
down by the creek with sweet feed.
Dave would hitch Sonny to the surrey
and we'd saddle Sixten and Syllabub
and he would guide us beaus
            around Little Sandy Farm.
Jokes, saved for our visit,
were the first order of business
and we'd pass the family burying plot
where your great grandfather's leg -
lost during the civil war -
            lies buried beside him.

When we got to news from the big city,
we were by the old family house
with its shanty foundations out back.
Here your Grandmother was born
and officiated the brewing of syllabub*
            Christmases.

At five o'clock sharp we'd stop
at Double Bridges across the Little Sandy.
The red dust cloud would settle
and into the well-stocked cooler,
carried like a treasure chest,
we'd dig for "a harness tightener,"
            as Dave termed it...

Soon enough my path through hell took me back to NYC.
The casualties from the crash were extensive, and companies cut
back to make up for vastly increased energy costs and a depressed
financial market. I finally found a company that had figured out
how to make money from the oil embargo—a chemical giant called
W. R. Grace. They went straight at the problem, starting an oil
and gas department by buying oil and gas properties in Texas and
elsewhere in the US. The CEO's son Peter Grace, Jr. in fact, would

manage the division. The company seemed secure enough and was the only offer I had at the time, so I jumped at it.

What I didn't know was that Peter Grace, Sr. was a visionary, hard-driving CEO who came down particularly hard on his son. In turn, Peter Jr. put additional pressure on everyone in his division. I didn't know anything about buying oil and gas properties and neither did Peter, but we learned together with consultants. Peter seemed to like me since I understood his situation. We worked 24/7 for six months straight. Our group would come out of work on Saturday at last light looking at one another when one analyst asked: "Do you think they do this at Exxon?" I never worked so hard and never had a weekend free, then discovered Grace was moving the division to Dallas, Texas to be in the middle of the action.

Georgia and I dutifully took the trip to Dallas and found a house in the River Oaks area, but our hearts weren't in it. This would be the end of Georgia's opera career, and though it was in the South, I wasn't ready to leave New York. I still wanted to conquer the financial market there and was determined to do so. I felt lost and unsure, though I knew that moving to Dallas wasn't the right thing. With my salary, I was not only paying the rent but paying off some of those loans. I just bit my lip hoping a miracle would happen. What I didn't know then and couldn't foresee was that the experience and education I was getting in the energy business would come to serve me well.

When I got back to my office at W. R. Grace, a telegram was waiting for me. We'd spent the whole weekend preparing a board presentation for the acquisition of a series of properties being divested from a major firm that was selling them off to secondary firms, such as us. I'd busted my chops preparing the presentation the chairman was to give to the board in London. The telegram was from the CEO himself; this was my big break! I thought he's going to tell me what a fine job I'd done, but the telegram informed me that I'd misspelled the name of the consulting firm that verified the key reservoirs. There was a special department at Grace—all the assistants to the chairman who proofread every presentation. This was Peter Grace Sr.'s fetish—the perfect board presentation. One of the proofreaders told me his secret to proofreading for Peter was reading the presentations backwards. They'd missed my mistake. I wasn't sure how long I could work for a firm with priorities like that, to gamble my future on Dallas, to move my wife there and sacrifice her career for certain and possibly mine.

I constantly networked with friends, and in fact, we ran together in the park on weekends. One of these guys was Johnny William (God rest his soul). Johnny was a consummate networker as well as a Georgia Tech and HBS graduate. Coming to the street in 1969, he had several corporate financial jobs shot out from under him with Wall Street still consolidating and ended up in the Mergers & Acquisitions Department of Chemical Bank, attempting to get into the big leagues of the merger business against the major investment banks. Johnny, who was from Atlanta, had just gotten his dream job at Robinson Humphrey & Co. in Atlanta—this was the best investment bank in the Southeast, headed by the legendary Justus Martin. It was a white-shoe regional investment bank, and Johnny had somehow gotten a job there. This was his ticket back home, and I was elated for him.

Having just been hired, he didn't want to hurt or embarrass his boss, Noble Welch—a wonderful man and long-term executive with Chemical, charged with the task of launching the bank into the investment banking business. Johnny proposed breakfast with Noble the following morning where he'd explain and introduce me as his replacement. He thought the bank needed my experience in the acquisition of oil and gas properties, as well as my venture capital experience. Georgia was ecstatic and got me to bed early in order to be rested for my interview.

We met in the executive dining room at Chemical's Pine Street headquarters. Noble was curious as to why Johnny had brought me along but took the news well. He saw Johnny wanted to go home and what a unique opportunity this was for him. He also didn't balk at the idea of me and got right down to the interview. I told him the truth and as it turned out, Noble needed a lot of talent because the merger business was about to take off and my next career with it. He hired me on the spot. Without hesitation the next day, I walked into Peter Grace Jr.'s office to tell him I was leaving, though felt a bit sorry for him having to live with a father like his. I explained I'd received another job offer and would be staying in New York. Peter being the gentleman he was understood and took it well, wishing me luck. I moved from the inferno to purgatory but wasn't out of the woods. I climbed up another rung with Dante words echoing:

"Thus, you may understand that love alone is the true seed of every merit in you, and of all acts for which you must atone."

Through this job turmoil, I discovered I was seeking some spiritual answer to my plight all along. I'd read, wrote entries and some crude poems in intermittently kept journals. Something was coming out from deep inside me I couldn't keep down. I was open for some kind of spiritual experience. However, I eagerly reported downtown to begin my two-year stint at the headquarters of Chemical. The M&A (Mergers & Acquisitions) Department was an ancillary group to the main banking business, that, for a large commercial bank, was making loans to major corporations. It proved difficult to get bankers to share their contacts with an uncertain and unproven M&A team. Some did, and those relationships worked well, but many wouldn't since most bankers assumed their clients were only interested in borrowing money and not in mergers that, at the time, weren't that frequent. Increasingly, however, there was enough interest to keep us in business. It was the early days of M&A, and the strategic implications the big investment banks could see weren't yet apparent to Chemical or corporate America. In the banking world, mergers was still an ancillary service department, but like foxes with a view of a henhouse filled with fat, lazy chickens, we were instinctively highly motivated.

I got a break early on when the president of Bow Valley Industries out of Calgary, Canada came in late one night from London to see his old friend, Noble. When Noble asked what he'd been up to, the man reached in his travel bag and on the table, rolled out a drilling log of a new find they'd hit in the North Sea. None of the assembled officers in the meeting, including the hastily invited president of Chemical, knew what that was. From my experience at Grace, I knew immediately and had never seen anything like it—over 800-feet of pay! This was a bonanza. I spoke up from my side chair and said something enlightening like, "Good grief!" Bow Valley's president knew I knew what I was looking at. After we jointly explained it, the bank president asked, "How can we help you finance this?" That began a long-term profitable relationship for the bank that eventually set up a special department to finance such oil and gas exploration. With their find, Bow Valley became a very big company overnight and a good bank customer. My tenure at Chemical Bank was starting off on the right foot.

The Bow Valley encounter was one of the more interesting meetings, but there was a ton of more mundane stuff—mostly trying to sell our merger services—that didn't appeal to lower-level company officials because most Chemical Bank officers never got beyond the treasurer's office. You needed access to the decision-makers. It was still early days, and we were doing missionary work, a lot of it.

One day I got a call from a headhunter looking for a junior officer to work for a major investment bank that was trying to get into and beef up their merger business. It was Blyth, Eastman Dillon. I was soon interviewed by three senior partners, one of whom did oil and gas deals—Tom Lovejoy, who had a saddle on a sawhorse by his desk from his time as a cowhand in Oklahoma. I hit it off with all of them. After being immersed in it, I could see the merger business was going to be a major strategic tool for corporate America and I was ready to move to a professional investment banking firm and to get deep into the mainstream. My experience in the venture technology and oil and gas businesses would be invaluable in this new job where it would differentiate me. I felt terrible telling Noble what I was doing, but again, being the good soul he was, he took it well. He also knew that the banks couldn't compete with the investment banks at that time for contacts, unless they used their balance sheets, that they eventually did as well as just acquire the investment banking firms when the law changed.

Blyth, Eastman Dillon grew from the merger of Eastman Dillon, a white-shoe eastern investment bank, and the small, but powerful West Coast boutique firm of Blyth & Co. The partners there had contacts in corporate America that were a step above the people I worked with at Chemical Bank; they really did have the essential contacts at large corporations needed to make strategic financial moves and importantly, to buy other companies. In turn, I learned the major firms of America were divvied up by the major investment banks—a sort of gentleman's agreement started by J.P. Morgan—and at that time, didn't poach on others' territory. With the rise of the strategic merger business, technology, and the banks trying to get in their line of business, this was all about to change big time.

Initially, I was working with my new boss, Noel Urban, a seasoned merger banker from Kidder, Peabody & Co., and who was a curler (I was his broom, so to speak—literally on the ice and professionally

in the office). The first weekend we worked together, he took me to
his curling club in Norfolk, CT, not far from my present-day home
in Salisbury. Noel treated me as his partner from day one. Mergers
were not yet a mainstream investment banking activity, but Noel had
quite a bit of experience and loved to sell entrepreneurs' businesses.
He related to these folks, and they felt understood by him. He didn't
relate to the formal corporate finance-types and that was eventually
his downfall as we had to step up our game to make larger corporate
deals. Noel and I were doing mergers with mid-sized companies
around the country, and I was responsible for initially visiting them
to see if they were real businesses we could sell. Our brokers were
very well connected, and there was a pent-up demand for more of
these businesses to get liquidity through a merger, since public un-
derwritings were becoming increasingly restrictive and harder to do.

I also worked with our senior bankers and their larger clients,
such as an assignment in Radnor, Pennsylvania for the Sun Oil
Company. Sun was still stinging from some bad advice they'd gotten
from Solomon Brothers raiding traditional relationships, goading
them into attempting an early hostile takeover of the McGraw Hill
Company. Rebuffed and shunned by the rest of corporate America
for this audacious move, they went back to using their regular, more
conservative investment bank: us. With the rise in the price of oil,
some genius in their Strategic Planning Department determined it
would be advantageous for them to acquire trucking companies
around the country and roll them up into a national network of Sun
Company trucks. My new Merger Department boss Eddie Stanton
and I were to be the project managers of a taskforce and travel
around the country to talk these independent trucking company en-
trepreneurs into joining a big oil company.

This made for good sport if you can imagine yourself with a
checkbook capable of acquiring the major trucking lines in America.
So off I went to learn the American trucking business, finding out
quickly they were largely a union operations, but there were many
independent and interesting firms. One problem was that they were
all independent and wanted to remain so rather than associate with
a major oil company. I began to recognize them all and remember
their stories, and even as I drive highways today, still see their logos
on trailer sides.

One early deal for Sun involved buying Smith's Transfer out of Stanton, Virginia, owned by Jake Smith, a wily Southerner. We negotiated a great deal for Jake, his family, their employees, and for Sun. Suddenly when we were about to close, Jake balked. I called him directly, and he hemmed and hawed, then I just said, "Jake, what does it take to do this deal?" He came right to it. "I'm going to retire in a couple of years after this deal, and me and the missus just want to go around the good old USA in an RV, so what I want is a perpetual Sun Oil credit card to pay for the gas. It might be really going up." I relayed that information to our client, who promptly sent the card before closing.

While I was intent on pursuing my intellectual and poetry paths, and my business path became more and more demanding when the economy picked up in the late-seventies, I was ignoring the love of my life who worked late, performing Wednesday through Saturday nights as well as Sunday matinees. Georgia was becoming an operetta diva. She spent a year on the road with Columbia Artists, singing in *The Merry Widow*, *The Student Prince*, and other light operas in every town across the United States. She traveled with her troupe via bus, and I'd fly to wherever she was on weekends, whether it was Oil City, Ohio or Boise, Idaho. I could usually end up close by on business. It was a tough, lonely life though.

I was walking home from work late afternoon on the upper East Side, and I noticed a lovely blonde lady walking ahead of me in a trench coat. She was holding hands with the tall man next to her. I froze when I realized. It was Georgia and her leading man! I tapped her on the shoulder, and much embarrassment and stuttering ensued. I thought better than to start an incident on the street, and instead went home and considered just walking out. I'd always thought he was gay, as most of the men in her troupe were, but he was bisexual, and we had a problem. I was stunned, livid, and ready to leave. After all, there was nothing wrong with me. I worked all the time to pay the rent while Georgia contributed little materially. I'd found other things to do the evenings like go to adult education classes at 92nd Street Y while Georgia was performing, and now I'd discovered she had other interests.

Georgia was savvier, however. She was trying to get my attention since I wasn't paying attention to her. When I calmed down, she suggested we go through counseling. Again, since I thought there was nothing wrong with me, I baulked, but agreed to at least see a marriage counselor. It didn't seem to work. Then Georgia suggested a psychologist she'd heard of, Thomas Waller. He had an office on the West Side of Central Park. Tom was an interesting man—an artist, a photographer, a sculptor and a thinker, who'd gone to school at the Sorbonne in Paris, even met Sartre and Camus. He was gentle and could see right through me. He held a mirror up and helped me see myself. I sat together with Georgia on his big leather couch, and after the initial interview, Tom told me, "You don't know who you are." And I didn't. Those words started many years of therapy for us both. We began going separately as we soon discovered both Georgia and I had some deeper issues.

At age fourteen, Georgia came home alone one day after school to find her father, a heavy drinker, passed out the floor in the den, so she closed the door and went to bed. Alma was away caring for her own sister who had cancer. In the morning, she found that he was still lying there. He'd tripped and fallen, breaking his neck. A 1929 HBS graduate and the oldest male in his family, he ran the family business. He'd trained in the Treasury Department of the Ford Motor company under Robert McNamara, and while he'd been a business prodigy, he was also an alcoholic—the family secret. Georgia had never gotten over the guilt and shock of this event.

I discovered I had issues as a workaholic and overachiever, but Tom plunged deeper and helped us put our lives and our marriage back together. Tom uncovered that my ambition to please my parents shrouded the real hero who wanted to be independent, an entrepreneur who didn't have to take orders from anyone. There was another side, however that seldom came out. He also uncovered a sensitive and far-seeing side that I continually ran over—the poet. I began to see work more objectively and to understand the longing in me to run my own show and to write more consistently and seriously.

Georgia became enamored with doing something else and retiring from the opera grind for a few years. She was talented and very creative and usually had her opera company eating out of her hand by the time the show was over. When we both realized how much we meant to each other, it changed our lives, and we began working together to support one another and help bring our dreams to ground. We'd come so close to throwing our relationship away. Tom saved our marriage. Working with Tom, I kept a dream journal. One of the first dreams I recorded involved a fence with a log running along the top that I balanced on while holding a long pole. I was trying to balance my life, and he encouraged me to do so, especially by concentrating on my writing. Given all my interest there was nothing else to do but try to balance these, but also I had to treat them equally or really see myself as I was. He also encouraged us to find a place outside of the city to visit and reflect in nature. It was Tom who helped me realize fulfilling the dream burning deep inside me: becoming an independent entrepreneur.

Lt. Harold B. McEver, US Navy Flight Instructor

Chapter 22
Passage to India

"Life never gives us what we want at the moment that we consider appropriate. Adventures do occur, but not punctually."

A Passage to India
E. M. Forster

My spiritual path began in childhood. My parents were pioneering parishioners at a little Methodist church in South Atlanta where I listened to Bevel Jones (who would become a bishop and my mentor) speak so eloquently and persuasively about finding Jesus through faith. My inability to walk down that aisle, to feel and truly be "saved" caused me angst and sent me searching. I wandered the fields and woods outside Atlanta with my dog King, a beautiful collie, and came close to God or something beyond and in me, particularly at sunsets, losing myself in that amber glow. Was I connecting with that great spirit that belonged to the Native American peoples I studied about diligently through Scouting? For me, at that time, God was in nature, where I could feel close to Him, feel some immense power that began like the tip of an iceberg in me, rather than one who resided in heaven and who could only be reached through some leap of faith, or organized path. He was there, and I deeply believed in Him. I felt this awesome power and saw His beauty displayed in nature and the stars I wandered under at night. I struggled to express this but mostly kept it to myself.

Throughout high school and college, I went to church, was religiously literate, enjoyed a good sermon, and occasionally felt spiritually refreshed by a service, but it was into nature I had to go to realize this and be with Him. I was always seeking the source of this peace, this knowledge of something beyond faith—that mystic connection, an original knowledge, an intuitive understanding I'd know instantly. I felt there was a prior knowledge within us that when crossed, enabled us to find our way on this spiritual path. I felt like an outsider, and sometimes met a pilgrim who was further down the path and recognizing this, quizzed them intently. Maybe that's why I bonded so well with my fellow Jabberwockies, and others I felt were seekers.

Though I worked most weekends while Georgia preformed, I found myself walking in New York one beautiful Saturday afternoon, and came across a film at a little art theatre by the Plaza Hotel that instantly appealed. It was Peter Brook's *Meetings with Remarkable Men*. It's the story of mystic Gurdjieff's life and search for esoteric knowledge he brought back to the West from the ancient secret schools in the remote mountains of middle Asia. I spent the afternoon watching it and changed my life.

Gurdjieff was a renowned "mystic" I'd heard of and read about in my seeking, and purportedly was, like Jesus, Buddha, or even Abraham Lincoln, a "realized" human being. His quest and the gusto and lengths he went to find enlightenment were humbling. I'd been lucky to run across some extraordinary human beings in this world, people who'd inspired and changed the way I looked at life. With his example at this time of my life, I was inspired to seek further and to never stop. The film was on my mind for weeks. I bought every book I could by him. I was always looking for such remarkable human beings.

It was during my time at the investment banking firm of Blyth, Eastman Dillon that I joined the Viking Health Spa with my group of friends who regularly ran Central Park. It had a fully equipped weight room, but also a pool and steam room. We'd exercise evenings after work or early morning. Fitness was always an obsession of mine, made tougher in the city. We tried to run in the park as long as the weather held, but winter forced us inside to the Viking.

The spa's manager hung out as lifeguard at the pool, occasionally surveyed the weight room, and took a steam bath after his shift ended. He always had his nose in a book. As I got to know Gordon Paterson—known as Gordo—I found his history had been a torturous one. As an Army veteran, he'd hurt his back in service and had resorted to meditation rather than pain pills. That took him to certain mystic texts—he was a seeker of esoteric knowledge par excellence—a monk out of his cloister.

His quest had recently taken him to India where he'd sought out the famous ashram of Ramana Maharshi. He'd read all his books. While staying at the ashram, he ran into some serious seekers who were all going to see a relatively new guru, Nisargadatta Maharaj. Gordon had visited this ashram in the slums of Bombay (now Mumbai) and had become a convert and devotee. Over eighty, the guru had been a small-time cigarette retailer, running a little shop. As a middle-aged man, Maharaj had met his guru and had become his devotee and the heir to his tradition. Gordon shared one of Maharaj's books, *I Am That*, and I was fascinated by the wisdom emanating from this seemingly uneducated man whose fame was now renowned in India and growing in New Age circles in America.

There was a good deal of travel involved with my work at Blyth, but it gave me plenty of time to read on planes. I began to ask Gordon for more material. He started me with the basics of meditation and recommended a master named Mouni Sadhu (which translates to "silent monk"), the pen name for a Polish man who'd been to India, studied with Ramana Maharshi, and who'd become skilled in concentration and meditation. Dutifully, I went to the Quest Bookstore on 53rd and Second and bought Sadhu's books. I became serious about meditating. I also looked forward to my evening workouts and conversations with Gordon. I began to read all sorts of quest literature and was wondering if at this stage of my mystical development, I needed guidance from a guru? As I got to know him better, I discovered Gordon had been a successful film producer, but when he lost his job, his wife and son left him too. He'd since become a sincere devotee of the Maharaj but was too broke to make the journey back to India since the Army was dragging its feet about sorting out his veteran's benefits.

I was curious as to how the guru might advise me, and I was ready to take another step on my quest. The problem was not only paying for the passage to India for both Gordon and me but also finding the time to do it. To supplement my income for the trip, I'd begun to speculate with bond futures. This is dangerous stuff, but I watched the economy closely, was working for an investment bank, and so was in constant touch with the market. Though an informed gamble, and on a hunch, I decided to make a bigger bet and was suddenly some $20,000 richer overnight! Providence was sending me to meet my guru. I called Gordon. We were going to India!

It didn't take much arm-twisting to get Gordon to go. He planned the trip, got us hotel reservations near the guru, and alerted the circle of devotees he was in touch with, he'd be bringing a new devotee. I told my wife, but not my co-workers or parents, who'd all think I was crazy. "Don't come back with a shaved head," was all Georgia said. She'd returned with me to see *Meetings with Remarkable Men* and knew it was something programmed into my karma. As the mystics say, when a guru is needed, he appears.

Luckily, working flat out for the past three years, I'd accumulated a couple of weeks' vacation I had to take before they expired and Georgia, who was starting a new show, couldn't take off, so I could go guilt-free. I was dying of curiosity, and I wasn't to be disappointed.

Gordon and I arrived in Mumbai in the evening. When they finally opened the plane's door, the waft of exotic and intoxicating humidity matched the hubbub and mass of people outside. There were crowds of spectators at the Indian airport, some who were curious onlookers, some wanting to touch us and even pick our pockets if not careful. But many had something to sell, pressing flowers, garlands, incense, or carvings and souvenirs in our way, or even services, offering to gather our bags or to find us their preferred cab choice to our hotel. The streets of Mumbai were an experience of crowding unfamiliar even for a New Yorker.

Surprisingly at that late hour, the streets of Mumbai teemed with life. Gordon guided our driver to the hotel. The city was steaming and humid, and the smell noticed at the airport lingered everywhere. The hotel was a low-rise building with a red neon sign, but the path to its front door was littered with bodies sleeping on the sidewalk in front of it and on the causeway up to the front door. It seemed routine for our driver, who casually gathered our bags and led the charge. Gordon and I picked up our carry-ons and began to step over the sleeping men, women, and children, undisturbed by our presence. The night clerk welcomed us, sending us up to modest, but clean rooms.

The next morning, I was awakened by a man who brought me tea and asked if "sahib" wanted anything else. I was confused, but soon realized I was on another continent, on the other side of the world from New York. Excited to soon see the guru, I washed and shaved. Refreshed, I went downstairs to meet Gordon who, with his bald head and white shirt, looked like a guru himself.

We had a breakfast of tea and toast and some sort of gruel, a kind of Indian oatmeal. There were eggs to be had, but I wasn't that hungry because my body was confused as to what time zone it was in. Gordon was chipper at the prospect of seeing his guru again. He'd instructed me on the proper bow and gift presentation. I'd carefully shopped at Tiffany's, settling on a crystal owl, thinking of it as a symbol for the guru's wisdom. I was so sure he'd be impressed and reward me with extra questions and attention.

Gordon decided we were going to walk—one of the more fascinating journeys I'd ever taken. Walking down the street from the hotel, I realized what all those people had been doing in the street—sleeping near their jobs as they became merchants, messengers, or porters carrying little trays of tea or coffee (usually balanced on their heads) between merchants and clients. There was thriving commerce on the sidewalks, then we came to a large open-air marketplace with fruits, meats, flowers, and all sorts of exotic vegetables piled in carefully crafted mounds and pyramids like they'd been planned by some color coordinator—a spectrum of new colors and fruits I'd never seen. Haggling was at its peak, and the market was alive with bargaining and animated negotiations. I remained most impressed with the splotches of color that begged to be painted, if only I could paint.

As we continued, the neighborhood became seedier. There were open windows and picture windows with scantily clad women hanging out or posing in them. We were skirting the edge of the red-light district! There was little commerce at that time of morning, but it must have been lively at night. We arrived at a four-story house with no signage and climbed the stairs. I'd traveled over 5,000 miles, had just walked through one of the most colorful markets on earth and through the red-light district to get to this place, and there I was climbing three flights of stairs to see the guru. It was surreal.

Maharaj sat cross-legged in a white dhoti at the end of the room on a raised platform. His shoulders were bare, and there was a neatly draped cloth across his chest, like a bandolier sans bullets. He was old and stern, very stern, with a scowl that took no prisoners and was surrounded by a circle of well-dressed Indians and a few ordinary folks. It was an impressive group that looked distinguished and well-educated. Beside him sat a translator who converted his native Mahrati into English. Later, I got to know many of those present. They were retired executives, and matrons, engineers, and doctors, a distinctly upper-class group of people who came regularly to these sessions.

When it was someone's turn, a participant asked a question and awaited his response. I was amazed at the level of questioning. It was as if they were interacting with Socrates—well, in a way, they were. He was daunting. I'd expected a sweet, full-of-love elderly fellow who was totally compassionate, sort of like how I imagined Jesus to be, but he seemed to simply answer questions, some very gruffly, almost with the attitude of, "Why, you idiot, did you ask that?" Everyone waited their turn. This was a serious interchange with some occasional humor and more chastisement.

A few of the circle recognized Gordon and motioned him and me forward. I'd thought of what I would ask but had kept changing my mind. What was the meaning of all this? No. What would he advise at this point in my life meditations? No. What was the efficacy of concentration for meditation? No. I was scared to death. Would he be impressed with my gift? Think it clever? Surely, he'd recognize the brilliance of the owl and engage with me about my career and why I had come so far to visit him.

Gordon stepped forward, prostrated himself on his knees and rose in prayer position. He greeted the guru, and the old man scowled at him. He had an ochre dot in the middle of his forehead. He wanted to know what Gordon was doing back, hadn't he learned enough on his last trip? Less than a warm greeting after traveling so far. Gordon explained he'd brought a friend who wanted to learn from the master directly and that he'd instructed me carefully. The guru glared at me and commented to his translator, "Maybe he has some spiritual potential?" Then he asked me: "Do you have a question?" I answered that I did, but also that I'd brought him a small gift I wanted to present first. I gave him the owl. He looked at it curiously for a moment, then threw it back at me like a baseball, saying, "What do I want with this? I can't eat it!"

I was scared, shocked, but believe I recovered by asking something about meditation.

"Yes, it's useful, but use it to meditate on a better question next time. You don't get many." I had tried his patience. Not exactly the greeting I'd expected, but there I was in front of a real guru. He was expert at ego deflation; I marveled how he managed the questions and answers that followed for the rest of the day.

Our remaining days we got to know the circle of people around him, one of whom was Mr. S. V. Sapre, an engineer who was writing a soon-to-be-published book about Maharaj's sayings and also served as a translator for Maharaj. He and his wife asked us over for tea, where he confirmed Maharaj was the real deal and was why he had such followers. There were other prominent Indians who'd also been dismissed by the guru. It was his method of waking someone up, thus Sapre encouraged me to screw up my courage and ask him other questions.

When it came my turn again, I asked about a three-minded person, someone like myself—a businessman, a writer, and a spiritualist. He bluntly told me that was illusory thinking, to go beyond that. "Meditate on the meditator," he told me directly. "Seek to know him, and all your problems will fall away." He looked me directly in the eye, then took the next question. Later, he talked of knowing awareness, and said, looking at me, "If you know the 'I am,' you don't need rules. Rules are for the ignorant, for religions, and those who dwell in a mind-body. Go after the 'I am,' dwell there—you don't need anything else."

When I asked him about a balanced self, he said you had to be balanced to understand the self, but that too much of any activity will cause you to dwell on that rather than on your true self. He told me what I knew from academic study would eventually strangle me.

"Seek the 'I am.' Meditate on the meditator. Don't worry about irrelevant knowledge. Let that be your mantra." As I was leaving, I gave him some chocolates and a little money. He was appreciative, even managed a smile, but looked like a tired old fellow. His final advice to me was not to follow himself or other gurus and mystics, but to look deep within and trust what I might find there.

His answers and advice were astute, and he spoke them in such a way that it seemed the answers came from somewhere else, like he was channeling from another source. They weren't the answers of a cigarette retailer who'd never been formally educated. He was an original, and it was like hearing the "Sermon on the Mount," or Marcus Aurelius' *Meditations* with a philosophically Hindu slant. Daily, I savored the whole environment until the guru tired, we were dismissed, and walked sublimely home. I'd met a most remarkable man indeed.

It was two Septembers later that I had a strange dream about him. I vividly saw his stern yet understanding face glaring at me. It prompted me to call Gordon and inquire if he'd heard anything from any of our friends in India. He told me it was strange that I should ask because someone had called to tell him Maharaj had passed away a few days before.

I was soon destined to see another remarkable man. It wasn't long after my return from India, I was home one night having supper alone since Georgia was performing. There was a knock on our apartment door. It was our neighbor Dona, who was a healer and mystic herself. She had a massage business as well, and I'd occasionally go to her to straighten out my shoulders, where I seemed to hold all my tension. She knew well my interest and about my India trip.

"Hurry. Come see this program," she said breathlessly. She took me next door to see Bill Moyers interviewing Joseph Campbell on TV. I'd never heard anything like it. Campbell had made a life out of studying the myths of the world and had begun to connect all the dots, at least he did for me. He was a comparative mythologist of all the religions and traditions. I had to find this person and discovered he taught at Sarah Lawrence College just north of New York, but moreover, he gave weekend seminars on various mythological subjects at his wife's dance studio, The Theater of the Open Eye.

That winter, I spent every available weekend listening to Joseph Campbell talk about early man and his cave paintings, the Arthurian Age, Eastern myths, Western myths, Christianity and the Middle Ages. I got to know Campbell better, relishing these weekends with him, listening intently. We didn't become personal friends, but he knew who I was and encouraged me to write and read. I have read, studied, and taught Joseph Campbell ever since. This man had examined the world's religions and myths and ordered them—connecting the stories, comparing them as no one else had done. While most academics are siloed, he rose above and beyond that. He had a vast vision of the world from ancient times to current events, and most importantly, put it all in context for his audience.

We were all heroes on our quests, but where were we on our paths? He believed in following our paths, following your bliss, and I could see I was on several paths that were crossing one another and con-founding me. I learned that poets were the visionaries. Once, they had been the philosophers, the seers. I thought I was one of those, could see, but just wasn't putting it together or writing it down. I started keeping journals more earnestly and writing my first poems. I began putting those feelings and emotions into words. Georgia joked that I was a poet and didn't know it, moreover, sincerely encouraged me to start putting it into practice.

After college, Campbell had studied in Paris and then Germany, then returned to the US after the 1929 market crash bankrupted his father. He couldn't get a teaching job, so read for six years, keeping a rigid reading schedule he set out for himself while hanging out near Woodstock, NY with his sister and an extraordinary group of friends. He knew Harvey Fite—the sculptor of "Opus 40." With a voracious and disciplined mind, he was largely self-taught, before entering academia. Much like Emerson—a self-taught public intellectual—he galled traditional academics who wouldn't look over the top of their specialty bunkers. Having read a lot about the bones, he was putting on the meat in his lectures, and he took the audience across regions, religions, ethnicities, as well as across time. He never talked down to the audience but explained, pouring out a clear spring of knowledge that has carried me far. I still think about his lectures, trying to find the patterns in the great poems he says sustain us. I went to his retirement banquet in New York before he and his wife Jean Erdman sailed for good to Hawaii where he passed away not long after.

The following passage from Campbell's *The Power of Myth* spoke to me and continues to speak to me:

> People say that what we're all seeking is a meaning for life. I don't think that's what we're really seeking. I think that what we're seeking is an experience of being alive, so that our life experiences on the purely physical plane will have resonances with our own innermost being and reality, so that we actually feel the rapture of being alive.

Bruce & Georgia McEver with John Robertson
and John's Glazed Turkey, Thanksgiving 1980s

Chapter 23
Risk Be Damned:
The History of Berkshire Capital—Part I

By 1979 the world had recovered from the OPEC embargo shock begun five years earlier. Ironically, the same seismic tremor that jarred me from my first job sent me through a couple others where I'd gained an accelerated education in the oil and gas business. I finally found job stability as a more confident vice president at Blyth, Eastman Dillon, and I was an active analyst back in those days. For my soul, I wrote more poetry and attended engaging seminars and classes at the 92nd Street Y and the New School. Life was much better.

Blyth was an old-line, white shoe investment bank where wages weren't bad, and our energy business was booming. It's strange where you get a good idea from. One of my clients was buying a major pipeline valve company and wanted me to accompany their due-diligence team somewhere out onto sage-brushed barrens near Midland, Texas to check it out. It was over 100 degrees, but so dry you didn't notice it was that hot. I was under the shade of a tin shed surveying a vast yard of every type and size of valve you could imagine for connecting pipelines. I'd never seen such a spread of metal valves, with the occasional lizard scampering over them, a distant relative of something once more dangerous and Triassic.

Matt Simmons, who'd graduated a year ahead of me from HBS, was representing the selling company. He'd started a little investment bank, Simmons & Co., in Houston and specialized in doing deals in the oil service business. While this may not seem unusual today, at that time there were no independent investment banks, much less ones that specialized in an industry, like a corner of the energy business. It was a unique idea that Matt and his brother Luke had seized upon because the oil service business was run by many of their friends and happened to be centered in Houston.

My client's team was carefully checking things over with his client's management, while Matt and I stood in the shade talking about his niche business. No investment banker did that at the time. Perhaps you worked for a larger bank as a generalist, but these guys defied custom by stepping out on their own and specializing. They seemed to be flourishing too and independently running their own business; I dreamed of such entrepreneurial freedom someday!

Matt and I negotiated the deal. My client expanded his product line to include valves in the pipeline business that was consolidating rapidly at the time. Matt's client got his price; both sides seemed happy with the outcome. We became friends, and I stayed in touch. Importantly, a seed was planted in my mind and stayed with me: now I needed to find an area where I could concentrate as Matt had done, with the same strategic advantage of deep industry expertise, contacts, and a hustle to survive. Meanwhile it was back to the developing my merger business.

The developing trend in the sixties was to conglomerate—building large and disparate companies with the stock boom—but this had cooled significantly with the crash of 1973, and the ensuing recession of the mid-seventies. The synergies imagined by the conglomerates of the sixties and seventies weren't panning out in the eighties. The mutual overhead savings and balancing cashflows between dissimilar businesses that the conglomerates had predicted proved illusory. As these companies turned out to be sub-scale or technologically obsolete, many divisions were spun off or put up for sale. I worked with our most astute industry analyst to confirm my suspicions about vulnerable divisions, and this diligence also generated leads for me. Many times we worked together on a project. It was great hunting and was both exciting and rewarding.

I would spot a likely target and persuade one of our senior partners to accompany me to a presentation for the CEO to lay out these ideas. Sometimes they acted and sometimes not, but I could leapfrog a long line of financial officers making presentations to corporate treasurers for financing and go right to the top with a solid merger idea and the CEOs appreciated careful thinking about their enterprises. Our business flourished. One deal led to another, and both our profits and bonus pool blossomed. At some point, it dawned on me that I was generating these ideas on my own. As I became more confident, I developed relationships with CEOs and other senior corporate officers who respected my thoughts and advice and took my calls directly.

It was getting a little heady when I got a dire call over the weekend from my boss Ed Stanton. The firm was broke. We'd been merged, actually bought by Don Marron of Paine Webber, at the time a firm many rungs below the corporate finance reputational standing of Blyth. The investment banking industry was an oligopoly with Morgan Stanley and Goldman Sachs at the top, Blyth in the middle, and Paine Webber and many regional companies considerably down the ladder. I couldn't believe it. Paine Webber was a firm we avoided partnering with. It was a retail firm, meaning one made up primarily of brokers with little reputation for underwriting or mergers. The wily Marron had snapped up our firm when our senior partners foolishly stepped up our fixed-income trading capabilities and added risk by hiring some Solomon Brothers bond traders. These guys bet the wrong way and lost the firm's capital in a week. Marron stepped up and acquired Blyth's people, reputation, and client base. We hadn't seen it coming. On the 32nd floor of the Mc-Graw-Hill building, we'd been making the money in corporate finance, while our senior partners were losing it on the floors below. Our bonus pool vanished like the time I sacrificed away from my wife who was performing brilliantly but was not being paid much for it either. We were both close to giving up the Big Apple and going back home.

At the time, Wall Street mergers were notoriously disruptive and bloody. Bonus pools shrank or disappeared as management changed. Harmonious working relationships broke up. Infighting began as clients and internal positions came up for grabs. The race was to the swift and greedy. Sure enough, a week into the merger, many of our senior officers jumped ship for other, more prestigious banks. Additionally, Paine Webber came with a powerful institutional sales and analyst team—Mitchell Hutchins—that sold research to large pension funds and money managers, so almost all the analysts I worked with and with whom I generated merger ideas were fired or had moved to greener pastures. Within a couple of weeks, the close cadre of my fellow bankers and co-workers had changed. Eddie Stanton had gone to Lehman Brothers to do mergers, as had many of the other senior bankers I'd collaborated with. Peter Slusser, an honorable, but tough investment banker and HBS grad, would run mergers at Paine Webber. I thought I could work with him, but the rest of his team was scrambling to pick up the client coverage left by Blyth's departing bankers, forgetting their own clients. It was going to be a political wrestling match as accounts were reshuffled while the remaining bankers nosed up to new bosses.

Then I got a call from the chairman's office. His assistant wanted me to come down for an interview with Mr. Marron. I was curious. Paine Webber's headquarters were downtown at 140 Broadway on the 13th floor. They probably didn't pay as much rent because of superstition.

This was typical of Don Marron who was practical, however, and a bit of a buccaneer. He didn't have a college degree but had sold the company he started, D. B. Marron & Co. to an institutional sales analysis research company called Mitchell Hutchins. He'd become president of Mitchell Hutchins and oversaw its merger with Paine Webber in 1977, and three years after was named CEO. In 1980, he found his chance to up his corporate finance game with Blyth and sprang when the opportunity presented itself. I gave him credit for being quick, shrewd and tough.

He was also a collector of modern art that lined the hallways of corporate headquarters. I gawked at Chagall's, Matisse's, even a Pollack, and many others I didn't recognize. He kept me waiting but was most affable when he finally got out of another meeting. He was tall, lanky, and had an angular face that reflected his experience.

"They tell me you're good at mergers. I want to share a plan with you and see if you can help me carry it out," he said.

He didn't ask me anything personal and got right down to work, walking me through a plan that the noted consulting firm of Booz Allen Hamilton had worked on for over a year. Their assignment was to speculate about how to make Paine Webber one of the leading financial service conglomerates of the future. To strengthen the enterprise, Booz told Don to take his broad base in retail brokerage, add Blyth's corporate finance prowess, and increase other retail capabilities to fill geographic holes and corporate finance opportunities. Mainly, he wanted to acquire investment management capabilities—a large mutual fund or institutional asset management firm—to stabilize the cashflow from the more volatile retail brokerage and corporate finance business. The mutual fund or institutional asset management firm businesses produce steady revenues, as opposed to the more cyclical brokerage business. Don asked me to systematically approach these firms and investigate the possibility of acquiring them. This would ironically be the modus operandi for my future company, Berkshire Capital.

From day one, I learned a lot from him and watched his moves. Don explained the goldrush mentality of the financial markets. When it was going up, everyone jumped in and bought stocks. Making money seemed easy; the bulls ran, sometimes stampeded. But when things got bad, something triggers a turn, and everyone panics. The bears—the short sellers and hard money types—have a field day. It was an endless cycle. There was tremendous leverage in brokerage firms that made a lot of money as the market was going up. But the real secret was survival when the markets were down. The key to getting through the crashes was keeping fixed costs down, paying commissions and bonuses that were variable with volume and profitability. Weaker competitors had neither economic nor franchise value. It was also the time to buy them.

Don was going to build a modern financial service conglomerate. He had a hole in some regional geographic territories, but most significantly had a hole in the asset management business. He wanted me to get to work filling that hole. He was also trying to decide whether to get into the insurance, banking, or commodity business. I would be his assistant for acquisition, as well as responsible for organizing a team of consultants to research new areas of the financial services industry that might seem lucrative or attractive.

Don was terribly persuasive. He previewed the secret corporate plans with me, assuming I couldn't turn him down. On top of that, I could have the pick of his staff for my assistant. He didn't say anything about more pay; this was to be a privileged position, a unique platform to work from if nothing else, and he wanted me to move downtown to corporate headquarters, leave the Corporate Finance Department behind. I didn't mind that since before it settled down into new leadership, it was turning into a hot bed of internecine political warfare. I went back uptown on the phone to Georgia the whole way explaining the position I was just offered who said it was about time I got recognized and maybe we should let this work out? In the office, I called my clients, carefully handing off my projects and contacts to my remaining comrades who were competent enough to handle them properly.

I started as assistant to Chairman Marron on Monday. I had a tiny corner office in the executive suite filled with inspiring original Ansel Adams photographs that I'd later begin to collect. I began interviewing some of the aspiring headquarters' analytical staff associates for my assistant finding that my future partner Bruce Cameron stood out from the rest. He was a Trinity College, HBS, and London School of Economics graduate. He really wanted to be in corporate finance, but with its typical arrogance, the Corporate Finance Department interviewer felt he wasn't aggressive enough, probably because, though he was very intelligent, he was also rather quiet, even shy. Silent waters run deep. I could tell he was a man of integrity. Having been an analyst at Prudential Insurance, he understood the insurance industry and, additionally, had a broad knowledge of the financial services industry beyond his years. We began a working relationship and business partnership that is still going today.

What I learned rapidly was that Don was a quick study, with his own ideas about what to buy, but he wasn't going to pay a premium for anything. This made it very difficult to present a compelling story to potential acquisitions. Don was a bottom-fisher but a persuasive and charming one. He wasn't going to listen to me about valuation but wouldn't embarrass me either. I learned to get meetings, and got to know the industry and its executives, reporting back to Don if we had an attractive prospect.

There was an exceptional group of executives working under Marron. Mike Johnston was the President of the firm and Don's right-hand man. He was principled, something he eventually paid for. Don Nicholson ran the extensive retail branch and generated most of the money. He was a broker's broker—a well-dressed cool customer who got immediate respect and exuded market savvy. We got to know each other well and still exchange Christmas cards, a man of tradition. Tom Wendel was the Chief Financial Officer, a real ruthless wheeler and dealer. He was a sometime friend, unprincipled and ambitious. He tried to recruit Bruce Cameron away from me but later hired us to sell a government bond trading firm he ran. Paul Guenther was the President of the holding company. Paul was most affable and helpful to me but said "yes" to Don Marron too much, seldom standing up to him. Eventually Marron would let him go, and he would chair the New York Symphony's board. Jack Rivkin ran Mitchell Hutchins and was the most interesting and intellectual of the group; I could always speculate about the markets in good humor with him. Howard Berg was Marron's axe man. He and I became really good friends. Every firm (if they are lucky) has a Howard Berg, an executive they send to fix the nasty problems by firing people, hiring people, or reorganizing departments. He could size up any situation and turn up with a unique solution regardless of the course of the markets. I was convinced he could turn any situation around.

Don was a player, so there was adequate deal flow, plus what I was scouring up. We were very selective, passing on some notable deals, such as Franklin Templeton whose executives came to see us, because, lacking retail distribution, they felt unable to expand their firm. They were contemplating going public and wanted to know if we would buy into them at a slight discount before that event. Don wasn't going to pay above what he saw as the true value of a company, but it was a deal we should've done. Lucky for Franklin, they remained independent and grew to the size they are today, with well over $700 billion of assets under management (AUM).

The next was ContiCommodity. The company had had some difficulties and was being offered at book value. Don was attracted by their being in extremis and the resulting price. I was sent to Chicago for a couple of months to learn about the commodity business and found out for Don that he could acquire any firm he wanted to for book value. They were all for sale, cheap! Afterwards, I was riding uptown in the corporate limo with our consultant, the former head of the Commodity Futures Trading Commission, hired to research Conti. He let slip there was a government suit pending against Conti for abetting the Hunt Brothers, who, with great hutzpah, had attempted to corner the silver market. This was the tip of an iceberg that would eventually sink the firm. Luckily, we avoided that one.

It was the Rotan Mosle deal that changed everything for me. The company was a Houston-based brokerage and investment-banking firm. A good friend of mine, Jake Taylor ran their corporate finance business. I'd previously interviewed with them for an M&A position and knew the company well. Luckily, I hadn't joined them since the price of oil had declined significantly, and their business with it. They were losing money, had little hope of turning the company around, lastly hiring Morgan Stanley to sell the business before they went bankrupt. Don and I met with their executives in Morgan's plush offices in NYC, and Don was a bit miffed when they all greeted me before him. They felt a little awkward being on the block and having to confess their sins before the infamous Mr. Marron.

Don knew a good deal when he saw one: a premier oil and gas investment banking firm for sale, provided we had the reserves to take on their debts and potential liabilities, even if the price of oil didn't improve. Bruce and I took the company apart, modeling it into pieces that could be changed given different growth-rate assumptions or that could be broken up and merged with other parts of Paine Webber. This model was interactive and was the basis of an extensive board presentation we gave pushing for the acquisition of the firm. The company sold below its book value. The executives were off the hook for the debt they owed, and the firm would move forward as a division of Paine Webber with its name maintained for a while at least. The owners had no choice since other speculators weren't as brave as Don in acquiring distressed firms.

The board presentation went well. The deal went through. There was to be a closing dinner in Houston, and I thought Bruce and I would be praised for our work. Our expectations were dashed. Don needed a new set of executives to run his freshly acquired division, so at the dinner when the toasts were proposed, he praised the firm and introduced the new slate of executives, but no one who had anything to do with the acquisition. No mention of our efforts. I was flummoxed and realized it would be a repeating pattern.

I was a cog in Don's wheel, expected to grind out acquisition after acquisition and expected, like a good soldier, to nicely cover over the fact we were stealing the business and would tighten the screws further after we acquired it. I was honored to be working for the chairman, and for being a principal with a checkbook rather than an always hustling investment banker. Still, from my vantage point at the top of this company, I could see there was a wave of these acquisitions on the horizon. How could I capitalize on that as an independent advisor, and help clients rather than taking advantage of them as a buyer with superior resources?

I had no capital, just my own wits, some industry knowledge, and the willingness to work extremely hard for much less than I was currently making to get my freedom. I couldn't see over the risk and expense; however, deep down I wanted to be calling the shots. I had to step up and take the risk.

After that dinner, I flew to Hartford the next morning. It was October, and the Berkshires were ablaze in color. I drove with Georgia through Bartholomew's Cobble—a unique nature preserve near our new home there—and began explaining the situation to her. I'd gotten no recognition for an exceptional job and told her I was thinking of starting my own firm. I'd had enough of working for this guy, or for anyone else for that matter.

Georgia took all this in, looked directly at me, and said, "You've been talking about this as long as I've known you. You're an entrepreneur. It's in your blood. You think up your own deals, create them in your sleep. Do this. As soon as you can. But do me a big favor—

if you don't do this, never come home and complain to me about working for someone else."

She threw me into the entrepreneurial pool. I never looked back. I knew my fate at that moment, and exactly what I wanted to do, had to do—risk be damned. But what would be the focus, and where would I get the money? We agreed to give it a shot and if we failed, well Atlanta and Little Sandy were good retreats. We could go back there and start all over as we thought we would do earlier in our careers. There were plenty of fall backs, but we had no children, no debt and lived frugally—we could also spend some time in the Berkshires as Georgia already planned. But the prospect of starting my own firm and tackling Wall Street as I had always wanted to do loomed like a bright brass ring before me. Georgia was 100% behind me. What did I have to lose? I went for the ring!

Founder and CEO Berkshire Capital Corporation, Bruce McEver, 1990s

Chapter 24
Something Said *Berkshire*:
The History of Berkshire Capital—Part II

I spent the next three months refining my focus, doing my due diligence, and raising the funds necessary to start my own independent investment bank that would focus on merger advisory work. For my specialty, I considered the oil and gas business, the telecommunications industry, and financial services. I had done mergers in all those industry segments, with the most experience in energy, but it was right in front of me the whole time. While the energy and communications industries were in the midst of major consolidations at the time, the financial services business (specifically the securities industry) was about to be supercharged, facing a tidal wave of consolidations when and if Glass-Steagall legislation changed. The Glass-Steagall Act was implemented post the 1929 crash and separated investment banking in the capital and stock markets from commercial banking. Its neighbor, the asset management business, was also ripe for consolidation from outside it. These management companies were stable cashflow businesses that grew as the assets under management (AUM) grew with a most-of-the-time rising market. Fees were derived from a small percentage charge on AUM and threw off a steady stream of profits. These profits were needed by the more volatile brokerage business, but also by the banking and insurance industries, which were hungry for more fee revenues as interest rates dropped and their core-spread businesses became less profitable. To add to the rush to merge, interstate banking legislation was about to change, allowing banks to acquire other banks across state lines. I could see it all happening with these businesses coming together, but reality was slower than my vision. I was cautiously gathering my courage to jump into the fray.

I had an interesting meeting with Morris Schapiro, a renowned bank analyst. He had a mining engineering degree from MIT and instead decided to mine the banking industry with his knowledge of it, both as an investor and investment banker. He'd managed the merger between Chase and Manhattan Banks. His fee for this milestone transaction was large enough to use part of it for a lease on entire 32nd floor of the bank tower. There, he thrived with his team, investing in bank stocks.

"What you want to do in the financial services industry is not be one of the Indians on either side of the river fighting one another but making the bows and arrows for them. Be a supplier of advice. Stay out of the consolidation that'll happen when interstate banking laws and Glass-Steagall change. Drive an ambulance in this war and it's going to be a big one." Morris felt the banking merger business had too many investment banks serving it. Banks reported all their statistics and financials to government regulators—it was too visible and monitored. He suggested I try the security markets or the investment management business where the numbers were still private and reportable only for public firms. A small firm would have an advantage in dealing with private firms, who could choose to give confidential financials needed for merger work only if they chose to. That was it. The Glass-Steagall Act was under attack. The banks needed new services and fee revenue streams from the investment banking and asset management industries. The asset management business additionally appealed to me because I liked to invest and liked the money managers who ran the industry.

The securities business could be a bonanza if the legislation changed. This was where I'd concentrate first. I could clearly see the allure of being an independent firm working among securities and other financial services firms. In fact, I wondered why others hadn't already done this. Traditional investment banks worked as generalists across industry segments, fighting over the quality of their client lists instead of specializing in these segments. When working for Don, I tried to convince our Investment Banking Department about the logic of concentrating by industry, but they would have none of it. That wasn't the way the traditional investment banking business worked, so why was I so sure it would? Most investment banks have something to sell, a product or a point of view, but my approach would be neutral, objective, and untainted by anything other than solid objective advice for the client. I just had to raise the money to enable my little firm to play among the giants and try not to be stepped on.

Bruce Cameron confided he also thought it would be a good specialty and that he'd be interested in coming along with me. He was tired of working for a big firm and was convinced—as was I—we were in for a period of consolidation. Bruce was key in my firm's formation because he had the technical and computer skills I lacked, plus I needed someone else in the office, a comrade.

I wrote a business plan and started raising money using industry statistics and thinking about who might chip in for the cause. We didn't need that much. I decided to take a salary of $75,000 and Bruce agreed to $35,000—frugal by industry-standards at the time. Marilee Scheunemann, who was my assistant with Don, was now unemployed, said she'd come with us as our office manager. We knew we could get a sublease cheap on Wall Street. I thought I needed to raise $200,000 to $500,000, eventually starting when I had $300,000. This wasn't a lot of money for a start-up, even then, but would be enough to get us through a dry year and a half. I'd made enough at Blyth to repay my loans. Importantly, Georgia and I didn't lead an extravagant lifestyle. If worse came to worse, I didn't need to pay myself. This was a strategic advantage compared to most middle-aged entrepreneurs with higher family overheads. I could eat sawdust, and for my freedom, it was worth it.

I made a careful list of friends and family. Neither my father nor his twin brother understood what I did. I didn't push them because I didn't want to live with them if I failed. But my in-laws were wealthier and could take the risk. Wallace Lanahan, my brother-in law's father, was one of the wealthiest men in Baltimore and had owned and run an investment bank he sold to Bache & Co. He'd also been a paratrooper who'd gone into Normandy. Wallace needed little explanation and wrote me a check on the spot. He never sent a contact but constantly encouraged me and profited handsomely. Perrin Long, the renowned security industry analyst working with Mike Lipper, was an important early endorser and investor who would supply invaluable industry connections. He, the industry's seer, was convinced there would be a merger wave as well, which added to my confidence. Another important early supporter was my HBS classmate, Tom Barry, who then was running the Rockefeller family office and was also a grief confidant. He enthusiastically wrote a check for twice what I asked him for and somehow knowing I was going to succeed.

Georgia's uncle, Ralph Johnson was the heir to her family's tent and canvas business that had grown and profited during WWII and Korea and was Sears' primary supplier. I sat down with him and explained what I was up to, and at the end of the conversation, he wrote me a check and wanted to nominate me to be a member of the Chicago Club whose members ran the city's businesses. He had amazing contacts and got us some of our biggest earliest clients, including Northern Trust, and

Chicago Title and Trust, among others. In starting a business, often the most unlikely sources turn out to be your most valuable.

Others proved quite illusive and disappointing—not every ask gained results. While still trying to complete my financing, I was surprisingly called by a most sophisticated man from Los Angeles. Rockwell Schnabel had a venture portfolio of mid-sized asset managers and securities firms he wanted managed and expanded. These firms were unremarkable in themselves, but it was remarkable they were all in the financial services industry; thus, Rock and I had congruent interests. Still, he was a principal and put his money where his mouth was. He heard I was raising money to focus on financial services and flew me out to LA to see his firms, including several money managers and a position in Wedbush & Co., a local respected brokerage company Rock was on the board of. We hit it off, and he initially wanted to hire me to run his venture portfolio.

I had to tell him I wasn't interested in his original proposal, but I persuaded him to make a large investment in my firm, arguing he would obtain a bi-coastal perspective. I'd feed him deals, and my niche business might even prove to be valuable as well. He agreed but asked for warrants or options for more stock that I couldn't give others. When he exercised his warrants, he'd effectively have acquired his stock for less than my other holders. I was trying to keep a level playing field and found it tough to go back to my other equity holders to explain this dilution for them, but they agreed to it, as his $125,000 investment sealed the deal and put us in business. Rock was invaluable as a mentor and backer, not to mention that he plugged us into his West Coast contacts. He would become the US Ambassador to Finland and later the EU, and in his living room in Finland, Gorbachev and Ronald Reagan had their famous meeting, ending the Cold War. Rock remains a good friend and confidant today and has sent us much business over the years.

I'd been in the market for almost three months, had talked to probably forty people, and found eight willing to write checks. With each of these investors, I got access to their contacts and their market wisdom. I didn't have a formal Board of Directors, but this was the closest thing to it, and as equity holders, they were all motivated to see me succeed in order to get their money back many times over, and they did. I told Bruce and Marilee we'd start in October and decided to take the rest of September off with Georgia at our new Berkshire home, but first I had to find an office.

I learned to look at subleases downtown where rents were considerably cheaper than in Midtown. It'd involve a commute for me, but I didn't mind. I would soon have my own company and office. I found a three-office suite on the 30th floor at 30 Broad. It was a two-year sublease from a bankrupt insurance broker, including the furniture. The building was filled with specialist firms. As a bonus each morning, in the building's elevator, just listening to the floor brokers and traders talk, we got to know Wall Street's heartbeat.

That done, I went away with Georgia to our cabin overlooking the Housatonic. I journaled about my experiences raising capital and read some of Campbell's books to assure myself I was on my own path. Business called. I had to find a name for the firm. I looked out over the foothills of the Berkshires, up the Housatonic Valley from Hulbert's Hill to Monument Mountain in the distance with the Taconic Range on my left. Something said "Berkshire" because Georgia and I lived there, loved the place, and felt the charm in the name. Berkshire Capital sounded wealthy and distinguished.

Georgia and I biked to the beach club down our road to swim in the lake, often having lunch there and sometimes staying to watch the sun set. I had time to read and write again and felt relaxed and confident about starting the firm. Georgia was proud of me and told me so, regardless of what happened. I had a great sense that the company was going to work and that I was at the right place at the right time. The Fates, however, wanted success to take much longer than I ever imagined, possibly to test me.

When I returned to the city, I saw Don and told him I was starting my own firm. He congratulated me and said he'd done the same thing. He wished me well, saying I'd never regret it, and if I failed, I could come back. He also said that if I never tried, I'd kick myself for the rest of my life. I said I'd prefer an investment or retainer from him, and he said he'd think seriously about it. Some thirty years later he would make good his intent and hired our firm for an assignment.

Bruce, Marilee, and I moved to our office at the beginning of October 1983. We were launched and found we also had a roommate that came along with the furniture, Milos Knorr. He was an insurance broker and taught Bruce and me that industry. He was also a genuine hero, having led the Czechoslovakian troops ashore on D-Day with the medals to prove it. We put a tombstone in the *Wall Street Journal*, and I waited for the phone to ring. I soon learned that wasn't how it worked. The only response to our expensive ad was a clipping I received in the mail a few weeks later from John McArthur, my section advisor and former dean of the Harvard Business School. Across our ad, he'd scribbled: "Wow. All the way from Georgia!" I learned I had to be on the phone constantly, calling my contacts to introduce myself and my firm's services to broker dealers and asset management firms. Better yet was to be out on the road to talk to potential clients face-to-face. It was pure hustle that generated business. I had to start a whirlwind to get a tornado going.

I learned the securities industry had a major conference once a year in November at Boca Raton, so Georgia and I went that year. I met the head of every broker dealer who attended. I learned that the industry leaders weren't anxious about the repeal of Glass-Steagall, relying on Congress to drag the process out. Beginning to make these contacts was invaluable and how I built the business. I really liked and respected the men who ran the securities industry, and they reciprocated by introducing me to many other contacts and explored entering the asset management industry with me. The key element for their confidence and referrals, I confirmed here, was being an independent firm and a neutral entity.

I called on the banks to try to convince them to stake out positions in the securities firms, but they were bureaucracies and had other priorities. They considered the brokerage business risky, but the fee-generating asset management business was attractive to them. A few were waking up to this reality as interest rates lowered and their traditional spread-business shrank. Asset management is a lucrative cashflow business that generates fees from the amount of assets a firm manages. Still, the best money managers didn't want to work for stodgy banks. Things needed to get worse in the market, or banks had to pay up to acquire these firms to convince them to merge. To convince them to do anything at all was going to be a slow road. I often felt like a missionary out there trying to convince the big banks to enter into more profitable and sometimes riskier lines of business, then painfully explaining how we'd charge them for this work. I didn't think we'd have a deal for our first annual meeting in October 1984. Fatefully I got a call from my former boss and friend Noel Urban. He'd been laid off at Blyth but had gone over to Banker's Trust where he ran a leverage buyout team where he'd made them and himself millions.

Noel had a good friend, David Halmrast, who was an assistant treasurer at Owens-Illinois (O-I), the glass company. Owning 35% of the world's glass industry, they were gushing cash and couldn't invest any further in the glass business because of antitrust concerns. O-I was forced to diversify into other industries and had hired an outside consulting firm Bain & Co., who had come up with the financial services industry as a place to invest and diversify their business—specifically the mortgage banking business.

David came to see me in New York, and we hit it off right away. He'd been an investment banker with a Midwest firm where he'd worked with Noel, before going to O-I. He oversaw their diversification program, and while there were plenty of consultants willing to offer advice, there were few investment bankers who were up for the trench-warfare searches necessary in the financial services industry's consolidation that became our hallmark. The big investment banks like to do large, one-off deals, but in a widely scattered and consolidating industry like the mortgage banking industry, the right targets weren't obvious, nor was the management who could then build a larger business from a base with O-I's resources. It required discernment and experience. I could smell a great deal coming.

The next call I got was David alerting me that he wanted me to meet his boss Jerry Boland, the CFO of O-I. We met on a sunny day at the NYC Harvard Club. Jerry was intimidating with big bushy eyebrows, and he looked right through you. Why should he—the largest glass company in the world—hire this upstart bank when he had the senior partners of the world's major investment banks calling on him, offering to help him spend that river of cash? While my background and experience weren't much at that point, I told him he was ahead of others since the financial services business was soon to consolidate nationwide as I'd learned while I was in charge of diversification for the chairman of Paine Webber. This project would put O-I ahead of the pack. We'd give him customized service that he wouldn't get from a larger bank whose senior partners would get the business and hand it over to some new MBA anyway, but with Berkshire Capital, I'd do it myself. I also had experience in digging out good merger deals, could talk with experienced managers in the mortgage banking business and be damn sure they got the best firm available. There wasn't a long list of investment bankers who would go company to company to find them the right firm. It must have been persuasive because David called back, saying we were hired.

Soon, I got a call from his assistant treasurer who said O-I had already targeted a factoring business—a company that financed a manufacturing firm's accounts receivables—out of Cleveland that had been brought to them by another firm. They'd done the analysis and wanted me to take an offer letter to this firm to negotiate a deal. I went back to the office, and Bruce and I took apart National Financial Factoring. We confirmed their estimate evaluation and made some suggestions on the structure, primarily reducing the amount paid down and increasing the earn-out. I was off to make my first deal.

The treasurer wanted to retain us and asked what we charged. I sensed he was not price sensitive and asked what he thought was fair. He said about $250,000, and then they'd take that out of the completion fee. Used to dealing with the big investment banks, this was so much above what we'd have charged, I agreed, and he sent me a check for an amount it had taken me three months to raise. I thought we were suddenly in the big leagues.

I had the offer letter in my briefcase and was on the train to the airport when I opened the *Wall Street Journal*. National Factoring Co. had been acquired that morning for a price well in excess of what we were willing to pay. Good for them, bad for us. I turned around when I got to the airport and called my client. O-I was not eager to get into a bidding contest, so I had to send that check back. We had a little ceremony in the office, disbelieving that we had that much money in hand one day and had to return it the next, but onward—the next one would be larger. We negotiated a more modest retainer for the mortgage banking project, but a higher completion fee. This long-term project involved going to Toledo during winter to visit O-I's high-rise headquarters by the lake and then turning around and spending time in their corporate apartment on Central Park South when the management team wanted to come to NYC.

We visited mortgage banking companies all over the country, even going to industry conferences and finally found the mortgage banking subsidiary of Florida National Bank. They seriously considered selling their mortgage banking subsidiary, Alliance Mortgage, because the parent bank needed the capital. It was the opportunity we were waiting for. This was the 17th largest mortgage bank in the country, a right-sized platform to build a much larger business since the mortgage banking industry could be scaled like manufacturing, a business O-I understood. Also, its Southeast location made it well situated for regional growth. The mortgage bank was headed by Mac McGriff, an entrepreneurial president, who wanted to grow his business and for a while, would do so with O-I behind him, but soon ran into industry and economic headwinds.

We negotiated the deal along with Lazard—O-I's investment bank—who had to give their blessing to the financial terms, something north of $120 million. Our fee would be over $1 million and needed to be approved by the O-I finance committee. David's call saying our fee was actually to be higher—at $1.2 million—made our firm. We'd come close to running out of money, and in the last months before we closed this deal, I didn't take a paycheck. Now, we'd never look back. We were covering our overhead with retainers from other projects, so I could invest this money in a core municipal bond portfolio that we didn't have to pay full taxes on and invest the rest with money managers, who, with prudent risk, could grow it nicely. This was to be our bedrock capital we grew for our initial years in business. We celebrated with champagne in the office before we went home. Georgia and I celebrated at a fancy restaurant that evening—the Box Tree in NYC. The next morning, I ran in the park, and watching the sun's first rays illuminate the top of a gothic apartment tower, knew I was never going to suffer for money again. I felt as though I'd finally arrived in the big city.

Bruce and sister, Sharon, with King, 1950s

Chapter 25
On Our Way Uptown:
The History of Berkshire Capital—Part III

The future is before us now; it's just unevenly distributed...
The Future Institute, Palo Alto, CA

We'd gotten lucky with O-I, but I wasn't basking in the glory. After launching my little ship, we had to change course drastically. During 1984, our first year in existence, we'd survived on some minimal retainers and those from O-I. Overhead had been chewing through reserves, and if we hadn't closed O-I in February 1985, we'd have been out of money. Our original plan to get rich quick on security firms' mergers wasn't going to happen anytime soon. Congress wasn't going to eliminate Glass-Steagall, and in fact, didn't get around to it for another fifteen years. The hype had been premature. We needed another game plan.

Again, we had the answer right in front of us. The banks we called on to persuade to buy brokerage firms were actually more interested in strengthening their asset management businesses. They began to realize these would generate good fee business in times of narrowing loan spreads. They could buy more assets under management (AUM) and acquire the talent to manage them. We ran across a little money manager—Howe & Rusling in upstate New York—that was a test case for us. Bruce did most of the work, since he had a natural affinity for money managers and was, unbeknownst to me, working on becoming a Certified Financial Analyst (CFA) to relate better to these companies. He also seemed to have an affinity for test-taking. We sold the firm to Key Banks shortly after we closed the O-I deal. Though bringing in a much smaller fee, it was a harbinger of our future.

There was a handful of managers in each city who managed money for wealthy individuals or institutions or both. These money-management firms did a nice business and couldn't be bothered to sell them until they tried to capitalize their rich cashflow assets and found there was no market, so they passed them along to their partners, and if lucky, they had partners capable of paying something for them, maybe book value, or possibly one-times revenues. Then we came along and found that there were banks that would pay as much as three times revenues or more for these small private businesses. We were pioneers, and Berkshire Capital was the first to discover this new marketplace for money management businesses. This was the beginning of a marketplace that we never looked back on and became the market leader in terms of number of transactions. It wasn't a clear path—the big banks were slow, but there was a market for asset management firms developing, and we were right in the middle of helping it happen.

After O-I closed, I breathed a bit easier, so I went to London to check out that market. I targeted and called on many money managers and brokers. Ironically, I arrived in the middle of the London market in turmoil. Regulators had unleashed Big Bang, meaning banks—including foreign ones—were allowed to buy entire brokerage firms. This was the end of the British equivalent of Glass-Steagall. It was a free for all—deals happening right and left. Phoenix Securities was an independent London investment bank, focusing on the securities industry like us and was enjoying the deal orgy that was underway. I'd been right and was in the right place, just fifteen years ahead of my time.

The epicenter of world finance moved with the dominant world power, but I could see the future market in the old one. As the former capital of the financial world, London had been succeeded by New York City after WWI, but I could see the future of the US market. There was consolidation among London's asset management firms before there was any consolidation in the US. So, in order to compete, they had to invest internationally. The center of international asset managers was actually in Edinburgh around Charlotte Square. These were the people competing with the Swiss managers, like IOS I had worked for in Geneva. I visited every firm there but couldn't convince any of them to sell a small portion of their firms to American firms needing to diversify their product line-up internationally. They were all doing very well on their own, thank you, but missed taking advantage of it and soon many would break up and their managers leaving to start new firms. International investing was to become the wave of the future.

In London, I learned never to ask for a breakfast meeting—no one does anything so crass as business before ten in the morning. That custom had changed with Big Bang and the influx of Americans. I filled up a week of appointments, making many valuable contacts such as Jamie Ogilvie and Andrew Martin Smith, both who would play a role in Berkshire's future. I also met Peter Darling who ran Warburg's asset management subsidiary, Mercury Asset Management (MAM) that would later hire us to be their banker in the US and acquire companies there. Peter was a colorful character, and Korean war veteran, who wrote an excellent book on the history of MAM and the London asset management business, titled *City Cinderella*. Peter became a good friend I saw many times I went to London who encouraged my writing. He sadly just recently passed away.

I could see that the smaller firms were struggling to survive with the cost and overhead from excessive regulation and merging, while the open-door policy of the British Regulator in the security industry (Big Bang) had almost eliminated their domestic brokerage industry, perhaps a mistake in hindsight. Many brokers lost jobs to cost efficiencies, and old, good names were shelved as history. This was a harbinger for the US. Mainly cost-driven, the consolidation of the asset management industry would continue at a slower pace in the US. But American firms with international investment expertise would have a strategic advantage necessary for future survival; if not, it was imperative they acquire or develop it on their own, which many did.

Also in London, I got to know Hikmat Nashashibi, a very savvy man who ran the Kuwait Investment Corporation. He was a Palestinian who'd studied at the London School of Economics and had a nose for the markets, and, through OPEC, insight of where the price of oil was heading. I spent many an enjoyable evening talking world economics with Hikmat. He was intrigued by the capital markets in New York and thought he could build a brokerage firm with a base in New York and attach an international investment company to it. He'd sell the broker and keep the asset manager. He wanted me to be on the lookout for a good base in the brokerage business in the US for him.

Upon returning, I spent my time calling on my security industry/broker-dealer friends. They were more entrepreneurial than the money managers or banks and always turned up deals for us. A number were either in the money management business or contemplating entering through acquisition. The financial service business was blurring, with everyone getting into the stable, fee-generating asset management business. We would benefit merging these businesses.

I learned to react quickly when an opportunity presented itself. I was in Philadelphia with Jon Buckley, the CEO of a brokerage firm conglomerate he put together called Moseley Hallgarten, Estabrook & Weeden Holdings. We were looking to buy a municipal bond broker dealer called

Dolphin & Bradbury that we'd represent the following year. It was a fine old Philly muni broker, probably fifty years old. Jon was having a serious conversation, coming close to making a deal when he was interrupted by an urgent message and returned to the room ashen.

He said we had to go back to New York on the next train. I asked what was wrong. John said the market for treasury bond coupons (called "tinnies") where his firm was a leader had collapsed—his firm was probably bankrupt. These coupons were early futures contracts on the treasury bonds, and the government had suddenly decided to issue them themselves, thus crushing the market and the dealers like him who "stripped" the treasury bonds of their coupons and sold them. Jon had a thriving business one day and was bankrupt the next. He was inconsolable as he ran out of quarters and his credit card line, frantically calling New York in the train's phone booth. I had a great deal of respect for Jon and what he'd built. I was proud he'd chosen to work with me and my firm to build his business. I felt awful for him.

Remembering the conversation with Hikmat, I told Jon I might have another solution, but he wasn't in the mood to listen. I called Hikmat anyway and got a call back later that week. He wanted to introduce me to his partner Omar, who was looking to buy an American broker in New York. Did I have a deal for him? I asked him to meet me the morning after his arrival, so I could introduce him to the CEO of such a firm. I called Jon and told him I thought I had someone who could help him out. He said it was hopeless, but he had no other solutions. Out of nowhere, we were going to put together a major brokerage acquisition, save a firm, and create an international money management company. Fate rarely aligns itself so perfectly, but this looked like the perfect storm.

We met at the Carlyle Hotel. Jon looked haggard but was ready to listen. Hikmat and Omar were curious. I asked Hikmat to begin with his background from rags (literally) to riches, his vision of the world, introduce Omar, and detail what they wanted to create. Jon perked up, a new man, so I asked him to explain what had happened to bankrupt the company and about the divisions that were being spun off as management left the sinking ship. We got through all the gory details, and Hikmat said they'd like to proceed. It was rare to find such a base, and a firm with this reputation and location.

Long story short, we put the deal together. We found a CEO for New York, Howard Berg, my friend and Paine Webber's former axe

man, and Omar would serve as CEO in London. Hikmat would be
Chairman. Jon took early retirement, and Moseley was saved and was
being rebuilt. We were so confident this was going to be a homerun that
we took our entire fee in the stock of the new Moseley Hallgarten. The
share certificate hangs on my office wall today—worthless.

As it got busier, we needed to add to our staff. We even corralled
Bruce Cameron's brother Ross, a photographer, to help put together
our presentations. I came in one morning and found Ross curled on our
couch with the books he'd put together for a pitch we were to give that
day. Such was his devotion to getting the job done. Diligence and per-
sistence run long in the Cameron clan. About this time, I got a letter from
the president of the New York chapter of the Chief Financial Analyst
Society, telling me that Bruce had passed his exams. I wasn't surprised
but wondered when Bruce had time to study working the hours we did.
To this day, we require all our analysts to qualify for their CFA designa-
tion—the asset management gold standard.

We'd opened a checking account at US Trust (UST) when we started
the company because it was the class act in private banking in NYC.
Our account officer, Barbara O'Connell, who always looked out for
us, wanted us to meet Chairman Marshall Schwarz because he had a
strategic plan we might be able to help execute. Bruce and I went to see
him and his CEO, Jeff Mauer. They laid out their project. US Trust was
the oldest trust company in the country, started by a group of Wall Street
tycoons to manage their money in trust after they passed away. UST was a
venerable and stodgy organization with only one office in NYC. Marshall
and Jeff decided they couldn't grow the firm unless UST got out of town
and bought or started branches in other, faster-growing wealth markets.
They were going to break out of the mold. The first place UST wanted to
go was California, specifically Los Angeles, the first of multiple locations.
Could we help? Naturally, they'd talked to other investment banks, but
our expertise was clear, and the big banks turned up their noses at these
smaller transactions. Ours was going to be a long-term relationship, and
we have repeated similar assignments for numerous larger financial firms
to this day. These deals take careful hunting and few of the larger firms
have the patience nor the expertise to do.

What I knew from my travels was that most large US cities had a
couple of brokers and a handful of investment counselors who knew
all the wealthy people in town and who managed their money. There

existed a network in every city comprised of a number of entrepreneurs and excellent investors running money in every town, usually not visible, beneath the radar, and rarely marketing themselves, thus our kind of firm, the type we had to dig out for our clients. Each deal plugged us into the high-net-worth circle of successive cities, rarefied spaces that are not easily accessible. This became an invaluable, almost nation-wide network of contacts for my firm.

The problem with most money managers, however, is while they are great money managers, they aren't interested in marketing for new clients, usually waiting for their business to walk in the door. UST was different and marketing oriented. They could add clients to the platforms they acquired. This was a highly replicable assignment. We took on UST and called on our shareholder Rock Schnabel and then Joan Payden. They gave us a list of managers they knew personally and could vet their quality for us. We began calling, soon finding Frank Ulf at Summit Management. We did the deal with him and after a year, had to tear up the operating agreement as the earn-out incentives, originally based on profitability, were meaningless. UST was spending so much money on marketing and expansion, there were no profits. US Trust would eventually do sixteen expansion deals across the country, fourteen that we initiated and sealed. They'd diversify the company spectacularly. Eventually, it would be acquired by Charles Schwab, who sadly destroyed its country-club-of-money-management-strategy culture.

In a couple of years, we'd also get calls from other banks to do the same thing for them—the principal one being Northern Trust. But then something exciting happened, we got a call from the Bank in Liechtenstein. The prince himself wanted to acquire a money manager in the US the way a French and an Arab client and UST had. We were becoming known as the place foreign firms could come to and find the right partner in the US asset management business. We subsequently acquired Trainer, Wortham & Co., one of the oldest money management companies in the country for him. This developed into a most interesting relationship, but the rest of the year was dominated by the securities industry where trouble was developing.

Bob Prindiville at Thomson, McKinnon Securities hired us to acquire Carolina Securities. Bob also introduced us to the top management of Commerz Bank, who were thinking of coming into

the US to buy money managers. By the end of the year, Dolphin &
Bradbury hired us to merge them with a local bank, First Eastern. We
were also hired by Integrated Resources (IR), a fast-growing securities
and financial services conglomerate, to acquire other broker dealers.
This assignment would lead to other significant contacts in the
broker/dealer community as the market was becoming overextended;
the bulls were about to run over the cliff. We were hired by Piper,
Jaffrey in Minneapolis when they were crippled by a rogue trader
forcing them to sell their venerated franchise to a bank as reflected in
this poem, "The Falls of the Mississippi:"

> At Minneapolis the Corps of Engineers managed
> to collar in a cement straight jacket
> the river's sandstone cliffs
> where the Blackfeet believed
> the Great Spirit once lived...
> [and] did away with any mist or roar.
>
> Along the river's bluffs
> the hulls of old flower mills
> that made this town's first money,
> await renovation into hotels or demolition.
> Glass towers defining the modern city…
>
> [whose] buildings have begun to lose
> their local owners to distant mergers.
>
> Like the one with the family's name on it,
> where I worked, after a rogue trader crippled it.
> They agonized over how to rescue the franchise
> their grandfather started. A big bank showed up
> making it easier to take a profit
> than save a tradition.
>
> At the bottom of the muffled falls
> the great river begins
> its 2500-mile course to the sea
> with a mad, muddy boil.

Even nature protested some mergers that was slowly consolidating away local ownership of the financial services business that supported local jobs, causes and charities. For IR we first tried another old-line brokerage firm in Philadelphia, Butcher & Singer (B&S), an over-200-year-old business. The meeting with B&S was a good one. We seemed to relate to the management, particularly the son of the founder, Jon Butcher, and his CEO, Dick Miles, but they wouldn't have anything to do with IR. The meeting proved fateful in many other ways the following year, but by year-end, we represented the insatiable IR, buying another firm in extremis—the Financial Clearing Company—it closed in two months. We'd done four deals that year. We moved from our downtown starter office to the 52nd floor of the Chrysler Building, sharing the floor with the largest producer of the Massachusetts Mutual Insurance Company, who became a major client. We were on our way uptown.

Harold McEver and Twin Brother, William, at Chattanooga
Air Show, 1930s

Chapter 26
The Crash of 1987: Meeting the Green Knight
The History of Berkshire Capital—Part IV

"As their meeting began, an elderly knight entered the hall. With him was the young man Lancelot had knighted the evening before. He was Galahad, Lancelot's son by Elaine. He took his rightful place at the Siege Perilous. Shortly later, an image of the Holy Grail appeared, floating over the table. It was a sign. It was time for Arthur and his knights to seek out the Grail."

Le Morte Darthur
Sir Thomas Malory

Joseph Campbell's nuclear theme was the hero's journey, exemplified by the Arthurian legends, and during the time of building up Berkshire Capital, I often thought what I was doing resembled the quest of these ancient knights. On a smaller scale and subconsciously, I came to feel that I was like King Arthur forming his Round Table, attracting both veteran and apprentice knights to be our shareholders, partners, and officers. They, in turn, were on their quests. We were all on the hero's journey.

We'd added expertise in new areas through additional partners: Steve Sheppard, who ran real estate investment banking at Paine Webber, and Glenna Webster who'd been a principal officer at the General Motors Pension Fund and who knew the asset management business cold. Glenna approached us, and she'd round out our expanded office. A Smith graduate and a great writer, Glenna brought much-needed balance to our all-male team. Additionally, Hoyt Ammidon—an experienced investment banker from E. F. Hutton whose father had been the renowned chairman of the US Trust company—would join us. Lastly was Don Miller, who was a first-class investment banker and who I'd mentored under at Blyth. He sub-let space from us, running the NYC office of Greylock Partners, the Boston venture capital firm. Here he concentrated on leverage buyouts for them and was an invaluable resource of advice and contacts for us. We continued to build a strong circle of associates and business contacts. Some of these friendships have lasted over the years—such as my long association with Don Miller, who became the

Chairman of Axiom Investment Partners—a firm that has enriched all who are associated with them including me.

In early fall of 1987, life was good and the market ebullient, hitting an all-time high in August. On a Friday afternoon, taking the most important papers and leaving the rest for the movers, we left our starter space overlooking the Battery and harbor for the Chrysler Building. Our office manager Marilee carried our beautiful carved wild-goose decoy on the subway to the new space, so it could grace the new central bookcase. We got some good furniture with the deal and a hell of a Midtown view from the 52nd floor that looked out over the building's gargoyles.

We got to know Joe Galgano, our suitemate across the hall. As a huge producer for MassMutual Insurance Co., Joe had introduced us to their Chief Investment Officer, Richard Dooley. Like O-I, Dooley and his company were considering diversifying into the mutual fund business for the first time in the company's history and would become a key contact. Building off our O-I experience and Joe's endorsement, we were the leading candidate for the job. To hit a big deal for MassMutual would be to find the Grail.

During the time I'd been in business for myself I'd learned three things. First, the industry was comprised of entrepreneurs who supported and trusted one another, and who helped other entrepreneurs out. When I first left Paine Webber, I didn't know where to go for technical and legal advice, but I found I could hire such advice or there was a network of CEOs who'd give guidance on a solution to a problem and/or who would identify the best folks in each technical area. Correspondingly, the CEOs called me when they ran across something that fit our strengths or recommended us to potential clients. It was a vast network of knowledge and connections—a safety net stronger than the intercompany connections I once thought secure, but that actually came with the additional baggage of political payback and jealousy.

Second, I learned I had to get out there and make these connections. Seek and ye will find. Go on the quest. I had to show up face-to-face because much of what I was dealing with was confidential, and people wouldn't tell me they were thinking about selling a company or acquiring something unless we sat across from one another. I had to pull it out of them, or extract it with my enthusiasm, and always display integrity in my dealings. They came to know they could trust me—that I'd act on the information with confidentiality and honor. I don't know

in the Zoom age—given that time and travel advantages are manifold—
what will replace in-person connection?

The playing field was on and around a hierarchy of investment
banking—an oligopoly—with a handful of firms at the top and many
regional players below. There were beginning to be some specialty
boutiques like us filling industry sectors. We competed fair and square,
respecting others' territory, but we also competed using our wits and
ideas, and our industry expertise gave us an advantage even over the
big guys. There was another advantage in being a member of this
club—as an oligopoly, the big guys didn't break on pricing transac-
tion fees, so we could price our merger fees right below them without
having to resort to charging by the hour. However, there was no end
to competition in this business, and soon, several specialty firms like
ours emerged. Berkshire Capital has survived to this day as one of the
largest and oldest independent firms.

Third, this industry ran on an honor code. Investment banking was
one of the last blood sports, but you had to play honorably. Your word
was your bond. Don't violate a confidence. Return a favor and go one
better. Some people traded in rumor and confidential information, which
was illegal. Don't go there. And don't go for the last cent because a deal
negotiated too toughly will come back to haunt everyone, like a rock
in your shoe. I found I got farther being clear, honest, and direct. My
principles were serving me well. Starting my business was adventurous,
but it was about to become treacherous as well.

The Green Knight, Arthur's legendary foil, rode boldly to challenge
our Round Table in the form of the 1987 market crash. Precipitated
by a seemingly innocent collapse in far eastern markets—starting in
Thailand—the crash spread around the world like a pandemic in a day. It
was accelerated by the Knight's modern guise of technologically driven
"program trading." This riskless "portfolio insurance" broke down under
old-fashioned panic and drove markets past their stops the first time
since stops had been instituted to help stabilize a market in extremis; the
next trading day the market continued its downward slide.

Being an investor who'd survived the 1974 crash and thus constantly
followed the market through our clients and contacts, I felt the markets
were ahead of themselves, but I hadn't experienced a bear market
from the merger business side. It happened on Monday, October 19,
1987— known as Black Monday—with the largest one-day percentage

decline (22.61%) in history. The market started to deteriorate Friday and thankfully closed over the weekend. I was in the Berkshires on a fieldtrip with Trustees of Reservations—the oldest land trust in the world, where I was a new trustee.

On a gorgeous fall day, Georgia and I were paddling on the Quabbin Reservoir, a placid lake in the middle of Massachusetts, hearing a nature lecture via canoe tour. There was an older couple in the canoe next to us. I recognized Mr. Johnson, the owner of Fidelity—probably the largest broker and money manager in the country. I introduced myself and said, "It looks like we're in for a downer?"

He smiled. "This is a big one. I've got to go back to the office this afternoon, but it's nice to be out here to take my mind off it. Good luck and be sure to fasten your seatbelts!" The man had built one of the great investment houses in the world and of course would survive but was wonderfully human about it with me.

While Wall Street panicked, all our deals seemed intact. Like a great storm at sea, the CEO's prayer is: "Please Lord, get me through this." The fallout was severe but precipitated opportunities as well. Thompson McKinnon had us rush to Charlotte to visit and bid for the floundering Carolina Securities. Meanwhile, downtown, Financial Clearing Company was going under when I arrived to answer an urgent call for help. They needed a life-saving idea. I knew Integrated Resources was fearless and could move fast. They acquired what was left of the firm before the end of the year. We brokered four deals before the end of that year, acquiring a reputation as a company that moved swiftly to assist firms in trouble, as well as one that found the right partners for our clients, even in extremis.

The crash was also terrifying because it dried up business confidence. Our brokered deals at the end of 1987 and into 1988 were with firms in trouble and that had to act. Everyone else retreated to their safe castles and looked out over the ramparts until it was all right to put down the drawbridge and take over some adjacent territory, but none ventured too far from home. It was touch-and-go with all our deals after the '87 crash, but then we got another call from a firm we'd tried to acquire for Integrated Resources (IR). This deal was to take up most of the next year and was unforgettable as it unfolded.

The management at Butcher & Singer (B&S) remembered us from our earlier solicitation for (IR). Butcher was a 200-year-old firm that started when Philadelphia was the financial capital of the US. They were unimpressed by IR but now needed our help. With the crash pushing them to the brink, they were losing money on a monthly basis. Needing to find a champion, they contacted their neighboring investment bank in Richmond, Virginia, Wheat First Securities, a venerable white shoe firm, headed by the epitome of a Virginia gentlemen, James Wheat. B&S wanted it to appear they had other investment banks willing to buy the firm if Wheat put the squeeze on during negotiations. So, my role was to create that illusion of many suitors, but after I reviewed the financials, it was clear they were hemorrhaging cash. Jon Butcher, the founder's son, now CEO, had sold some oil and gas deals that had gone sour with the declining market. Additionally, they'd sold a minority interest to the Count and Countess of Thurn & Taxis who'd made their fortune owning the German Post Office. They'd seen the same financials and put the pressure on Jon to sell his firm while he still had a book value and could. The firm was truly unsalable now, but how to dress it up so Wheat would take it?

I had my job cut out for me, but luckily I had help from Richard (Dick) Miles who was their president, a solid citizen, and experienced investment banker from Merrill Lynch (and would later become one of our partners), and Jon who could sell anything. B&S headquarters was on Market Street with a lovely mural of brokers and merchants from the late 19th century, gracing its main banking floor. It was the beginning of the summer when I took the train to Philadelphia to meet with my client in their beautiful historic offices with roll top desks and brass sconces on the walls. We then went to the airport and took their small twin-engine plane to the airport in Richmond. As we taxied up to the executive hangar, the Wheat team appeared—all very cool customers who were waiting for "us" Yankees (including me who now lived in NYC) to discuss "terms." We conducted our initial negotiations between these two airports at the executive air terminals on alternate weekends, to be sure that only a small core team knew what was going on. If sophisticated brokers got wind that something was amiss, they could take their books of business, i.e. customers to another, more stable brokerage house and soon we'd be left with an empty bag.

Because Mr. Wheat was blind, the way negotiations worked was this: we'd introduce ourselves to Mr. Wheat and speak with him until he recognized our voices. He'd been blind since he was a young man and had a college student accompany him to read to him. He recognized voices, could adroitly conduct negotiations, and discuss the implications. He was a natural leader, and when things got tough, he told a bawdy joke. He kept us going. His lieutenants were courteous, competent characters—Jack McElroy, Mark Green, and Danny Luderman. Each could easily run the firm, but Mr. Wheat was clearly the general on this battlefield, and McElroy his chief lieutenant. Jack was courteous, but quick and deadly, ready to pounce on a mistake.

They would see right through us once we produced the financials. When they did their due diligence, they'd also discover the oil and gas deals. Should we come clean initially or let this be a slow discovery? The losses were unabating; every time we went to Richmond, the numbers got worse. We'd negotiate a deal, and the next week I'd deliver another set of operating statements showing further red ink. Jack McElroy verbally amputated another one of my fingers by lowering the price, tightening terms, or worse, threaten to let us have the company back. It was becoming a long, uncomfortable summer. We needed to get this deal done quick and receive more than the book value that was eroding daily before our eyes and the Germans tanked the whole thing. There was no turning back, there was no alternative, and the market kept getting worse.

It was late Friday evening and confident that no one would see us, we'd moved from the airport to the boardroom atop the twin towers that Wheat occupied in central Richmond. You could see the James winding through the city, rushing over the rapids, shoals and the brick wreckage of the old Confederate armament plant, the Tredegar Iron Works by the river. The red setting sun was ominously burning through the haze on the horizon. Jon Butcher was slowly jogging around the big board room table to get some exercise while the other side was out deliberating. This is a poem I later wrote about this city and its current and former citizenry:

Richmond

> Undeterred by over a century
> of industrial progress since the War
> the cold stone-cobbled James
> runs through this city's heart.
>
> The river floods the brick
> clutter relics

of old cannon foundries, tumbled tobacco warehouses,
and wracked bridges, dams, and locks.
Now on the banks, modern glass towers taint pink
toward sunset and shadow Corinthian columned porticos.

It's charming and everywhere:

I negotiate with a landed banker whose family financed the Cause
or casually chat with an ex
Marine cabby back to the airport.
His great-granddaddy dug and manned those earthworks
strong holding and surrounding this sacred capital.

It even seems alive in the glimmering eyes
of the great generals' oils arrayed at the Commonwealth Club.
JEB Stuart, Stonewall, and Lee
whose stares of determination and damnation
glow like the end of the day
and secretly ember
in the bosom of the citizenry:

that certain, courteous,
soft-spoken southern character,
somewhat deceptive,
but capable of taking on vastly
superior forces
and sometimes
whipping them.

"What do the firms look like together if they take out most of your
overhead and back office and just keep your brokers and bankers, and
this market turns?" I asked.

"We'd have to lay off a lot of people and would be really unpopular, but
it would be a homerun for them when these markets turn—low overhead
and more revenues, more money all around." Jon was slightly panting. "As
it stands today, they're going to lose their jobs anyway if this keeps going."

"Right, so we stage layoffs, take an earn-out, maybe get severance
packages paid?" I said.

"How much do you think we could get?" Jon said in sync with his pushups.

"Book value plus maybe 20% of an earn-out for the combined firms but try for more."

"Let's go for it, before there's nothing left."

Jon confirmed he'd take book value at closing and a pay-out for 20% of the value (to be defined) of the combined firms in not more than five years. He sent me to meet with the war council in the adjacent room to get just that. The proposed deal cleared the impasse, and we got an earn-out that wasn't payable until five years later, when, if it worked, there would be plenty to be shared. It was based on their projections, so they had to accept them, but five years away was also out of sight, out of mind. It turned out to be a bonanza, unfortunately accruing only to the Germans, since the liabilities from the oil and gas went against the shareholders of the company, principally the management, in the interim. Wheat eventually merged with Prudential Securities, a deal we also worked, and they became one of the largest brokerage firms in the country. We owned 20% of the profits of that firm.

The market turned, and the earn-out was worth a fortune. We had no idea this would happen, but Butcher was saved from the brink. Had I not been out there calling for Integrated Resources, I wouldn't have gotten inside B&S. The participants in this deal kept it to themselves. Luckily, no rumors leaked that could have panicked the B&S brokerage force and left us with an empty bag. Dick Miles would join us shortly thereafter and open our first office outside NYC. Danny Ludermann would become a client and run the combined Wheat and Prudential Securities business.

Jim Wheat was eighty-two and still very spry as we saw him in action. Howard Butcher, the son of the founder and Jon's father, was ninety-two. The two scions finally got together and shook hands after the deal closed at a meeting in Philadelphia. Howard was giving Jim a tour of their auspicious banking floor, and as they were leaving, he turned to Jim and said, "I hope you stay in this business young man, as you show real promise!"

We closed no other deals that year because the market was still traumatized from the shock of the crash. In its aftermath, there was an expansion opportunity for smaller firms, like us, that could survive such a crash and even benefit from it. We acquired some excellent people who'd been laid off elsewhere: Peter Bain, who was unknown to us from Merrill Lynch, and Richard Foote who I'd worked with from Paine

Webber. Peter was a Harvard Law School trained attorney and deal-man extraordinaire. The first thing Peter told me was he was real smart; it took us a couple of years to tone him down. He was, but Richard Foote, who came to help Steve Sheppard in the alternatives and real estate asset management area, was brilliant, though cantankerous.

Dwight & Margaret Anne (Peddy) Meteer

Chapter 27
Reaching for the Grail—Oppenheimer
The History of Berkshire Capital--Part V

"Many of Arthur's knights sought out the Grail, but most returned badly wounded, or worse. Then three knights went out in search of it: Sir Bors, Sir Perceval, and Sir Galahad. And they were the only ones to achieve it."

Le Morte Darthur
Sir Thomas Malory

Then, in early 1990 we got our big break. At our urging, the management of Oppenheimer Funds came to visit with us and our client, MassMutual. They'd been spun off from the famous investment banking and brokerage parent and were owned by a firm in the UK going into bankruptcy—British and Commonwealth (B&C). We spent some quality time together with John Fossil, Chairman, and Bridget Macaskill, CEO of Oppenheimer Funds and Dick Dooley CIO of MassMutual, as well as with their teams. We seemed to hit it off, but the parent company wouldn't entertain an offer. They were staving off bankruptcy courts and weren't paying any attention.

Later that year, MassMutual was approached by a banker representing B&C in bankruptcy. They were forced to sell Oppenheimer Funds. It would be a big auction, but it seemed we had management on our side. Our early introduction had worked. We needed to prepare the winning bid. The rest of the bidders had their own managers and wouldn't need the present management, while Mass Mutual needed and wanted them. The management team would help us through the process, as it was a complicated property with a commodity trading subsidiary plus twenty others that had potential hidden liabilities. A regular bid with contingencies wouldn't work. We had to take our best shot without contingencies but had considerable help from the management who wanted to save their jobs.

MassMutual also had an investment in Wertheim Schroders—a small, but prestigious investment bank—that they wanted to retain to also work on the deal as a sister company. Dick Dooley assured me we'd found the deal, and it wouldn't affect our fee. In fairness, they were masterful negotiators but didn't really understand the industry. It was a hard-fought contest, but we bid the most we could without contingency. Others bid more, but with all manner of contingencies that a bankrupt company couldn't accept. Ours was all-cash, quick with no earn-out. We won.

There was great jubilation because this was a name-brand. It had over $20 billion AUM at the time and was bought for close to $200 million, a large deal in those days. The largest deal of the year in fact. It was a real coup for MassMutual. I thought Dick Dooley would be pleased, but he called, and because both Wertheim Schroders, and Skadden, Arps had been in the picture, fees had gone way over budget. He hoped I understood and wanted me to take $300k, be a good boy, and come back another day, which a larger bank could do, by selling investments and other products to the insurance company or its clients thus making up for a discounted merger fee. That's not how we worked since our only product was advice and initiation creativity that, after all, had produced this extraordinary merger. We were owed $1.3 to $1.5 million. I tried to explain, but he hung up. I dealt with a dial tone for weeks.

What he chose to do was perfect big-company strategy. He stonewalled me—wouldn't talk to me and wouldn't pay me. He'd wait me out, knowing I couldn't afford to sue him and would eventually have to settle for less. I decided I had to get his attention, using a tactical nuclear weapon—a contingency lawsuit. Of course, I was loath to do this, as we'd never been sued, nor had sued anyone in our ten-year existence, but the attorneys agreed that we had an airtight fee agreement. I called our law firm—Proskauer Rose. The partner Alan Rosenberg was a great attorney who helped me get Berkshire started. I asked if he would handle the case on contingency, meaning I wouldn't have to pay a retainer, and we'd divide the spoils. He went to his management committee, and in an unusual precedent, they agreed. Then I went to my brother-in-law, Mason Cargill at Jones Day, who'd incorporated us. His management also agreed. With two major law firms ready to back and fight for us, I put a call into MassMutual's attorney at Skadden and told him that two firms agreed to help recover our fee, and that both were working for a contingency. Would we see them in court, or would they settle? Within half an hour, I got a call back and picked up a check for $1.3 million that afternoon.

It was a bittersweet victory. There was now an animosity between myself and Dick Dooley, who I'd guided through the mutual fund industry to find a premier property. While he was stonewalling us, he proceeded with the traditional closing dinner and didn't invite us. It had taken three months of our management time wrestling to get our fee. It was unprofessional for such a large firm to act the way they had over what was a homerun for them. It would have been the attainment of the Grail for us all if Dick had just picked up the phone to talk. It was moments like this that made me wonder why I was in this business and heard something else calling.

On the Road

I love early mornings in a new hotel,
traveling West on East Coast time,
before room service starts delivery,
searching the lobby or even down in the kitchen
for coffee, to greet dawn with the night clerk,
who starts his wake-up calls.
I find a newspaper by the revolving door
and a town map from the tourist's rack
to discover where I am and what's happening,
having missed the previous day, sequestered
with clients in a windowless conference room.

I notice a busboy picking up
last night's glasses and emptying ashtrays,
to start the lobby over with a worn smile by seven.
I begin to feel oddly comfortable
before the stir of day,
unhurried and at home
in the contrived elegance
of overstuffed couches, mirrors, and marble.

I wonder, how much of my life
has been spent, just like my father's—
in rented rooms and strange beds,
with our time neatly folded and packed
into suitcases and carried
between the unforgiving schedules
of people and planes?

Chapter 28
A Cat Curled in My Lap
The History of Berkshire Capital—Part VI

The Oppenheimer deal was a real feather in our cap to start the 90's. Later, it helped us to market ourselves for Mass Mutual, this extraordinary platform in the mutual fund business though it was debilitating for the wasted time we lost fighting over the fee. The platform is significant today with over $300 billion of assets under management, a ten-fold increase and the core of their retail investment management business, as well as a significant cash generator. For the rest of this decade, life for me was a succession of deals as we built the company; one led to another and another, and even to some memorable ones that got away.

I had been calling on Lord Abbott since working for Don Marron. They were larger mutual fund complex than Oppenheimer at the time, probably an even better industry name. It was a private partnership, as many of the older investment management firms were, just transferring ownership at book value among their partners as they retired. I had gotten to know the CEO, and senior partner, Ron Lynch, extremely well. He had grown up in Hawaii, a military brat and had wonderful landscape paintings of his home islands adorning his office walls, high in the General Motor's tower overlooking Central Park.

One day, I was called by Ron who took me for lunch at the Links Club, his favorite haunt. After settling in and pleasantries, he broke the news to me that he had been diagnosed with a fatal cancer. Shocked, I listened carefully: After discussing it with his partners they wondered if there was a foreign firm looking to coming into the US that might be interested in taking over the firm, or a part of it? In his case, he wanted to endow a charitable foundation before he passed. Could we help him out? After our Oppenheimer deal, we had many inquiries, most recently, the Generali Insurance Company of Italy, one of the country's leading financial institutions; they would be a perfect fit.

Not long thereafter, we had a great meeting with Generali and the senior partners of Lord Abbott in NYC who wanted to negotiate some preliminary terms, even getting to a letter of understanding that we signed before going to Italy to meet their senior management and do further due diligence. We were on our way to Trieste to meet with their management the next week.

Ron Lynch took his wife, me, and his junior partner and successor on the Concord to London. It was a most pleasant and exciting flight breaking the sound barrier and being in Europe in two hours when it was still daylight. From London, we flew on to Venice. Then the company limo took us to Trieste along the gleaming Adriatic coast.

Generalli threw a big dinner that evening, in an ancient town square, even with fireworks. Still, I sensed we were in trouble when the President, who I had gotten to know in the course of our negotiations, when he whispered in my ear at the end of dinner that he wanted to delay the signing for a month while he checked with his investment bankers. He may have been hesitant to approach the Medio Banca, a merchant bank-like organization and the financial mafia of Italy that owned part of the company; he naïvely hadn't cleared the deal with them.

For Thanksgiving we left from Rome on the Concord to be with our respective families. Around that time, I got the call I was fearing from Generalli's President; Mediobanca wouldn't approve the deal. I took the news to Ron, who took it badly, and tragically, soon after, got sicker and passed away. Had I to do it all over again, I would have gotten back on the plane and gone to negotiate directly with Medio Banca, not leaving until it was done. Lord Abbott was never again for sale; the insurance company had missed a huge strategic opportunity to get into the US asset management industry with it. After Ron died, the new management at Lord Abbott had no intention of selling. The insurance company was to be soon run by the former president's dynamic and savvier assistant, Giovanni Perissinotto, who we got to know in the Lord Abbott deal, who hired us several years later to do a similar search, but there were no companies around like this one.

There was a demand for US firms from Europe and the UK, and there was a demand among US firms themselves. Like early native Americans, I followed the game, in this case the deals, wherever they were. There was much travel involved. Between her shows I sometime took Georgia with me or, more-often, met up with her traveling company, Columbia Artist, on weekends. We seemed to orbit around each other coming back to our NYC apartment or increasingly traveled out to our house in the country in Salisbury, CT, through Hartford's Bradley airport. Weekends would find us gathered in front of our barn going out or returning from a ride on our own trails up and around a pond meant to center a 125-acre development we stopped by buying, to be named the Blackberry River Run. Weekdays began with a commute into the city and ended back on

Friday afternoon, sometimes a Thursday night escape. My horse, antici-
pating this rhythm, would throw his bridle out into the saw dusted barn
isle at these times to be ridden.

The diverse personalities encountered in my business fascinated me
as much as the deal doing. I had been calling for years on Dean Lebaron,
the legendary CEO of Batterymarch Financial. Dean was brilliant and a
gentleman. He was famous as the inventor of "value" investing and wrote
and talked about it constantly with great flair. Investment conferences loved
to have Dean as their keynote speaker. Dean, however, was loath to share
the ownership of his firm with his employees. A number of famous money
managers left him to start their own firms, most notably Jeremy Grantham
and Eyk Van Onterloo whose firm became legend and many times the size
of Batterymarch. I continue to see Ike in Naples, Florida today.

I made a point of calling on Dean every time I was in Boston. He was full
of investment savvy and was always on the frontier of current investment.
Early on, Dean was interested in investing in Russia just after its opening to
the West. He thought it would significantly expand his global business. He
went over as a guest of the Russian government, even got to sip vodka with
a cosmonaut before he was blasted off to space. Dean decided on the next
trip to take a select group of his big pension fund clients, AT&T, GM, and
other large funds he managed along for a due diligence trip. They found they
would be getting in on the ground floor but would also be paying under the
table for the access. He discovered corruption rife and part of life there, as
it is today and called it off.

Dean called from his home in Switzerland shortly thereafter. He said to
me simply, "It's time." And I asked, "Time for what?" He paused… "For
me to sell the firm. Would you represent me?" He would be in Boston within
two weeks where we met to sign a contract. He signed without question, but
then told me how we would conduct the process. Dean gave me five names
and said that was it.

I suggested some others and we compromised on a combination of
six, one I insisted he include was Legg Mason whose CEO, Chip Mason,
I knew would hit it off with Dean, and who also needed an international
manager. However, Dean's assets were highly concentrated in a few large
pension funds; it was not that easy to sell or without risk. Nonetheless, all
six firms were interested. When we opened up the envelopes, Legg Mason
wasn't on top but had made a fair offer. After meeting all the other firms
Dean chose to go with Legg, because he had the most respect for "Chip,"

leaving considerable money on the table. Dean wasn't concerned about the money. He had enough of that. What concerned him was getting the right future home for his firm.

Raymond Mason, whose family was in the brokerage business too, started his own firm right out of college in Newport News, Virginia, later moving his firm to Baltimore. He was one of the first CEOs in the securities industry to begin to acquire asset management firms and did the deals himself with no staff or corporate development officer doing either the initial work or sorting out candidates. He took the measure of each executive personally and did the deal on an envelope. What he could fairly pay and not much more, but people loved him for the exceptional personal touch.

I experienced this myself, after an overnight ice storm staying with my sister in law, Holly Lanahan, who lived in the same neighborhood in Ruxton as Chip, in Baltimore Maryland. Chip, knowing we had an appointment, surprised me the next morning when he called to ask if he could pick me up and take me downtown. Apparently, the local cabs weren't working with the ice storm. That was the kind of man he was. His honesty and integrity were infectious. Dean sensed the same thing and a good home for his firm. His CEO, Tanya Zouikin would lead Legg Mason's entry into the international asset management business. She was an energetic HBS graduate with a Canadian background and global view, the more traditional Legg lacked. At the closing dinner, Dean and Tanya gave Chip a beautiful model of "The Constitution," the historic frigate tied up in Baltimore Harbor. I still see Chip who also winters in Naples, Florida.

For Alleghany Corp., a holding company much like Berkshire Hathaway, we worked with John Burns, the Chairman, who directed us to work with Stu Bilton, who was to build their asset management business introducing them to Montag & Caldwell, a renown Atlanta growth manager we represented. For Boatman's Bank in St. Louis we worked for Greg Curl, the President who turned the job of expanding over to the head of his Trust Department, Peter McCarthy, one of the most decisive executives I've ever worked with.

I was not doing this alone either as I had an eye on institutionalizing the business, so it was just not me bringing in the business. I felt the best way to do this was to develop teams with a leader for each team that became expert in the various segments of the asset management business, a Berkshire within a Berkshire. Bruce and I worked together a lot, but he was developing into his own man, doing more in the private wealth and the investment counseling business, working principally with US Trust, Legg Mason, Mellon Bank and Northern Trust. Steve Sheppard, an expert in real estate finance, who had developed some of the original specs for mortgage futures that now trade on the CBOE, and Richard Foote began to develop a practice together in the real estate asset management business. About this time, there was an interesting article in the financial press reporting that we started our board meetings with a poem.

In the mid-90's we did a number of international deals representing the Commerz bank group that acquired a quantitative asset manager led by an industry pioneer, Arnie Wood. That was Martingale Asset Management. We had worked for over two years with Commerz Bank, who had been originally introduced to us by Bob Prindiville of Thomas McKinnon when they were originally inquiring in the US. Heinz Hochman was the fair-haired boy who led the charge for Commerz Bank coming into the US. He was helped by his sidekick Robert Hoch who was bright and tough. Heinz and Robert remain friends today, but our journey together hasn't always been smooth as Heinz used other bankers on some of his other transactions. There was one in particular with a hot handed manager in the UK, that blew up the firm. Heinz overpaid for it and it sank him as well as eventually the German bank's whole international asset management business.

The second cross border deal closing in 1995 was representing a joint venture of Hypo Bank in Munich and Foreign & Colonial Management in London ("F&C"). The latter was run by Sir Jamie Ogilvie, who I had met in London a few years earlier. Jamie was the middle child in his family, so under the prime genitor system inherited the title, but not the family fortune. He had to work for a living, first in the British Marines in the Mau-Mau conflicts in Africa. He was a colorful character in all aspects, accent, dress and sayings that were memorable. One in particular involved "the long spoon," that is the marrow spoon he referred to that was long and the proper way to finish the roast beef bone. He said our eventual venture in the UK called for a "long spoon" approach, i.e. required time and patience as indeed it did. He would be an extraordinary representative as we worked our way into the UK marketplace, but this was after we represented him and established a distribution beachhead for his joint venture in the USA in Boston with Mass Financial (MFS) Mutual Funds.

F&C was the epitome of an advanced international asset management, with a team of specialized analyst divided for most countries and geographies, in their modern London tower headquarters. Here is a poem I wrote while visiting there, looking out over the city at dusk:

St. Paul's Dome

lords over low sooty sandstone flats,
packed to the Thames bounding
the griffin-guarded City
on the winter eve of my visit.
Wren wanted his cathedral to raise, a marble phoenix,
from the ashes of the Great Fire
and center the New London.
Like a gigantic bare breast
of an ancient amazon's statue,
it dominates the skyline
of glass towers and old church spires...

Sir Christopher's vision
seems lost in gothic zoning laws
perfected over hundreds of years of bureaucracy.
Thriving behind high wrought iron fences,
they make progress like rush hour traffic, queued-up
in boxy black taxis along ancient Roman
and Anglo-Saxon roads named Barbican,
Eastcheap, and Houndsditch.

At my next appointment, the Dome's framed
from a pinstriped banker's carved oaken window.
Backed by ancestral portraits, he's convinced
that real estate is the only hedge
against a falling pound.
He can do nothing about his country's slow slide
into socialism, secure in his knowledge
nothing will ever change here
but the guards.

Jamie inspired the pinstripes mentioned above, had sagely and jointly ventured with one of the largest banks in Germany to get distribution for in-

ternational investments products there. You couldn't get into Germany unless
you had a distribution partners. Rather than selling out, the two formed a
joint venture. While Hypo had asset management capability, they were better
distributors. F&C had the investment expertise. He also had a very talented
head of asset management at Hypo and they got along together exquisite-
ly. Gunther Dunkel was a bright star at the bank as international investment
product was coveted and couldn't be found. Now the two of them set their
sights on the US to distribute their international product, rare at the time and
chose us to represent them.

We were honored to have the job. It was a pleasure working for
Jamie and Gunther. We scoured the east coast for a partner finding Mass
Financial Services (MFS) a venerable Boston establishment institution, so
they and the British got along just fine. It was run at the time by Jeff
Shames, a hard driving but very astute New Englander. Ironically Jeff was
going through his wife' deathly struggle with breast cancer that unknow-
ingly Georgia was about to undergo.

Soon another and more impactful deal for us was headquartered in
Boston. I had been in touch with one of the original personal investment
managers that had become institutional as well and a household name,
David L. Babson. It was headed by a mustached gentleman who was David
Babson's, then Brad Lee Parry's protégé, Peter Thompson. He was backed up
by a business school classmate of mine, Peter Schliemann, who was simply
one of the best small cap investors in the US. They had received a number
of offers and were pressured to grow the firm. Having investigated minority
positions, they felt it was time to take some money off the table, to capitalize
an otherwise illiquid asset. They had decided to sell and wanted us to represent
them. Peter Thompson and I went down to a Dunkin Donuts in Back Bay
behind the Union Club overlooking the Granary where the Boston Patriots
were shot in the massacre are buried and oh yes, Paul Revere, is there too.
Over coffee there we casually signed a million-dollar deal. Then, I walked
back to the Union Club where I stayed and ordered a celebratory red wine that
evening. Our club mascot, Vidalia, the cat, I had talked the Club's manager into
getting to solve their mouse problem, was curled in my lap. There was history
here and with this deal. As it turned out, the Mass Mutual Insurance Company
would ironically be the successful winner of our auction and Babson would be
a central part of their future asset management business.

Chapter 29
Succession and 9/11
The History of Berkshire Capital—Part VII

By the end of 2000, Berkshire Capital was a prosperous and successful company, however in the first year of the new century, I found myself living with the devastating loss of Georgia and spent much of 2001 navigating that grief. It was a handicap I couldn't simply shake; I finally gave up on my efforts to return to work fulltime as CEO of the company and designated Bruce Cameron to run the firm day-today, while I'd continue to work with larger clients and on the firm's overall strategy, particularly international expansion, even into Asia. Everyone seemed fine with the change. I tried to pick up a number of projects—balls in the air that I'd left.

These were deals I'd started in 2000, not completed by year's end—I just had to rise to the challenge. Upon reflection, these were also opportunities to travel that I took at every opportunity, eager for the chance to get out of returning to my ominously empty apartment. The first deal in our pipeline was Atlanta Capital Management Co., an institutional value manager run by Chip Reames. Chip had also gone to Southwest High with me—and we'd both been on the football team together, though he was a couple years my senior. Chip was a big bird hunter and had an office full of taxidermized ducks. Not being a hunter and thinking of Georgia's reaction, I was uneasy in his office, but they were good asset managers.

We ran an auction for Atlanta Capital Management that was won by Eaton Vance Group in Boston. The management teams bonded primarily because Jim Hawkes, another Georgia boy, ran the old-line Boston firm. Hawkes related directly to the Atlanta Capital team of Southerners. Ironically, Jim's relatives, the Malcom family had a cemetery on Alma's Little Sandy Farm. This was a very friendly deal, and the participants soon understood and were sympathetic about what I was going through. Atlanta Capital had over $5.0 billion AUM and was our largest deal in 2001—it got Eaton Vance, a mutual fund and private wealth manager started in the institutional asset management business.

In 2001, I slowly got back to my work, though I could see that the road ahead was going to diverge, as I started thinking about beginning

divinity school. I had great hopes, but the world as we knew it was about
to change. On the morning of September 11, 2001, the entire firm stood
in my office looking downtown along the cavern of Madison Avenue
toward a smoking twin towers. Then we saw another plane hit. People
panicked and tried to make calls, but the cellular networks were jammed.
We turned on the news and watched in horror as the first tower went
down. I looked at that plume of grey-black smoke and said to myself,
"Where have I seen this before? Of course, the film at Pearl Harbor's
park headquarters, with Mom." That same evil plume born of hate and
treachery turns the pages of the world's history book.

We watched as the second building went down. By now, the streets
were packed with people fleeing uptown. We tried to send the admin-
istrative staff home, but they returned from the train station reporting
that nothing was running. Phone lines and cell lines were clogged; I
managed to get a landline call out to Connecticut. I told Eli to phone my
family in Atlanta and tell them I was okay and walked down 19 flights
of stairs. Walking home, I stopped by St. Bartholomew's Church where
people were praying. I sat and contemplated the beautiful carved marble
angel in the chapel and being alone in this world. The world was full of
hatred and revenge. Could I be a peacemaker? How might I help those
who would be mourning as I still was? Could I share my experience?
Whatever had happened, it was going to be a time of change. I was going
home to an empty apartment. I needed to do something besides business
to fill my life—maybe write more, travel abroad, or go back to school.
Life was so short and getting shorter. What was my mission now that
Georgia was gone?

The world was unsure of itself and what the attack on the Twin
Towers meant. At Berkshire, I held an all-hands meeting at the end of
the week to discuss our anxieties and suggest how we might help one
another, and others affected by the tragedy. I'd forgotten about it until
the following note, written by one of our administrative assistants fell
out of one of my diaries covering this period:

> This is an overdue expression of appreciation for your
> words of encouragement at the firm-wide meeting last
> week. Hearing your thoughts on the devastating tragedy
> helped so much in gaining perspective at this difficult time.
> I was particularly moved by your suggestion that each of
> us find our inner light so that we may pass it on to others

in pain. It is reassuring to know that the leader of this company has so much spiritual strength. Thank you for sharing that light with all of us.

I'd changed, was sobered by the death of my wife, and was somehow encouraging others to share their light. I was fanning a small, still-glowing coal as hard as I could to keep it from going out in me, trying to heal a psychological wound. I attacked it directly through prayer and meditation, but also indirectly by drinking more wine than I should and by traveling to see friends and business acquaintances—excursions around the US and abroad on the pretension of seeking new business. I was searching for another path. Like the knights on the quest for the Grail, my encounter with death was just another stern lesson on the path to eventual enlighten or destruction. What did this shift in world tensions mean for my and the company's future? I felt strongly my paths weren't all business related; Berkshire was doing fine and would carry on. I was luckily healthy, too. It was my soul was what needed tending.

Paulson Family Farm, Carroll, NE

Chapter 30
Kinesis
The History of Berkshire Capital—Part VIII

As a country, we faced a new mysterious enemy—terrorism, and we seemed bent on revenge for an attack on our home soil. This would be played out in the new century, but there was an uncertainty about how business would be affected in general. I'd planned a trip to Europe and the UK to leave on September 12th. Of course, all flights were delayed. On September 22nd, I finally got on the first flight out to Europe, almost empty, due to the scare. Sated and tired from a half-night's sleep, I was in a first-class railroad car the next morning, traveling up the Rhine bound for Cologne to see my friend Ingolf. At a window seat, looking out on the Rhine and its romantic castles nestled in the picturesque hills, I was arranging future appointments on my cell. Suddenly I was surrounded by a group of neatly attired German businessmen. I thought they were going to protest my talking on the phone, but they most respectfully expressed their sympathies for the attack on my country and the world. They told me they abhorred the attack and were behind us trying to punish the culprits. International relations with our allies was never so close. Sadly, we have frittered away those friendships since.

The train traveled right along the Rhine, north, past historic fortresses on the vine-laden hills of Rheingau country into Cologne, where there is the grandeur of the gothic-spired Cologne Cathedral, purportedly housing the relics of the three wise men. I loved this cathedral and felt a strange presence and energy whenever I was in it. The gothic structure—600 years in the building—had been built on top of the site of a Roman temple as well as even earlier Druidic temples—an ancient and sacred spot. I spent a great weekend in Cologne with my Ingolf and Marie Ange Mayer-Plate, catching up and all mourning Georgia's passing. He was assistant to the chairman of a large German conglomerate—Humboldt, Klockner, Deutz. His 6'5" stature towered over all on the street and in the bier halls. It was good to see those two souls and reminisce about Georgia with Ingolf, who'd known her almost as long as I had. This is the opening of a poem I wrote about my friends and their ancient city:

> A failing moon rises between the twin spires
> of a ghostly Cologne cathedral
> that looms over the old Roman city on the Rhine
> like great spaceships that never got home.

Traveling on, I arrived in Munich unsuspecting, but just in time for Oktoberfest—an event I'd experienced as a student in the city back in 1965. Early in the day, I was visiting with a self-confident woman in charge of strategic planning for Bayern Vereinsbank. Petra Enthofer took pity on me as a widower when I told her my story, something I often did at this stage of my grieving. She invited me to come along with her, her husband and his law partners to the festival held in the great halls and tents just outside the city. She was the designated driver, and we all got on famously, though I didn't have my lederhosen on as the rest of the jolly crew did. The hospitality of the Bavarian's have always amazed me as well as the serving ladies at the Oktoberfest who can carry no less than two or even three liters of bier in each fist. Leaving the next day I stopped in Munich's Cathedral that always rekindles my admiration of its builders and their age:

> I try to imagine being a citizen
> at its consecration five centuries ago,
> awed by the sacred stories
> luminous in the stained glass and blessed
> by their light…
> beholding the Master Builder's plan
> complete, and my father's and grandfather's all
> consuming work done.
>
> Outside, I pass Sunday strollers,
> bundled in western denims…
> We rustle through linden leaves
> littering the churchyard,
> unable to fathom
> when great faith
> was last in fashion.

I left Germany for London to meet with our new London team— Glenna Webster and Andrew Martin Smith. The issue of how we would service London, that, next to NYC, was the most important financial service capital and was an on-going problem for our small firm. We'd almost come to the point of drawing lots between our partners for temporary coverage, when Glenna came into my office to resign. "Why?" I asked. "He's English!" she'd responded. Glenna was marrying an Englishman and moving to England, and here all the partners had all been nervous one of us would have to move to London. It was like some kind of movie script. On the spot, we worked out a deal for her to open an office for us there.

Looking back, I stayed on airplanes, running from my grief or trying to catch up on business neglected because of Georgia's death. I felt bad about both. In our business, it's important to work several deals at all times because we never knew when one would come home to roost. There was a global opportunity for us, and I'd later spend much time in Australia and Asia, laying the groundwork for our future work there. Georgia and I had no children, and my family was thin and mostly in Atlanta, so my large network of friends was a sort of surrogate family for me to travel among and still is.

In late October Buzz Schulte's daughter was getting married in Carmel. I'd known Buzz from my time at Harvard Business School, where we'd been suitemates. I decided to call ahead to my friend, Mary Drew, who Georgia and I had known when we lived there. I stayed a couple of delightful days in San Francisco, where we got reacquainted. Mary had just been made secretary of her AA chapter and was intent on getting me sober. She took me to a Friday morning chapter meeting, where I confessed to over-imbibing because of my grief. The release I felt from the confession was amazing and even better were the folks who came up to confess their same experience. Though awkward, it was a wonderful lesson for me. Afterward, feeling unburdened, Mary and I went across the Golden Gate to Muir Woods and hiked to the top of Mt. Tam, where we watched the sunset and the fog roll into the bay, dramatically leaving only the red tops of the bridge pillars visible as the day faded. I felt renewed!

In Carmel, I attended Buzz's daughter's wedding, a lovely event with the reception held at Pebble Beach Golf Club. The following day Jake Taylor, Buzz's college roommate at Williams and our suitemate at HBS, asked me to go with him and his wife Lisa to Yosemite Valley. Jake had a lumber camp just outside Yosemite Park that'd been in his family since his father acquired it in a poker game during the Depression. It was a wonderful pine log lodge called Fish Camp, and boasted huge fireplaces, a great cook, and working logging trucks. We took expeditions into the park to see the spectacles of nature there—Half-Dome and Bridal Veil Falls.

We even wandered up into the cathedral-like Mariposa Stand of giant Sequoias.

Jake and Lisa drove me to Fresno where I took a plane to Dallas/ Ft. Worth and visited Georgia's sister, Suzy and her husband T.O., an ex-marine entrepreneur. They'd acquired a house on a duck pond in an upscale suburb there. We had dinner and caught up. I hadn't seen Suzy since Georgia's funeral. I also hadn't met her mature children, my nephews, who joined us with their significant others. It was like a family reunion but being around her sister made me miss Georgia intensely. Upon my return from this odyssey, NY to Europe to California and back to Utopia on October 26th, I wrote the following entry in my journal:

> I'm so glad to be back here, just to touch this wonderful earth… I've missed the passing of fall—my favorite time here—for a life on the road seeing friends and family, but home is best.

Escaping the shadow of her death, I had become kinetic, traveling at the slightest excuse to avoid being alone. I missed my companion more than I understood, and it was taking its toll.

It was time to slow down and let my soul catch up with me.

Baby Bruce McEver, 1940s

Chapter 31
Pilgrimages: What Kind of Sign Was This?

"Your begging bowl may be of pure gold, but as long as you do not know it, you are a pauper... you cannot imagine the taste of pure water, you can only discover it by abandoning the flavored... Discovery cannot come as long as you cling to the familiar. It is only when you fully realize the immense sorrow of your life and revolt against it that a way out can be found."

Sri Nisargadatta Maharaj

I sadly continued to engage in all my peripatetic activities in order to avoid the tragic loneliness of Georgia's loss. Like that fateful day in Sharon Hospital, my mind was split. On one hand, I struggled to fill the huge hole in my heart with my business and personal relationships, and on the other, there was a curiosity—a calling to explore something different—maybe the Far East and to begin to write about it. Backgrounding all this was my faith, shaken—but still steadfast.

On Saturday, October 27, 2001, I went to our church's men's retreat held at Camp Chimney Top in Becket, MA. There was a dusting of snow on the cars and picnic tables when we arrived. I rode with our pastor, Dick Taber, who charged us to think on the meaning of our faith, specifically on the famous passage found in Hebrews 11: "Now Faith is the assurance of things hoped for, the conviction of things not seen." That evening there was a video called *Wresting with Angels*, where people who suffered loss were interviewed. Strangely enough this included an interview with a woman named Georgia. This reminder was too close to a still open wound and tested my faith. Dick counselled me that almost nothing that makes a difference can be proved and that he'd come to see that faith was a belief that what happens will be understood in the future. As I reflect, I see this more clearly, but it was hard to convince my raw soul at the time.

I was with my congregation—a wonderful group of sympathetic and understanding neighbors. I needed such fellowship and the time to reflect and see the deepening of my faith. A road was taking me elsewhere, if only I listened to the Lord and let him guide me. Through this, my faith grew stronger with regular prayer, meditation, and reflective writing in my journal, as well as increasingly, creatively through my poetry. I had read some of my poems at our retreat and Dick told me privately as I was leaving: "You have a gift; use it."

After a business meeting in Richmond the Tuesday of the following week, I was off to Atlanta to attend the advisory board at Georgia Tech. The Tech trustees were a prestigious group—the power behind the school. I served on the investment committee, working closely with Dr. Wayne Clough, the President of Tech, and who would later become the Secretary of the Smithsonian. He asked me to help him at Tech and then later at the Smithsonian with its initial religious exhibitions. I also met Dr. Henry Bourne, a former president of Tech, who, like me, endowed a Chair in Poetry at the school. We sat together in the president's box at a football game Tech won. Sitting with my sister and these men, I thought about how far I'd come from the Boy Scout who sold Cokes at Grant Field during the games. I looked out from the president's box and saw my fellow Scouts still working the cheering crowd, as well as the Atlanta skyline in the background that had changed dramatically.

My excuse to travel East was already in place. I'd forgotten that before Georgia died, I'd deposited money for a trip for us to Burma and Angkor Wat with my Salisbury travel agency. At the time, it was hard to get visas to visit, and it would be several thousand dollars to cancel. I also wrestled about asking Mary Drew to go along with me because it would foster gossip and real guilt in me for being with anyone after my wife's death, but I didn't want to go alone. My physician Dr. Bruce Janelli encouraged me. In fact, he'd asked me at my recent check-up if I was dating yet. The doctor advised about the power relationships had to heal these wounds.

I'd always wanted to see Angkor Wat and had wanted Georgia to see it with me. Burma was exotic, but I had no idea of the beauty of that country and its people, nor the spectacle of Bagan, an equally ancient and mysterious archaeological monument. I decided not to cancel the trip but to share it. Anyhow, it was doctor's orders. I got excited about the prospects and began reading the background material.

In the meantime, when I returned to New York, I had dinner with Tom Lux. He announced proudly that he was going to take the permanent Chair at Poetry@Tech Dr. Bourne had endowed. He was very excited and had great plans for the program, including having Billy Collins as the first McEver Chair that was a rotating position. Tom was leaving Sarah Lawrence and moving to Atlanta. I'd changed his life as he'd changed mine by getting me started writing poetry. He was also going to write an introduction for my chapbook that would be published the following year. He urged me to apply for a trial summer session of the MFA program at Warren Wilson in Asheville, NC, as I promptly did. There was much else for me to do and to write about as well.

I left for San Francisco on November 17th with several books on Buddhism to read on the long flight over. There, I met an excited Mary, who was taking a steamer trunk of stuff that I helped her slim down into a suitcase for the trip. We left for Tokyo on the Monday, then on to Bangkok, crossing the International Date Line and losing a day. My journal records an impression after our arrival: "The Chao Phraya River is a scramble of activity this morning. I was up at sunrise to see an orange ball rise through the heavy haze and Bangkok's pollution. This hotel is the lap of luxury... There is a bustle of barges and little water taxis on the river below..."

We spent a day in Bangkok and left early the next day for Angkor Wat. After checking in at a half-full hotel, we took a taxi on the great causeway to the Shiva's mountain at the center of the earth. We followed the crowds to the central edifice—richly carved with bare-breasted dancing maidens or angels who gave a haunting sensuality and beauty to this most sacred of monuments. We climbed to the top and sat perched on a pedestal where the sun glowed redder and redder and finally fell into the gloam of haze overhanging the jungle. It was a powerful feeling, heightened by some strange energy emanating from the mysterious stone mountain. My mind seemed to resonate with a heightened rush of energy pulsing up my spine.

We walked back to the causeway and caught a cab to the hotel, where we had Thanksgiving dinner Cambodian-style. We were tired from our travels but elated at the prospect of further exploring the edifice we'd visit again the next day. Our guidebook said Angkor Wat's temple complex was the largest religious monument in the world, then occupying over 400 acres. It was constructed as a Hindu temple of the God Vishnu for the Kamer Empire towards the end of the 12th century. The middle tower we'd sat at was in the form of a lotus bud, and represented the sacred mountain, Mount Meru. Amazingly, the monument was made of five- to ten-million sandstone blocks, with a weight of up to 1.5 tons, far more stone than in all the Egyptian pyramids. It once covered an area larger than the city of Paris.

The following morning, we headed off by cab to see Bayon in Angkor Thom, another city with a magnificent temple complex graced with famous mysterious giant faces. There's a bridge into Bayon, carved in sandstone, depicting an ancient battle of the gods who used the sacred serpent to churn the sea of milk, setting the cosmos spinning. It's a remarkable piece of sculpture in itself, but the carvings throughout are truly magnificent to behold. All the temples are carved, and the relief is different from different angles. The carving is equivalent to the magnificent sandstone carvings of Europe's cathedrals, or at the Rosslyn Chapel in Edinburgh, depicting the story of Matthew, but Angkor Wat is on an exponentially different scale, telling the story of Mahabharata in stone, the Hindu epic longer than the *Iliad* and *Odyssey*.

The following day we had to go back to Bangkok to get the plane to Yangon, where we were greeted by a guide with a British accent. He gave us a tour of the city and palace with an historic British backstory. Then we visited the great Stupa and began to discover more about Buddhism in Yangon but returned to the very British Strand Hotel to meet our tour group. We went up country for our next treat—an overnight stay on Ile Lake in a hotel on stilts. There we had a sumptuous meal and were entertained by Burmese dancers.

From the stilted hotel, we took long canoes with motors to visit more stupas, each grander than the last, and the next day boarded our boat, the RV Pandow, for a most pleasant cruise up the Irrawaddy River. This boat was something like a repurposed passenger tug built in Glasgow in the 60s. We had pleasant state rooms and met on the large fantail late afternoons for tea and cocktails. The upper decks were great for watching sunrises and sunsets and the parade of river traffic. The boat took us back in time. There were no electric lights, so we watched a civilization along the river illuminated by fire and candlelight at night. We made stops at major trading ports, stupas and monasteries. There was a stupa on most major hills along the river; piety was in the people here. This was an impression in my journal from an afternoon sitting on the upper deck, dated Friday, November 30:

> You can feel everywhere the deep impression of the enlightened one in this land around, feel the ineffable, the silence beyond the memory. The feeling is that the religion seems everywhere in the land and gets into you as you come under its spell.

The highlight of the Burma trip was Bagan, a plain of ruined temples and stupas as far as the eye can see. Located in the Mandalay region of Myanmar, Bagan was the ancient capital of the Pagan Kingdom from the 9th to 13th centuries. During this time, over 10,000 Buddhist temples, pagodas, and monasteries were constructed on the Bagan plain. Today, the remains of over 2,200 temples and pagodas still survive. This prosperous city became a center for religious and secular studies, specializing in Pali scholarship. It attracted monks and students from India, Sri Lanka, and the neighboring Khmer Empire. Religion dominated, but Theravada Buddhism co-existed with Mayahana and Tantric Buddhism, various Hindu (Shiva and Vaishnava) schools, as well as native animist traditions. It must have been the Athens of the Far East. The Pagan empire collapsed in 1287 due to repeated Mongol invasions. We spent two days exploring these temples; it was the biggest surprise of our trip—the enormity of this ancient city and its import for the ancient world. There was a party one night where we lit fire balloons (that use candles to produce hot air). We released almost a hundred into the air and watched them drift over the plain. Then hot air balloons arrived the next day, and on them, we took an aerial survey of the great ruin. It's hard to imagine the wealth and diversity of the citizenry when this was at its height. It was a once-in-a-lifetime experience.

In Tokyo, I said goodbye to Mary, who was off to SFO. I went on to NYC where I took my bags full of souvenirs and books back to my apartment before heading the next day to Salisbury. It was good to get home. When I prepared to meditate, as I'd been accustomed to doing twice a day, I walked outside to the greenhouse off the basement where I found a young hawk had flown into its window, breaking its neck. I took the bird to the great pine tree in my backyard that I consider sacred. It had snowed over six inches during the night, but the next morning, I buried the hawk ceremoniously, preserving some of the larger feathers. What kind of sign was this?

Chapter 32
Advent 2001
The History of Berkshire Capital—Part IX

I went back to work the next week, recovering from a cold and adjusting to the time zone change. Exhausted from the travel, it took me much longer than I expected. I realized I couldn't keep it up, nor did I want to, but I had seen the potential in the Far East for us since Berkshire Capital—mainly its clients' businesses, asset management—was truly a global business. I needed to return to Asia to explore those possibilities and let Bruce run the company day-to-day. In the meantime, the return from Burma resulted in a burst of business for me in early December 2001. Still mystified by the mystic symbolism of the dead hawk outside my meditation space in Salisbury, the vision of the grieving pigeon hovering over its dead mate that I'd seen just before Georgia's death haunted me.

But it was back to business. I set off to visit Bob Bagby, the CEO of A.G. Edwards in St. Louis where my partner Dick Miles and we proposed the merger of Wachovia and A.G. Edwards that would form the largest securities firm in the US. We were swinging for the fences! Bagby greeted me, and when he understood what we were proposing, brought in several other officers. His office was that of a big game hunter—full of large taxidermized animals. He heard us out but said he didn't want to have another shareholder influencing the firm. He'd only agree to a deal where he'd acquire Wachovia for cash and be in control. This was not what our client Danny Ludermann had in mind. Danny wanted to eventually run the whole thing himself. Bob said he'd think it over. He walked us to the elevator joking nervously the whole way, as he could see the power in the two firms together.

Next stop was Charlotte, where we reviewed the meeting with Danny Ludermann and continued to go down our priority merger list. We'd eventually merge the company with Prudential Securities, not as desirable as A.G. Edwards that, ironically, owns the remains of Wachovia today. That evening, I also took the opportunity to have dinner with Jim Morgan, former CEO of Interstate/Johnson Lane Securities, a company we'd merged with Wachovia back in 1999 when Glass-Steagall was finally repealed. Jim was one of the most ethical and outstanding examples of a

leader I'd ever met. He exuded confidence and took a chance to merge
his little company with the larger Wachovia Bank since the company's
CEO Ken Thompson had promised to keep him independent and at the
center of the bank's security business.

Tragically, this was abrogated when Wachovia was itself merged
into First Union. Suddenly, all bets were off. First Union had acquired
Wheat Securities, and Danny Ludermann was put in charge of all of
First Union's combined securities operations, including Jim's former
firm. Jim was now running his own investment management company
and enjoying serving his old clients. It was a great dinner conversation
as we reflected on the state of the world after 9/11 and the security
industry post Glass-Steagall. Our meeting caused me to contemplate the
world around me. I wrote this poem reflecting on Charlotte, a regional
southern town ironically headquartering the largest firms in America's
banking industry. And after 9/11, it was a very different and difficult
Advent from many perspectives:

Advent 2001

The moon smiles through bare branches of old oaks,
mum druids of Charlotte suburbs.
Christmas lights outline manor hedges,
boxwoods scenting of stability.

Defiant stars and stripes drape every house.
This year we've learned the crescent
marks the end of Ramadan
as well as the start of Advent.
The peace prince has much work.

I walk a sidewalk buckled by the oaks
downtown where bank towers—
the city's cathedrals of commerce—
dominate the skyline.

They loom silver at dusk,
ghostly erections conjuring
ancient San Gimignano.

It is near the anniversary of my wife's death
and the world has changed:
Many grieve and question
the wisdom of tall towers.
I saw them burn.

When I go back to my empty room,
progress is not crying.
I light a candle;
it's all I can do.

It was a day at a time for me then. Returning to New York, it was my first Christmas without her. Warned this would be difficult, I'd agreed to allow Georgia's best friend Paula Vemeyer to clear out Georgia's closets in the apartment while I was gone. I didn't need to be reminded of her absence. However, I still found little notes in drawers, or a knick-knack that reminded me of her that triggered memories. I went through her jewelry in our safety deposit box, deciding that I'd divide it among the women in our family for Christmas.

I left NYC for Del Ray Beach on what would have been our 32nd anniversary—December 20th. My sister Sharon had acquired a condo near an international tennis camp for her daughters, Ansley and Kristin. Ansley had just been named an All-American her freshman year at Duke, and Kristin was playing top seed for her high school team in Atlanta. Sharon assisted Mom and me find a penthouse apartment next to a state park. The place had a grand ocean view, and the girls loved it, so we made it our headquarters during our stay. Sharon and I rented bikes and rode up and down the road between Boca and West Palm Beach. It turned out to be a great gathering for the holidays and helped take my mind off my grief. On Christmas Eve, however, I couldn't repress the memories of Georgia's death, and the tape replayed—the whole sequence of events—over and over again in my mind.

My family was helpful and supportive. We found a couple of benches out on the intercoastal waterway, facing west, and at sunset, we gathered there with a CD player. After her death, I'd luckily found Georgia's audition tape and had it copied onto CDs that I'd give to people as a memorial for their friendship. Georgia's voice sang out that evening, and each family member said something in remembrance. The girls teared up, as did I, and we sang some of her favorite songs and carols. I read a few of my new poems about her and her death. It was a poignant and proper memorial for her. She'd always been so bubbly and vocal that time of year. I felt a hell of a lot better after that, sharing the grief and exorcising it with family.

Afterwards, we attended a memorable candlelight Christmas Eve service at the local Presbyterian Church led by Dr. Bush. His red-robed choir filled the church with the sounds of "Holy Night" and transformed the tropical setting outside the windows. My family was impressed, and Kristin would be married by the same pastor in this church some years later. On Christmas day, overlooking the beach, we unwrapped presents. I handed out Georgia's jewelry. We then all went to Palm Beach for a Christmas service at the Royal Poinciana Chapel, an interdenominational church. Each year, Jack Jones, a friend of Georgia's and the music director at Royal Poinciana, had arranged for Georgia to come to Palm Beach to sing with the local Gilbert & Sullivan group. It was good to catch up with him at this historic church next to the Flagler Museum where Georgia performed in a concert Jack helped arrange.

During the week when we weren't at the beach, we biked and toured the nature center and orchid gardens. Del Ray is much more laid back than Boca, and certainly humbler than Palm Beach. For me it was closer to "old Florida" that I remember from family vacations. I came to love the town and biked around it. I also took much time walking on the beach and talking my new situation over with Mom, who was so wise about it. I began to question what I should do for the rest of my life in this poem:

Delray Beach

Here, pelicans patrol the space over sand and sea.
They glide in prehistoric formation,
like old PBY's my uncle flew in WWII.
Sharp eyed, they peel off
and plunge into the waves.

I bike along the inter-coastal waterway,
where yachts at anchor seem posed

for mutual fund ads.
Both sides of the road are chock-a-block
with condos, leaving little of the native
mango hammock between this path
and the waterway, save some landscaped
sea-grapes and gumbo-limbos.

High rises to the dunes down the coast,
like Manhattan moved south.
And above block-like towers, buzzards
feather afternoon thermals,
unemployed and patient for roadkill.

The snowbirds, up from their naps
walk the beach afternoons,
their tracks soon scrolled smooth by the surf.
Retired from work and winters,
their time's suspended,
slowed like the traffic waiting for those yachts
to parade under yawning drawbridges
over the inter-coastal.
Along this path, trees are dedicated to departed
snowbirds with a biography on a plastic plaque.
I want to know their stories: that third date,
when they gave up the hassle
and came down here for good,
content to walk
          by the sea.

At the time, I felt a need to review my life and thought about writing
my life story, musing on Maharaj's quote about realizing the immense
sorrow in our lives that I recalled when I found the detailed outline of
my life history that I'd written in my journal at that time. The gaps were
the most interesting. I wasn't aware of what I'd lost in those holes but did
have some coverage in other journals. As I reviewed this outline, I saw
the turning points were abrupt; many were outside my control; life's plan
was not mine and the angelic influence she had on me:

Georgia took me on a path and jolted me from it. I think about how a year has passed since her death and that I miss her so deeply but have accepted the fact that I will never physically see her again but have an incredible relationship with her spirit that I know is here. I light a candle for the mistress of this valley, now in another form, but who left part of her soul in mine. She taught me kindness, love of life, love of animals, love of beauty all around me. She opened my eyes, ears, my senses to every possibility, and that was also her gift. She was a bodhisattva in disguise and took me on the path to enlightenment. I knew that, and like the sunrise, it is always in me, but I have self-doubt she had to pull out of me.

Georgia McEver as "Anna" in the Merry Widow, 1990s

Chapter 33
Mystery School

Right Speech, Pure Heart, & Compassionate Action
Mystery School Motto

There were some interim steps on the way to the rest of my life after Georgia died. On one of my trips to San Francisco in early 2002, I caught up with my cousin, Caroline McEver, a feisty redhead who looked remarkably like my sister and me. She was a graphic artist working for a New Age group out of Petaluma, called Noetics, that astronaut Edgar Mitchell had started after a religious experience he'd had during his return trip to earth. The organization dealt with consciousness, awareness, meditation, religious tolerance and understanding, particularly for the more mystic side of different religious traditions. It was a questing group of people, with a surprisingly strong science background—astronauts, psychologists, neuroscientists, etc. It thrives today, known as IONS and has over 10,000 members with chapters all over the US.

Caroline took me to an introductory meeting in Tiberon where I met Gay Luce and her husband David Patten, who ran a Mystery School as part of Noetics' event-programming in the spring and fall. My confidants and friends had advised that I should be open to new experiences during my grieving Georgia, and this piqued my interest. Mystery School explored the mysteries of ten traditions and was a guided tour of the non-traditional sides of the major religions without having to take trips to remote monasteries to experience them. It sounded damned interesting. The words "many paths" reverberated in my mind. I got an application, and in early 2002 sent it off with the deposit.

I was accepted and given some background reading. In late April 2002, I would go to Santa Barbara, where we'd gather at Casa Maria, a former convent just outside of town. Mary wanted to go as well. Casa Maria's cloistered grounds had ocean views and contained great old oaks, a wonderful chapel, and a meeting hall transformed into our temple. Bordering the property were great rows of grand shag-bark eucalyptus that brooded over all our proceedings. This fragrance always reminded me of Georgia and my blissful days together on Yerba Buena Island, a eucalyptus forest. Central sessions and ceremonies were held in the temple with participants dressed in ceremonial robes. Before leaving, I'd found an ornate ceremonial robe in my closet from the Egyptian trip Georgia and I had taken. Finding that robe convinced me I should make this journey. I was always been curious about the Greek and Roman mystery schools that thrived in ancient times. We still don't know their full mysteries since people were charged with terrible fates, including death for revealing their secrets.

The school's mantra was "Right Speech, Pure Heart, and Compassionate Action." These were our guiding principles through the different lenses of the various traditions we'd explore. We pledged this mantra to each other in our opening circle and ceremony. The altar was a gallery of the participants' loved ones, where I placed a picture of Georgia singing. I noted in my journal: "It began last night. We stood outside our temple waiting to go in. Finally, we came into a big room with people gathered in a circle in all sorts of colorful ceremonial robes. I felt it was a new home."

Open to the new experience, I was going with the flow. The first morning we were up early and with no coffee were walking barefoot in the cooling lawn to reconnect with the earth. A full moon was setting. This is a powerful and mystic sign—a sun rising or setting with a full moon opposite. We were on a path of discovery and rebirth, like snakes about to shed their skins. David Patten was the first speaker. Working for our intelligence agencies, David had learned the language, later in life going to Bali to help preserve their ancient wisdom and was translating the sacred Balinese text written on palm leaves. He spoke about the first chakra located at the foot and how our feet connect us to things, grounding us. He said that the ancients could tell things that happened miles off, being more connected to the earth with the sensors our feet provide—our "soul" where sun never shines.

After our lecture, the first initiation was rebirthing—the shedding of our old skin, a real birthing reenactment where we crawled down a live birthing canal created by fourteen people on all-fours, urged by a birthing initiator to leave our heads and let our hearts take over, as we each inched down the canal. The staff pulled each of the forty of us into the world. At first, I thought I'd make it through with no emotion, but Georgia's loss still weighed on my heart. I lost my composure with her soprano voice singing in my head and wept. At the end of the live rebirth, we experienced a spiritual one. We approached the pool where we performed a self-baptism. In white linen robes, we pledged, "Right Speech, Pure Heart, Compassionate Action" aloud before jumping in. For good measure I added, "Thy will be done."

The school was about energy, turning up that energy, and feeling it as we progressed through the different filters of these traditions. I felt close to Georgia's spirit after my rebirthing because I was followed by a black and white cat that seemed to attach itself to me. It was like a playful spirit sent from

Georgia. I went to the chapel, where at its center window, a suffering Jesus hung on a cross. The window framed a dead elm mysteriously curled, its frozen arms messaging something from purgatory, or another ungodly place. I needed to examine how I would live with this spirit and memory, on one hand inspirational—in fact, my muse—and on the other, a melancholy millstone, that could take me down. How would I balance this love for someone who'd passed with my feelings for Mary, who also had strong feelings for me, and who was sharing this experience with me?

As an initiation into the second chakra, we were blindfolded and taken into a room where our feet were submerged in water and massaged. We were then each put alone in a mirrored room and admonished by the priestess outside, "Go inside, strip, and behold your divinity. Then urinate in the glass and drink it, as it could one day save your life." Afterwards, I wasn't sure about the divinity part, but had added to my survival knowledge bank.

The second session was on community and tribal bonding, taught by an African woman who could make a drum sing. The drumming and singing greatly bonded the participants, and we left this tradition by walking out of a labyrinth constructed in the middle of a great field. I walked barefoot and was the first one out, only getting stuck once, but retraced my steps. David said the point of the labyrinth walk was to make us think about taking back the years of our busy lives as we followed the twisting path until we reached Nirvana, then returning and thinking about how we would give back in service until our deaths. This was where I hesitated, still not having an exact answer, but felt it would involve teaching or writing. I walked that labyrinth many times during my visit, trying to un-knot that question. Towards the end of the school, the clouds parted, and it became a little clearer.

The following sessions were meant to release the next layer of emotions. They were taught by Gay. We reenacted certain emotions—love, hate, anger, envy—and then went through true confessions with a randomly drawn partner. Our next spiritual experience was with a Navajo shaman in a sweat lodge. We sat gathered in a circle and drifted into a trance-like state, propelled by low drumming. All experienced different visions and shared them. I imagined my earlier dream image of an eagle dancer. We were urged again to shed our skins, like being in a hot confession booth—our sins sweated out of all of us to cleanse our souls.

The Sufi session was our most interesting because of its combined music, words, and religion with powerful intent. We whirled like dervishes, inducing a meditative state. Many slogans and mantras were repeated while turning: "Speech is most powerful; do things that are simple first; music is optimistic;

pessimists miss opportunity; beauty is bringing order to chaos; empty yourself to make room for God; make friends with your life." I felt elated, elevated, and like I was still spinning, even after we finally stopped.

We left in early May, retracing the ritual walk and labyrinth before our exit. The day had clouded. Our energy levels had been turned to full, and now, we were empty and exhausted. Time to sober up and get back into the world, reintegrate with it. I was inspired to rearrange my life to fit a new pattern with the new knowledge and energy I'd gained there. I was on a new path, but where was it taking me?

Georgia McEver as "Mabel" in the Pirates of Penzance, Central Park, NYC, 1980s

Chapter 34
Among the Joshua Trees

Back in NYC from Santa Barbara, I went to work, but after Georgia's death and my mystery school experience, it would never again be the usual jumping on airplanes to pursue every piece of business that may promise revenues. I left this to my younger partners and became more selective and focused. Also, just before her passing, I'd secured a new corporate headquarters for us on the 19th floor of 535 Madison with stunning views of Madison Avenue south and north. We got the most favorable deal on a ten-year lease. As part of the deal, I'd purchased the full floor of built-ins and office furniture. With this office, we were set with plenty of space for expansion. It was now up to me to recapitalize the firm and rebalance my life as well. I had much to think about, and I found I did my best thinking at Utopia.

The Metro North's Harlem Line was my method of escape from NYC on weekends. After rumbling through the Bronx, this straight line north borders the idyllic reservoirs that Robert Moses built in the 1930s to quench the Big Apple's thirst. Just past a stop aptly named Valhalla, there's a population of swans gracing the lakes that I believe screen negative thoughts, so that they get left behind in the city. One of the first poems I wrote is about these birds:

The Swans at Goldens Bridge

Those elegant white hooks slide by, sustained
on their long lake,
along MetroNorth's Harlem Valley line.

Through the perpetually
filthy commuter car
windows, I religiously
search for my totems.

Hello, my mystic friends:
pen, cob, and cygnets,
floating on your halficed waters.

You are Friday's first salutation
and Monday's aesthetic farewell.

Viewing those beautiful birds never failed to inspire me. I was reading *The Tibetan Book of Living and Dying* in preparation for my return to mystery school in Joshua Tree in September. Most of Wall Street flees, heading for the Hamptons or the Berkshires at the end of summer, so I traditionally took the last days of August off. Since 1983, I've retreated to Utopia, overlooking the Housatonic River winding through an impenetrable wetland I own on the opposite shore.

Over Labor Day weekends, Georgia's opera company, the Light Opera Company of Salisbury ("LOCOS"), gets together and puts on a weekend of light opera, usually Gilbert & Sullivan pieces. When Georgia tired of the rat race of constant auditions, she retreated to our farm and started LOCOS in 1995. It was a great success because she had her friends from NYC, who were professional singers of some renown, come up and sing leading parts, while the locals sang in the chorus, occasionally performing a lead, and prepared the sets and backdrops. The orchestra was local as well. The event was held at a large auditorium at Hotchkiss School every Labor Day weekend. Georgia sang the female lead, coaching the chorus and directing the production, a true player-coach. The years she directed were sell-outs.

Harriet and Paul Tomasko—with whom Georgia had toured—took over the production after Georgia's death. They had talent, energy, and good voices, plus the determination to keep LOCOS going. Georgia's other friends kept up the tradition as well, volunteering their time to come up for a long weekend in the Berkshires to carry on the tradition. Harriet and Paul managed to keep LOCOS alive until the summer of 2012.

Over Labor Day of 2002, the performance was *Pirates of Penzance*, and LOCOS was in fine form. Georgia's sister Holly visited for the weekend to help me through the show. A type-A personality, Holly took charge of things for me, but her keen sense of humor made some heavy moments lighter. There was a lot to manage. In addition to the performance, there was also a party for the entire cast and neighborhood. Our caretaker Eli was to be one of the pirates. He'd diligently learned his lines and sang while caring for the horses in our barn, "Oh, I love that pirate's sherry..."

Holly and I helped the troupe put up the sets and dismantle them. We traditionally held the cast party at the old lodge, overlooking where the rivers converged. I had one of Eli's friends, Ritchie, a former chef, cater the affair. He barbequed ribs and chicken, to be washed down with a keg of beer, and cases of red and white wine. Nature took its course, with the locals and the New York crews mingling. The show was good, the cast jubilant, and the community grateful. We held a joyful party, all toasting, and at the end of the day, missing our diva.

Having fulfilled my business and end-of-summer obligations, I was finally on my way to the desert and out to Joshua Tree. I'd never been in the desert, so it was a new environment for me. I looked forward to picking up where I left off in spring, listening to the quiet voice inside, trying to divine a future course. We were assigned cabins—concrete and glass triangular affairs strung along a desert road down from our temple meditation center. It was a fantastic natural cathedral. We were in the desert with the Joshua trees and the cacti and the most fantastic rock out-cropping—sandstone or something more substantial that became more and more bizarre.

We gathered ceremoniously robed in our community circle that evening, affirming our vows to all: "Right Speech, Purity of Heart, and Compassionate Action." It was good to be back with this group and hear everyone's interim journeys, but then we went into silence. We had spiritual work to do. Dinner was silent, and there was an auspicious rainbow that graced our gathering as we came out of the dining hall, followed by a showy sunset. The passing storm's clouds billowed, ribbing the sky in shades of pink like a Frederick Church painting.

The next morning, we met in the refectory to experience the Christian mystic tradition. We were there with a woman appropriately named Mary, who at sixty-five, had left the Franciscan order after over forty years to devote her life to a mystic Christian path. There was something saintly about her calming presence that resonated with me. Though she addressed the group, she seemed to just be speaking to me, coaxing me out. Soon, she had us kneel in prayer that evolved into prostrations. After a couple of bows, I felt the underlying sadness leave me, but lurking beneath was ego, pride, and a haughtiness that ran out before the Lord. He'd broken me finally, and I allowed his greatness and my humbleness to find their balance. The ego dump was cathartic and flowed out of me when my head to the touched floor. My eyes filled with tears as I began to feel a burden lifted. I was open to a much higher feeling. These feelings went on for the next few days. I had shed some part of my ego, and the world was more alive. I was more aware.

We did more ego-stripping meditations with Mary the following morning after a spectacular sunrise. The desert was reciprocating the respect we'd shown it with dramatic heavenly displays for sunset and sunrise, and star-spangled skies to humble us at night. After a long day of mind management and discovery, we put on ceremonial robes. After our procession that halted at the pool near dusk, we were admonished to give up our worst elements, then plunged in the pool to be purified. We sang "Gloria en Excelsis Deo" while marching up Om Hill where there was a scripture reading from the Thomas Gospel and a sermon by Mary and Gay. As the sun was setting, we were given the sacraments and went into silent meditation.

The next session would be Hindu with a guru who was a monk from a line of gurus that practice the fire ceremony in Banaras (now called Varanasi). He'd also gotten an MBA as I found out but had given up his business pursuits to be an active guru and yogi. Babaji has a flourishing ashram in Sonoma County, and we've become friends. He led a fire ceremony the first evening where we burned all the bad thoughts and habits. We also paid respect to our ancestors and loved ones lost. His yoga sessions also put me at peace, an incredible peace. He said when you wake up, have a word, talk to, and bless the divine in you. "Speak to God and keep your word." He also had another tidbit of advice: see which nostril is open when you first wake, use it as a sign, and start the day on that foot."

Our last teacher was a martial arts specialist in the Taoist tradition who led us in Tai Chi exercises. We stepped outside into the exercise circle while the sun rose. It was a quite dramatic start of the day with the desert backdrop. I find this tradition most appealing, as it is symbolic, the intertwining circles of the yin and yang—the world is in balance. It's us who are out of balance, and we should try to get in sync with the mysterious "way."

The last day of school we were supposed to die and go into bardo—the intermediate state of existence between two lives on earth—the space between death and a rebirth. We'd been working up to this moment over our time there. We were going to die that evening, so we spent the afternoon saying goodbye to everyone and our loved ones. We were to sit at the foot of the creator. We stayed up all night chanting for the dead and reading from the Book of the Dead. Before that we were asked to envision our life as a movie. I ran out of time reimagining my life because

I had too much to tell. We were paired to go through the experience. I was paired with a lady ironically named Anne. She and I were the first ones through the darkness of an imagined death. Afterwards, we were placed on pillows under the arms of pines looking at the stars and were released of all illusion.

The next morning, we walked up Om Hill and had a communion of bread and apple juice—repossessing ourselves—watched the glorious sunrise and were rebirthed. When asked to comment on the experience, I simply said, "Awareness" and walked back holding hands with Gay and the others.

Before we were to die, we wrote down what we wanted to complete for the rest of our lives, and I wrote the following that remains surprisingly relevant:

1. I wish to complete building my company and leave a whole, viable, competitive entity capable of carrying on 100 years. It should be an example of a successful, prosperous entity that has right intent and practices compassionate action.
2. I want to complete my relationship with my family, particularly my mother before she leaves the planet, reconcile things with my sister, and love my nieces and nephews.
3. Find, again, a stable, loving life partner.
4. Complete my chapbook for Georgia and write more poetry that is powerful, compelling, and moving for others on the path that tells of my experience.
5. I wish to explore putting together a mystery school, seminar, or retreat for other corporate executives to teach them how to enter and stay on the path, how to blend a spiritual life so their businesses will be more meaningful and thoughtful. I think there is longing in many leaders for this path.
6. I would hope to find spiritual enlightenment in this lifetime.
7. Lastly, I wish someday to just be a poet living with someone I love at Utopia.

What I realized rereading this journal entry was that these points were to be, in fact, guiding metaphors for me over the ensuing years, indeed were long trails persisting today and well into the future.

Chapter 35
Trip to Greece: Living Waters

It was hard to fathom our trip was still on. Our minister Dick Taber was taking a contingent of the Salisbury Congregational Church on a pilgrimage to follow in the footsteps of Paul through Greece on the eve of the start of the Iraq War in March 2003. The US began its attack on Iraq the same evening our trip was to begin. When we showed up at the airport, crowds were glued to the TVs, watching laser-guided missiles find their targeted refinery or ammunition bunker, resolve with a bright flash, then a serious moderator who began with great solemnity, "Today, allied forces bombed…"

I couldn't believe we were at it again, this time starting a war to avenge the towers. What I couldn't get out of my mind was my time at the Pentagon and my knowledge of how war was waged. I could imagine the current Pentagon analysts debating the same kinds of targeting issues we'd had in the late sixties as we became mired in Southeast Asia. Now those analysts did not even understanding the religious differences within the country they were going to blitz and liberate. I didn't think it would go well. Would we ever learn?

The next morning, we arrived in a much more heavily trafficked and polluted Athens than I remembered from my time as an exchange student in the spring of 1966. The classic ruined grandeur of ancient Greece that reached heights not surpassed for centuries thereafter, hovered over and out of a cloud of bronze pollution produced by our new age carbon-dependent society. Choked in congestion, we crawled through to our hotel. It made a great poetic statement but a poor post card. The trip's premise was to retrace the pilgrimage that Paul had undertaken to bring the Good Word to the gentiles. I felt close to my traveling companions and fellow congregants. They'd taken me in and become an important part of my support network after Georgia died. I felt this was the community I wanted to live among, so it was fitting that I was embarking on this journey with them, together on a spiritual and historical discovery trip of sorts.

As we traveled the early spring landscape of Greece, looking out the bus windows at the white clouds of blossoming olive trees across the countryside, the guide recounted the history of ancient Greece and its gods. We traveled into the sacred valley of Delphi, one of my favorite places on earth and where I feel something speak to me, an ancient presence, and I wished the priestess was still prophesizing. I wondered what she'd say about this war to tell our leaders today? I doubted it would be a thumbs up.

We then journeyed on to the monasteries atop the rock pillars of Meteora, where black-robed monks were carried in baskets and ferried with supplies up to their sanctuaries.

The devotion of these ancient fathers always amazed me. A pilgrimage to Mt. Athos and similar momentariness has always been on my bucket list. The dark mysticism of these places still reeking with incense and reverberating with chanting has a strange appeal; maybe I was there in a former life and these places trigger a memory washed away by the river Lethe?

Meditating on Paul's pilgrimage, I also thought of my early church upbringing. Other than semi-regular attendance at the Methodist church as a child, I had little spiritual life other than my nature wanderings. At heart, I was a Southern Methodist by Sunday-schooling and a pantheist by practice. Now wrangling with myself about whether to attend Divinity School, I remember attending church in college and graduate school, and Georgia and I had continued to go to church in NYC. Georgia went when she became in demand as a soloist. We discovered our true community however, when we became members of Salisbury Congregational Church. The community made the difference. After Georgia's death and Dick's interpretation of my vision had been personal turning points. The grieving, meditating, deep-reading, and soul-searching had all served to deepened my faith. I was becoming intrigued by the idea of divinity school.

Paul had begun his conversion with a vision so powerful that it blinded him, knocking him off his horse. Subsequently, rather than persecuting Christians, he became their principal evangelist. He seemed guided by dreams. One night, after preaching in Alexandria Troas, or ancient Troy, he had a vision that a Macedonian man invited him to cross the strait to help them. Thus, the gospel came to Greece and eventually spread to Rome and beyond. After crossing into Greece, Paul was thrown out of Thessalonica and Berea—places we visited. We followed Paul to Athens, where he'd gone for sanctuary. There, he'd gone to the public market, the Agora, to preach where he encountered Epicurean and Stoic

philosophers and students. He was taken to the Areopagus, the rock of
Ares, where the high court asked him to explain himself. Acts 17:23-24
recount this event:

> And Paul stood in the midst of the Areopagus, and said,
> Ye men of Athens, in all things, I perceive that ye are very
> religious. For as I passed along, and observed the objects
> of your worship, I found also an altar with this inscription,
> TO AN UNKNOWN GOD. What therefore ye worship in
> ignorance, this I set forth unto you. The God that made the
> world and all things therein, he, being Lord of heaven and
> earth, dwelleth not in temples made with hands....

Acts 17 is the most dynamic and the fullest record of Paul's teachings
we have. It's also the hub of Christian teaching. I love that he chooses
to base his sermon on the statue to the Unknown God.

On the morning of our third day, we went up to the Parthenon,
and on the way down, stopped at the rock of Ares where Paul made
this speech. We had a good view of the city and a better one of
the Agora ruins. I tried to imagine listening to Paul as one of those
philosophy students. Almost every ruin is devoted to a different god,
and I could picture his incredulous look upon his seeing the plethora
of them. I also felt his skepticism and frustration at trying to persuade
the hard-nosed philosophers, who doubted everything, that there was a
man-god who'd risen from the dead. That's a hard sell, and the reason
Paul spent much of his time in and out of prison.

It was beautiful spring weather as we headed north to Philippi.
In a stream running down from the mountain top at Philippi, Paul
had baptized Lydia, his first woman convert. I was so overwhelmed
by the history, place, and day that I asked Dick to rebaptize me there.
Graham Davidson, our church moderator and my roommate for this
trip decided to join me. Graham would pass away from esophageal
cancer not two years later. The crystal-clear stream ran through the
pits, all along the streambed, where purple goods had been dyed in
ancient times. At the stream a monument commemorates Lydia's
baptism. She was not only the first woman, but the first convert in
Europe. From that spot, Christianity began its march to Rome and the
rest of the world. Dick rebaptized Graham and me out of this stream
in Philippi. This occasion was a rededication for me, a stepping up to

recognize that the good Lord had gotten me through a dark valley with my faith intact and thriving.

Living Waters

I go back to my rebaptism in Greece.
My church group following
Paul's footsteps 2000 years later in Philippi,
along the river snaking through
the clay pits where Lydia
dyed her purple cloth
and became the first woman
he baptized.

I was moved to ask my pastor
to baptize me again while a friend
who passed two years later,
sprung to join me, to be
sprinkled with those living waters.
Beyond, I saw blue mountains
whose high springs sourced the river,
sluicing down and over ancient
aqueducts to the town…

I thought of this water
bubbling from the earth
to cleanse me, to rededicate
my life to creative service,
and fellowship with friends.

Ideas gushing from the pressure
of what's right inside you—
quenching a long thirst from wandering a desert
with distrust as a companion.
I find those living waters inside me,
sourced out of hard rocks
at Saratoga, Horeb
and the mountains above Philippi.

There was a lady from Saratoga, referenced in the poem above, wasn't a member of our congregation but accompanied Debbie Marks a church choir member and one of Georgia's LOCOS troop on our trip. Debbie was always talking, while Brooke Conklin was quiet, thoughtful and a master photographer. She quietly took a picture of me meditating behind St. John's house on Patmos and sent it to me after we returned. We talked on the trip and became friends later when she became LOCO's costumer.

Bruce McEver & Wally Lanahan at Dedication of Opera Studio, Peabody Conservatory, Baltimore, MD, 2001

Chapter 36
The Selling of Berkshire
The History of Berkshire Capital—Part X

The world and my bereaved mind seemed clearer after my travels in Paul's footsteps. I realized my practical and mystical life revolved around that unknown, like a wheel around its axle, or numbers around zero. I plunged back into my business life, pursuing deals while trying to balance my personal and writing lives around my travels and responsibilities. As early as spring 2002, Richard Foote had confided that the troops were dissatisfied by my majority holding in Berkshire Capital, in light of my increasing travel and devotion to other interests. Bruce was too polite to tell me. Knowing this inevitability, I consistently sold down shares. However, the fact was that the company was still too valuable for our junior officers to purchase control of it. Thus, we needed to sell a partial interest of the company so that I could realize the value and recapitalize the holdings, simultaneously giving the junior officers a larger stake in the company. Strategically we needed to expand internationally, as the asset management business and many of our clients were global firms. To accomplish this, we needed an outside buyer.

For the next two years, I knew that my principle responsibility was to find a new business partner, one who could help me rebalance the financial ownership of the firm; as well as make money for myself and the original shareholders from the sale of part of our equity. The buyer needed to have the wherewithal and international presence to help us expand overseas. If we wanted to be leaders in the industry, the business needed to head in this direction. I didn't have the capital personally, nor did I want to undertake the liability that entailed. Most likely, I would have had to sell a minority interest in the firm since my partners wouldn't tolerate giving up control. My legacy and the firm's were also in the balance. I wanted the name to continue, and with a total sale, that was at risk. These factors made it a much more difficult sale, and there wasn't a huge market or a clamoring demand for small financial services firms. To get on with the other parts of my life beyond Berkshire, I had to sell an interest in the business and balance the ownership with those who'd be running it. It was no easy feat—indeed, it would take most of my focus and energies, but my two-year goal was clear: give my partners back some of my control in the company, make a profit for all involved as I did so, and become a global firm.

I learned quickly that it was a tough task I'd set for myself. In late fall 2002—a glorious time in the Berkshires—I went on a long bicycle ride with my neighbor Scott Bok, an investment banker who'd trained at Morgan Stanley and co-founded Greenhill & Co., a boutique firm specializing in M&A. He lived in the former Borden family estate, down the road from Utopia. He was a friend, so I could confide my plans to him, and as an experienced M&A banker, he'd tell me what was possible. First, he said it was a job that Greenhill couldn't undertake because of its size and their minimum fee standards, meaning we needed to make over $10 million. This job would be like finding a needle in a haystack, and something I'd have to do myself. However, it was doable—we'd developed a name in the industry and a unique niche. I'd also institutionalized the firm and had some good partners. Importantly, we'd built an excellent reputation. Scott reassured me that with persistence, and some luck, it could happen.

At a spring 2003 shareholders meeting, I reported about this and similar meetings with other industry-savvy folks and laid out my plan to my partners and shareholders. We agreed we needed to take this course of action to properly transition the firm. We put together a small internal team consisting of Bruce Cameron, Richard Foote, Desmond McCarthy, and me because we didn't want anyone outside of the partners and shareholders to know we were trying to sell the firm. In a confidential memorandum that succinctly told our story, we pulled together our deal history, some summary financials, and a brief overview of the firm. At that point, I needed to contact each potential target personally and let nature take its course. I fashioned each sale pitch based on a potential buyer's reaction and interest.

We made a list of approximately fifty firms—both domestic and international—that could potentially be interested. We researched them carefully and began to make top-level contacts. There were large banks and financial service firms, but also smaller regional investment banks and boutiques, as well as wealthy families I'd run across over the years who'd expressed interest in getting into the financial services industry. It was a fascinating list, and over the next year, I got to know the businesses intimately, developing a rapport with the decision-makers in order to ascertain their strategies and how we'd sync.

In a planning meeting later in 2003, I made a presentation with Bruce and Desmond to our shareholders, outlining what I'd discovered about our prospects for finding a good partner:

1. To sell about a third of the company at a value of six- to eight-times pretax profits (the standard way financial service firms are valued).

2. If we made between $2-4 million, the total valuation would be $18-24 million, one-third of which would be sold. Typically, half of this sum would be the down-payment with the balance to be paid out over three to five years.

3. It was a good time to sell because we were coming off record earnings of over $3 million pretax from the Wachovia/Prudential deal, that, at the time, was the largest securities firm merger on record.

4. Currently, the economic future looked bright, and the prospects for the merger business in our corners of the financial services industry seemed endless.

The Canadian banks, specifically their investment banking branches, were by far the most interested. They needed to expand into the US, and all realized the potential of doing this quickly through us and the financial services sector. The only rub with the Canadians was that they insisted on owning control of Berkshire Capital. They wanted to expand our product offering. This was also true of the US regional investment banks that would help us expand into the banking and insurance M&A business, as well as into underwriting. I couldn't find anyone interested in a minority stake, so I went back to my friends at Caledonia.

I'd visited Jamie Cayzer-Colvin in London in April 2002. We'd begun discussions about what I knew would be coming regarding Berkshire Capital. His family's company liked to invest in companies in management transition by taking a minority position and holding it for a long time, while helping management but not interfering with the governance. Minority stakes were their modus operandi, realizing cleverly that they often could never control partners, but could share in economic interests. They would thus pick up a large part of both my and our outside shareholders' stakes in the business while working with the partners to increase their ownership stake. They'd also help us expand internationally, especially in the UK and Europe. It was pretty ideal, but I'd discovered others interested as well.

My friend Richard Goblet d'Alviella ran Sofina out of Brussels and was also interested. Sofina was a publicly traded closed-end shell of a company once owning Belgium's steel industry that Richard's family controlled, and that he'd liquidated. He was interested, but wasn't as organized as Caledonia, nor worked as fast. Sofina tended to take minority positions and bought public blocks of stock like Caledonia did. During this process, I introduced Jamie and Richard, and they now each serve on the other's company board.

During this process I met other fascinating people who would prove valuable contacts for future business, such as the foundation that owns the Swedish Match Corporation and private banks in Switzerland and Germany—both Vontoble and Metzler—that would have helped with our European expansion. Through slow and careful work, what I ended up with was the competitive horse race I wanted to foster all along. In the deal business, it's amazing how you start with no interest, and as industry knowledge grows, somehow word gets around, and the project gets competitively bid. I didn't want the world to know about our desire to sell but needed those interested to know they weren't the only bids and thus, couldn't low-ball me. It worked. After we issued a bid letter, we got four serious responses. The strategy and efforts that I used for my clients had worked for us as well.

The partners and shareholders meeting I called soon thereafter was memorable. Settling the group, I opened: "You've probably been wondering what I've been doing these last months and the progress on the sale you authorized. Well, I have here three formal bid letters. One from Caledonia, a publicly traded, closed-end fund in London. Two from Canadian banks—Scotia Bank of Canada and the Bank of Montreal's investment bank, Nesbitt Thomson. I also have an indication of interest from Sofina, another public closed-end fund in Brussels."

"You must be kidding," was the initial response. Most were surprised at the breadth of the list and the positive response by a handful of quality names, and three actual bids. They were still in denial that I had found any interest at all, and certainly not at a respectable level.

"I've provided you with a copy of the letters in the folders in front of you, and Richard has a detailed analysis of each proposal, also enclosed."

We went through each bid in detail. Predictably, they didn't want to sell control to the Canadians, so the outside shareholders and I would leave some money on the table to go with Caledonia. Sofina's bid wasn't as good and was a bit vague. In the end, my partners and shareholders decided to take Caledonia's offer, and though with Bruce, the outside shareholders, and myself, we had a controlling vote, we didn't want to ruffle any feathers with a power play. We needed everyone's cooperation so as not to lose control of the firm or its name.

After this meeting, however, the internal partners ganged up on me and wanted better terms than the outside shareholders, so personally, I had to make concessions to get the deal done, but it was worth it. I took a sizeable capital stake off the table in order to be free to pursue my interests, as well as to be able to continue in the business with a salary and participate in the bonus pool if I produced. Everyone was benefitting from this sale, and in the end, we had a strong international stakeholder. I wanted to get this fish in the boat.

After this coup, I celebrated my 60th birthday in Atlanta on February 8th at a great party that my mom and cousin Billy Mitchel threw at the Peachtree Driving Club. I had all my Atlanta friends and relatives, including Tom Lux. Mom was my date. I got a number of journals and good books, and best wishes for carrying on with life and finding the right person to share it with.

By early spring, we were deep into the details of the deal. Problems weren't over, however, and as with all deal vectors, they're fine one day only to become a problem the next, as I noted in my journal on April 5, 2004:

> It was the day the deal fell apart, or almost fell apart. The first issue involved our status as a sub-S corporation that will be blown up by selling shares to an outside foreign shareholder. Our accountants and attorneys didn't pick up on this issue early enough, so it required a whole re-structuring of the company and an examination of the tax implications. The second issue involved a projection sent by our COO that was a couple of million off a previous projection, so they wanted to have a conference call tomorrow. Richard Foote has been the main problem here. I was livid by the end of the day and retreated to the Harvard Club for a good dinner and to watch the Tech/UConn basketball championships to calm down.

Several things were happening. The folks at Caledonia were savvy and looking for ways to reduce their first full price. We supplied them with the excuse by providing a set of projections that were a couple of million off from our originals, and they pounced on the opportunity to lower their cost. One of my partners, who was trying to crater the deal in a most blatant attempt, made the mistake. The legal structure of our firm was a sub-S—an ideal start-up form of corporation—but had to be changed to a more complicated limited liability company, so a foreign company could own part of it. The problem then became paying the taxes on the gain in the value of the firm since its origin as a sub-S business.

Richard Foote was our best deal guy, though sometimes erratic in his negotiations. He and the proper British gentlemen at Caledonia didn't see eye to eye. Richard also got the idea of leveraging the firm and having the partners buy it from me. Leveraging a cyclical firm like ours was not a prudent approach. By selling to a wealthy company and family, I was attempting to reduce the risk for my partners, not increase it. I had to have several serious talks with him about the deal and keep his personality out of it. We buried the hatchet a few weeks later over a lunch. After Richard passed away suddenly a few years ago, I wrote this poem describing him in action:

For Our Partner
(Richard Stuart Foote, May 28, 1963-April 25, 2014)

It was at the time tulips
soldier-up straight and brighten
Park Avenue's corners early spring.

In a mahogany chaired conference room
overlooking the traffic tangle on that avenue below,
we gathered to review his deal.

With swept-back hair and a broad smile,
Richard was in fine form—
lean in a tailored blazer,
he exuded confidence,
As he explained the subtleties
of his model, you saw the path

to the gates of Golconda open wide.
It all meshed, like a Bach fugue—
the notes complex, yet ethereal
in hearing, even hum-able.

We parted, shaking hands and joking,
and Richard scootered-off to chemo,
like Jesus rode the ass's colt,
through cheers and waving palms to Calvary.

Our partner and friend—
a brilliant, courageous warrior-banker
we could always count on,
till his Lord called him
that day of tulips.

I somehow had to get the deal back on track. We changed our legal
structure and paid back taxes. Then it would only be a matter of time
and passing British regulatory issues, which proved to be minimal. There
was a significant price adjustment in the end, from eight- to six-times
estimated pre-tax earnings, but I decided to proceed anyway. I also had to
adjust the prices my outside shareholders would receive, so my working
partner shareholders would get a better price. It was not a clean deal, but
in the end, it enabled me to take away a significant chunk of cash, and
depending on age and length of service, it also enabled my shareholders
and senior partners to take something off the table as well. Cash, at the
time, was a more valuable commodity than currently and, more impor-
tantly, knowing excellent money managers; I could invest it with them to
diversify as well as grow my holdings.

The deal closed in mid-May 2004. My day of freedom had arrived.
I could now begin to think about continuing the other parts of my life
that were waiting. It was also important that I begin traveling in the East
since I believed the future of our firm was its ability to be a global player.
Caledonia would help significantly with our presence in the UK and
Europe. I needed to figure out what was going on in China and Australia.
In the back of my mind, I had the thought of becoming a student at
either Warren Wilson for an MFA in poetry or Harvard Divinity School.
I also needed to find someone to share my life with, but this sale would

enable my growth to another stage. My life suddenly felt more stable and from this base I felt like I might be able to take off to a different level, as C. S Lewis once intimated:

> God became man to turn creatures into sons... to produce a new kind of man... like turning a horse into a winged creature... But there may be a period, while the wings were just beginning to grow when it could not do so, and at that stage the lumps on the shoulders—no one could tell by looking at them that they were going to be wings—may give it an awkward appearance... That someday we may ride bare back.
>
> *Mere Christianity*
> C. S. Lewis

Chairman of Berkshire Global Advisors, Bruce McEver, Madison Ave., NYC, 2010

Chapter 37
Go West, Young Man, Go West to the Far East

I began my trips to Asia thinking, today Horace Greeley would amend his famous advice. I was excited about exploring where the future growth of the planet was supposed to take place. I needed to assess whether it might and if we could realistically conduct business in Asia. However, I had to take care of some business closer to home before leaving.

After Memorial Day 2004, I headed to Atlanta to attend my first meeting as a trustee of the Georgia Tech Foundation. Mom was proud of me for being asked to join this auspicious group who ran all things Tech, as well as much of Atlanta. Because of my background, I was assigned to the investment committee. Since the state had cut back its funding, the Foundation had to maintain the school's excellence—acquiring real estate for campus expansion, as well as underwriting scholarships and exceptional professors' salaries. With an endowment of just over a billion dollars, shrewd investments mattered for state funded school with budgets tightening.

This trip I also introduced my friend, poet Tom Lux (who I'd persuaded to come to Atlanta) to Penny Thompson—one of Georgia's best and oldest friends. Tom needed someone to acquaint him with the city and the South. Penny was just the woman for the task, and like him, she was a voracious reader. Both suffering from divorce hangovers, they soon bonded. Tom had acquired a four-story townhouse in Midtown, the top floor of which he'd stuffed with books, creating a memorable literary nest. No one read more than Tom—a self-educating junkie. He literally had stacks of interesting books—everything from the lives of poets to war histories and forestry at various stages of reading. Penny didn't end up with Tom; Jennifer Holley, a wonderful lady and writer, did, later inheriting his incredible library. Penny, however left her classic Bluthner Grand piano she inherited from Georgia ironically to the Peachtree Luthern Church (where we held Mom's memorial service).

That Sunday I went with Mom to Northside Methodist to hear Gil Watson, a remarkable preacher. He would later preside at the marriage of my niece, Ansley, and at Mother's memorial service. His message that bright spring morning was that it wasn't our endgame that mattered, but what we became along the way. "You are not the love you are meant to be until you give it away," he said, reminding me of one of my favorite poems, Cavafy's "Ithaca," whose message is similar—the joy of a well lived life.

In June 2004, I was off to China just in time to make the opening of the Harvard Business School-sponsored conference on the future of China after its absorption of Hong Kong—its only door currently open to the West. On the way to China, I stopped off in San Francisco to meet up with Mary, who was eager about the trip. We didn't sleep well going out and crashed at our hotel, situated in the Shanghai financial district that was then under construction with crews on bamboo scaffolding working around the clock—impressive.

I'd been to China before—principally to Hong Kong—several times but only once to Shanghai. I saw a tremendous difference between the city that I'd visited ten years earlier. Now pollution permeated, not only was it in the air and stinging our eyes, but it also made us cough. When I'd first come to Shanghai in the nineties, there were thousands of bicycles in the streets. Now cars dominated, and the traffic was tied in knots. This was progress?

After a full day of conferencing, Mary and I changed for dinner then took a bus to a folk ballet based on the last five dynasties of China. It was a beautiful blur of color, movement, and dashing choreography. The dinner was a stand-up champagne affair. Though the evening was thoroughly a spectacle, we left early, still exhausted and very jet lagged.

At the end of a most informative week, we took a plane to Tibet, a last-minute decision. I'd never been there and might not get another chance. I was also curious about Tibetan Buddhism but paid for my curiosity. Within an hour of landing, I realized this trip was a mistake because we hadn't properly acclimated enough to be dropped into Lhasa at over 11,000 feet in elevation. Mary and I were aching, as was half our group. When we got to the hotel, some of the debilitated crowd improved with oxygen from portable tanks, but that evening proved hellish. The next morning I had no relief from a splitting headache and a painful rash that had developed along my ribcage.

The guide took four of us to the emergency room where we were examined and given oxygen—an instant relief! The physicians there determined my rash was herpes, pointing it out in a medical book.

It turned out to be shingles. After all the stress of finalizing the sale of Berkshire, a trans-Pacific trip, and severe altitude sickness, shingles attacked when I was weakest. Walking out of the hospital to continue this adventure, I felt very mortal.

One of the trip's highlights was the Dalai Lama's summer palace. Decorated in gold and yellow and with an incredible view of the highest mountains in the world, it's symbolic of the Dalai Lama's power, yet also represents the power of a monk to rule a people. On one wall, there was the curious story of the Tibetan creation myth. The picture showed the founding monkey—an Adam-like character—meditating and becoming lonely, wandering over to the cave of the rock ogress. Their union produced a family of early man, who were happy in their valley home. Later, in the museum, we were to see the implements of the earliest humans who'd lived there. The painting was remarkably Darwinian for its suggestion that men descended from monkeys, and equally bold was a picture of the Dalai Lama, who the Chinese loathe because of his popularity, but who was still on the walls of his palace.

On the last day, I was recovering slowly and finally found some peace at one monastery that until the altitude sickness, I'd thought I would find in Tibet. There was a large group of monks touring the Norbulingka Palace with us, paying reverent respect to the Dalai Lama—none spoke English. How I wanted to sit down with a monk, as I'd heard the afternoon tour was able to do. I found some respite in the garden across from the palace—two teahouses in the middle of a rectangular lake. A crew of blue-coveralled workers with red helmets—both men and women—were repairing a bridge to the teahouse islands chanting a work song. I walked around the lake and on the steps, realized great peace watching a pair of ducks, like those in ancient Chinese paintings. Pure serenity, the first I'd felt since I'd arrived.

In Lhasa, the tallest building is the Portola—the Dalai Lama's former winter palace. It was once full of monks, but the brotherhood had been significantly cut because of defections, political prisoners, and general discouragement. The second highest building is an ugly, brown, almost-windowless modern tower—the headquarters of the secret police. People enter for interrogation but don't come out. The Chinese have also built highspeed trains to

move people, supplies, and armies into Tibet. They are steadily re-
populating the country with the Han Chinese, so, soon, the Tibetans
will be a minority in their own country. It's a tragedy being enacted
in our lifetime as reflected in this poem:

Prayer Flags

Just landed and leadened with oxygen sickness
I climb its Acropolis, to the Portola,
the Dalai Lama's winter palace.
It is painful to breathe, to put one foot forward,
but imagining thousands of saffron robed monks
once chanting up there keeps me going.

In an inner chamber, a painting
depicts the Tibetan peoples' origins from monkeys.
A playful and prayerful lot,
they decorate their land above the tree line
with prayer flags of symbolic colors.

Up the shoulders of ridge trails, at every turn,
cairns hold those tattered scraps,
colorful sacred scarecrows.
Flags fly from poles on corners of Tibetan homes
with smoke curling from central hearths helping prayers to
heaven.
Tattered bits of cloth, blue for sky, red, earth,
green for water, and yellow, spirit, pray,
Farmyards with adobe walls hold the family fortune:
scrawny chickens, a withered cow, and shaggy yak.

Their windows wear heavy eyeliner,
like the all-seeing eye of Buddha.
Monks spin prayer wheels for tourists and wink,
sneaking us little gold framed glimpses
of His Holiness under the folds of their robes.

On the way to the airport our bus
falls behind a military convoy;
red-starred liberators on maneuvers
allow no one to break their ranks.
Scraps of cloth on hillsides
flap in stiff breeze,
praying they will someday
find their way home.

Bruce McEver and Randolph Kwei in China with Daoshi (Taoist Priest)

Chapter 38
Along the Swannanoa River: The Warren Wilson School

After my recovery from the China trip, my writing interests took me to North Carolina for the first session of the Warren Wilson's 2004 summer MFA program that, courtesy of Tom Lux, I was fortunate enough to be able to sample. The program opened with an address by Ellen Bryant Voigt, the program's founder and intellectual inspiration. She pioneered its low-residency MFA program where students attended school with workshop leaders and their classmates for a concentrated couple of weeks in the winter and summer, and then worked long-distance, corresponding weekly with a mentor for the rest of the year. Voigt challenged us to work intensely and breathe in the atmosphere of this gathering of writers. I jumped in with both feet.

The opening speaker the following morning was Heather McHugh—a woman so verbally acute and perceptive that I inscribed and underlined the following sentence in my notes: "I wanted to tape her craft talk on poetry." I got soaked in a Southern summer downpour going out afterwards to the store with Tom for coffee and soap. For the evening student reading, I read my poem "On the Road" (see pp 207) that was upliftingly cheered by the supportive assembled writers.

The next day writer-teachers gave stimulating lectures. There were talks on prosody, as well as on the topic of infusing a philosophical idea into concrete writing, followed by a treatise on river poems as metaphor. The place radiated writing ideas. I sat next to Heather for lunch, and she encouraged my work and enrolling in the program. She'd read some of my chapbook and commented specifically on it. I was flattered she'd taken the time.

My assigned advisor was poet, fiction, and nonfiction writer Stephen Dobyns. Stephen was a bit intimidating, but I soon warmed to working with him. I was very impressed with his breadth of knowledge, and he provided me with a solution for one of my thornier poems that eliminated a character I was emotionally attached to but who blurred the poem's focus. Very helpful, I got excited at the prospect and recorded the following on July 4th: "He is an ideal person to work with. This new approach inspired me; I want to go on believing I can create. He's an academic and a pro, but now he says, writing is a real option. This could be serious, and I could produce real work with him. Wow!" In a session the following day, he told me, "Don't do it until you want to do it for the thing itself." He also recommended reading Shakespeare's sonnets, and a lot of Philip Larkin.

That evening, I had a most significant dream about my father, which I noted in my journal:

> I was trying to fly a huge seaplane, and he stood on top of the wing, taunting me, which overwhelmed me and kept me from flying his damned plane.

Ironically, the next day Tom Lux gave a talk on Theodore Roethke's "The Lost Son," a wonderful sequence poem, exploring Roethke's search for his father's approval: "A lively understandable spirit / Once entertained you. / It will come again. / Be still./ Wait." The poem was a story of Roethke's journey to this realization and what it took him to get over the shadow of his father, as I did too.

I went to classes all day, and afterward, was drawn down to the Swannanoa River meandering along a farm. It was stocked with handsome draft horses with large, swishing blonde tails. In a pasture next to a garden was an inviting stone bench where I meditated on all that I'd learned and that had happened. I threw a flower into the river. It was my time to write. I had lunch with Tom that day, putting the finishing touches on my first full book of poems he was publishing and writing the forward for. Without Tom, I wouldn't have had the courage to pull it together. He wouldn't have had his job at Tech without me twisting his arm to give it a try. He gave up his comfortable chaired position at Sarah Lawrence and restarted from scratch in Atlanta. How we'd affected each other's lives!

Walking along the river, I ran into Brooks Haxton who I'd known through a poetry workshop I took in NYC. He told me about his creative writing teaching at Syracuse and his three new books, particularly about his book *Uproar: Antiphonies to Psalms*. He'd become more openly religious. As he'd explained: "It's putting your energy into making something to communicate effectively with a reader yet to be an idea that brings credibility with it and you. Take pleasure in your work and be excited by it. To create, to find an idea from within oneself and craft that for an audience, a few people who will listen and hear your story."

I reflected on the rich environment of the school, having rubbed shoulders with the writers whose works I admired, who could relate seriously to my work and what I was doing, even at this stage of my life. I was developing a circle of writing friends that I could work with going forward. Tom Lux encouraged me to do this as well. This program came at just the right time in my life, giving me the tools as well as the contacts to push my writing further, whether I chose to go back into the program or not. I looked forward to implementing my knowledge, but how to put the time in, and improve? At the end, I came to the conclusion that I should write more poems, as well as the story of my life.

In New York I've been to the Poetry Society's annual lecture called "The Education of a Poet." I've often fancied giving this lecture because my education seems so different from the poets who surrounded me at Warren Wilson and elsewhere. I admired these folks, but they'd all started writing early or were English majors, then became teachers, who later became professional writers. How differently I had come to this craft.

I didn't start writing early, though I was always a voracious reader as I've discussed. As a child, my handwriting was awful, and I couldn't spell, therefore, was embarrassed about my writing. When I got to high school, I detested writing essays, but enjoyed the literature assigned, often reading more than was required. I enjoyed the Romantic poets who Major Fariby taught at GMA. I read epic novels on my own, always carrying one around with folded pages to mark my progress, reading such authors as much of James Michener, Edna Ferber, Willa Cather, some William Faulkner, and much of Ayn Rand.

At Georgia Tech, I took James Dean Young's course—an elective in my junior year, when there were few elective courses offered. It was a poetry course featuring Wallace Stevens and WB Yeats. He changed my life. Jim had gone to Stanford, then taught at Rice and then Tech, where he befriended and later collaborated with James Dickey, even consulting on *Deliverance*. For my three naval voyages across the Pacific Ocean, Jim had provided me with a fantastic reading list (that I wish I could find) that included some of the classics I continue to teach in my class at Georgia Tech. There was much to ponder, surveying a vast empty ocean, but it provided a time to read. As Thomas Jefferson said and I have put up in my library today: *I can't live without books.*

Some of my earliest teachers were Hugh Seidman and Kathy Pollock at the New School in NYC. What really change my life was taking a course taught there by Pearl London. She was a true pearl. In any case, Pearl picked me out of her class after reading some of my early poems and took me under her wing.

She suggested that I take her course that went through all the mechanics and history of poetry. It was a yearlong and met during lunch. I must've seemed out of place— on my lunch break, an investment banker in a pin-striped suit, trying to be inconspicuous in the back of a classroom filled with women of all ages, all of us learning the guts of poetry. I still have Pearl's criticism and the extensive and intricate notes she made on my early poems. I now think the poet was born in me and Georgia pulled it out of me while Pearl taught me the craft. I began writing and submitting my poems. The first I published was in 1992 in the local *Berkshire Review*. It was a thrill to see it in print, a real joy that kept me writing. It was originally called "Cow Heaven:"

How Things Never Change
In a hieroglyphed wooden box
stiff miniature men wearing white kilts and sandals
sit tending tiny exquisitely
carved black and white cows,
just like the Holsteins

along the Housatonic
at the Shady Maple Farm,
manned by my mustached neighbor, John
and his suspendered crew,
who know all about cows
and slog galoshed
through mud and manure
savoring the stench of their dairy
daily and spreading its abundance on their fields.
They work on unending chores for their cows,
somehow making ends meet
until the day they drop.

Like their ancient brothers
who tended Metuhopte's herds by the Nile,
four thousand years ago,
they travel together,
an eternal memory,
ka from the Middle Kingdom.

It footnoted the ancient Egyptians believed ka was the spiritual duplicate of a person that after death traveled back and forth between the land of the living and the land of the dead. Funny, it's publication kept me going between the worlds of business and poetry. Later, poems that I sent out were picked up by journals, such as *Westview* out of Oklahoma, whose editor seemed to like what I wrote, publishing several of them. *The Cortland Review* and *The Connecticut River Review* also picked up poems. I even had a poem appear in the prestigious magazine *Ploughshares* when Tom Lux was the guest editor. As Tom and I became better friends, he introduced me to Kevin Pilkington at Sarah Lawrence as well as Ron Egatz, who later published my first chapbook and who taught there as well. I later took evening workshops in NYC with David Lehman, Richard Howard, and J. D. McClatchy. One of the advantages of the big city was the pool of writers available there. This was my hands-on writing university.

When Georgia died, I was really still dabbling in poetry, sending out a few poems. I had no idea how to manage the chaos and grief her death caused. I resorted to writing, and it helped. Initially, I took the poems from this dark era to Kevin Pilkington to test their sentimentality. He encouraged me to write on. I continued to attend the summer writers' programs at Sarah Lawrence where I also worked with Mary Cornish and Stuart Dischell, along with both Tom and Kevin.

My first chapbook *A Place by Water* came together in 2002. Before its publication, I happened upon a cache of love letters I'd sent Georgia principally when in the Navy at sea that she'd saved in a closet in Connecticut. We published one of them in the introduction to my first book and there's excerpts in Chapter 19 as well. In the foreword Tom writes: "These beautiful poems you hold in your hand are a celebration of a 31-year marriage, a 31-year love affair. There has been no more fit subject in the history of poetry."

Tom also encouraged me to put together a full-length book, and then reviving his dormant press Jeanne Duvall Editions in 2005, he published *Full Horizon*, containing the poems I'd written to date. *The Atlanta Review* took a poem from *Full Horizon*—"Snow Geese"—that was also set to music by a local composer and was memorialized by the Berkshire Chorale Society. Tom again wrote the introduction, and the cover is an original oil by my friend and neighbor Margot Trout, who is a great Berkshire landscape painter. This book I dedicated to Georgia.

Shortly after that first book appeared, I'd begun working with Kurt Brown, who inspired me to self-publish another chapbook, *Quartet for Daniel*, about my farmer-neighbor's fifteen-year-old son who I became close to before he died of throat cancer. Kurt had been born at the Wandering Moose Café across from the old covered bridge in Cornwall Bridge, CT, not far from my home in Salisbury. It was an immediate friendship after Tom Lux's introduction. This smaller work was at the core and incorporated into the next full-length volume. Kurt encouraged steady production. We met at the Harvard Club every few months to catch up and review my recent work. Kurt was married to the Belgian Laure-Anne Bosselaar, also a poet. Kurt convinced me to join him on the board of Poet's House. Sadly, Kurt passed away in 2013. He was the founder of the Aspen Writers Festival and was one of the most generous good guys in this world.

Eight years later—in 2013—C&R Press published *Scaring Up the Morning*, which contains poems about my many travels to Asia and Europe, as well as the courtship of my second wife. It is dedicated to my mother, who'd recently passed away. Chard deNiord a friend and poet I'd worked with at Sarah Lawrence, wrote the introduction for *Scaring Up the Morning*. Travis Denton of the Poetry@ Tech program helped edit the work and designed the cover, featuring a Monet painting of sunrise. I asked Billy Collins and J. D. McClatchy to blurb the book. Billy generously observed these poems were "observations of a world traveler… delivered with a musical balance and a quiet authority."

New and ambitious management took over C&R Press in order to build one of the country's fine small presses. Andrew H. Sullivan and John Gosslee—the new editing team—accepted my third book of poems. *Like Lesser Gods* appeared in 2017. With all my many other activities, spending the time to send out my individual poems suffers most, though *Five Points*, *Town Creek Poetry*, and the *James Dickey Review* printed some of them. Help also came from workshops with David Bottoms and Jeff McDaniel at Sarah Lawrence, and invaluable editing and proofing came from the team of Travis Denton and Katie Chaple, who came to Utopia to assist. David Bottoms, Stephen Dobyns, Eavan Boland, and Stuart Dischell gave blurbs for the back cover. In his direct style, Stephen sums it up best: "This is a brave book: a book for grownups." For me, the book was cathartic. I got a lot of anger off my chest and moved on.

I wrote this memoir in a gap year, occasioned by enrollment in the Distinguished Careers Initiative (DCI) program at Stanford University. When I first came to Palo Alto in 2016 to explore the possibility of taking a year off, I was introduced to Eavan Boland, an Irish poet who runs the Creative Writing Department. We were to talk for a half-hour, but it delightfully stretched into over an hour then two with a surprising agreement on one Irish writer's personality that assured me we were on the same page. She insisted I work with John William Evans, who taught memoir writing. I am indebted to Eavan for her introduction to John, as well as the time I spent in her department and classes and some memorable outside lunches ; she sadly passed away this past year, a loss for the literary world and those who knew her.

At Stanford, I worked closely with John. He'd experienced the tragic and gruesome death of his first wife, and the subject of his first memoir. We related from the start. John has been a personal and professional mentor, dragging a long story out of me and showing me how to utilize words to tell my life story effectively. John likes to compare a good memoir to a good Romantic poem. Hopefully this work blossomed into one of those.

Bruce McEver and Tom Lux at Utopia, 1990s

Chapter 39
Girl in the Green Bikini

Going through my journals for memoir fodder, the photo fell out. It was an image of a cute, red-haired, lanky teenage girl in a green bikini. She lies on her side, her head propped up with one hand, while the other rests against her hip, elbow cocked in the air—a trying-to-be-sexy-before-her-age pose. Her eyes squint in the bright Mediterranean sun at a resort near Nice where her dad vacationed every summer with the jet set. Her face is alert, but uncomfortable, maybe from the sun or lying on the rocks where those who wore both pieces of a two-piece suit sunbathed. The topless monopolized the stretch of sand. She smirks with told you-so confidence or maybe with slight distain for the tuxedoed waiter about to bring her a Shirley Temple. She had the world before her but wanted it only on her own terms.

The photo reminded me of when I met Christina on a blind date that was supposed to occur with another woman. A little over a year after Georgia's death, Jim Awad, an HBS classmate and friend, and his wife Pamela were taking friends to a charity production of *Oklahoma* in the spring of 2002. Jim and Pamela had invited both Christina and an attorney who'd been slated to be my date; however, in the confusion at the theater, Christina got the seat next to me. The fact that Jim and Pamela and she were neighbors at One East End Avenue, and that she was a breast cancer surgeon were enough to break the ice between us— Georgia's death had been brought about by medication she'd taken for breast cancer treatment. At the end of the night, Christina, the woman who was supposed to be my date, and I rode in the same cab. I offered both my card. Christina snapped it up; I never heard from the lawyer.

Christina was silent for about a month, and then I got a shy email inquiring if I'd like to go to a movie. I was still burning candles for my wife, and Mary and I had an increasingly close relationship, so it took me a while to respond. After I did, Christina and I went to see *The Man from Perdition*, a gangster, cops-and-robbers-type movie that I soon learned was her favorite genre. She liked intrigue. Afterwards, at a local burger joint near the cinema, we sat in a corner table and unpacked baggage, as people initially getting to know one another tend to do. She was a divorcée with two sons fathered by a prominent plastic surgeon, who, according to her, had tried to kill her. She was a Harvard honors graduate with a major in history, intending to be a criminal lawyer, but a life-changing experience as a student volunteering at Bingham Hospital in Boston radically altered her outlook. There, she'd witnessed a little girl who'd been crippled since birth walk after a transformative operation. Overwhelmed, Christina hid in a nearby closet, crying for over an hour. When she came out, she called her father and told him she was going to medical school. She first entered Stanford for a year to cram in Chemistry and Biology before going to med school at the University of Pennsylvania. Her residency was at Duke, where she was one of its pioneer woman surgeons and where she also met her husband. Munching bacon cheeseburgers, we soon got our resumés behind us.

Christina was a brilliant person, a dedicated professional, and I enjoyed her company, but at the time, I wasn't ready for another relationship. The next time I saw her she invited the Awad's and me to the Annual Amory Art Show benefitting the Settlement House, a charity her mother supported and served on the board of. We had a great time wandering from booth to booth, viewing the spectacular array of art from some of the best dealers in New York and other major cities. I met Audrey, Christina's mother, and Christina's older sister Laurie, neither of whom were initially warm nor welcoming.

We came back to her handsome apartment, overlooking the East River just a floor above the Awad's. Here I met her manny, Nelson, who after sizing me up, cautiously got me a drink. Christina explained that her son Edmond had some challenges and was asleep; while her other son Oliver had problems going to bed. As if on cue, a naked Oliver ran through the living room pursued by Nelson. Christina caught Oliver and finally corralled him into his pajamas and into bed. She and her manny had their hands full with these boys, and I soon found the rest of her family wasn't terribly sympathetic.

There was a slow burn to our relationship. We went to a cabaret and some plays together after that. I remember most distinctly one evening when I was getting ready to go to Europe on business and was stricken with a flu that was going around the office. It was too late to call a doctor, and I needed to go on this trip, so I called Christina to ask her advice. Though I tried to dissuade her, she was at my apartment in a flash. She stuck a thermometer in my mouth, declared that I had a temperature, and was going nowhere. She'd brought some chicken

soup and put me to bed, saying I could go to Paris once the fever had
been gone for at least twenty-four hours. Doctor's orders.

I liked her bedside manner. She started narrating her favorite
vacations, like my mom telling me stories when I was sick. There were
stories of Paris, and since I was going there, she wanted me to know it
was her favorite city. She'd gone to the Chapin School in New York,
where she excelled in French. She traveled to France often, especially
to the Riviera where she stayed at a fancy hotel with her father after her
parents had split. She loved the hotel and the two weeks she'd spend
there every year, practicing her French with the rich and famous, and
even had some old photos of her as a teenager taken there, she showed
me and must have left. I tried not to fade while she talked. She told me
she'd gone to all the three-star Michelin restaurants in France with her
boyfriend in college, and we, too, should try them sometime.

She admired her dad who was a floor trader on the Stock Exchange.
He was a bit of a playboy and had a couple of wives she'd gotten to know
during those weeks on the Riviera. Christina had sided with her father in
the divorce, citing her mother's coolness. He was obsessed with growing
orchids, eventually selling his seat on the Stock Exchange and moving
to Santa Barbara where he currently lived as a master orchid grower. She
loved him very much and wanted me to meet him the next time he was
in NYC or I was on the West Coast. Thankful for the chicken soup, but
achy with a headache and fever, I would meet her father another day, but
when she reiterated we should go to Europe together, I filed that away.

Over the next couple of years, we became good friends, but with
Georgia's memory lingering, I was in no hurry. I dated other women,
and both because of my travel schedule and the fact that Mary was all the
way across the country, our relationship became increasingly strained.
I found my attraction to Christina and her intellect growing. She also
lived in NYC, and thus had the home court advantage. I finally took
Christina up on her idea of our going to Europe together. I was headed
to Amsterdam and invited her to meet me there. She took time off and
arrived in Amsterdam early morning, where that first day we walked and
biked all around the city, taking in the Rijks and Van Gogh museums.
The following day we biked into the countryside and cycled around
jubilant patches of tulips, abundant north of the city. We figured out the
transportation system together, and with the bikes, took a train back to
the city from our tours of tulip fields and windmills. Christina traveled

on with me to Zürich. We'd gotten to know each other over the course of this trip in a way that we couldn't on our home turf, and something between us had shifted. I found out Christina excelled at just about everything she did, even summer camp:

When She Showed Me Her Paddle
I knew I loved her. The one she earned
at sleep-away camp in Maine, where
her newly re-married parents sent her
to get her out of their hair summers
 too early. But she showed them,
winning every honor,
memorialized like merit badges,
little "A's" painted on her paddle
for master canoer, sailor, and swimmer.
She climbed every mountain,
walked every path on the camp
and wrote home she was lonely.

 One day on a trail, examining
a knotted bundle of pine root, she realized
why they named a little red-headed
Jewish girl, Christina.
That she was indeed like Christ,
had his healing spirit
coursing her veins, could
figure out disease and save people.
And has every day since she was licensed
to wield a scalpel.

A camaraderie developed as we began to spend more and more time together. She accompanied me on my family's annual Christmas pilgrimage in Florida. I felt I was ready to move on. I'd discussed my desire to propose with my mother who sagely predicted I wouldn't be able to coexist with Christina's sons. My sister agreed with her. Despite their words, I was tired of being alone. There in Delray Beach in 2006, I asked Christina to marry me on the bench by the Intracoastal Waterway where we'd held Georgia's memorial. I asked, and Christina accepted.

To celebrate our engagement, we took a trip to Australia and New Zealand with my friends John and Jane Robertson. Since I'd discovered Australia's rich money management environment—fueled by their superannuation savings system—and had subsequently convinced Berkshire that we should open an office there, I combined this trip with some business. At the beginning of the vacation, we stayed at a sheep station in the Australian Outback where watching the sheepdogs work the wooly flock multitudes was a delight. In New Zealand, we explored the countryside and geysers on horseback, and the glaciers and fjords via helicopter. Returning, with the help of a savvy wedding planner, Christina and I jointly planned our wedding that would occur in less than three months. We sped up the timeline because Christina's mother's lung cancer worsened, and my mother, in her nineties, was rapidly becoming immobile with arthritis.

We were married on June 2, 2007 at the Congregational Church in Salisbury in a beautiful ceremony with our family and friends. The reception was at Naumkeag, and we held a posh dinner dance at the Wheatly Estate where I had to insist that her ex-boyfriend—the jeweler who owned Harry Winston—be removed from the honeymoon suite he'd occupied since his arrival. Having been a student of Arthurian romances, I should have known that sometime in my life the Green Knight would appear in Camelot. What I didn't know was that the green knight would be an enchantress disguised in a tiny green bikini. Like the old boyfriend, the signs were subtle but ominous, and were even reflected in nature, and cutting a long story short...:

The Turtle in the Road

The day we were married,
after the recessional,
through the cheers of friends
and pelting rice and petals,
your son wanted to ride
with us to the reception.

The limo took the back road,
and we were high, talking about the service,
how funny the preacher had been

when the driver slammed the brakes
for a hulking snapping turtle crossing—
something from the Triassic.
Armored, she took her time
to cross the road after laying her eggs,
clomping to the safety of the swamp.

It was a sign—
mother earth's symbol:
the beast that carries the world
on her back, saying to us,
go slow, consider.

Every year we have a mother turtle
cross the road from the river
to our farm's pasture and lay her eggs.
I see her sometimes close-up
in the Blackberry, ancient
and beastly, having survived
longer than we will.

The weekend after you served divorce papers
for our anniversary dinner, I biked
along our road. There was a fresh
turtle nest just dug up by a raccoon.
The feathery shells lay scattered, sucked dry.
The animal had scat on the nest.

Soon after your affair was dug up,
I went for a walk by the wetlands
near friends, and there I saw a mother turtle,
her head just out of her nest
laying her eggs, looking at
me to say—the world goes on.

We spent seven peaceful and happy years together, but never in
a single setting. On weekends, we rotated between my house in the
Berkshires and her mother's home in East Hampton. In the city, we

alternated staying at her apartment on East End with the boys or taking a break from them at my place that I'd had since arriving in New York in '73. Her place had views of the East River and magnificent sunrises. Together as a family, we'd weathered Hurricane Sandy in it, watching the East River lake over the highway. As if it was a trial marriage, we never merged our apartments together in New York nor thankfully our weekend retreats though Christina pushed me to build a much larger house there and inexplicably abandoned it and me before its completion.

Bruce McEver and Dr. Christina Weltz, Wedding Dance, June 2, 2007

Chapter 40
The Road to Divinity School

This journey began as a vision in a barnyard. It was a vision that grew in me, but a gentler vision than Paul's or Jonah's. It had a bright light, a circle of compassionate animals, and an energy that coursed through me like an electric shock. The day after my wife died, an internal voice whispered and reverberated in a moment of rare clarity: *Many paths.* Thinking I was psychologically vulnerable and this no hierophany, I simply did not know how to handle this tragedy nor its revelation, and I sat with it for six months. I shared that moment with Dick Taber on a late summer day when we launched a canoe from the place on the Housatonic where we'd scattered Georgia's ashes on Easter weekend of 2001. We traveled down river to the dam at Fall's Village.

Dick was a biblical scholar and after hearing my story like a confession, suggested I might want to consider Divinity School, Harvard specifically, because it taught across religious traditions. I felt and knew he was right. Deep down, this was something I'd always wanted to do. A confluence of events had opened a door, and I needed to figure out how to go through. After our discussion, we were paddling in the deep water at the dam, and a great carp jumped out of the river. A woman struggled with the fish on her line and lost it. I thought Georgia was there saving the animals, and discovered later that for the Japanese, the carp is a symbol of luck and good fortune.

After Georgia died, I was in grief's grip. I wanted to shut myself away like a monk, read much scripture from all traditions, burn candles, and meditate. In this idea, I found strange comfort and thought I longed to be a pilgrim in every tradition but didn't have the time, nor was I that ascetic. I wanted to study them intellectually. It was a burning desire. I was a modern-day Gurdjieff looking for other remarkable persons to search out the sacred with me. I made some dry runs. During a visit with HBS Dean Keith Clark in late 2001, I tried to suggest that religion play a larger role in the school's mandatory ethics courses. Clark, a Mormon, felt the school was not ready for the "R" word and suggested I see Bill Graham, the Dean of Harvard Divinity School, but I wasn't ready for that step yet.

I looked for churches all over Manhattan where I prayed and meditated—my favorites being The First Presbyterian's large wooden sanctuary on 5th Avenue near my office; the Lady Chapel in the back of St Patrick's Cathedral, and the silence and awe of St Bartholomew's byzantine sanctuary with its chapel hosting a great marble statue of an angel. I read Emerson and Wordsworth, and like it had for them, nature called to me from every direction in Salisbury. I communed with God in my valley. At Utopia, I constructed a little chapel, re-arranging Georgia's former practice porch. I went to Mystery School. These were the places where I got my soul in shape, practiced spiritual exercises to take on a real study of religion. I wanted to do it right. I worked to assure the business was secure and my partners comfortable; I was no longer the CEO. After several years, I decided I could relax, take some time off, and study part time.

In late spring 2006, through HBS Dean Jay Light's introduction, I scheduled an appointment with Dean Bill Graham. We had much in common, being both from the South, he from North Carolina, and, ironically, had both been to Germany the same year as exchange students, just in different cities. Bill was effusive, short, quick in mind and movement. He ran the Harvard football stadium steps every morning. He was also an Islamic scholar and spoke both Arabic and German fluently. I told him of my recent history, the vision, and my desire to study across religious traditions formally. Also, I confessed ignorance of real scripture study. I wanted to dive into it as literature. I ventured that with more knowledge, I'd perhaps be able to do something about the misunderstandings between the traditions.

Bill responded that he had a couple of spots available in his next class as a "special student" that wouldn't require me being full time. I'd have to find my own housing, but I could also take courses in HDS and the college. That all sounded wonderful to me, capped with a visit to a student gathering underway in Aldrich Hall, where he introduced me to students and faculty. From this afternoon of interviews, I knew that our arrangement was going to work and moreover, would be exciting. Bill sent me a reading list that I worked on over the summer. It was early in my marriage to Christina, and though she was proud I'd gotten into her alma mater, she was wary of me going to Divinity School, being agnostic. However, she was a very busy and sought-after surgeon, often operating late evenings, so we didn't have much weekday free time anyway. To compensate, we began to orbit our weekends around Utopia or the Hamptons.

Over ninety but still sharp, my mom was delighted, as were the ministers in my life—Bev Jones and Dick Taber. Christina's family, who were secular Jewish, didn't seem to care one way or the other. Most friends who knew me were happy for me. I had to handle this most carefully with my clients and business partners, but Bruce got it right away. He both needed and enjoyed the space at Berkshire, also part of my plan—to have him work into taking control of the company with me gone a few days a week. I wanted to be out of his way, but nearby if needed, so I promised him I'd only be away two days a week. While this limited some course choices, it also set a pattern that I'd follow for the next four years via shuttle aircraft, train, or car.

On September 17, 2007, I went to Harvard Divinity School's 340th convocation in the gothic-paneled Memorial Hall, built to honor the school's Civil War veterans. The amphitheater was over four stories tall, drawing me to first look up rather than down at the black-robed faculty solemnly filing in, accented by their varied vivid hoods. Bill Graham presided. He reminded us that the Divinity School faculty was the university's oldest, as well as the only one that followed the tradition of beginning its academic year with a convocation, and that HDS was the only divinity school to globalize its curriculum, thus promoting the study of other traditions. The School's Hindu specialist, Dr. Anne Monius delivered the keynote, reviewing her tradition with its different yogic paths: Bhakti yoga, the path of devotion and love; Karma yoga, the path of action and service; Raja yoga, the royal path of prayer, meditation, and self-discipline; lastly, Jnana yoga, or the philosophical path of self-knowledge through study, practice, and experience. She reminded us these were not separate paths, but how we approach God at various times of our spiritual lives. She urged us to take the course catalog and "wallow in it like a water buffalo," to go through the courses and have a great first week shopping them, as was the tradition here. Later, each professor would pitch a summary of his or her course to start shopping week. Monius also closed with a challenging question, "What kind of thinker do you want to be?"

This first quarter, I stayed at the Irving House near campus and across from Henry James's house. I'd read his *A Variety of Religious Experience* while crossing the Pacific and was impressed; he was one of my hero thinkers. Bill Graham suggested the perfect advisor for me—Dr. Ron Thiemann, the former dean. Ron was a bearded, handsome man and an ordained Lutheran minister. He was a theologian, philosopher, and since he was practical, related well to businessmen. Ron and I really bonded. He'd tried to start a center at Harvard for Religion in the Public Square—his specialty—that didn't quite work out. Bill advised that working together, Ron and I could start something that would take off.

Ron was an extraordinary man. He was the Lutheran church's representative to the Vatican for the reconciliation talks that have been going on in Wittenberg, Germany for the past 500 years. Religions move on Divine Time. He was also Harvard's academic representative to Iranian universities. Ron had an office on the third floor of Divinity Hall, down from the dark-paneled hall where Emerson gave his famous "Divinity School Address," recommending that there be less passing out of the eucharist, and that students act more like Christ. He also criticized the then-current dean and was banned from Harvard for twenty-five years.

Early on, Ron leveled with me academically: "Take as many courses as you like, but only two for credit. Even though you're a special student, if you really like this and become full time—and I bet you might—you'd have some course credits behind you. The only real way to learn is to take the tests, and most particularly, write the required papers. I know that sounds like a pain now, but I think you'll thrive here. Also, remember, only two courses per semester. Drop the others as soon as the real work escalates." He was so right. I sampled many courses across HDS and Harvard, but when it became crunch time, I concentrated on my designated two and did as well as I could, particularly enjoying the research and the writing.

I wandered around campus with an increasingly large backpack of required texts. The Buddhist professor who ran the Center for Study of World Religions, Don Swearer saw this and took pity on me. He arranged a permanent locker that I kept through all four years. As a commuter student, this was a godsend and saved my back. Don practiced compassion and became a confidant and advisor. He eventually let me stay at his center. In 2010, Don gave the commencement speech on "enoughness," igniting a meaningful exchange between the Divinity School and the Business School, a project I worked on with him. He got this concept from the Buddhist King of Thailand. His address happened to be attended by some business school professors looking for the answer to "How much is enough?," and we filled classrooms on both sides of the Charles River discussing the topic.

My first two courses were "Storytelling" and "Literature and the Christian Experience." Michael Jackson, an anthropologist and poet from Australia, taught "Storytelling." I learned he'd also lost his wife, which had motivated his writing poetry. It was a powerful connection.

Michael's class focused on the philosopher Hannah Arendt's research on the value of the story in communication for healing troubled situations, such as Apartheid with the Truth and Reconciliation Commission, and similar public confessionals after the massacres in Darfur and Rwanda. That idea of the power the word could have over the chaos in our lives was inspiring and hopeful. It was a lesson both he and I learned regarding how we might assuage our grief.

Dr. Stephanie Paulsell from Chicago's Divinity School (and who eventually became my advisor) taught "Literature and the Christian Experience." To get into Stephanie's overly demanded course, we had to write an essay on our literacy background, and since mine was sufficiently barren, I got selected. I thought I was lucky, but Stephanie's was a massive reading seminar. Not familiar with the classroom's location, I was late to my first class and was also unaware that everyone had already chosen a book to present. I got the only book left, St Augustine's *Confessions*—the longest and weightiest tome. Not only did I have to read this but present it in the next week's class. Once the work was assigned, we were asked to introduce ourselves and read something we admired that was religious, but not overtly so. While the others told of their ministerial experience, I talked about starting an investment banking firm and read one of my poems:

Manhattan Morning
It is in the early hour,
as first light just, pinks
the apartment canyons,
when Gotham stirs and stretches.

Then confusion's messenger
is easily dispatched,
my thoughts let go
of the traffic din, and all

fades to background.

Sadness passes,
and I come close
to something still and vast,
like this city after a heavy snow,
silent, yet alive.

Thereafter, Stephanie and I seemed to respect one another, resulting in an independent study course, one of my most enjoyable, with her my final year. Not out of the Augustine assignment, however, I began to panic and soon found Dr. Charles Stang, working out of Center for the Study of World Religions (CSWR), was the expert on the Bishop of Hippo. He ominously clued me in at our first meeting: "Most famous people are rivers, but Augustine is an ocean!" His crash course stayed with me when I taught Augustine later.

The first real paper I wrote was for Stephanie's class: "The Thread of Attention." I linked messages concerning spiritual exercises with attention and concentration, while taking the reader on a classic art trip through Rome. The paper opened with my first viewing of Caravaggio's *The Calling of Matthew*. Ron took a look at the paper and said I had the big ideas from my life experience and intuition but lacked the "meat on the bones"—the details and connections only extensive reading, study, and writing would bring. He liked that I opened with the Caravaggio painting, a painting he'd used as the cover of his last book. How right he was. I'm still putting meat on those bones.

Harvard's treasure is its seventy-eight libraries. Bill Graham's wife Barbara oversaw them and told remarkable stories of finding famous people's letters between the pages of old books. I spent much time reading and writing in the vast Widener Library, sitting upstairs in the winged chairs of the huge central study room, where glowing chandeliers hang over long oak tables. I also enjoyed the Lamont, where the poetry library is housed, also the Andover Library at the Divinity School, and especially, the Houghton Library, containing rare books and maps.

Since Christina was in NYC and all my business contacts in Boston went back to the burbs in the evenings, I didn't have a big social life and mostly hung around Cambridge. When winter was over, I discovered the joys of riding a bicycle around the campus and along the river where the rowing crews practiced. I related to a few students, but it soon became apparent that with my life experience, I related more to the professors and became close to some of them.

Being a student was daunting at first. It was humbling going from CEO with an assistant who provided anything I needed, and associates to research, write memos and create spreadsheets to a student who took notes on unfamiliar subjects, conducted my own research, and wrote papers. Certainly, I had life experience over these younger students; however, they could run circles around me technologically and pull all-nighters. This experience was going to be more difficult for me. There was much more for me to learn and absorb, not only from my reading and research, but also from the wisdom and knowledge of my professors and classmates.

At HDS, I started out thinking I'd specialize in Comparative Religion, but after Stephanie's course and having written "The Thread of Attention," I wavered and began to see how religion could be explored and delivered more effectively in literature. Through literature, I saw how I could cross traditions and deliver the message through good writing that excited readers in the way Brooks Haxton and I had discussed while walking along the banks of the Swannanoa River at Warren Wilson. Dr. Ken Knoespel and I would later develop a class at Georgia Tech that was a religion and literature course called "Witness to Consciousness," similar to Robert Coles famous course using the literature of exemplary people that Christina had taken while she was at Harvard.

I took Ron Thiemann's Religion in the Public Marketplace in the spring of 2008. For this course, Ron and I agreed exploring religious literacy was a subject worthy of further study and an in-depth paper. I reached out and met with Stephen Prothero whose book on religious literacy was a classic and used his book as the basis for my paper, "Religious Literacy: Revival Time?" The essay begins with a call for peace, which I argue is only achievable if we all become conversant in the origins of religious roots and beliefs—often fervently held—and that paths to God are numerous. The end of the introduction says: "... the paths to God are more numerous. We will need to know more than our own path to survive." Ron and I had many discussions on the need to address these growing concerns, and in the future, we'd work together and form the Foundation for Religious Literacy.

Dr. Michael Cogan's Introduction to the Hebrew Bible led me to write a paper on King David and his poetry. I drew heavily upon Robert Pinsky, who was our poet laureate and lived in Cambridge at the time. Pinsky had just written a book on David, and a most generous man, allowed me to interview him on the subject. Although tradition has it that King David wrote the Psalms, I learned that he didn't, that he actually wrote a remarkable poem of parallel construction that's in the Book of Samuel. David was a poet-king, but also a flawed warlord, who, some say, invented chainmail, maybe how he survived his many battles?

I also took a course on the sacred tree by polymath Dr. Kimberly Patton and wrote "Branches from the Tree at the Center of the Meso-american World," centering around the ancient, mythical tree that appears in both the Mesoamerican and Nordic cultures. In the London Warburg Library, by chance I found a text documenting that both cultures shared the same constellations, though named differently for their respective creation myths. I wrote the paper in our London office. Here is an excerpt: "One of the more dramatic examples of a central and linking symbol that reappears throughout the world's mythical and religious traditions is the cosmic tree. In the Mesoamerican traditions, the tree's branches seem taller and roots deeper from the formative Olmec through the Classic Mayan to the post-Classic Aztec civilizations. The cosmic tree acts as an axis mundus, linking heaven and the underworld with earth. Moreover, it became a symbol and succor for the ruling elite, mediating between their subjects and the gods." In the conclusion, I point to Wendy Doniger's discovery that the image of the tree is echoed in northern European mythology. The image is strikingly similar—rare birds at the top, snakes at the bottom, and the tree, similarly to the Mesoamerican symbol, connects earth both to heaven and the underworld.

Even today in the Western world there seems a resonance with trees, where large trees or memorial trees are placed next to houses in the European culture and we still preserve yule log and Christmas tree traditions, which, given the latter's evergreen nature, could imply a res-urrected element. I've often thought the conservation and ecological movements are indeed forms of a religion, a kind of worship of land and trees, now increasingly necessary for our preservation. The whole basis of Druidism is of course the knowlege of trees and their sacred groves.

I wanted to learn both the Old and New Testaments as literature. I studied the Old Testament in a series of courses from Michael Cogan.

In one of Cogan's classes, I wrote a paper on William Blake's images of Job that he produced at the end of his life. I was able to view some of Blake's original illustrated and illuminated texts housed in Harvard's Houghton Library. It was quite a treat to review them on their foam rubber holders as the librarian turned the pages.

Damon his biographer regarding these illuminated illustrations: "both the clearest and the profoundest of all his [Blake's] pictorial diagrams charting the spiritual life of a man; for this book like so many others of his is not primarily a set of illustrations to a given text, but a map of the mystic way." As such, Blake's *Illustrations* chart the legend of loss and the chronicle of an innocent's suffering, purposefully left unanswered. Blake was uncomfortable with the unanswered question and answers it himself. He tries to tell us his philosophy of life through illustrations. Blake has always interested me because he has the dual ability to address such a deep question aesthetically, both through his poetry and art. This is a poem I wrote while at HDS in a somber mood meditating on some flowers bought to cheer me up:

Tulips

surprise me like a yellow sunrise,
igniting from my coffee table.
Bought last night in a cold rain,
they stand, radiant, in a tall vase,
leaning toward the window,
savoring the morning light.

How perfectly they spill
with each leaf folded to embrace
the tumbler's edge.
Flown from Holland's fields,
where we biked last spring
between astounding rows of color,

they were the fancy of Turkish sultans.
Gifted to Dutch botanist who
hybridized them to be dazzling:
"tulip mania" became endemic.

Then the deluded traded
their homes for a single bulb.

Today it's big business,
this bounty of bulbs, fresh cut,
and air expressed around the world.
These bright missionaries

come to spread joy
through impersonal cities,
come to roust
from our comfortable beds,
and wake us
from our morning slough.

When Ron Thiemann went on sabbatical my senior year, I began working on an independent study program with Stephanie Paulsell. We devised a list of authors, including Flannery O'Connor, Meister Eckhart, Dante, Rilke, Mann's *Joseph and his Brothers* (that I think is one of the finest novels ever written), among others. For my final paper, I wrote The Great Works of Two Wandering Bards: Dante and Rilke in Retrospective, strengthened by my interview of Dante's major translator, John Hollander of Princeton and by spending time with Galway Kinnell, who'd just published a translation of Rilke.

In my time at Harvard, I was able to combine two great loves—a study of religion and a study of poetry and literature. In Professor Michael Jackson's, Poetry and Religion, we were invited to work with poets of our own choice, exploring religions as a poem. We worked from a central book of Octavio Paz's—*The Bow and the Lyre*—where he further expands this thought:

> "Sometimes without apparent cause, we truly see that which surrounds us, and that vision is, in its own way, a kind of theophany.... Suddenly, any day, the street leads to another world, the garden has just been born, the weary wall is covered with signs."

For my paper, I chose to focus on Patrick Kavanagh and Herbert Reece: dirt farmers turned poets, with the gift of transforming simplicity into erudition. For both these poets, the divine was in the

land, nature, and especially in the commonplace. They describe the
ineffable presence, a thread that runs deeply throughout their poems
made visible in the quotidian. Both men lived hard lives—Cavanaugh
dying of lung cancer and Reese committing suicide, but they both
wrote beautiful poetry.

In my final year, inspired and challenged by Dr. David Carrasco
in his course Religions of Latin America, I wrote an epic poem instead
of an essay. The poem, "The Path of the Plumed Serpent," is about
Quetzalcoatl, the legendary plumed serpent of mythology, but also
the historic leader of the Toltecs, the peak civilization of Mesoameri-
ca. He was a god/man like Christ, and legend has it, he would return.
Montezuma mistakenly thought Cortez was Quetzalcoatl because the
Spanish landed at the predicted time of his return. This is from the
prologue to the poem:

> He was a man-god,
> a traveler between existences, like his name:
> *Quetzal*, the precious green-feathered
> plumed bird of paradise,
> master of the air and climber to heaven;
> and *coatl*, the serpent, master of earth
> descender into underworld
> shedding its skin each year,
> eternally renewing.

After he tries to stop human sacrifices and builds an incredible civili-
zation, he succumbs to an incestuous relationship with his sister, and so,
like Aeneas, is sent wandering into the underworld and is finally immolated
by the sun. I write about his return in the epilogue of the poem:

> And every year at noon on the spring equinox
> his shadow body waiting and wreathing
> crawls down the stair-side
> to the base of the great pyramid
> at Chichén Itzá,
> joining the plumed head
> of the grim-grinning serpent
> for his annual return.

Across the plaza in arid fields,
after eight days in mother earth
rows of little green forked
shoots of corn emerge
like serpent tongues, flickering
in the faint breeze before
the returning rain.

Carrasco took me to lunch after I turned in the poem and told me he'd never had anyone request or turn in an epic poem instead of a term paper before.

On a fine May morning in 2011, black-robed and crimson-hooded, I queued with my classmates to parade into Harvard Yard for the commencement exercises. Divinity School was one of the most interesting things I'd ever done. I loved commuting to Boston in order to study with these scholars. I was a scholar at heart and enjoyed the contemplation and the exposure to new ideas that came along with the reading, research, and writing it required.

That day Dr. Drew Faust spoke first, followed by the keynote, delivered by Liberian President Ellen Johnson Sirleaf. Hers was a remarkable story of overcoming the establishment. We then adjourned for an interfaith service at the Memorial Church. As I found my way to the steepled sanctuary where the degrees were conferred for divinity students, I remembered Anne Monius' opening convocation speech about the different yogic paths. Then, I identified with the Jnana path and had been on it these four years. I remained excited about continuing it.

Christina arrived for my degree ceremony wearing a green flowered dress that complimented her red hair. As we filed across the sanctuary's stage, she waved. After the ceremony, we showed each other our version of Harvard. She showed me her haunts first—Adams House where she lived and the Griffin Pub where she hung out. Next door was a Chinese restaurant where she got sick over-indulging in rum punches. Then we went to the imposing and cavernous Widener Library she'd haunted like I had. This was good ground for both of us, but Christina was uncomfortable with religion and sharing of our spirituality was barren ground between us.

I don't know that HDS deepened my faith, since divinity school tends to take belief apart, focusing on scripture origins and construction. However, I did feel better-equipped to write, think, and talk about religion and literature than ever before. From this new confidence, I was going to write more, build the Religious Literacy Foundation, and speak or preach when called upon. Thus, I would put my faith into action.

Bruce McEver Accepting the Bronze Medal at the
Global Business and Interfaith Peace Awards, Rio De Janeiro, Brazil, 2016

Chapter 41
Archeological Trip to China

My archeological tour of China in September 2011 with the AIA was something I had been wanting to do ever since reading Fairbank's history of China while crossing the Pacific in the early seventies. It was in a way my HDS graduation present to myself, but also was combined with business in Beijing. Christina couldn't go, busy with surgery, so I was free to travel.

In a way, it was an indulgence since ancient civilizations and archeology have attracted me since I secretly wanted to be an archaeologist from an early age. It started when I assembled an arrowhead and potsherd collection from the Indian mound my uncle Fletch had on his farm's field outside Gainesville, Georgia, now covered by Lake Lanier. He had it plowed every spring when I would add to my treasure.

There was no chance of scratching my itch for things ancient in a technology or business school. When my job future was secure in NYC, I jumped at taking a tour of the Mesoamerican civilizations sponsored by the Archaeological Institute of America (AIA) with Georgia in the eighties. Our guide was an astro-archaeologist named John Carson who became a great friend. It was an extraordinary adventure, and Georgia loved it as well. At the end of our trip, she put on a little skit, parodying our group of archeological geeks to the delight of all. We learned of the amazing Mesoamerican civilizations, starting with the giant stone face carving of the Olmecs to the Aztecs' capital city (now Mexico City) destroyed by the tragic Spanish Conquest. We also learned from John that these ancient cities were also aligned with the heavens but that the Chinese were the first to align their cities to bring the control of the cosmos down to earth. "As above, so below" chant mystics across the ages. I wanted to see ancient China.

I flew to Shanghai in September 2011. Our group spent the morning after our arrival at the Shanghai Museum with its collections of paintings, stone sculpture, furniture, calligraphy, jade, Ming porcelain and my favorite, the rare bronzes. I've always marveled at the skill of the ancients that produced these pots. There, our guide, Donald Sensabaugh, gave us a lecture on those remarkable Chinese painting poems that involve three skills—painting, poetry, and calligraphy. We then walked the Bund and went back to the Pudong New Development Zone.

We flew out the next morning to Taiyuan, the capital of Shanxi province where our tour would center, starting with the massive Chang family manor to get some idea of how the wealthy merchant class lived in ancient China and an adjacent temple. In this province, we dipped back into the history. For me, the Jinci Temple was one of the highlights of the trip with its amazing spring said to be the haunt of a water spirit. The spring is steeped in ancestor worship from the emperors who came here and set up resident temples, composing poetry through the Daoist and Confucian traditions, finally subsumed by the Buddhists. There was a 3,000-year-old cypress and 1,000-year-old locust trees surrounding pools of colorful carp and goldfish, entrants greeted by fierce-looking guardians meant to protect the water goddess.

We bussed to the most impressive Pingyao Ancient City, an exceptionally well-preserved example of a traditional Han Chinese city. It was like a mythological castle town, a fortress-ringed city designated a World Heritage site. The ancient city walls date to 827 BC when it was a rammed-earth fortification, later rebuilt during the Ming dynasty into a brick and stone defense wall, one of the most complete in China. The city's mysterious narrow cobblestone streets also contain the Rishengchang Financial House, the first money exchange shop in China and precursor to the modern Chinese and universal banks. We rode horse-drawn buggies with our baggage to the hotel, oddly named the International Financier's Club (IFC). I detail this remarkable city in my poem lamenting the absence of my wife:

Celebrating the Moon Festival at the Pingyao International Financiers' Club

"Why does the moon tend to be full when people are apart?"
Su Dong Po, 1076

I.
Over its bar, the Club shows global pretentions:
four clocks tracking time in London,
Moscow, Beijing, and New York,
yet no one speaks Russian anymore,
and barely enough English to manage a red wine.

But here in the Qing dynasty, the first financiers

gave up prosperous dye works
after discovering paper could carry
the same value as silver.
They convinced other merchants to leave deposits
in their vaults who in turn, traveled lighter
and safer without bodyguards.
Setting out under the ten-foot-thick walls,
still surrounding this city, on shaggy horses,
their clients carried coded paper
they later exchanged for coins
at other Rishengchang branches
when they got to Peking,
Nanking, or Chang'an.

Last night, I strolled those streets
the first bankers left long ago,
past their courtyards of carved screens and intrigue,
protected behind the huge walls and watch towers
from plundering Huns, like an obsolete
giant dragon guarding its hoard, unable
to contain an idea that has since
spilled around the earth

II.
As predicted, the moon showed up
for her festival though
subdued behind a misty veil.
In honor of the silver goddess
(who carries memories of loved ones)
the city streets were littered with the red rubble
from the autumn festival's fireworks,
being bunched
and swept away by old women
bent over branch brooms.

This morning, hot water swells green tea leaves
in my cup, after climbing from a raised bed
to munch a left-over moon cake.

I remember her shy appearance
over the curved court-yard eves last night,
inspiring a dream:
a vision stumbling from my bed
this morning and showering first thing,
as my love always does
and did on the other side of the earth
while I watched her shining.

In a morning lecture, Dr. Sensabaugh discussed "The Archeological Treasures of Shanxi." After lunch, we departed for yet another World Heritage site that seemed to abound in this part of China. On our way between these treasures, we drove through the countryside along manicured highways but beyond could see the heavy industry and coal-fired power plants, as well as the massive housing projects outside the cities that house millions of Chinese citizens. The Shuanglin temple we visited that afternoon was impressive for its porcelain statues, each shockingly individualized to capture a 2,000-year-old personality, now dusted with coal ash and for a memorable swarm of bees. It was spared during the cultural revolution reflecting the past and future in stanzas from a poem I wrote about it called "When Bees Swarm:"

There are thousands of porcelains,
Whose monk makers wanted
to show through self-knowledge, all
can be enlightened. Unlike the hordes
carrying little red books—those
who attacked, but luckily spared this temple—
those who would erase their history
and build a new collective future…

As we cross the river over a lyre-
like bridge, through the coal haze,
block towers and high-rises
emerge and march across the plain
like an emperor's invading army.

Impressive, row upon row,
block after block, as far
as the eye sees—
brown pylons, of honey-
combed humanity, the first fruits
of the last five-year-plan;
homes of harmony,
the Red dream rising.

The next morning, we departed by bus to Wutaishan, one of Buddhism's four sacred peaks and yet another World Heritage site. Mount Wutai ("five terrace mountain") is the highest peak in northern China, boasting over fifty-three monasteries and temples. I took the chair lift to the top and walked down the 2,000 steps that penitents usually climb on their knees. I saw many such individual pilgrimages in progress that day. Strongly supported by the government, Buddhism has been revived in China with restored buildings and sacred places in contrast to other religions.

From the Buddhist sacred mountain, we drove cross country and stopped at a beautiful mountain pass with a large pasture of shaggy-footed horses that ran up to the railings to greet us and nibbled at offerings of the tall grasses from the other side of their enclosure. We were on our way to the famous Hanging Cliff Monastery built in AD 491 into the base of Mount Heng, one of the five Chinese Daoist sacred mountains. Quite amazingly the natural topography of the cliff face forced the buildings to hang on its edges. I took the twisting trails up the cliff to the ancient temples that reminded me of the Greek Orthodox monasteries perched atop rocks in Meteora. I wanted to learn more about Daoism, and these monasteries later becoming Buddhist.

We breakfasted to a lecture on the famous Cave Temples at Yungang and spent the entire day in the Datong area visiting the famed Yungang Buddhist Grottoes and nearby Huayang Monastery. These grottoes were cut into the cliffs of Wuzhoushan and contained more than 50,000 statues. Designated a World Heritage site, it's an extraordinarily masterful work of early Buddhist cave art. This is quote from my diary on Friday, September 16th, 2011:

I don't think I've ever been as moved as under the giant gilded-faced Buddha in cave #5 (or was it #6?) this morning where we started out tour. His cobalt blue headdress was stunning, so giant yet perfectly shaped with his aura spread over the ceiling...The rim of evening reddens and now enlivens [the rich world here].

It was notable how the government spent massive amounts restoring this site and redeveloping the city center for a town with over 2.5 million inhabitants. Our guide, who was born here, said she didn't recognize it today as they had cleared out the town center, preserving the Buddhist temples and part of the old city wall to clear access for the train station and government buildings. The most impressive building, however, was the museum at the grottoes. This new and magnificent grotto center has a giant floating hologram of Buddha levitating over the center of the hall. An exhibit of the former city's history of being overrun by various "barbarians" from the steppes of the north—the Huns and Mongols—who assimilated into the Chinese ways was instructive and impressive.

From there we flew to Beijing where we visited, among other historical sites, the Great Wall, the Forbidden City, Tiananmen Square, and the Arthur Sackler Museum that houses more than 10,000 objects that span a period of 280,000 years from Paleolithic hominoids and their stone tool remains to costumes and ceramics and paintings of the present age. We had a special Beijing duck banquet that evening and saw the Beijing Opera another, including acrobatics, magic, martial arts, and dance. David gave a lecture on the Forbidden City's lay out like a grand triangle with the inner sanctum at the top. The whole complex is aligned with a variety of symbols around the number nine, it being the largest single-digit whole number.

On Sunday morning I left the group to find a Protestant church in a back alley, an old missionary outpost. It was a more exciting visit than I expected, as religious services weren't advertised; you have to find them. The people were enthusiastic in their welcome and ushered me into their sanctuary. I sat in the back, and they placed earphones on my head that had an interpreter on the other end of the line. The preacher was a woman, and the service went on for three hours, but the length wasn't noticeable because of the joyous singing and an excellent message and testimony. These people were so happy to be able to worship, though they were surveilled continually. Earlier in the year, a larger congregation was jailed during their Easter service because they had rented a space in a modern high rise and attracted too much attention. It seems sad and unlikely the Chinese government will be able to contain the natural human longing for the spiritual. I think they fight a long-term losing battle; witness the enthusiasm of this congregation that makes me appreciate more our freedoms we take for granted at our peril.

The day we went to the Temple of Heaven, my friend Randy Kwai joined our group from Hong Kong to tour the temple where the emperor plowed the first furrow with a steel plow before steel was known in the West. Randy left us the next day, but I had many adventures in Asia with my friend who wrote *East to West to East*, a memoir of his life as a financier in New York and Hong Kong. He sadly recently passed away of lung cancer.

At the end of the trip, I had one of the most interesting meetings with my friend Gerhard Hinterhäuser, a German married to a Japanese woman. Fluent in Mandarin, he was recruited to be the chief risk officer for the largest Chinese insurance company, Ping An. Gerhard wanted me to meet his boss, the CIO of that company.

After battling crippling cross-town traffic to get to the former summer palace, and almost not making it, we had dinner together in a complex of low buildings by a beautiful lake outside Beijing where the emperor used to keep his concubines. Gerhard interpreted, but his boss could speak English and understood everything I said. This company was the largest property casualty insurer in the country and had a massive portfolio, but at that time, he could invest only in China. He desperately wanted to diversify his risk and invest outside China and told me so, saying it just a matter of time before the government would allow it. What a revelation and what a contact!

When I look back at this trip, I see again how all men and civilizations seem similar as they rise and fall, following the hero's path and grow old and pass away, some leaving amazing achievement and artifacts to be discovered, keeping archaeologists employed. My interest in archaeology is growing. The year following this China trip I went with Dr. John Carlson to Chichen Itza with a group of archaeologists, new agers and old hippies to observe the "end of the world." On December 21, AD 2012, our Winter Solstice really did mark the end of the great 5,125-year Maya Long Count "cycle." It also marked the alignment of our solar system with that of our galaxy. Pretty good for stargazers on platforms in the jungle without telescopes or computers to calculate!

I have since joined the board of the Archaeological Institute of America (AIA), immensely enjoying their meetings. I have set up a trust supporting real scholars and diggers through the dust of our ancient past, who utilize a variety of new technologies available to us now and in the future that will keep unlocking the mysteries of the past.

Utopia Farm Main House, 2015 (Photo by Phillip Spears)

Chapter 42
Finding and Building Utopia, Ltd.

"Once Jesus was asked by the Pharisees when the kingdom of God was coming, and he answered, "The kingdom of God is not coming with things that can be observed; nor will they say, 'Look, here it is!' or 'There it is!' For, in fact, the kingdom of God is among you."

Luke 17:20-21

Being from the south and with all my world travels, it seems ironic that I would find in Salisbury a home, and like in Yeats's "Lake Isle of Innisfree," its landscape calls to me when I'm away. Because the place is so special, Georgia and I named it—audaciously so— "Utopia, Ltd." Even with tongue-in-cheek modifier, it says there's something special here.

Its story began over 400 million years ago when the ancient seabed that laid underneath was upended in the Taconian Orogeny, smashing, and compressing that idyllic beach up into our Taconic Range, forming a continuation of the Appalachian chain. Part of that ancient shore became an exposed quartzite, an acidic rock and marble, an alkaline stone deposit now cut by the Housatonic River that defines and bifurcates our valley thus sweetening the surrounding soils. Consequently, unlike much of the rest of the world, our dirt is chemically basic, not acidic, resulting in a plant diversity not found anywhere else in New England, and quite rarely in the rest of the US. At the end of my road, Weatogue Road, this outcropping is visible—a tumble of grey marble boulders forming a natural rock garden called Bartholomew's Cobble. This sanctuary hosts over 800 different types of plants. Every year, the reservation's parking lot fills with nature photographers and worshippers of its spring wildflower blooming.

For over 200 years, this place has attracted naturists who've written about it. Notably, Brighton Cobb wrote his handbook on ferns based on the diversity found there. The former nature editor of the *New York Times*, Hal Borland owned a farm right next door that I bought from the local bank after his widow passed away. Borland was so enamored of this valley, he made it his home and wrote his weekly "Reports from the Country," as well as twenty plus books about it, documenting its seasons and plant diversity in books of days, novels and short stories.

Several times, glaciers passed through, rounding off the Taconic Range behind my house and polishing the big granite dome mountain looming in front of it, called Canaan Mountain, named by the Puritans who settled the valley. Modern settlers followed and founded the Land of Nod Vineyard right under Canaan Mountain. As evidence of its former presence, the glacier deposited a huge marble limestone boulder in front of my house like a big, pocked white egg. This serves as a centerpiece for the garden in front of my house. These boulders are sparse, like ancient eggs scattered by some wandering stone giant throughout the surrounding forest. The indigenous peoples who lived here, a branch of the Mohicans, named things too, calling the river that defines the valley and this region of the state, "Housatonic," meaning "beyond the mountain place."

Salisbury was settled by the Puritans, who, as was their custom, sent a missionary preacher to build a church first and then gathered the congregation, while trying to convert what Native Americans he could. My Congregational church was "gathered" in 1744. We had our 275th annual meeting in fall 2019. Ethan Allen had been a member but differed with its pastor about the efficacy of smallpox vaccinations. A sore loser, he left to form his famous Green Mountain Boys in Vermont. They played a key role during the Revolutionary War, raiding the British frontier forts for vital cannons, later to be produced in Salisbury.

There were rich deposits of iron ore discovered about this time just outside of the town. Since the British forbade the production of iron by the settlers, local entrepreneurs—led by Samuel Forbes—set out to build an iron industry, utilizing the surrounding natural bounty of the land. Soon, foundries stoked by bellows and pumped by the swift-running streams were charged with the abundant local limestone (from that old seabed) and fired by wood from the surrounding hardwood forest. The woods were soon cleared by an army of colliers, organized for the dirty task of producing charcoal that denuded the countryside by the beginning of the twentieth century.

The remnants of charcoal mounds—large circular scars on the forest floor—still dot the hills around my home. It was dangerous work, but they succeeded clearing the countryside for the shepherds and cattlemen who followed. Iron was big business here, making the area the Pittsburg of that era until the center of production moved west and to Birmingham, following the new Bessemer technology. Along the local streams like Blackberry River, there are the remains of over thirty-five stone-blast furnaces. The original steel master was Sam Forbes, while the ore body was owned by the Scoville Family who endowed the local library—the oldest public library in our country.

After the novelty of the Big Apple wore off, Georgia and I escaped steamy summers in the city to visit Chris Covington, an HBS classmate of mine. Georgia and I first came to the area in around 1980. North of Salisbury, in Lanesboro, MA, Chris had an idyllic cabin that overlooked Mt. Greylock. His front yard was graced with a country pond ideal for swimming, and yes, even skinny-dipping. The over-four-hour drive from New York got old, so we decided to look further south and found our friends, Rick and Jenny Stowe, who had a house on Twin Lakes, near Salisbury. My former boss Noel Urben also had a house in nearby Cornwall. The choirmaster at the Congregational Church, Al Sly, soon discovered Georgia and tapped her for solos on most holidays. We found the people in the community most congenial and rented a house for the summers of '81 and '82 to try it out. We soon fell in love with the area and its people and began to work with a real estate agent. We saw everything answering our specs—"a place by the water with a view of a mountain," like Chris's cabin where we'd spent many a happy weekend.

We looked for two years and were at the point of giving up. On New Year's Eve, 1982, Georgia performed her usual gig at the Bardavon Opera Theatre in Albany, NY, singing light opera favorites with other artists from NYC. We'd agreed to give it another month before starting to look farther south, when we got a call from our agent, "Petie" Robinson, informing us there was a home on a bluff overlooking the Housatonic with a drop-dead view of Canaan Mountain that we had to see before it went on the market.

The following day we drove to Salisbury from Albany and up a steep driveway. It was bright and very cold, with the clean remnants of the last snowstorm still on the ground. I won't forget turning the corner and beholding the grand twisted white pine ahead of me. It was so impressive I thought it must be sacred. Later, I learned it was a wolf pine because an insect embedded into the growing sprout, causing it to split into many arms and preventing its straight growth, thus saving the magnificent, contorted giant from the lumberyard—pure serendipity, a phenomenon that appeared to circle my life when Georgia was in my presence.

There was something special about this place. The cabin was modest, built on three levels with a deck out back that overlooked the river and the mountain. I was charmed, but Georgia was particularly taken because, the owners being cat people, had jig-sawed an image of a cat through the entrance door to the litter box in the basement. The cabin's woodwork was impressive. It was paneled with local wood; the view was magnificent, and the price about right—$150,000. Georgia told me in no uncertain terms not to bargain—just hit the bid. I did. We closed and were in by my birthday on February 8, 1983, spending the first night in sleeping bags on the bare pine floor. I thought back to that night in one of the first poems I wrote about this place, in a lament for Georgia called *Dark River*:

> It was winter, like now.
> We searched long for a place by water.
> The first night in our unfurnished house
> we lay in a sleeping bag
> joyful on plain pine boards.
>
> Through sunrise's haze,
> we overlooked the river
> defining the valley.
> It wound south
> between bare tree-lined banks
> fresh with snow.

That next morning, I rose to fix coffee and looked out the curtain-less picture window at Canaan Mountain, anointed white from overnight snow. The dark river snaked down the valley, edging the bare cut cornfields below the house and across Weatogue Road.

We had great fun decorating the house and furnishing it with objects purchased from local antique fairs and auctions that periodically popped up over the Berkshires weekends. Nestled in a woodland rim of a glade on a plateau overlooking the river, the house was cozy, well protected from storms, and safely above the inevitable flooding that came with living by the river. In the meadow, there was cleared space for gardens and a toolshed. We cleared more and put in two perennial gardens— one in the shade in front of the house and one in the sun in front of a stone wall restored as a backdrop. A friend and neighbor and renowned perennial horticulturist, Fred McGourty, designed both of these. His fees were the martinis he consumed sitting with me on our little cabin's porch. Each summer we grew and picked vegetables until Gordon Whitbeck inherited his father's farm down the road, bringing a bounty of organic vegetables to the valley.

I discovered a number of springs and a mud hole next door, and we later bought the property to dig out a pond for fishing and swimming. We had everything we needed, and even glassed in the downstairs patio for Georgia's year-round practice studio. Her clothing and effects are gone, but I can't erase the memories of the time we spent together in our little treehouse, and though it was the last house Georgia ever lived in, I felt strangely comfortable there after she'd died.

Georgia named everything she loved. She decided on Utopia, but modified by calling it *Utopia, Limited,* the name of Gilbert and Sullivan's thirteenth opera. She had sung the lead in all fourteen of Gilbert and Sullivan's operas, but *Utopia, Limited* was her favorite. In 1993, I managed, after months of negotiations to acquire the land south of our little cabin, once a boys' summer camp. Soon after we bought the land, we placed a permanent conservation easement on the fifty acres that are adjacent to similarly conserved acreage owned by the Trustees of Reservation—the world's oldest land trust. This poem tells this story:

Utopia Farm

> When lilacs scented
> Housatonic hedges
> we walked from our weekend cabin
> to the old boy's camp next door.
> We wrestled this from a failed developer
> who planned a subdivision
> of country estates to be named
> the Blackberry River Run.
>
> Touring our abandoned camp
> after the closing, past
> the boarded and tumbled cabins,
> the months of haggling pay off
> with a periwinkle ground cover

in azure profusion.

You're dressed in a red checked shirt,
faded jeans, and tattered straw hat.
Our path cuts across an overgrown field:
we talk of horses pasturing there,
renovating stalls in the old barn,
and building a pond edging the wetlands,
sourcing the stream meandering the meadow.

This is so distant from the city
where we could barely pay
the rent when we started.
You were singing late nights and weekends,
and I was traveling weekdays
and working spreadsheets the rest.

In a seed-heavy sea of green,
high before the first haying,
flaked purple-white with flea bane
and yellow with buttercup and hawkweed,
we leave a wake
of trampled grass across our prairie,
a dew soaking
our trousers bottoms.

Indians camped at the fork of these rivers
and settlers left stone footprints
of cabin cellars and walls across the acreage.
They knew this alluvial land was rich,
the forest's full of cedar and ash for fence and rail,
straight white pine's for barn sides
and oak's for stall interstices.
From our hillside, an artesian well gushes
that watered the camp and filled a pool
where 120 buttnaked little boys
bathed summer mornings!

It is strange we should settle
here…under Canaan mountain,
in Weatogue valley,
so far from our native places
seeds scattered,
but now sown,
taking root,
feeling home.

The new property became not only home, but the center of farm activities. Many fine evenings, we invited our friends for "harness tightening time" at the new barn we built from our timber milled on the spot with a portable bandsaw. Georgia and I talked of renovating the lodge on the hill above it into a pavilion for entertaining. There, we held an annual Halloween party for the road (which soon became an annual social event with a high-stakes costume contest), as well as cast parties for Georgia's opera company. Those were such happy times. In that barn, we stabled five horses. Windsor, Georgia's Morgan horse, started the whole equestrian thing. In fact, our caretaker Eli used to jokingly call the barn Windsor's Castle. My horse, Cinnamon, was a big chestnut quarter horse with a white blaze that Georgia's sister Holly sent me as a Christmas surprise.

Eli Butcher is a horse whisperer whose day job was at a paper mill. Georgia met him on the farm down the road where she bought Windsor and was impressed by the care he took with his horses. He owned Manny, a solid black thoroughbred mare, and mother to two horses, PT or Perfect Timing and Elijah's Prophet, also known as Prophet. The latter two horses were born in the new barn, both sired by the famous racehorse Mr. Prospector. Prophet was born on the night a tornado came through; we thought this a good omen for a racehorse.

We'd trailer both horses to Saratoga racetrack with Bongo, a brilliant goat skilled at calming these high-strung animals. At Saratoga, they worked out, and sometimes got in a race. PT came in dead last on each one of his outings, but Prophet came in an exciting second on his first race in Boston. We had great hope for his future and sent him to training camp where he jerked a halter out of a groom's hand and ran into the open tailgate of a pick-up truck, thus ending his racing career.

The house I currently live in at Utopia is made of stone and wood with most of the stone quarried from the site. The floors are oak and pine, both milled from the property as well. Created by an Atlanta architect and devotee of Frank Lloyd Wright's, James Choate, the house's architecture follows Wright's design principles, meaning the rooms center around the fireplaces, and nature itself seems to be invited in. The house looks like it belongs in its environment, using materials from the surrounding land. It surprises you when seen from the road, bold yet blending with the wooded background. The central space in the house is a large circular library containing all the books I've gathered over the years. Its entrance way is whimsically held up by an uncarved oak trunk, like an unfinished totem pole.

The little cabin Georgia and I lived in so happily for over thirty years became a guest house next door to this big house. Christina was not into Waldenesque cabins in the woods, nor a rustic swimming pond, and after we married, she strongly lobbied for a larger house and formal pool. She finally convinced me the cabin was not good enough and that we should build something grander on Weatogue Road.

In 2007, I found Jim Choate, a Georgia Tech architect, and we worked together for two years to plan the new house. We walked the property, visited Falling Water together, and went back and forth getting all of my and Christina's dream house wishes on paper. Initially, I didn't want anything like this home, but Jim's creativity impressed me, and I let him and Christina drag me into it. Today, I'm overjoyed to live in the artwork he created.

In 2009, after the crash, I began to interview contractors who, in the recession, had no work. Though several large Connecticut contractors bid on the job, I found an impressive local contractor, Fred Laser. He'd meticulously prepared for the bid, putting together a team of local subcontractors. I chose Fred over my architect's objections because he most wanted the work, and with local workers, I felt he and the subcontractors he selected would pay the most attention to the detail the job required. The house was scheduled to take two years to build but was completed in a year and a half.

I walked the site and bonded with the workmen, who were remarkable masons, carpenters, and iron fitters. They thanked me for the work and actually competed with one another through their craftsmanship. Instead of a chore, building that house was a pleasure, and it was an education working with Fred and his foreman, Moe Benson. Moe had a "wall of shame" in his central construction shack for anyone who screwed up that day to build morale. The house became an interactive and instructive process, as well as one of great pride for the craftsmen, many of whom lived across the river in Canaan. The house was somehow meant to be.

Ironically, Christina wasn't there for the completion of the house she'd persuaded me to build. While that was shock enough and another chapter of my life, it also took me a while to move in from the little cabin next door. I was not used to so much light, wood, stone and space, vaulting ceilings and changing vistas. However, it was a beautiful space, inviting and seductive in a strange way. Each corner showcased a changing landscape. Even now, I constantly move around to try out a new view. It's a magical and kinetic environment.

When it was move-in ready, I threw a party for all the workers who built the house and their families, as well as all my neighbors who'd tolerated its construction. My pastor came to bless the house, and we had great fun properly christening it. On a bluff overlooking the river and mountain, the house looks like it grows out of the local stone. Like its namesake, it's a living piece of art—Utopia Limited.

Utopia Farm Main House Library, 2015 (Photo by Phillip Spears)

Chapter 43
On the Island of the Smiling Loon

The person who helped me organize Utopia's housewarming party was Brooke Conklin, a friend who I dated after Georgia died and after Christina left me. Brooke and I met on my church's trip to Greece but got to know each other much better when she became a costumer for LOCOS in the summer of 2005, run by our mutual friends, Harriet and Paul Tomasko who directed and carried on Georgia's troop of musicians for ten years after her death. They brought Brooke into the LOCOS circle, who borrowed costumes and sets from the Manhattan Savoyards in NYC and were in constant need of alterations. This poem records one of our early gathering with the Tomasko's near Woodstock, NY:

Concert at Opus 40

A monolith stakes the sky,
an exclamation point
of a massive Stonehenge,
measuring the mountain beyond—
distant blue in the haze,
an aloof overlord, last-lighted
by a setting sun.

Below, the band is spread out
on the stone earthwork
like a platoon ready for a fire fight.
Refugees and rhythms from the love-in
at not-far-away Woodstock,
the audience dances, enthralled,
drawn in by the primordial beat
of tom-toms turning on libidos,
liberating picnic blankets and chairs...

Nearby, after the concert, our hostess
Harriet sits by her koi pond,
ringed by the same blue stone and calls

the circling school by their names:
Smokey Joe, Chinese Checkers,
Lemon Meringue and Mrs. Moby,
like she's auditioning carnival clowns.
Around the house, Paul's well-tended garden,
fodder for their cooking and pickling,
and an oak hangs
with druid-like offerings
of bird feeders, shading all.

We sit around the tree, talking
of the scars of former loves,
healing them with our fellowship
lasting through it all.
The mountain looms distant,
a good father listening
to our confessions.

Brooke and I became good friends, but this became difficult when my relationship grew more serious with Christina. After Christina and I married in June 2007, Brooke and I seldom communicated, but I had a great deal of respect for Brooke, her family, her photography, and her missionary work for the Methodist Church where she worked at that time. Somehow, we remained friends.

After it became clear Christina had gone outside our marriage, I re-contacted Brooke. We first went to a Shakespeare & Co. play in Lenox. The poem below reflects Brooke and me getting back together during this most difficult time in my life—when I was still stinging from a betrayal. We tried rebuilding a relationship. She had a beautiful and restorative island in the Adirondacks with a quaint cabin on it. The environment was a primeval wilderness, that, even now, is hard to describe, but I sensed it deeply, harkening something beyond us:

On the Island of the Smiling Loon

Afternoon rain tingles
on the cabin's pane, washing
the memory into the lake
moating the pine island…

Despite all efforts to forget,
betrayal pits your stomach.
You know you must forgive
or give it up to God.

Compassion sleeps beside you,
sharing her island, and somewhere
in the water lilies, a loon wails
that haunting sound, harkening

something timeworn,
going way back to the primordial—
clean living and faith,
keeping your word.

These white- and black-feathered birds
seek clear waters,
stand their ground
and mate for life.

We enjoyed some wonderful times exploring the property around
our respective retreats together as well as the horseraces and spas
in Saratoga. I hosted her daughter and children from Australia for
Christmas that year, as well as her son Steve, his girlfriend, Jessica
and her two adorable children, Branden, and Aislinn, who produced
a Christmas coloring for me as a present. Fond memories of that
Christmas at Utopia, including a gourmet goose that year with the
children spreading their innocent joy, leaving me a coloring that
remains still framed on my wall.

Brooke was a good and generous person who helped me transition
two voids in my life:

Camellias in the Moonlight

I was up before the cold dawn
looking out the kitchen window
watching a full moon setting—
a luminous lamp turning night

into a ghost-like morning. Below,
a camellia bush bloomed full white,
its petals, vulnerable and inviting—
risking all for an early spring.

My companion, gracing mild winter
days until the freeze—
this unrequited love, dressed
for a prom that didn't come.
The camellia's buds, now shriveled
are scattered in the garden
where I swept them
with a sadness hard to say.

My relationship with Brooke began to wane after my longtime friends, the Staglin's introduced me to their friend, Anne. As I spent more time with Anne the following year, some in Florida, I soon came to the realization that we clearly had more in common. Indeed, it seemed fateful the way we met and bonded. I had become simply in love with Anne, and it seemed that we were destined to be long-term companions.

Chapter 44
The Foundation for Religious Literacy

While I was still a student at Harvard Divinity School, Dean Ron Thiemann and I decided to partner in a venture for a series of evening lectures at the Harvard Club. He and HDS supplied the intellectual content through lecturers, and I funded the endeavor and supplied the audience from my business contacts, augmented by HDS alums, and sometimes the members of the NYC Harvard Business School Club. We called these seminars Business Across Religious Traditions, or BART programs—echoing San Francisco's rapid transit system's acronym. Little did I know these popular lectures would become the programmatic foundation for the public charity Ron and I would later establish. We thought by employing teachers with international reputations in the study of world religions, the BART program would develop into a unique educational resource for professional leaders worldwide, hoping our message would trickle down from the leaders to their organizations. In 2007, there were to be three programs across three major traditions to kick things off. We started with Michael Puett, Professor of Chinese History whose class in Chinese philosophy was one of the most popular at Harvard, and his lectures for BART were always standing room only. It was a sell-out. The next program was on Hinduism, featuring Anne E. Monius. The last program was Buddhism led by Donald Swearer. Encouraged by the turn out and feedback, we ran programs like these, rotating among religious traditions, for the next four years I was at HDS, even branching out to San Francisco, Boston, and London. Nancy Birne, organizer extraordinaire of HDS's development office; Charlene Higbe, Ron's indispensable assistant, and my assistant Claire Durka sent out invitations, organized the gatherings, and made them happen.

Early on at my fortieth HBS reunion in 2009, Ron and I made a presentation and held a seminar for the reunion classes where a handful of interested business leaders of different faiths gathered to discuss the distinctive resources that various traditions provide for ethical leadership in the business community. This became our BART support group. Interest and participation as well as membership expanded. When Ron was on sabbatical, we held roundtable discussions in the back-conference room of Berkshire Capital. Ron set up the topic for discussion, and we chewed-over each subject with the group of executives and continued into dinner.

In 2011, my last year at HDS, Ron and I decided to set up The Religious Literacy Foundation. We both thought things had gotten a bit Harvard-centric and needed a more diverse entity, both for the lecturer line-up and the impact of religion across more professions. The following year Ron was on sabbatical to write a book and decided to fundraise for the Foundation after he returned.

We decided 2012 would be the year of the CEO lecture and got some excellent people lined up for talks at the Harvard Club in NYC. Our first was a homerun. It was an evening with Stephen Green, Group Chairman of HSBC Holdings that Ron moderated. After I'd graduated from HDS and was back at work, we had one more New York CEO lecture with Bill George, Professor at HBS and former CEO of Medtronic. A year ahead of me at Georgia Tech and at HBS, Bill taught business ethics courses at HDS, and because he also knew Ron, was helpful to me after Ron's passing.

After the June meeting 2012, the advisory group was dining outside at an Italian restaurant, San Pietro, just across from my office. It was a beautiful evening, not too hot or steamy yet. We ordered wine, and Ron didn't have his usual glass. He complained of heartburn and excused himself to get an antacid. He came back, still not feeling well and left for Boston without dinner. He was to see his doctor the following morning, but I didn't hear from him for four days, which seemed ominous. When he finally called, it was brief and direct. He had pancreatic cancer, and it was inoperable.

I almost dropped the phone. I called Christina and told her. She said Mt. Sinai had one of the best surgeons for the Whipple procedure, but it was a dangerous operation. I called Ron back, but he calmly said it was too late. He was on advanced chemotherapy and had begun to put things in order, including rushing to finish his book. We talked about convening a religious literacy conference and decided to do so in the early fall before Ron was too sick to attend. Over the summer we put the project on rush and got it together, gathering all the luminaries in the field—academics, practitioners, and funders.

In collaboration with the Coexist Foundation, the first Religious Literacy Roundtable was held in October 2012 at the NYC Harvard Club. Representatives from diverse organizations and educational institutions attended to discuss how best to promote national and international understanding about various belief systems and how to promote collaboration among leaders in the academic, programmatic, and funding communities.

The insights were then captured in a substantive report. The conference included scholars, like Stephen Prothero of BU and Charles Haynes of the First Amendment Center as well as entrepreneurs, like Steve Waldman founder of Belief.net who focused on media and technology; we also singled out religious literacy program funders. Though Ron was visibly in pain, he stayed for the whole conference, his wife Beth by his side. At the end, he stood and summarized the proceedings in a masterful performance. The participants gave him a standing ovation. They took up his challenge to keep going and continue the good work we were all trying to accomplish.

I visited Beth and Ron at their home in Concord, MA for a last time in October 2012. We went to the neighboring airport where I had rented a two-engine plane to fly us out to Utopia for lunch on the shore of Twin Lakes with David Ford, the Regius Professor of Divinity at Cambridge. The Berkshires were ablaze in color, and our lakeside discussion was blessed by the Great Spirit when a bald eagle landed on a large pine bough at the edge of David's property. Ron had wanted to come out to Salisbury to see me, and I knew there was no other way but to fly. He faded fast thereafter, passing away in late November 29, 2012 at the age of 66.

I wrote a poem for Ron's memorial service, held at Memorial Church in Harvard Yard in April 2013. This work blends a combination of Ron's favorite Bible verses and excerpts from Emerson's infamous "Divinity School Address," delivered July 15, 1838 to the senior class in Divinity Hall at the old chapel, just down the hall from Ron's office:

The Bearded Man of Luther
For Ronald Frank Thiemann (Oct. 4, 1946–Nov. 29, 2012)

I.
The idea came to us on an island
in the Atlantic flyway shrouded
white with snow. A distant pine—swept
and bent by the ocean blow officiated
like a priest, a big bonsai, painfully trimmed.
Here, we first talked of the gatherings.
Here, where flocks descended as if on schedule
into gloam's Götterdämmerung,
amber orange and blood red—
arrow after arrow of gangly "Vs"

honking and cacophonic,
coming to peace on the coastal ponds.
Grand swans circle the island
like elegant ideas.
Their graceful necks grope
the half-iced waters for sustenance.

It was in the refulgent summer,
the season that gives up its mystery
of corn and wine, when our friend
was given the bitter cup:
to learn suffering's lessons
of endurance and character, and hope
that sometimes disappoints, though
God's spirit is poured out in each of us.

II.
We saw him sit hours in pain
through a confessional first seminar
of aspirations for religious literacy
and summarize so simply and eloquently
its content; we glimpsed, for a moment,
at a promised land where he could not go.

This bearded man of Luther,
acquainted us firsthand with the Deity.
His church sent him to end the schism,
and his school sent him to salve Iran's intellectuals.
He loved his family, the Red Sox, and scholarship.
He explained the absence of God
in our public square and His troublesome
re-appearances. Shamed, but unbroken
he stood. We took courage in his suffering,
and hope for change in the world's order.

Carrying on after Ron was going to be very difficult. His death
took the wind out of my sails. I hired Kay Johnson as interim director,
and she helped me carry on and organize the Faith, Leadership and

Ethics (FEL) seminars. Each seminar hosted a leading academic and/
or practitioner who addressed how approaches to the resources of
various religious traditions could increase professional effectiveness,
ethical leadership, and personal conduct.

We put forward an exciting list of speakers for the 2013-2014
season, but the effort to organize lectures and seminars dragged since
I had limited assistance. It was like we started over with each seminar,
though the response from the programs was great. I gave up on this
approach and began to seed programs that would have a more sig-
nificant impact. Since 2015, this has resulted in some surprisingly
successful projects.

For example, starting in January 2017, Harvard Divinity School
and Boston University hosted a successful symposium on religion and
humanitarian action through The Religious Literacy and the Profes-
sions Initiative, initiated by a symposium on journalism in November
2016. Similarly, followed by a two-day symposium on religion and
government in December 2017. In the fall of 2018 in Boston a
symposium on business and media was the most successful of this
series. At Harvard Divinity School, we also supported The Harvard
Religious Literacy Project, led by Dr. Diane Moore that offers courses
via its most successful massive online course, that has reached over
125,000 students through Harvard EdX. The man who got me into
all of this, Boston University's Professor and the world's leading
authority on religious literacy, Dr. Stephen Prothero, led BU's side of
the initiative.

This Harvard program was preceded by the Leadership and Multi-
faith Program (LAMP), a project between Emory and Georgia Tech.
where I was on their respective advisory boards once. These univer-
sities hosted a well-attended conference in Atlanta, the most popular
on science and religion. Again, like the Harvard/BU model, the
symposium was organized by professors at each school—Dr. Deanna
Womack, an Interfaith Studies Chair at the Candler School of Emory
and Dr. Ken Knoespel, a professor from Georgia Tech's Department
of Literature, Media, and Communication in Ivan Allen College.
The Arthur Vining Davis Foundation provided generous additional
funding for the events.

One of our most impactful investments was the Smithsonian's
exhibition titled *Religion in Early America*, in 2017/2018, focusing on

America's diversity, freedom, and growth of religion. This exhibition started out of my work with the former secretary of the Smithsonian and President of Georgia Tech, Dr. Wayne Clough, and the 2015-16 series of three symposiums led by Stephen Prothero focused on the religions of America. The Lilly Endowment provided $5 million in additional funding in order to create the Lilly Endowment Curator of American Religious History at the Smithsonian. The holder of this curatorship, Peter Manseau developed a book, *Objects of Devotion: Religion in Early America*, based on the exhibit that richly displays this collection.

We also seeded the funds to create a religious literacy specialist position at the Religious Freedom Center (RFC) of the Newseum that was held by Benjamin P. Marcus, currently an advisor of the foundation now at Yale Law School. Ben is an HDS alum with us from our start, who, in his capacity at the RFC, led a team of national experts to create a religious study companion document to the C3 Framework, a landmark achievement in religious studies in K-12 education. It was at the RFC visiting Ben where I met its director and our current director of TFRL, Rev. Dr. Nate Walker. Little did I know that Ben and Nate, when working at the RFC, had nominated me for an award.

In the summer of 2016, I was surprised by the visit of an official from the United Nations who informed me I should plan to travel to Rio for the Special Olympics. I was going to receive a medal from them for the work I'd done in the interfaith arena. In Rio, I was awarded a bronze medal at the Global Business and Interfaith Peace Awards. These awards were hosted by the Religious Freedom & Business Foundation, a US-based nonprofit organization, in collaboration with the United Nations Global Compact's Business for Peace Initiative in Rio de Janeiro. The trip was most satisfying because The Religious Literacy Foundation got recognition for all the organization's work and investment. I only wish Professor Ronald Thiemann had been there to receive it with me.

Since my return from Stanford in 2017, Nate and his firm, 1791 Delegates, has been managing the foundation and conducting its fundraising efforts. At the start, Nate led us through a strategic planning process that helped us see three patterns of our previous success: our ability to convene leaders, to seed initiatives, and leverage assets to scale our investments. These have become our primary methods for now managing the foundation, approaches we feel preserve and build upon the work that Ron and I began in 2011.

For instance, we seeded a national religious literacy fellowship program and helped each award recipient find additional programmatic and funding support to continue their projects. Our current fellows are: Dr. Andrew Henry, whose *Religion for Breakfast* YouTube series has millions of viewers, Katie Gordon, developer of the *Nuns for None's* program, Usra Ghazi, community organizer with the US foreign service, and Eleesa Tucker, developer of Utah's 3-R's program. We seeded the curriculum development for an anti-religious-bullying curriculum for the Cub and Boy Scouts in the New York City area Dr. Kate Soules another TFRL fellow developed with Dr. Walker. We also convened a dozen of the nation's leading funders in the field of religious literacy to learn that the programmatic and philanthropic space is thriving and growing every year.

Looking back over the last decade, I see that Ron was prescient and correct in advising me to invest in this emerging field. I think he would be proud that we honor his life by convening leaders, seeding innovative projects, and inspiring donors to leverage our investments. In the last two years alone, we have increased our operating budget six times and broadened our philanthropic investors to dozens of investors. I could not have done this without Nate Walker; he is simply a blessing and bodhisattva. We continue this work with a great sense of purpose and gratitude for all those who made it possible.

Chapter 45
The Signs of a Beautiful Life

As an HDS graduate, I'm asked to preach occasionally, and these sermons reflect my developing philosophy. I find sermons take about two weeks of deep thought. The church follows an annual lectern of scripture readings that are read at most churches around the country on any given Sunday, so you have the subject laid out for you. What I really love is to research the text and background, bringing in my life experience. Mine are more academic and much too long. I wish I could give those short direct punches that, like a Meister Eckert, knock you off your feet.

The first sermon I gave was to my congregation in Salisbury for July 4th, 2010. I based *Our Freedom, Lost or Found?* on a reading from Galatians (5:13-15) that says we're called to freedom but also cautions that we do not use freedom "as an opportunity for self-indulgence." My opening point was we can and do enslave ourselves; we give away our freedom through our activities, interests, work, and ambitions. I concluded: "We live in constant outside noise that fills up our inner-space and peace. We suffer from an overload of information—TV, the internet, newspapers. The technology that was meant to free us is the biggest user of our time. How much time do we spend with our faces in a computer or phone screen? Leave your cellphone home, and it's like being naked. Try a day without it—it's blessed."

In August 2011, I gave my second sermon, *Poetry, a Bridge to the Sacred*, and again addressed the Salisbury Congregational Church:

> The experience of the sacred and love is similar: every love is a revelation, a jolt that causes the very foundations of the ego to tremble and utter words not very different from the mystic. In poetic creation, something similar happens absence and presence, silence and words, emptiness and plenitude are poetic states, as well as religious and amorous ones—in each of them the rational and irrational elements occur simultaneously.

I believe the sacred is indeed within us, and if this is true, the whole world is changed. If we incorporate the divine in us, each day is a communion with our maker:

> In order to be, man must propitiate the divine, that is, ap-
> propriate it. By means of consecration, man has access to
> the sacred, to the plenitude of being. This is the meaning of
> the sacraments, especially that of communion.

The starting point of poetry, like that of religion, is the original
human situation—knowing we have been thrown into a hostile and
indifferent world. By a path that is in its own way negative, the poet
comes to the brink of language. And that brink is called silence; a blank
page. Sterility precedes inspiration, as emptiness precedes plenitude. The
poetic world crops up after periods of drought. I mixed the sermon with
selected poems and came back to my title as the concluding argument:

> The poetic image is the bridge. It does not conceal our
> condition from us: it reveals it and invites us to realize it
> completely. The act by which man grounds and reveals
> himself is poetry. In sum, the religious experience and
> the poetic one have a common origin in their historic ex-
> pressions—poems, myths, prayers, exorcisms, hymns,
> and dance... This is not the dilemma: life or death, but a
> totality—life and death in a single instant of incandescence.
> In this troubled time, our sin may indeed be the littleness of
> our being—let's take wing and go beyond.

This sermon was picked up and published by my friend, Jeff Zaleski,
the editor of *Parabola Magazine* who was excited as it fit neatly into his
winter 2011 issue.

On Sunday May 13th, 2012, I delivered *A Mother's Gift* for Mother's
Day to the Peachtree Road Lutheran Church in Atlanta for my good friend
Rev. Kurt Bridges, who was receiving an honorary degree in North Carolina.
Kurt was a pioneer in Atlanta race relations and organized Atlanta's pastors
during the 1996 Olympic Games. This church was next door to Canterbury
Court, the assisted living home where my mother spent her last years.
It's the church where we held her memorial service and where Georgia's
Bluthner Grand piano resides. In this sermon, I cited Mom's favorite poem,
Billy Collins's *Lanyard*, an autographed copy of which hung on her wall, and
I made the point the poem was a rumination of our inability to repay our
mothers for the gift of life and all their love for us:

My mother even has a cabinet of cha-chas from all over the world that I, my sister, and her granddaughters have brought her to try to pay tribute. In closing, let me say there is no way that we can repay our mothers for what they've done for us, given us the gift of life. We make feeble attempts like this day.

My sermon for the Congregational Church of Salisbury on a Sunday in June 2014 was *An Introduction to the Sermon on the Mount*. I think *Sermon on the Mount* continues to play an important role as a core ethical rudder for modern societies. It is the touchstone of the literature I teach at Georgia Tech—its course runs through Augustine, is the core of Jefferson's remarkably edited Bible (in four languages). It was the life-changing center of Tolstoy's new religion and the development of his non-violence theories in the last thirty years of his life. These theories resulted in Tolstoy's correspondence with Gandhi, who was thrown out of the "whites only" train compartment where he was reading Tolstoy's book *The Kingdom of God Is Within You*, that led Gandhi to non-violent action in South Africa then India. *The Sermon on the Mount* was also at the core of Martin Luther King's non-violent philosophy. This torch passed onto Thich Nhat Hanh, a living Buddhist saint who protested Vietnam. This literature pushes ethics and morality to a new level that we can only attempt to live up to.

In July 2016, my sermon before the Congregational Church of Salisbury was *In the Presence of the Divine*. I spoke of hearing David Brooks talk about his book *The Road to Character* at the recent Aspen Ideas Festival. In the book, Brooks says we strive throughout our lifetimes for four things (1) material things (2) ego things—status, fame etc. (3) generative things—kids, service, contributions to community, and (4) lastly, transcendence—how do we develop that inner light? What are we doing for our souls?

His book is about people who achieved transcendence. Brooks goes on to say we work on getting to the transcendent through long-term commitments—first to our spouses or loved ones, secondly to our vocations, thirdly through development of our philosophies and beliefs about life, and lastly, through building our community around us. We must risk commitment to gain anything in the long run. I pointed out the parallels between Brooks' heroes and those I use in my course: Brooks' book, in fact, is about a series of his heroes who, over time, achieved transcendence over their lifetimes. The class I teach at Georgia Tech tries to do much the same thing through studying the literature of these people. At the end of his book, Brooks shows that the victories for notable people who commit themselves to ideas and faiths nobler than any individual ever could be follow the same arc:

> ...from defeat to recognition to redemption, the humble path to the beautiful life. Joy is the byproduct experienced by people who are aiming for something else Joy comes as a gift when you least expect it. Those moments are blessings and the signs of a beautiful life.

But it comes when there is a unity of effort—when moral nature and external skills are united in one defining effort. I am seeing some signs of that showing up in my life, but I believe this is only through the grace of God.

Georgia McEver at Tanglewood Concert, July 18, 1994

Chapter 46
Crossing the Void

Early summer 2014 I went for revival walk in Central Park before heading off to work at Berkshire Capital. I loved to take the route from my apartment that allowed me to climb to Belvedere Castle, sitting atop a dome-smooth, dark granite outcropping. There's a great view of the Park's acreage and the vast treasure house of the Metropolitan Museum. The placid surface of the pond below was occasionally pocked by turtles coming up for air. It was idyllic. That morning I took in the view as well as well as took the time to meditate on recent troubling events. I sat on one of the castle's lawn benches made from artfully twisted grape vines.

It was the first anniversary of my mother's birthday following her death, and I so missed her. The previous year, in November 2012, I'd lost Ron Thiemann. He and Mom were doers, and people I could bare my heart to. They understood me. Both were gone within a year of one another. Inexplicably, my marriage had now fallen apart. Christina and I were separated for no good reason that I could see. I faced the prospect of a summer alone in my new home in Salisbury, a project that my wife had urged upon me, and that we'd started together. She'd inexplicably abandoned both our new house and me. The life we'd built together had fallen apart before it really started. The world seemed flat and bare. I wandered through the Shakespeare Garden deep in thought where I wrote this poem inspired by the one of the garden's inscriptions:

On Mother's Birthday
"Here's flowers for you
Hot lavender, mints, savory, marjoram
The marigold, that goes to bed with the sun
And with him rises weeping…"
Shakespeare, *The Winter's Tale (IV, 4)*

With my estranged wife refusing
to see or even speak to me, I wander
to the Shakespeare Garden in Central Park,
bustling with its gardeners who trim
early spring blooms for summer's fullness.
Edgy and tired from another fitful night,

I can't explain to my mother
just one year passed.
What would she say?
She saw through me, uncannily right.

Shakespeare's words wash over me,
and I soak in them in long silence
on a cold bench, listening to the shrill
whistle of just fledged red tails.

Be a man, son, like Shakespeare,
write the true hurt, get it out.
Face your destiny.
It's been in there all
along, my son.
Write, write, write.

I didn't include the poem in my last book but found it before I started to write this chapter. It says what I want to say now. I'd looked into the void when Georgia died. I'd looked deep depression in the face when it had flattened my world to shades of gray, as it was doing again. The vision I had after Georgia's death had sent me to Divinity School to explore those many paths. I took my first shot at organizing, taking charge of the chaos, pain and grief by writing a chapbook, *A Place by Water and later,* a full-length collection, *Full Horizons.* Before, I self-medicated with liberal amounts of wine, but this time I wasn't drinking. The pain was coming straight through:

Mother's Day

After she went into hospice,
my mother refused offers
of morphine "cocktails"
just as Jesus refused
the wine mixed with gall.
And so I quit drinking
to feel the full tilt of my separation
because there is wisdom in this pain...

This is my first Mother's Day

without mother or wife.
I, too, will be changed.
Just returned warblers' songs peal
from barely green trees.

Those warblers, like Blake's larks—a symbol of the transcendent—would bring me sanity. In the meantime, I also had to rely on my mother's memory. She was wise, I knew, and asking her for spiritual guidance seemed prudent. As I discovered with Georgia's death, one answer was to start writing poems. A few poems at first, then it cascaded. Writing became my ritual, my consolation. I kept a journal and wrote in it each morning, and now the story of my separation with the divorce saga following became the backbone of my book of poems, *Like Lesser Gods*. Writing can be cathartic in confronting chaos. With the delivery of the divorce papers by a rain-coated sheriff at our anniversary dinner, the drama rose to opera.

Friends said I was dealing with a passive-aggressive personality, so for good measure, I found Dr. Scott Wetzler, a brilliant psychologist out of the Montefiore Einstein Medical College, and the world's expert on this disorder. He informed me I was dealing with much worse. After much background discussion, he cut to the chase and told me that along with writing about the pain, developing another relationship was key, his practical prescription for getting across and out of this void.

Soon thereafter a friend of Christina's sheepishly came to my office, closed my door, and confided in me the reason behind my wife's behavior; I did it to myself. After seven peaceful and, I must admit, happy years, I had introduced Christina to an Irish poet ...and nature took its course. He had been introduced to me in Dublin by theologian Dr. David Ford as his close friend. On a US reading tour for a new book, I helped this man find readings in the US, even insisted over Tom Lux's objections, he read at Tech. I felt empathy for him—his wife was dying of Parkinson's. Later, Christina confessed that she'd loved him from their first meeting—a dinner the three of us had at The Dutch Treat! I was seething:

Last Walk Down 72nd in Hard Rain

My shoes and my pant legs were soaked going for cigars—
a new place complete with every brand
and a busty lighteress who smiled
when she bent over, gave a view

of her cleavage and lit my Davidoff #2.

Someone who didn't want to talk,
but thought it right,
had visited me this afternoon
having seen my wife
and her new lover...

I walked out in the rain—pouring
down 72nd Street...

past trash piles, wet dogs
in raincoats out for a piss...

Down to the end of 72nd, I looked out
over East River Drive to Roosevelt Island,
the illuminated reef beyond, out over
the stream of white lights going south
and red going north
to the light in her apartment window
at East End Avenue
where they were together.
I threw the butt of my Davidoff
in a cold puddle of muddy street water,
and walked on.

I wrote this poem, among others, to describe my pain and to drain
the anger. How right the doctor was, but to find another relationship
is like waiting for the grace of God. I still had a court battle on my
hands and had retained great legal advice in Barry Berkman and his firm.
Initially, when I desperately wanted to save the marriage, Barry, hearing
the facts and being so experienced, told me straight—it couldn't be. I
would be divorcing Christina. As he predicted, my assets were targeted.
But I was prepared, and the process I wanted to avoid began to unfold.
Since many of her relatives were divorced, and her uncle was one of New
York's top divorce attorneys, there was precedence for her actions, and
her attorneys might have convinced her she could profit as well. For me,
it was a new and shameful experience. No one in my family had ever
been divorced.

Eventually, providence came through. Christina's son Oliver decided he wanted to attend the Rose in Switzerland and needed my help in procuring a recommendation from board members I knew. The hurtful silence was broken and the stone wall tumbled. This enabled a meeting between she and I where we settled our differences without lawyers and shortly thereafter signed a binding agreement. Finally, in August of 2015, we were divorced. At that point I began to see across the void, but the stress had taken its toll, unbeknown to me.

In the interim, I was at an interfaith conference with my friend, wisest of men and my counselor, Dr. Yehezkel Landau. He followed the progress of my separation and the divorce, having experienced something similar. At one of our meetings, he told me, "What you don't realize, is that God is already in the process of preparing someone for you. Just keep your faith." Little did I know, how right he was.

Bruce McEver and Holly Lanahan at Family Wedding, 2016

Chapter 47
My Recent Unpleasantness

Like divorce, cancer was another club that I never wanted to join. It wasn't in my family as far as I knew. Early into the divorce with Christina, my friend Randy Kwei visited from Hong Kong and told me he'd been diagnosed with lung cancer. He said it came from him being a smoker in college, but also from stress. He said I should be extremely careful about stress at work, and particularly careful with the additional load from divorce proceedings. He advised to look at my diet, to drink more green tea and meditate more often. I thought nothing of it, but as the summer wore on, I noticed that I was sweating through my t-shirt nightly. I dismissed the night-sweats as too much summer beer but had my annual physical coming up in August with Dr. Bruce Janelli.

I felt fine, had no real symptoms. I worked out, biked, or hiked every day and so would have noticed any diminishing in my physical capability. That August morning in 2014, I biked over to Bruce's office, a two-story white-framed house in Canaan. It was a beautiful day, and I felt great, up early for this routine event that I usually passed with flying colors. Bruce had told me the previous year that he wanted my test result numbers when he reached my age. Christina had seconded something similar in friendlier times.

Bruce was an affable and highly intuitive doctor. I went to him when I came to Salisbury and after my first Yale-trained doctor retired. Bruce noticed things other doctors wouldn't pick up. He listened attentively to what I told him, and he looked me over, rather than burying his face in a computer. I dropped that I was having night sweats, and without missing a beat, he said, "It's been a number of years since you had a chest x-ray. Why don't you stop by Sharon Hospital Monday morning on your way to the train and get one?" As I was leaving, he added: "How's that divorce going?"

Bruce knew my entire history and come to that same hospital when Georgia was dying and tried to tell me she was brain dead. He hunted geese in the fields in front of my house at my farmer-neighbor John Bottass's place, and when I needed a shot, he met me at his son's hockey practice at the Salisbury School rink to give it to me. He was never too busy when I was sick and picked up the phone within an hour to give me advice. He was the ultimate country doctor.

The Tuesday morning after the x-ray, I got a call from him while I was in New York. "Bruce," he started, and I knew it was serious. "There's a lesion or something in your lower right lung lobe. Can you get a CAT-scan as soon as possible and send the results back to me? I'm sending you a prescription for the image. Your insurance company will argue, but get it done right away. Sorry to interrupt your day. Have them call me if there're any problems."

I arranged to have a CAT scan at East Side Imaging in the basement of a townhouse a few blocks from my apartment. After a struggle with our insurance carrier that required me threatening to switch providers, they reluctantly approved the procedure. A sheet-draped cigar, I was gently but dramatically inserted into the donut-shaped machine. As I was being scanned, I wished I hadn't had those relaxing, symbolic cigars with brandy or port, but reconciled that it hadn't been that often.

I dressed and then waited for the disc with the results. They were sent to Dr. Janelli as well, and he called me to say I needed to have someone read them closely, preferable a thoracic surgeon. As I knew none, I reluctantly called Christina. Our divorce had only recently been finalized, but like the time I had the flu, she was courteous and professional, asking me to come by her office right away. Before I'd arrived, she'd summoned a radiologist for an expert opinion. Wearing her name-embroidered and starched lime-green smock, she took the disc, and closed her office door.

When she came out, she didn't need to speak. After our years together, I could see the answer in her eyes. I had something serious. She didn't say anything to me, but calmly arranged for a biopsy while I was standing in the middle of her waiting room. Then, I realized what I had—lung cancer. I was the only male in the middle of a room full of already anxious women waiting to hear their own cancer verdicts. All my anger at her and her betrayal disappeared in a moment like a snowman melting in a heatwave, and tears streamed down my face. She gently escorted me to a vacant office and sat me at a plain grey-metal desk where I composed myself.

"I was so angry," I gasped.

She looked at me and said: "I'll be with you through this…and uhm…I don't ever remember seeing you cry?"

Christina switched into her professional self, becoming even compassionate, changing our acrimonious relationship to a positive one. She arranged for me to see Lisa Post's (her boss's) husband at Columbia. He would be available the next day and wanted to schedule a biopsy.

Looking like a stocky wrestler, Dr. Larry Post wore hospital green scrubs and sat behind his spotless mahogany desk. He said there was a lesion that he'd need to have biopsied in order to tell what we were dealing with. He minced few words. It looked suspicious and in fact, had already spread to a lymph node. That put a shiver up my spine, and I tentatively asked about the procedure. On a blank sheet of paper, he drew a lung and pointed out where the spot was, then drew a small line where the incision would be and showed what they'd take out. They would cut through my back. I asked if there was any other way, and he said, "Not with the current state of medicine. Let's get that biopsy ASAP and go from there."

The following Monday morning I entered the imposing façade of Columbia Presbyterian on the East River only six blocks from my apartment. I went up to the appointed floor and put on one of those stupid gowns open in the back so that your bare ass hangs out and deposited mine on an ice-cold exam table. An orderly came in and took me to a room where a cheerful fellow in a green bandana began to line up my CAT-scan against my back. Like a delinquent, he drew on it with a black magic marker, his assistant helping him ink the target. He told me he'd just returned from Iran where he'd been a medic but had also directed missile and drone strikes. Halleluiah! I knew this was the right man for the job and instantly relaxed. He drew his target on my back, anesthetized me, then found and speared his microscopic target with a long needle, taking a sample of the new enemy he now looked to annihilate. I was informed Dr. Post's office would be calling me with the biopsy results as soon as they were available.

In the dressing room afterwards, there was a nice-looking fellow at the locker next to me, lamenting to his brother, "I don't know why I stayed in shape all these years. It seems all useless now." He broke down crying. After he left the locker room, his brother explained that he'd just been diagnosed with pancreatic cancer. I prayed on the spot the Good Lord could do something about that man's cancer and mine as well.

The following week I headed to Sarah Lawrence Summer Writers Week in Bronxville where I worked with David Bottoms, the poet laureate of Georgia and a good friend. David had some great poems to inspire us before our daily workshops. Each afternoon, I hid in the college's library, really diving into poem creation and revision, trying to take my mind off the inevitable call and what was going on with my biopsy. Tom Lux, who ran the conference, was in constant contact. He knew what I was going through, having dodged a prostate cancer scare recently. Each day he checked to see if I had any news.

After Friday's morning session, I sat under a large oak in a field of clover in front of the old brick building where we had class. The phone flashed "unknown caller," and I picked up. "Mr. McEver?" It was Dr. Post's office, some nurse who didn't speak English very well asked if I minded if she read the results. I couldn't understand what she said but knew the last word was "carcinoma."

Damn. I'd been hopeful it was minor lesson and had even been increasingly convinced by my fellow would-be poets, that it was just a scare. I'd almost talked myself into believing that the look on Christina's face and Dr. Post's reaction weren't true. I had to face cancer, lung cancer, and it had to be exorcised sooner rather than later. I went to find Tom, and we hugged one another, not saying anything.

The week after Sarah Lawrence I had tickets to Aspen to visit my new love Anne and to attend the Aspen Ideas Festival for the first time. I called Anne, who encouraged me to take a break, insistent I needed to clear my head in the mountain air. I could get away to look at lofty mountain tops, think about life, and be with her and her friends. There, I'd start to absorb the impact that cancer would have on me. I hesitated to put the burden on Anne. She took it calmly when I told her, as it was the new reality between us.

I told my sister, my partner Bruce and a few friends in David's workshop. I called Eli to say I wouldn't be home to Utopia that weekend but would head directly to Colorado. Anne met me at the airport. I took oxygen sickness pills and was prepared for the altitude change, enjoyed a beer at dinner and was glad for a reprieve. Clever Anne already had a plan. The very next evening at a dinner, Anne had us seated next to Ken Davis, the head of Mt. Sinai. Both she and Ken served on the Aspen Institute board. She'd briefed him, and Ken was on the case, telling me he'd just hired the entire thoracic surgery team from Sloan Kettering, headed by Dr. Rajas Flores. Dr. Flores would see me first thing the following Monday. I made the appointment the next morning as well as a plane reservation. I'd work on simply enjoying my next days at the Ideas Festival and being with Anne.

Biking along the river and hiking the mountain trails, I thought a
lot and decided I'd face it when it came. In the meantime, I was with
someone who cared about me and who'd helped me arrange the correct
treatment. She made me feel braver. I also had Dr. Post as a backup.
What was interesting was how trivial some of the conversations at the
conference seemed when I knew I had cancer. In this context, many of
the lofty Aspen ideas became distant like the snow-covered mountain
tops reflected in this poem:

The Roaring Fork

We bike a trail by the rain-swollen river—
muddy, boiling, and hell-bent downstream
over rocks and rills under poles of pines
reaching skyward, and the eternal aspens
quaking riverside. The stream cuts
a "v" through bedrock and swaths
down-valley. Impressive,
this power of water—the yin.

Verdant slopes reach to red peaks
patched with remnant snows
above the tree lines of Aspen's mountains.
Like noble muses they stand
over this town bustling
with the summer crowd here
for the annual Ideas Festival—
Its congregants, their world
swiftly simplified, all tagged and imbibing
inspiration from the mountains
and speakers in the tents and halls.

If only we would follow
the logic proposed here,
work together with goodwill.
But then the cancer of reality, always
intrudes once we travel home
from these summer meadows.

> I try to forget the adenocarcinoma
> found a week ago in my lung,
> I must face when I leave this place.
> But I'm together with my friend,
> a lady, who brought me here,
> makes me brave,
> and rides beside me
> into this dark valley.

Dr. Flores was a tall, oddly handsome man with a nice bedside manner. He drew two lungs, pinpointing where my problem was and how it could be cut out. This still seemed crude. He said there was no other way because he didn't know what he'd find when he got in there, but I'd be cured. His attitude was that the only good cancer was one entirely cut out and put in the trash. Crude? Yes. But effective. Because I didn't feel sick, all this seemed remote until I did more study and realized how dangerous those mutations were. Dr. Flores was polite, but an in-a-hurry guy. He was in scrubs for our meeting because he'd taken time out of his operating schedule to see me. Would the following Thursday, 8:00 am be, okay? I said yes.

I went home to tell Dr. Post, informed relatives, close clients and a few friends. In the meantime, I was probed, scanned, and tested all over to ascertain there wasn't cancer anywhere else in my body. I was also given a stress test that I maxed. The nurse administering it wondered why I was there and how I could have lung cancer. I wondered the same thing.

I slept the night before but got up without the alarm. Anne went with me. There was a crowded public waiting room at 6:30 am until they separated the lines. Speedily, I was sent to surgery prep and given something to calm me. I said goodbye to Anne and went into the operating room where they verified what side they'd operate on. In scrubs, Christina was there to reassure me, but wouldn't be staying for the operation.

Dr. Flores gave me assurance as well, then the nurse gave me a shot, and I don't remember what came afterwards. They were in there for a while and took out my lower right lung lobe as well as a lymph node, sent them for biopsy. The team removed a thumb-sized tumor, containing over thirty mutations, many deadly if they ever recurred. It's a nasty, deadly disease.

When I came around, I remember it was still daylight. Ken Davis and Anne were there, and Dr. Flores said it had gone great, not to worry, just to concentrate on recovery. I was tubed up and on something for the pain. I only felt groggy. I was so glad to see Anne and Ken, who sternly told me I'd be fine. My partner, Bruce soon arrived, as well as later my other partners, Jon Stern and Mitch Spector. I ended up in a room with an inspiring view of Central Park.

Damn. It was done. I was glad it was over and braced myself for the pain I knew would come but didn't that week. Whatever drugs they had me hooked into were highly effective. Two tubes that fed into my lungs hung from my side, and those wounds had to heal before I could go home. I tried to write about the surgery, but with the drugs neither could I write nor read well, though I could carry on a conversation and contemplate the great park view. What I hadn't reckoned on was that the switch from hospital meds to conventional opioids would not be easy. For Salisbury, I'd arranged for visiting nurses to pay a daily visit and for my sister to come for a week. Anne was heading back to Aspen once I was home at Utopia.

Finally, the day came when the doctors agreed the tubes could be removed. As I was still on the intravenous painkillers, I had no idea how much pain I'd be in from the removal of my lower lung, but I was about to find out. They removed the last tube one Friday afternoon before the hospital shut down for the weekend schedule. Anne drove me to Salisbury where we met up with Sharon and her husband Mason, who was always good for a comedic quip, but I wasn't that chipper. We had lunch at Manna Dew, a restaurant in Millerton, NY, and dear Anne left the following morning.

Sharon headed for the golf course, and Eli and Nancy Rutledge, my assistant in the country, checked in on me regularly, as did the visiting nurses. Eli and Nancy rented a soft recliner they put in the space where I usually write, overlooking the river and Canaan Mountain. I spent two weeks in that chair. I tried to get in bed that first night and had never felt so much pain. I popped a handful of pain pills that didn't help much. It was going to be a slow recovery. I got into bed with a pillow across the scar that circumnavigated my side and back. The nurses showed me the next morning how to get back into bed, hugging a pillow to moderate the pain. I learned what life with intense pain was like. Frankly, that next week was hell. I wanted to reduce the pain medications but didn't see how I could.

It was hard to walk around. Each step was torture and lying down was worse. I went back to Mt. Sinai arranging to see the doctor, and one of Dr. Flores's assistants said it was a normal recovery. The scar was healing, yet the pain was intense. Then I went over to see Christina, who wanted to see the scar and focused on the red sores across my side.

"My god, you've got shingles!" she exclaimed. She called her expert colleague. Sure enough, when I was weakest, I'd developed a case of shingles just like I'd had in Tibet. She gave me a prescription, and I immediately started feeling better. I asked the Salisbury nurses why they hadn't discovered my case of the shingles, and they had no explanation. After that, I was able to reduce the pain meds but still had to lie in bed with a pillow covering my side. It was weeks before the pain was gone and I was totally off the meds, but I was feeling stronger.

I went back to work in October to take my mind off things, but I had to decide on chemo since I'd had type IIA cancer that had gotten into a lymph node. I didn't want to take any chances if there were any cancer cells floating in my bloodstream. Christina was most helpful. Throughout the process, I talked with friends in Atlanta, particularly Dr. Walter James, a lung doctor and former roommate who helped greatly. In the end, I chose Dr. Jorge Gomez, who worked with Dr. Flores at Sloan Kettering. He's been treating me ever since.

Dr. Gomez recommended a cocktail that was a combination of Cisplatin and Pemetrexed. I had to take Folic Acid for at least two weeks before I started, then I went to chemo every other week for three months. Gomez varied the cocktail throughout. I think chemo is much like alchemy, but I was reassured by Dr. Gomez there was an upside to these treatments, a cancer insurance of sorts.

My chemo treatments over three months were not as bad as Georgia's. I didn't lose my hair, nor suffer any apparent immediate damage, but I soon discovered an aversion to some foods, particularly the smell of overly ripe bananas and fruits, as well as a craving for others, particularly cheeseburgers. About a year later, I developed a terrible itch on my forearm when exposed to sun. As it turns out, there's no telling what the effects of the treatment are. Initially, I was tested for hearing loss, but afterward, none was apparent; however, in an ancient perfumery in Florence two years later, I discovered my olfactory glands had been impaired.

The most instructive thing throughout this bout of chemical warfare, however, was my afternoon stroll through the cancer ward. I made conversation and new friends, many with harsher treatments and eventually deadly cancers. For a brief time, we were in the same lifeboat. I realized how fortunate I was, and how good my doctors and their teams were. I go back every six months and recently passed a statistical milestone of four years cancer free.

Bruce McEver with beard grown for chemotherapy, 2015

Chapter 48
Meeting a Remarkable Woman

One of the special sacred spaces in New York for me is the domed byzantine sanctuary of St. Bartholomew's Church. It's right down Park Avenue from my office on the way to Grand Central Station. I often stop to meditate and unload my tension burden. I love the beautifully carved marble angel in the back chapel, visible from the sanctuary. It is a place of peace and special happenings for it is here on the evening of October 21, 2014, I met Anne McNulty. We had agreed to rendezvous in the chapel to hear a concert of ancient music, to be performed by my Salisbury neighbors.

The origins of the meeting went back to a summer morning walk with my good friends Garen and Shari Staglin through their still dew-wet vineyard in Napa Valley. Over the long stroll, I told the painful story of my recent separation, and about the time we reached a pond with a dozen wild geese cruising it, Shari, moved to compassion insisted, "I know just the person for you." That was late summer, and sure enough, Anne and I both got a dutiful introductory email from our mutual friend. Subsequently, I got an email from Anne. She was going to be in New York for only a day and a half and offered to meet me during this brief window of time, but no commitment.

This seemed a little pushy, so I let the email age thinking of the right venue and suggested we go to the concert. My friends were scheduling a light dinner afterwards, though I could beg off. I was skeptical about the meeting. In the meantime, Sheri followed up sending me an interesting article about Anne's running of the wine festival in Naples, Florida; naïve me had no idea what a big deal that was. With my blinders on, I only saw that after a career as a managing director at Goldman Sachs (a competitor since I'd come to Wall Street), she was now running a foundation. Interesting, but I needed to upgrade my attitude to get through the evening.

We both arrived early. I recognized Anne from her picture in the article and hesitatingly introduced myself. We began chatting in low voices in the back pew of the church. She was quite a woman. Charming, alert, attractive—she had a presence, a real gravitas, as well as the most beautiful and infectious smile. She seemed such a positive and basically happy person. We talked in the back of the church until the concert began, and then again at the break. I determined quickly that this was someone I wanted to get to know better. Scrambling, I begged off dinner with my friends, and since we were close to my office, I thought I'd first impress her by taking her up to my empire in the sky with its great view down Madison Avenue.

At the office, the bullpen was still at it, and must have thought it odd me bringing this stranger into our office, even into my inner sanctum. I turned on my office light and asked Anne to sit down while I babbled on about my background. From forty years of experience, my corner office was loaded with deal mementoes that filled the bookcases and spilled over to the tabletops. For some reason, I just couldn't stop talking. I was so excited and wanted to know more about her. She knew the business, so we talked easily about the market, charity and foundation work, the Staglin's' wine business, and art. Anne was smart and witty. I found out she was Catholic, so we could talk about religion as well. I called San Pietro, the Italian eatery next door, to make a reservation for a supper that I hadn't planned on.

I don't remember what I said but must have told her my whole life story; she might as well know it. I wanted no baggage between us, and I wanted to hear more of her. In retrospect, I think I behaved like one of those ruffled grouse cocks we have in the woods around Salisbury that puffs up, beats his wings, and sounds like a little tom-tom while turning in furious circles, dancing around his unimpressed hen. The head waiter at San Pietro is a friend and likewise performs his specials menu like a melodrama. Neither he nor the meal disappointed. As we left to go our separate ways, she asked me if I liked opera. I instantly answered in the affirmative, and she surprisingly asked me to the opera the following evening.

I, of course, said yes and we saw *The Marriage of Figaro*, but I wasn't entirely paying attention because I was concentrating on her. At the opera, I cautiously spoke of the times when Georgia sang these roles, worrying I may have overdone the Georgia stories. After the performance, we dashed across the street in a cold driving rain to a restaurant where we shared a medium-rare cheeseburger. Maybe both liking our meat done the same way was a promising sign? We said goodbye, and I didn't see her for several months—our family Christmases taking us to different geographies. In the New Year, her Advance Leadership Institute (ALI) classes at Harvard began in Boston, and her duties as former chair of Naples wine festival escalated. However, we started making evening phone calls.

We began dating in the early spring. Anne had started her program at ALI class of 2015 at Harvard, and I thought it a good idea to ask her to come to Utopia. I couldn't wait to see her and got the house ready. It wouldn't be proper for her to stay in my new house, but the guest house next door would work. Then I got a last-minute call, she'd been on her way, but was going to have to cancel, since she'd forgotten her suitcase in her rush to leave. I had to talk fast and told her Christina had left a complete wardrobe behind and asked Anne what she needed. She admitted she only needed basic toiletries and a tee-shirt as a nightgown. Relieved, I said, "No problem. Come anyway, right away."

I wanted her to see Utopia so that she could understand me better. She arrived, and we had a polite, sane dinner conversation, having already covered so much territory in earlier discussions. I was proud of my property in Salisbury and wanted her to like it as well. We walked it the next day, and then she drove back to campus.

We grew close and spent time together that summer. That fall, I visited Anne in Cambridge when I was there for an HDS advisory board meeting. Anne was completing her ALI class and was thinking of following up immediately with a program at Stanford. Distressed, I was making the case for her to stay in Boston.

"I don't understand why you don't just stay here at Harvard," I pleaded. "I've been to school twice here; first across the river there." I pointed across the Charles River toward the Business School from her top floor apartment with its panoramic view. "And then four years at the Divinity School. I could probably get them to let me back in and get a PhD there, then we could go to school here together and spend weekends at Utopia. I loved my time here and you'd also be closer to New York and your kids."

She'd just gotten off the phone with Phil Pizzo, the dean and founder of the new, haughty-sounding Stanford Distinguished Careers Institute (DCI). Phil had invited her to join him in Palo Alto for the 2016 January class. She'd applied and been accepted into both Harvard and Stanford in 2015 and had chosen Harvard. In winter of 2015, it had snowed a record of 110 inches in Boston, so Palo Alto was looking very attractive for the following year. I knew I was going uphill and couldn't get this woman to change her mind, but I might be able to slow her down. "It's beautiful out. Let's go for a bike ride along the river to watch the crew's practice and talk it over."

"I have a class starting soon. You go, and I'll join you for lunch," she said.

It was "The Head of the Charles" weekend, the intercollegiate rowing meet pitting the best oarsmen and women in the country in competition along the river I so loved to bike and walk along. It would be an exciting weekend together with her ALI classmates and in fact, one of her ALI classmates was crewing. This weekend was the pinnacle fall event. Next door to the Charles Hotel was my favorite place to meditate and pray—the episcopal monastery of St. John's. When I was in school, I went there for all my serious thinking and decision-making. I stopped in when I could. It was a sacred space that resonated with silence, and it drew my spirit out. I could also worship and for a big change, could share worship with Anne, whose spirituality I appreciated, particularly after having been married to an agnostic.

Anne and I had looked across a similar void together—the awful experience of losing a spouse suddenly and unexpectedly after thirty-plus-year marriages. Her husband John and my Georgia had both been only fifty-three when they'd died. We had each been with our spouses when they passed. We had each gone to a hospital to witness fruitless efforts to save them. John died of heart failure, Georgia an aneurism. Anne had three teenage children to inform and comfort. Georgia's close family and I had to take her off life-support.

Anne took more time to return to the world of relationships than I. Maybe she was wiser, remaining unconnected. Christina had left me to live with a former friend of mine and had sued me for a costly divorce. With this surprising turn of events, I had looked across the void twice, exacerbated by the almost concurrent losses of a business partner and a foundation partner. I didn't like the renewed prospect of being alone. Though I had many fine and loyal friends, coming out of this almost acrimonious divorce, I was searching for a real companion by my side. Anne was pulling me out of this valley, and, I fervently hoped, I was reciprocating. I was beginning to feel almost whole again and didn't want to try a bicoastal relationship. It wasn't easy to come back to love.

The following January, she invited me to Florida, which sounded great with the New England winter beginning. At that time, I was also teaching a course at Georgia Tech every Thursday, so I could easily hop down to Naples for the weekend via a simple hour flight. I so clearly

remember our first Florida dinner at Sea Salt, a restaurant in downtown
Naples. We sat in the middle of a covered porch in the center of the
lively commercial district. I savored the balmy evening after freezing
New York and cold, rainy Atlanta. We dined with her close friends,
Roch and Carol Hillenbrand. After dinner we went to the same parking
lot for our respective cars. I hadn't noticed hers, but Anne started up
her red Maserati; what a distinct rumble that car makes when it starts! I
followed her home in my rented Chevy. She put me in the downstairs
guest bedroom in her beautiful home in Port Royal on a shimmering
canal reflecting all the grand houses along it. Initially intimidated, I was
afraid to touch anything and was on my best behavior.

While the house was lovely, its art was tasteful and impressive. I
found out she'd won the Maserati in a raffle. She was also lucky in other
ways. One of six siblings, she'd grown up in a middle-class, Irish-Catho-
lic family. She hadn't come from wealth, nor had her husband.

The next night Anne hosted a dinner, and as was her custom, asked
everyone to introduce themselves with a personal fun fact to break the
ice. This enlivened the evening prompting mini performances enacted
by the various guests. I think I said something hokey like I had a farm in
Georgia. Afterwards, I kept thinking I was never going to be invited back.

Anne is a brilliant conversationalist. She pulled off the dinner party
without seeming the least bit stressed. She was the center of conversa-
tion and conversant on most subjects. This is great for me, an introvert
at heart. There was a whirlwind of activity around Anne; keeping up with
her would be invigorating. We continued to see one another in New
York, and we relished one another's company, introducing each other
to our friends. Late in the season, at another charity dinner at her house,
the stars aligned as I describe in a poem called "Restarting the World:"

> Under a scattering of stars, we talk
> of constellations and our zodiacs aligning
> since our meeting through friends.
> A half-moon holds an ethereal lantern
> for summary life-histories
> while a soft sea breeze
> encourages palms.
> Relaxing in two chaises side by side,
> we survey a dreamscape—

from a groomed slope to a canal, dancing
with the glittering lights of villas
on the opposite shore, only broken by the silhouettes of sloops
hulking in the channel.

Gingerly, we go inside to light candles…
and speculate with a kiss…

Anne and I have dated steadily since this time. I relished being
around this woman and hoped the feeling mutual. This was getting
serious....she had simply restarted the world for me—changed it for the
better. To close out the season in Florida in 2015, we went to an Easter
sunrise service together:

Easter in Naples

We sit by the club pool for Saturday's vigil,
lunching on grouper salad and soup.
We watch children thrill
in the splash, while beyond
stretches a white line of beach,
the Gulf divided into gradients of green
like a ladder to blue heaven.

A row of palms crowning the skyline
is buzzed by a string of pelicans,
like ancient guardians challenging
a straining bi-plane's
banner proclaiming: *Poker & Racing
Tonight—Ft. Meyer's Track.*

Jesus still has temples to cleanse,
but Naples' streets with jacarandas
flowering gaudy yellow
seem far from His grim trail…

There's no time for grief
along these placid canals nesting

boats tied in pace at their piers.
We all suffer though.

Till the old story is retold—
the empty tomb.
My ego gutted, but that was nothing
to begin with. Who was really hurt?
If these are my nail holes,
hopefully I am wiser, can
even forgive my trespassers.

I stay with a woman with a smile eternal
yet who carries a deep grief inside like mine.
Together at a sunrise service
we enter the mystery
as the sound of birds and gulls
harken the growing glow
in the east. Her hand in mine
is assuring, while behind us
is the cold extinction
of a full falling moon.

The New York psychologist had been right. As our relationship
deepened, my bitterness faded—as it is wrung out in this poem—and
I could forgive and forget the hurt. We spent the Christmas of 2015
together with her family snow-deep in Aspen. I got to better know her
children, Johnny, Brynne, and Kevin, who seemed to accept this new
man in their mother's life.

In late January 2016, I experienced for myself the remarkable Naples
Wine Festival that benefits a local charity called the Naples Children and
Education Foundation (NCEF). I was blown away by an auction that
seemed to resemble the Dutch tulip bulb auctions of the 17th century.
People bid hundreds of thousands on special events or trips to exotic
locations with cases of excellent vintages thrown in. At the end of an
exhausting day of frenzied bidding, the festival had raised $15 million for
the kids! Anne was often at the center of the auction, with an enthusiastic
and effective way of getting things done with positive outcomes. I saw
the gravitas that encircled this woman.

In the calm of the summer of 2016, I began to consider going out to Stanford for the 2017 Distinguished Careers Institute, starting that fall. As noted before, Anne had already been accepted into the class of 2015 but had been granted a deferment. She hadn't gone in 2016 because of my illness. She very much wanted to join the class of 2017 and was actively persuading me that it would be interesting to go through this experience together. I welcomed the opportunity of being with Anne. I did need space to write, and besides, I'd fallen in love with this remarkable woman.

Bruce McEver and Anne McNulty in San Francisco
while at Stanford's DCI Program, 2018

Chapter 49
Field of Wildflowers

"The Stanford Distinguished Careers Institute is a dynamic program for highly accomplished individuals from all walks of life who seek to transform themselves for roles with social impact at the local, national, and global levels."

Stanford Distinguished Careers Institute (DCI) Website

The story goes that Dr. Phil Pizzo was looking for a new challenge after running Stanford's Medical School and drew inspiration from the Advanced Leadership Initiative (ALI) program at Harvard. At Stanford, he created DCI thus fostering a community of successful people over the course of a year to create a new chapter of their lives, by providing them access to the university's full facilities, faculty, programs, and libraries. Centering his program on wellness by teaming up with the Stanford Longevity and Health Center—a concierge health program included with the Institute's tuition—Phil made a clever and essential twist on that model.

One difference in the Harvard program was each ALI member had to undertake a social-impact project. For Anne this was creating a strategic plan for a comprehensive center for women's leadership at her alma mater, Villanova University. The Anne Welsh McNulty Institute for Women's Leadership was officially launched in October 2017. There was no project required at Stanford.

Anne remained determined to have the Stanford and West Coast experience. Because of Anne's more than thoughtful deferment on account of my cancer diagnosis and treatment, we talked it out, and I agreed to apply as her partner and go with her to join the Stanford DCI class of 2017.

There was an obligatory telephone interview with Phil and his assistant dean. I explained my educational background and that I was both a businessman and a want-to-be writer. When I got to the campus, Phil had arranged a meeting for me with Eavan Boland, an Irish poetess running the Creative Writing Program who later introduced me to memoirist John Evans, resulting in this book, and Scotty McLennan, who'd taught ethics classes at Harvard Business School, where we'd met several years earlier. Scotty was just retiring from the chaplaincy at Stanford and someone with whom I'd had a long due diligence beforehand and who endorsed it wholeheartedly. After the introductory orientation in Palo Alto in November of 2016, I was convinced this experience would be a doorway to a new life chapter and was excited to fully engage in the program and find new friends among this extraordinary group of folks.

After we got back, however, I had to carefully disengage from Berkshire—I still had the corner office. We had a newly hired executive who was going to be co-CEO with Bruce—Nick Sheumack—and I could turn my corner office over to him. Staying late one Thursday before the Christmas holidays, it was more traumatic than anticipated to load boxes and separate stuff accumulated from over thirty years on Wall Street. Though I was willingly leaving a now-thriving enterprise, it was traumatic, sorting out the physical evidence of the history of Berkshire Capital I've now written about in earlier chapters of this book—tombstones, overstuffed deal files, photos and other mementoes that triggered and reran old tapes as I culled the treasure from the trash. This would be my last night in the office I'd spent over a decade in and strategically positioned the firm to last into the future. It was from this office with most of my company around me, we watched the Twin Towers fall into that terrible plume of smoke changing history.

At the initial DCI Program meetings, I was most impressed by Phil's intelligent, yet humble approach. I could see he was clearly on to something. At our opening reception, Scotty set me straight, taking me into a courtyard where we walked around the most memorable dramatic and substantial pine tree. I was still considering working a couple of days a week, and he explained this program was like a wildflower field. I had to wander around in it to see, smell, and appreciate those spring flowers—even pick a few. It turned out, the secret of this extraordinary program was in our cohort, and its binding glue was storytelling to each other.

My initial interview with Eavan Boland was to be for a half-hour, but after an hour, we were still deep in conversation, and I asked her if she knew a certain Irish poet. Eavan had no idea how I knew him but answered memorably with a thumbs down. I knew then we were on the same page—I could trust and work with this woman! She was most excited to pair me with John William Evans, who taught memoir writing and shared the story of the tragic death of his first wife with me. That angst had galvanized us both to writing our stories. This book is the child of our subsequent weekly luncheon meetings where John coached me through my memoir. It took a year and a half to shape this, and I'm grateful he took the time to pull it out of me so effectively. He's intuitive and instructive. His insight and inspiration made him and our DCI memoir class one of the most popular for our class.

In my mind, the real experiment was Anne and I living together. Though this was her idea, she was a little nervous, particularly if space was too tight; we'd need to respect that. After our introductory meetings in November, Anne stayed and looked at apartments, finally settling on the Marc on Forest Avenue in the middle of Palo Alto that would house eleven other of our DCI classmate couples. It basically became an upscale, dormitory for our class. I agreed to go first and set us up, returning to Palo Alto one January evening from Christmas in Aspen with Anne and her family, the apartment only contained the rental furniture. My flight was delayed, it was pouring rain, and nothing was open. After driving up and down El Camino Real, I found a 24-hour CVS and picked up the basics, finally sleeping under my rain coat with my backpack as a pillow. The DCI adventure would hopefully get better! I soon recovered and located all the necessary stores, a retail education for me as I don't really shop. I came to appreciate the genius of IKEA and put-up bookshelves, bought lamps, and found a kitchen store for plates, pots, and pans. By the time Anne arrived, the place was comfortably furnished. The refrigerator and pantry were stocked, and we had both wine and coffee. Anne enjoyed helping to fill out the rest of our new little nest, but was much better at it than I.

We had a two-bedroom apartment on the 8th floor with a balcony that ran the length of the apartment. There was only one heating unit in the living room and electric units in the bedrooms, and none in the bathrooms. For the Palo Alto scale rent we were paying, it was damn cold. It eventually stopped raining, but not for the next two months and not before the drought conditions that had prevailed in California for over a decade were abated in a single season.

Anne and I got used to biking to class. Initially, it was a little difficult with the rain, but between storms, it was a truly unique experience. We went everywhere around Palo Alto by bike, mainly because parking was such a pain. The DCI group compared notes, professors, and classes, and the exercise of choosing courses was a bit of bonding as well. We settled into a routine. At four on every Wednesday, we met in the faculty lounge of the law school for a lecture or presentation by a professor or campus notable, including George Schultz. When someone like Shultz or a Nobel Prize Laureate showed up, we had formal community dinners. Later, this time and these meetings became our moments of individual storytelling.

At noon on Thursdays, we had lunch with a professor or other luminary who taught a case study on, say, negotiations, or stand-up comedy, or sharpening our practical skills. We were also enrolled in a wide variety of classes, though usually didn't have to take tests or write papers. We began to enjoy the newfound freedom, appreciating the many wildflowers in Stanford's beautiful field. We had some all-day sessions, one with the famous Design School, where we "designed our lives." We spent a fascinating afternoon at the Institute for the Future and took a long-distance look discussing various implications. Scotty's words, the start of writing this book, and the plethora of great classes kept me on campus. From time to time, entrepreneurs from Silicon Valley visited classes, and there were also continuing studies options in the evenings, so if we wanted, we could go to school all day and into the evening. Anne and I took some thoroughly engaging classes—courses on James Joyce's *Ulysses*, Cervantes' *Don Quixote*, and even went to wine tastings in Napa disguised as a geological fieldtrip.

We took a class in designing presentations with the objective being our life stories. All were nervous when the turn for our individual presentations arrived. Each of us—the fellows and their partners—had to tell their life stories by standing up before the rest of the group and present our histories using PowerPoint slides. This was not to be a business resumé— those had already been distributed. Instead, we were encouraged to tell our real stories—details of emotional and traumatic events that had shaped our lives and bent and brazened our characters. In order to prepare, we all searched family albums and files for suitable, poignant picture-points to illustrate and enliven our presentations. These stories were amazing. There were stories of an expatriate couple enmeshed in Indonesian intrigues; a judge from London; couples from Singapore; Indian executives and scholars; a South African Iron Lady—a real United Nations of experience. We went beyond being merely a program of successful people and their partners, aged between fifty and seventy, who wanted to come back to school. We were trying to sort out our futures. Life-long learners, we weren't retiring to golf courses, but would make further impact on the world in an as-yet-to-be-defined way. We were pilgrims and were ready to forge more confidently along new twisting paths. We were all exiting the labyrinth and this experience helped us find the way out.

On most Wednesday evenings after one of our story sessions, we went to Gotts—a local burger and beer joint—to cheer our classmates' performance and they improved with each telling, in turn lowering the barriers between us, showing all our humanity, foibles, and blunders, as we shared the victories and joys, as well as the disappointments. The group seemed eternally bonded, gathering for a party at the slightest provocation. Anne was one of the leading organizers.

We took trips to Yosemite and Carmel, and a number to Napa. We had much larger travel ambitions but more often found ourselves hanging out in Palo Alto, working or going to football games, and socializing with our newfound friends. We found traveling back East was a real time killer, and prior obligations or holidays with family were suddenly a strain. It was strange how appealing this area was, and we extended our initial DCI commitment for another six months. Actions, clearly, spoke louder than words.

Anne and my life became intermeshed, getting up mornings, doing yoga on the balcony, biking across the eucalyptus forest to the Spanish tiled sprawl of Stanford for classes. I began to spend more time in the Green library writing a chapter of my book a week to review at a lunch with John Evans on Wednesdays. My normal peripatetic work and call schedule faded into my class and writing schedule, and Anne and my social life intertwined nicely. In my mind it was a successful integration that made me look forward to our life together.

Chapter 50
Totems

I have written and edited large parts of this book in a quiet vast hall of tables and students mesmerized at their computers, backgrounded with the Green Library bookstacks looking out over a view over the campus Leland Stanford so generously endowed. To the east is the lingam-like Hover Tower, the contemporary university symbol with a red-tile roof reflecting the Spanish heritage of the region. To the west is the circular lawn of the law school decorated with modern sculptures and a symbolic totem pole. A closer inspection of this carving provided the idea for closing of this book. It's made of traditional red cedar and was dedicated by the Native Americans in the memory of Mr. Stanford, his wife, and son, whose death motivated the donation of this priceless idyllic 8,000 acres scattered with the university's buildings and a giant eucalyptus forest, where in late spring, Native Americans hold a colorful pow-wow all, in the middle of Silicon Valley, some of the most expensive real estate in North America.

Thus, I circle back to where this story began, with an omen at New York's Natural History Museum. In its Northwest Coast Hall, arrayed with Native American totem poles, the first interview between Joseph Campbell and Bill Moyers was taped. It was this conversation that inspired me to find Campbell and take his seminars in NYC in the eighties. These expanded my wider thinking and started me writing poetry. Those mystic faces coming out of those totem poles around Campbell and Moyers have to do with the myths we unconsciously live by, the things that drive us to action, the path the hero follows to find and fulfill his destiny. As Campbell said, myths are great poems we travel on into the world, the invisible road maps of our unconscious actions; my life so far has been a filling out of those early vague hunches and visions.

Writing this book, I began to see more clearly those emergent faces on the paths I have followed and am still on. I realized these were the same paths I discovered I was on while quiet and reconnoitering in the desert at Joshua Tree. Each of those seven points recorded in my journal at that time was a totem that could be represented by an animal stacked on a pole outside my lodge.

Ironically, there is an uncarved oak tree designed into the front of my house at Utopia maybe awaiting its totems. Let's imagine what they would be...

At the base of the pole would be a great whale representing my interest in business and investing, as well as the company I started, supporting everything above it. What I hadn't considered was the longevity of the security industry and asset management business cycles or their size, global reach, and impact. It turned out we were in the right place at the right time. I've followed this totem, this path most of my adult life starting Berkshire Capital Corporation in 1983 surmising an ideal place in the market was as an investment banker's banker—a neutral party to help consolidate these businesses—and it has grown into a global company. When I returned from DCI; I found my partners had already changed its name to Berkshire Global Advisors to reflect this emerging reality. Though this path was important, something more than business has always motivated me.

The next totem on the pole would be a pelican, representing my mother and family. She gave our family a great part of her life and would have given more. In ancient Europe, it was believed the pelican opens her breast to feed her young (and even bring back its dead). In Florida, watching the pelicans dive bomb their prey, is a new pastime:

Ode to Pelicans

I love these birds.
they look like flying dinosaurs---
survivors of the Jurassic extinction.
They soar wingman-to-wingman
in a formation over the channel,
on morning's bay breeze defusing
sunrise over the following waves.
Ancient hunters, the flight soon spots
their pray and like dive bombers,
plunge to stun the fish,
then scoop them up, and flip
breakfast into their yellow pouches,
swallowing it down head-first.

The only species to so stun their victims
they're off again for another run,
working together over the length and breath
of the channel between the estates on the canal bank,
agnostic of the neighborhood.

Evolution's lab gave them an impact
resistant skull and a membraned eye covering
to survive their high dive hunting technique.
They follow fish schools in and out
with the morning tide.

As they have before this development of dredged
mud, rock and shells ate canals
into their mangrove swamps and moved
their rookeries further south.

They are older, and maybe wiser than we:
in them the world rebalances.

Pelicans demonstrate social responsibility acting as a savvy choreo-
graphed unit for their survival. We must act environmentally responsible
for the planet and its inhabitants. The bird also represents familial love,
like my mom who was a life force and kept me on and true to my paths.
My mother died fully aware at age ninety-six on Labor Day weekend in
2013, telling my sister she was going to "cross over" to get a new dress.
I had a wonderful relationship with her that only deepened at the end of
our time on earth together. Mom always had my back. This poem was
the title piece for my third book of poems:

Like Lesser Gods

We wing south in a full plane, strapped-in
and bumping through heat-hazed skies.
Sudden thunderheads rise
as high as we fly to quench
an exhausted earth below.

Sun pinks the massive billows
internally pulsed and illumined
by Thor's lightning bolts. Like lesser gods
we've conquered in our age of radar,
our jet plays between the white mountains.
With this vista, my father spent his working life.

We continue south, jostled
home to Atlanta where my mother,
keeper of our family's memory,
is bedfast and can no longer
answer her phone
to tell me she has left
the keys out for me
as she always does.

My family is a small one—my sister and her remarkable daughters, my two nieces Ansley and Kristin and their spouses and their children. Through my marriage to Georgia, I developed a close bond with her sisters, and they, Suzy, and her children, Luke, and Matt and, recently deceased, Holly and her husband, Wally, along with their children, Will and Ashley, are another family for me. I have a new family developing with Anne and her grown children, Johnny, Brynne, and Kevin, plus Anne's family and siblings. My future is these relationships. Also, because of my small family and no children of my own, my friends are and become increasingly important. These relationships are dearer and dearer as I age.

Anne—my beloved has a beautiful and smiling face. She's a serious, but permanently cheerful person who doesn't let much get her down, despite having experienced deep tragedy. However, Anne is a woman of action, fortitude, and compassion, and has proven a delightful life companion. She has a strong family life with her children and recent grandchildren, as well as her siblings and their spouses and children. The next totem on my pole would be the sun disk, representing Anne's smile and the gravitas of her charitable works. I begin to see our life together as a pair of twin stars, suns that have begun to orbit one another, their gravitational fields in balance, creating a new solar system between them, their influenced planets intermeshing.

Another totem on my pole would be a hawk, the messenger of the ancients, that represents the poet and scholar in me that has been slow growing but recently soaring. I've produced three full-length poetry books and a couple of chapbooks. In service to the craft, I've endowed a Visiting Poets Chair at Georgia Tech that developed under Thomas Lux and Travis Denton into the Poetry@Tech program. I sit on the board of Poet's House in New York, and in memory of Georgia, I also started the Georgia Poetry Prize with the University of Georgia Press.

This memoir represents a branching out of my writing into prose. It seems a vehicle toward future works—I am searching for the great subject like Ahab's hunt for the great white whale. In the meantime, I follow my poet, friend, and deceased teacher Kurt Brown's advice, and write a poem whenever inspired by my muse, heeding the hawk's call…

The Religious Literacy Foundation www.tfrl.org that I co-founded with Dean Ronald Thiemann needed revitalizing after Ron's loss. It's doing good works, initially bringing executives together in learning circles revolving around different religious traditions and then ethical discussions. It helped seed the first-ever exhibition of American religion at the American History Museum; established interfaith programs through partnerships between Georgia Tech and Emory University, as well as between Harvard and Boston University, while underwriting the largest on-line course at Harvard. Our new director, Rev. Nate Walker, is helping me reorganize and revitalize this foundation, adding online courses for students, teachers, and leaders—something so necessary in these quarantined and contentious days and in service to the lofty ideals of equal opportunity and the democratization of learning. Hopefully we inspire growing circles of seekers and learners and through better understanding of the other, foster peace. I don't know what totem best represents this endeavor—perhaps it would be the image of a dove, trying to bring peace to the fractured world, or mourning doves in their beautiful balanced dialogue with one another.

Lastly, spiritual enlightenment—respect for and seeking the ultimate mystery. For the native peoples, this path is represented by the eagle who flies closest to the great spirit. Ironically in October 2019, I received the Distinguished Eagle Scout award from the Boy Scouts of America, becoming one of the few so honored. That's the top bird on my totem pole symbolizing my spiritual path, that took me on remarkable journeys and internal voyages to reconcile my grief over the loss of Georgia and, beyond loss, to pursue wisdom. My faith is at my core. It has gotten me through deaths of loved ones, partners, divorce, and cancer. For gratitude and for spiritual nourishment, I attend church—different churches across the various communities where I live—and sample other traditions when possible. But beyond organized faith, I've also had visions and brief glimpses of elevated awareness. I seek this mystic contact and peace in nature and sometimes find it in the most ordinary of places and experiences. It's the grist mill for my poetry and, when discovered, some call it grace.

I see my path of knowledge connected to my spiritual path—providing enlightenment. I am an education junkie, constantly reading, a life-long learner, a trait that has led me to both Harvard's Divinity School and Stanford. At Utopia Farm, I have a great circular library and intend to spend much more time reading within its circular walls as part of my future life. I sometimes think of my path as that of jnana yoga—also the purpose of this book—to trace and reflect upon my many paths to make further sense of them.

Anne and I have been blessed with many beautiful homes. Like migratory birds, we begin to synchronize our time at these with the seasons. Returning from California, Anne and I began balancing our lives and interests between our respective homes, in Salisbury, CT., Aspen, CO., Short Hills, NJ. and Naples, FLA., reflective of our interests and life's pursuits. It's been a long trail…well, many paths! I hope I can balance the remainder of it in good health and humor, keeping in mind all that I've learned.

AFTERWORD

I was editing my memoir on December 20, 2019, when I was flying with Anne to her home in Florida to continue our experiment as snowbirds for the 2020 season in Naples. As fate would have it, this day would have been my 50th wedding anniversary with Georgia. I thought I'd be soon finished editing this book, looking out at a gold and amber sky at sunset as we winged south. In Florida, I was looking forward to writing and reading more, mostly from a porch at Anne's house festooned with bougainvillea and overlooking a canal alive with watercraft, their motors mummering. I had no idea when I began writing the afterword, I would still be editing my memoir at the end of this year and would have plenty of time to do so because our current pandemic, pushed off publication and isolated most of us for the surreal year of 2020.

Sometimes a different mood overtakes me, actually two personalities appear as I discovered the day Georgia died, maybe from the left and right side of my brain or as the ancient Egyptians believed, both my Ba and Ka become visible then? Interestingly one of my early poems from my first book was a poetic self-portrait and captures this whimsical/soulful personality:

My Silent Partner

vacations with me best.
He's up for the early profits
of sunrise, golden over tropical
mountains. He delights
in jungle ruins, sad
for the secrets of their tumbled stones.
He's curious about exotic leaf and bird
and prefers verandah reading,
while I tennis with the ladies.
He's quiet at the cocktail hour,
not mixing, but moody by a window,
absorbed and gnostic in sunset.
In these things he is stubborn
and will go on being so
when I am gone.

This was written at Ma Mora, the Lanahan home in Jamaica on vacation with Georgia and her sisters and their husbands, shortly after we were married. Reading through the book, I muse at the character described as my silent partner. And 50 years after that poem was written he's still there, but has a few more scars, one visible around my waist where a third of my lung was exorcised and a couple of deep psychological scars from the loss of Georgia and a failed marriage. However, without these, I would not have my current loving relationship with Anne. There are also scars from the losses of friends and partners, always ongoing as we age, possibly accelerated by this pandemic, though a hopeful breakthrough vaccine was just announced.

Before we left for Florida my company had their 36th annual Christmas party at a restaurant called Manhatta, after Walt Whitman's name for the city. It was one floor above one of the top floors of what was once Chase Plaza; this is ironically the same floor where I interviewed Maurice Shapiro in 1982, who wisely advised me to go into BGS's corner of the business after a breakfast of scrambled eggs served by his butler in his office, one of the spoils for his merging the Chase and Manhattan Banks. Luckily I heeded his words.

Berkshire has flourished, and one of my partners asked me at that party what my biggest surprise was. After reflecting, I said it was the longevity of our run. We're enjoying record markets, and it looks like they'll keep going, with the brief interludes as we experienced in the spring this year. The consolidation of the financial services business seems unending, and it's global. I'm proud my company carries on, indeed thrives through this plague. I am less involved but like a deep spring the company and subsequent investments has enabled my funding Chairs in Engineering and Poetry at Ga. Tech and Theology at Emory. Also a Religious Literacy program at Harvard and a Foundation to carry on this work and through the AIA, the more technological search for ancient civilizations. These will be ongoing programs after I am gone.

There is much more coming from this fount. We get the most satisfaction giving more than we get as we grow older. This pandemic is making monks out of us all and hopefully we are all learning something if nothing more than cooking for ourselves and others. I've had time to read and reflect and recall a paper I wrote for one of the best courses I took at HDS on the *Thomas Gospel* first introduced to me by Joseph

Campbell. (If you haven't read this Gospel, I highly recommend you do.) The paper concludes talking about a passage strategically placed right in the middle of that remarkable text written over 2000 years ago that moved me greatly at the time, one I continue to ponder:

> Logion number 50 is about the "Children of Light" trying to find rest. The seeker is challenged before entering the kingdom of God:—"What is your sign?" The answer is most relevant —"It is movement and rest." It is in the movement, the things that we do in life, the seeking, the struggle along our path, doing good works, spiritual exercise, that takes us to the final rest, the reward for the seeking... We are moving continually between these two worlds as we grow and mature. We can draw deeply from prayer and meditation during important times of solitude; however we are in the end moved by God's love. It is from this love that we gather strength, gain divine insight, hear the whisper of Jesus from so many years ago in the [scriptures], and drink...from his bubbling pure spring.

We are always moving between movement and stillness and, recognizing this energy, utilize it to make the best of our current circumstances. It is also interesting, that even then a password was required! Over the winter and into late spring I was in Naples with Anne and her growing family, now blessed with grandchildren, Kelly Marie and Griffin Charles. I wrote this poem about how we coped with the initial shock of forced isolation down there:

Flattening the Curve

It was at the time of the quarantine.
Governments panicked, ordering
social distancing, the law of the land
to flatten the surge of the stricken.

A strange virus from China had flown
with bats out of Mongolian caves
and jet-sped to spread its curse
around the world.

Here police cordoned off
park benches and beaches
like crime scenes with yellow tape.
We soon rebelled as did our neighbors,
who came out, quiet at sunsets
like the ancients gathered at Stonehenge,

to pay their respects to the waning day,
observing the orange orb sink
into the placid gulf, feeling
in its absence a new presence,
watching close as slack waves
lapped the forbidden sandy shore
and dared to read poetry.

Tired of isolation, we and our neighbors went to the beach to
observe sunset, properly socially distanced, of course, had cocktails
and read poetry. Mankind can always figure a way to make the best of
adversity and enjoy themselves. I've been blessed to have finished this
book, part of it during a magical Indian summer quarantining here at
Utopia Farm this summer and fall. At dusk the sun sets early now on a
rusted Canaan mountain top turning it near-red like Ayer's Rock on the
other side of the world. There is much that connects us. It's a good way
to end the day.

ACKNOWLEDGMENTS

The seed to write this book was planted by Tom Lux when we were having dinner together one evening at the Warren Wilson School summer session in 2004 that he had gotten me into. I was telling him about my recent trip to China and my adventures there and he said to me: "You know you've lived a damn interesting life and besides using it for your poetry, someday you should write your story."

I remember also reading articles encouraging telling your story, particularly in Rod MacIver's *Heron Dance* magazine I used to take, as well as a conversation with him. He was a businessman and cancer survivor turned artist and literary magazine publisher who promoted lesser know people expressing themselves through their art. Shortly after I came to New York City and was almost ground up by it in the late 70s, I began keeping a journal for sanity. Lo and behold, poetry began to appear in it and I started to go to writing workshops to learn what I was doing and improve it. Luckily NYC is a place with abundant adult education where great writers help novices—they inspired me.

My daily journaling remained the grist of my memoir mill. There were some false starts as well, the Christmas break a year after Georgia's death in 2001 and after mystery school at Joshua Tree in 2003, evidenced by pages of chapter outlines in my journals warming up for a biography. The problem was, as you will see from this book, there wasn't enough accumulated experience. I had to get through death, divorce, and cancer for an adequate launching pad plus those emotional boosters to get me off of it.

The real start of this book was my sabbatical year in 2017, accompanying Anne McNulty to Stanford's DCI program. I had a year off and the full resources of a great university at my disposal. As part of that program's initiation, Phil Pizzo, the head of that program had me interview poetess Evan Boland, who ran Stamford's creative writing program. We were to have perfunctory half hour interview that turned into a couple hours conversation where we bonded. Evan, being the daughter of a diplomat, was most persuasive and insisted I begin work with John Evans who taught her memoir classes.

After John and I met, we realized we shared a tragedy in the sudden loss of our wives, driving the need to write our stories. John gave me excellent guidance, structure, and purpose and precise assignments weekly at religiously kept lunches on Wednesdays at the back of the Green Library under shading eucalyptus trees. There he critiqued my previous week's production and suggested topics for the following week, patiently pulling my lifetime out of its shell. We did about a chapter a week and, luckily, Anne and I extended our stay. We were having such an enriching experience and we agreed I ought to complete this work. I brought 60 chapters and 600 pages back East.

I had had, of course, discussions with agents and publishers who were memoir specialists, meetings which were set up through the creative writing department's contacts, however, C&R Press had published two books of my poetry and was under new management. I was impressed by John Gosslee and Andrew (Ibis) Sullivan who had taken it over. Andrew was a particularly solid citizen who suggested they might consider the publication of my work. I respected Andrew's thinking, so decided to go with C&R.

For practical publication, the work needed further editing and downsizing. Both Andrew and I previously had work well edited by Travis Denton, Tom Lux's righthand man at Poetry at Tech. Travis and his wife, Katie Chaple, helped me to cut the tome—all my treasured storie—down to size. We would sit down together in the lobby of the Tech Hotel in Atlanta when I was there teaching. About three months later we had a tight 350-page manuscript. We turned this into Andrew, who went through it and helpfully suggested I might want to mix in more of my poetry. About that time, the pandemic surprised us all, putting everything on hold, including publication of my book. This gave me adequate time to tighten the manuscript further and stir in some poetry.

Serendipitously, out of a conversation about my book with *Parabola*'s editor, Jeff Zaleski, he chose to publish my chapter about my Indian trip as an article in his Spring 2020, Quest issue of *Parabola*.

This book is laced with my poetry. The following poems were first published in *Full Horizon* by Tom Lux's Jeanne Duval Editions in Atlanta, Ga. in 2005: My Silent Partner/Flying/Ma Mora/St. Paul's Dome/Cathedral/A Little Liaison/Richmond/The Falls of the Mississippi/On the Road/Harness Tightening Time/Manhattan Morning/Dark River/Fallen Flowers/Refuge/Line Dance Heaven/The Vision/Snow Geese/Candle/Advent 2001/Swans at Golden's Bridge/Utopia Farm/How Things Never Change.

The following poems were first published in *Scaring Up the Morning* by

C&R Press in 2013: Many Paths/War Games/At the Stress Reduction Center/Delray Beach/Prayer Flags/When She Showed Me Her Paddle/Tulips/Celebrating the Moon Festival at the Pingyao International Financier's Club/When the Bees Swarm.

The following Poems herein included were first published in *Like Lesser Gods* by C&R Press in 2018: Reunion/Living Waters/For Our Partner/The Turtle in the Road/Concert at Opus 40/On the Island of the Smiling Loon/Camellias in the Moonlight/The Bearded Man of Luther/Mother's Day/Last Walk down 72nd in Hard Rain/The Roaring Fork/Restarting the World/Easter in Naples/Like Lesser Gods.

So, thank you, Tom Lux, whom I miss...as well as the literary world, for the idea. Appreciation for Travis Denton's organizational editing and particularly Katie Chapel, for her close editing. Also, my Salisbury neighbor Tom Shachtman, author of over 30 books, for his edits of the early chapters, helpful suggestions and general encouragement. Thank you, Andrew (Ibis) Sullivan for your astute questioning of my text and careful edits. And thank you, Andrew and John for your confidence in my work to put the resources of your new, growing and thriving enterprise behind its publication. Thank you, readers for your interest—I hope you can gain something, as the native Americans advise from walking in my moccasins with me on my *Many Paths*.

Bruce McEver
Utopia Farm
Salisbury, CT.
May 26, 2021

Bruce McEver and Anne McNulty in Tel Aviv, May 2019

C&R PRESS TITLES

NONFICTION

Mnay Paths by Bruce McEver
East Village Closed by Billy the Artist
By the Bridge or By the River? Stories of Immigration
from the Southern Border by Amy C. Roma
Women in the Literary Landscape by Doris Weatherford, et al
Credo: An Anthology of Manifestos & Sourcebook for Creative Writing by
Rita Banerjee and Diana Norma Szokolyai

FICTION

All I Should Not Tell by Brian Leung
A Mother's Tale by Khanh Ha
Last Tower to Heaven by Jacob Paul
History of the Cat in Nine Chapters or Less by Anis Shivani
No Good, Very Bad Asian by Lelund Cheuk
Surrendering Appomattox by Jacob M. Appel
Made by Mary by Laura Catherine Brown
Ivy vs. Dogg by Brian Leung
While You Were Gone by Sybil Baker
Cloud Diary by Steve Mitchell
Spectrum by Martin Ott
That Man in Our Lives by Xu Xi

SHORT FICTION

Fathers of Cambodian Time-Travel Science by Bradley Bazzle
Two Californias by Robert Glick
Notes From the Mother Tongue by An Tran
The Protester Has Been Released by Janet Sarbanes

ESSAY AND CREATIVE NONFICTION

Selling the Farm by Debra Di Blasi
the internet is for real by Chris Campanioni
Immigration Essays by Sybil Baker

Death of Art by Chris Campanioni

POETRY

Leaving the Skin on the Bear by Kelli Allen
How to Kill Yourself Instead of Your Children by Quincy Scott Jones
Lottery of Intimacies by Jonathan Katz
What Feels Like Love by Tom C. Hunley
The Rented Altar by Lauren Berry
Between the Earth and Sky by Eleanor Kedney
What Need Have We for Such as We by Amanda Auerbach
A Family Is a House by Dustin Pearson
The Miracles by Amy Lemmon
Banjo's Inside Coyote by Kelli Allen
Objects in Motion by Jonathan Katz
My Stunt Double by Travis Denton
Lessons in Camoflauge by Martin Ott
Millennial Roost by Dustin Pearson
All My Heroes are Broke by Ariel Francisco
Holdfast by Christian Anton Gerard
Ex Domestica by E.G. Cunningham
Like Lesser Gods by Bruce McEver
Notes from the Negro Side of the Moon by Earl Braggs
Imagine Not Drowning by Kelli Allen
Notes to the Beloved by Michelle Bitting
Free Boat: Collected Lies and Love Poems by John Reed
Les Fauves by Barbara Crooker
Tall as You are Tall Between Them by Annie Christain
The Couple Who Fell to Earth by Michelle Bitting
Notes to the Beloved by Michelle Bitting